DANUBE CANAL

STEPHANSDOM
QUARTER

HOFBURG
QUARTER

BELVEDERE
QUARTER

D0486471

DK EYEWITNESS TRAVEL

Vienna

DK EYEWITNESS TRAVEL

Vienna

Main Contributor **Stephen Brook**

Project Editor Carolyn Pyrah
Art Editor Sally Ann Hibbard
Editors Marcus Hardy, Kim Inglis
Designers Vanessa Hamilton,
Andy Wilkinson
Design Assistant Elly King
Production Hilary Stephens
Picture Research Ellen Root
DTP Designer Adam Moore

Contributors
Gretel Beer, Rosemary Bircz, Caroline Bugler,
Deirdre Coffey, Fred Mawer

Photographer
Peter Wilson

Illustrators
Richard Draper, Stephen Gyapay, Chris Orr,
Robbie Polley, Ann Winterbotham

Printed and bound in China

First American edition 1994

18 19 20 21 10 9 8 7 6 5 4 3 2 1

Published in the United States by
DK Publishing 345 Hudson Street,
New York, NY 10014

Reprinted with revisions 1994, 1995,
1996, 1997, 1998, 1999, 2000, 2001,
2002, 2003, 2004, 2006, 2008, 2010,
2012, 2014, 2016, 2018

Copyright © 1994, 2018 Dorling
Kindersley Limited, London

Published in Great Britain by
Dorling Kindersley Limited.

A Penguin Random House Company

A catalog record for this book is available
from the Library of Congress.

ISBN 978-1-4654-6819-2
ISSN 1542-1554

Floors are referred to throughout in
accordance with British usage; ie the "first
floor" is the floor above ground level.

Introducing Vienna

The Prunksaal, the largest Baroque library
in Europe

The distinctive roof and one of the Heathen Towers of Stephansdom

◀ **Title page** The Karlskirche, a Baroque masterpiece **Front cover image** Michaelertrakt's impressive dome, Hofburg Complex
Back cover image Schönbrunn Palace and its elegant courtyard

Contents

Golden shield from Theater an der Wien

The Neo-Classical Gloriette arcade at Schönbrunn Palace and Gardens

The Burgtheater

HOW TO USE THIS GUIDE

This Eyewitness Travel Guide helps you get the most from your stay in Vienna with the minimum of difficulty. The opening section, *Introducing Vienna*, locates the city geographically, sets modern Vienna in its historical context and describes events through the year. *Vienna at a Glance* is an overview of the city's main attractions. *Vienna Area by Area* starts on page 68. This is the main sightseeing section, which covers all the important sights, with photographs, maps and illustrations. It also includes day trips from Vienna, a river trip and four walks around the city. Carefully researched tips for hotels, restaurants, cafés and bars, markets and shops, entertainment and sports are found in *Travellers' Needs*. The *Survival Guide* contains practical advice, from what to do in an emergency to using the transport system and its ticket machines.

Finding Your Way Around the Sightseeing Section

Each of the six sightseeing areas in the city is colour-coded for easy reference. Every chapter opens with an introduction to the part of Vienna it covers, describing its history and character, followed by a Street-by-Street map illustrating a typical part of the area. Finding your way around each chapter is made simple by the numbering system used throughout. The most important sights are covered in detail in two or more full pages.

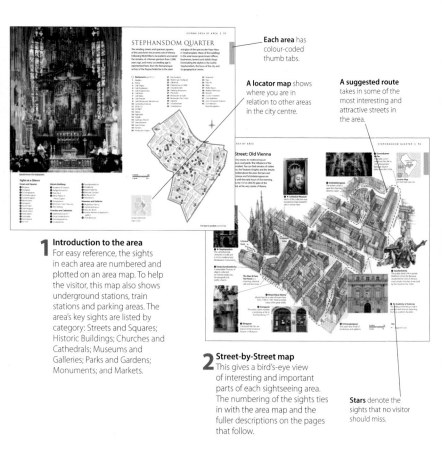

Each area has colour-coded thumb tabs.

A locator map shows where you are in relation to other areas in the city centre.

A suggested route takes in some of the most interesting and attractive streets in the area.

1 Introduction to the area
For easy reference, the sights in each area are numbered and plotted on an area map. To help the visitor, this map also shows underground stations, train stations and parking areas. The area's key sights are listed by category: Streets and Squares; Historic Buildings; Churches and Cathedrals; Museums and Galleries; Parks and Gardens; Monuments; and Markets.

2 Street-by-Street map
This gives a bird's-eye view of interesting and important parts of each sightseeing area. The numbering of the sights ties in with the area map and the fuller descriptions on the pages that follow.

Stars denote the sights that no visitor should miss.

Vienna Area Map

The coloured areas shown on this map *(see inside front cover)* are the six main sightseeing areas used in this guide. Each is covered by a full chapter in *Vienna Area by Area (pp68–181)*. They are highlighted on other maps throughout the book. In *Vienna at a Glance (pp42–63)*, for example, they help you locate the top sights. They are also used to indicate the location of the three guided walks *(pp182–9)*.

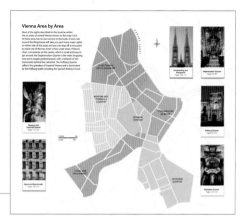

Numbers refer to each sight's position on the area map and its place in the chapter.

Practical information provides all the detail you need to visit every sight. Map references pinpoint each sight's location on the *Street Finder* map *(pp262–7)*.

The visitors' checklist provides all the practical information needed to plan your visit.

3 Detailed information on each sight
All the important sights in Vienna are described individually. They are listed in order, following the numbering on the area map at the start of the section. Practical information includes a map reference, opening hours, telephone numbers, admission charges and facilities available for each sight. The key to the symbols used is on the back flap.

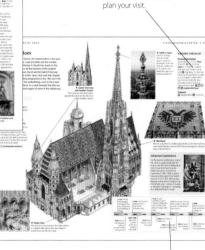

4 Vienna's major sights
Historic buildings are dissected to reveal their interiors; museums and galleries have colour-coded floorplans to help you find important exhibits.

A timeline charts the key events in the history of the building.

INTRODUCING VIENNA

GREAT DAYS IN VIENNA

Whether you are a history buff, an art lover, an outdoors enthusiast or a fan of thrill rides, in Vienna you will be sure to find something that appeals to you. From imperial palaces and art galleries to parks and a funfair, Vienna has attractions to suit everyone.

Listed here are some ideas for themed days out and suggested itineraries to get the most from the city on 2-, 3- and 5-day breaks. Prices include all travel, food and admission costs. Family pricing allows for two adults and two children.

Schönbrunn Palace, whose formal gardens contain a palm house and zoo

Vienna of the Habsburgs

Two adults allow at least €110

- **Visit the vast Hofburg Complex**
- **Dine on Emperor's Pancakes**
- **Take a tour of Schönbrunn Palace and Gardens**

Morning

Start the day early with a visit to the huge **Hofburg Complex** (see pp98–9), which includes the former Habsburg winter residence, a church, chapel, the **Spanish Riding School** (see pp100–101), museums and the Austrian National Library. Take a tour of the former **Habsburg State Apartments** (see pp102–3), the **Sisi Museum** (dedicated to Empress Elisabeth of Austria) and the Silberkammer, which houses the Imperial Silver Collection. For lunch, dine in the complex at the **Café Hofburg** (see p212), where traditional specialities such as *Kaiserschmarren* (Emperor's Pancakes) and *Rindsgulasch* (beef goulash) are served.

Afternoon

After lunch, take a trip out to the impressive **Schönbrunn Palace and Gardens** (see pp174–7), the former summer residence of the Habsburgs. The "Imperial Tour" leads you through 22 of the palace's grand state rooms, with a free audio guide providing snippets of interesting information. If you still have time after the tour, head out into the park and admire the picturesque gardens. The **maze** (see p174), a favourite feature of European stately homes, provides a unique outdoor adventure.

The Mozart monument in the Burggarten, by Viktor Tilgner (1896)

Green Vienna

Two adults allow at least €100

- **Tour the Butterfly House**
- **Dine in a historic café**
- **Stroll through one of the city's largest parks**
- **Climb a 252-m (827-ft) tower**

Morning

Start the day with a trip to **Burggarten** (see p104), a park in central Vienna that was created by the Habsburgs on land around the Hofburg. Here you can wander among the trees and view statues of Goethe, Mozart and Emperor Franz I. The park is also well known for its greenhouses, designed by the Jugendstil architect Friedrich Ohmann. Among them is the Butterfly House (*Schmetterlinghaus*), home to over 150 different species that fly around in a recreated rainforest environment. Next, take a lunch break at the nearby **Café Mozart** (see p213) on Albertinaplatz. In this historic and elegant coffeehouse, first established in 1794, you can dine on gourmet vegetarian or traditional Austrian dishes and enjoy some pastries for dessert.

Afternoon

After lunch, pay a visit to **Donaupark** (see p163), which was created in 1964 and is one of Vienna's largest parks. Here you can go for a leisurely stroll or jog, or rent a bike and ride along the cycle paths. For a relaxing moment, sit down by Lake Iris, an artificial lake at the centre of the park. One of the park's highlights is the **Donauturm** (see p163), a

◀ *Carriage race in the Prater in Vienna, 19th century*

Gustav Klimt's Beethoven Frieze on display in the Secession Building

252 m- (827 ft-) high tower with a revolving restaurant, a café and an observation deck. A lift takes visitors to the top of the tower where views of the whole Vienna metropolitan area can be enjoyed. On a clear day, the view stretches to beyond the city.

The elegant exterior of the historic and popular Café Mozart

Art and Architecture

Two adults allow at least €100

- Tour a Jugendstil contemporary art museum
- Dine on classic Greek food
- Explore an imperial art history museum

Morning
Begin your day with a visit to the **Secession Building** (see p142), which was designed in Jugendstil style and is now used as an exhibition hall for displays of contemporary art. Exhibitions have included work by Oswald Oberhuber and Maja Vukoje. The building is also home to Gustav Klimt's famous *Beethoven Frieze*. After viewing the art, try nearby **Kostas** (see p216) for a classic Greek lunch of moussaka.

Afternoon
Having eaten, head over to the **MuseumsQuartier** (see pp120–23) and, for an unforgettable experience, visit the **Kunsthistorisches Museum** (Museum of the History of Art) (see pp124–9). Here you can easily spend a whole afternoon viewing magnificent works of art and antiquities, many of which are from imperial Habsburg collections. The Picture Gallery on the first floor is especially impressive and features paintings from Giovanni Bellini, Titian, Pieter Bruegel and Diego Velázquez among others. Afterwards, stop off at **Café Eiles** (see p214), a typical Venetian coffeehouse and nearby in the Museums-Quartier, for a drink and pastry, or light meal.

A Family Day

Family of 4 allow at least €200

- Explore the Volksprater Funfair in the Prater
- Lunch at the Prater's Schweizerhaus restaurant
- Ride a rickshaw along the Hauptallee

Morning
This day starts with a trip to the **Volksprater Funfair** (see p164), the oldest amusement park in the world. Take a spin on the famous Ferris wheel built in 1897. Older kids might then like to ride on the daring Volare roller coaster, while parents with smaller children might enjoy the carousel, or the 4-km (2.5-mile) miniature railway. For lunch, visit the **Schweizerhaus restaurant** (see p218) inside the park and try one of the tremendous-value daily specials of beef or chicken.

Afternoon
After lunch, families can rent a rickshaw (or mountain bikes, tandems or children's bikes) from the Bicycle Rental Hochschaubahn stand, near the Hochschaubahn roller coaster. Go for a two-hour ride down the **Hauptallee** (see p165) in the Prater's green area, which is a boulevard famous for jogging and cycling, or just enjoying a pleasant stroll. Return to one of the funfair's fast-food stands for an ice-cream cone or soft drink.

The Ferris wheel at Volksprater Funfair

2 Days in Vienna

- Take a stroll around the streets of Old Vienna
- Watch the elegant horses of the Spanish Riding School
- Enjoy the panorama from Vienna's famous Ferris wheel

A traditional horse-drawn carriage (Fiaker), a fun way of getting around Vienna

Day 1
Morning Start at the landmark **Stephansdom** cathedral *(see pp74–7)*, then wander around the pedestrianized medieval streets of **Old Vienna** *(see pp72–3)*. Take a stroll along **Kärntner Strasse** *(see p107)*, the city's main shopping street, to the **Opera House** *(see pp140–41)* for a tour and perhaps tickets to the evening show.

Afternoon Pick up a **Ring Tram** *(see p254)* for a bargain 30-minute ride around **Ringstrasse** *(see pp34–5)*, Vienna's grandest boulevard. Then head to the **Wien Museum Karlsplatz** *(see p150)* to learn about the city's history, or to the **Belvedere** *(see pp154–9)* for some fine Austrian art and attractive gardens.

Day 2
Morning Head to the **Hofburg** *(see pp98–9)*, the imperial palace of the Habsburgs, where the main draws are the sumptuous **State Apartments and Treasuries** *(see pp102–3)*. But first, see whether there are any tickets available for a performance of the **Spanish Riding School** *(see pp100–101)*, held on Saturdays and Sundays at 11am.

Afternoon Walk a city block from the Hofburg to the **MuseumsQuartier** *(see pp120–23)*, a superb cultural complex next to the **Kunsthistorisches Museum** *(see pp124–9)*. Choose carefully from the various museums here; it's all too easy to attempt to see too much. Afterwards, head out to **Prater** park *(see pp164–5)* for some fresh air, and take a spin on the famous Ferris wheel.

3 Days in Vienna

- Explore the imperial marvels of the Hofburg palace complex
- Tour Vienna's grand opera house
- Take a ride in an old-fashioned carriage around Old Vienna

Day 1
Morning Visit the vast imperial palace of the Habsburgs, the **Hofburg** *(see pp98–99)*. Most visitors head straight to the lavish **State Apartments and Treasuries** *(see pp102–3)*, but be sure to leave time to visit the **Neue Burg** *(see p97)*, home to three interesting museum collections. If you can, get

The Kunsthistorisches Museum, housing Habsburg imperial art and treasures

tickets for a performance of the **Spanish Riding School** *(see pp100–101)*, held at 11am at weekends.

Afternoon Take the Ring Tram *(see p254)* for the 30-minute loop around the elegant **Ringstrasse** *(see pp34–5)*, before getting off at the **Opera House** *(see pp140–41)* for a tour and perhaps tickets to a show. Wander up **Kärntner Strasse** *(see p107)*, Vienna's main shopping street, en route to the cathedral, the **Stephansdom** *(see pp74–7)*. End the day with a ride in an open horse-drawn **Fiaker** *(see p251)* around **Old Vienna** *(see pp72–3)*.

Day 2
Morning Choose from several interesting art and culture museums at the **Museums-Quartier** *(see pp120–23)* and the adjacent **Kunsthistorisches Museum** *(see pp124–9)*. Afterwards, stroll over to the **Naschmarkt** *(see p142)* for an alfresco lunch from one of the food stalls here.

Afternoon Leave central Vienna, with a stop at the playful, fairy-tale-like **Hundertwasserhaus** *(see pp166–7)*, to explore **Prater** park *(see pp164–5)*. Be sure to take a ride on the Ferris wheel.

Day 3
Morning Head southwest of the city centre to verse yourself in Vienna's history at the fascinating **Wien Museum**

Karlsplatz *(see p150)*. The beautifully ornate **Karlskirche** *(see pp148–9)* is nearby.

Afternoon Spend a peaceful afternoon in the vast **Belvedere** *(see pp154–9)*, with its lovely gardens and impressive art collection.

5 Days in Vienna

- Take a tour of Vienna's musical history
- See the work of Austria's finest artists at the Belvedere
- Explore the beautiful Schönbrunn Palace and Gardens

Day 1
Morning Start at the **Stephansdom** *(see pp74–7)*, Vienna's great cathedral, before wandering the pedestrianized medieval streets of **Old Vienna** *(see pp72–3)*, which are packed with shops, cafés and restaurants. Consider a pricey but fun introduction to the city by horse-drawn **Fiaker** *(see p251)*, leaving from the front of the Stephansdom.

Afternoon Drop in on Mozart's old home, the **Mozarthaus Vienna** *(see p78)*, and continue the musical theme at the **Haus der Musik** *(see p82)*. Then, admire the musical monuments in the pretty **Stadtpark** *(see p167)*, or take in decorative art at the **Austrian Museum of Applied Arts** *(see pp84–5)*.

Day 2
Morning The old Habsburg imperial palace, the **Hofburg** *(see pp98–103)*, can easily occupy a whole morning, so be sure to prioritize seeing the **State Apartments and Treasuries** *(see pp102–3)*. The **Spanish Riding School** *(see pp100–101)* holds performances on Saturdays and Sundays at 11am, so before visiting the palace see whether there are tickets available.

Afternoon The Hofburg has several excellent museums and galleries, particularly in the

The distinctive Secession building, built in Jugendstil style

Neue Burg *(see p97)*. Once you have had your fill of art, stroll down **Ringstrasse** *(see pp34–5)*, Vienna's historic boulevard, or see it from the **Ring Tram** *(see p254)* for a quicker ride to the flamboyant **Opera House** *(see pp140–41)*.

Day 3
Morning Begin the day with a lesson in Vienna's history at the magnificent **Wien Museum Karlsplatz** *(see p150)*. Look in on the elegant **Karlskirche** *(see pp148–9)* on your way to the **Naschmarkt** *(see p142)* for lunch from one of its many food stalls.

Afternoon The unusual **Secession Building** *(see p142)* is worth a closer look; but save some energy for the superb **MuseumsQuartier**

(see pp120–23) and the world-class art of the impressive **Kunsthistorisches Museum** *(see pp124–9)*.

Day 4
Morning Start at the **Belvedere** *(see pp154–9)* to see works by some of Austria's finest artists: Gustav Klimt, Egon Schiele and Oskar Kokoschka. Head a little further out of town to visit the **Central Cemetery** *(see pp170–71)*, the resting place for many famous Austrians, which also has a fascinating funerary museum.

Afternoon Lighten the mood with a look at the unusual municipal apartment block **Hundertwasserhaus** *(see pp166–7)*, en route to the **Prater** park *(see pp164–5)*, where you can take a spin on the city's famous Ferris wheel.

Day 5
Morning Leave Vienna for the Rococo masterpiece **Schönbrunn** *(see pp174–7)*, the Habsburgs' former summer residence. Spend some time exploring the beautiful palace gardens, which include a zoo, a maze, and some "Roman ruins", actually constructed in 1778.

Afternoon It's easy to spend a whole day at Schönbrunn, but to explore more widely, take a walk around the attractive adjacent neighbourhood of **Hietzing** *(see pp186–7)*. The quiet streets are filled with interesting architecture.

The Vienna Opera House at night

Putting Vienna on the Map

Vienna has a population of about 1.8 million and covers an area of 415 sq km (160 sq miles). The River Danube flows through the city and the Danube Canal winds through the city centre. It is the capital of the Republic of Austria, of which it is also a federal state, and is the country's political, economic, cultural and administrative centre. At the heart of Central Europe, it makes a good base from which to explore cities such as Bratislava, Prague, Budapest, Zagreb, Salzburg and Munich, as well as many Austrian towns.

Karlovy Vary
CZECH
Plzen
Strakonice
Cham
Heilbronn
Regensburg
Deggendorf
Zbior
Lipiens
Aalen
Ingolstadt
Passau
Donauwörth
Schärding
GERMANY
Donau
Landshut
Ulm
Braunau
Augsburg
München
Ried in Innkreis
Wels
Landsberg am Lech
Vöcklabruck
Memmingen
Lech
Ammersee
Chiemsee
Salzburg
Attersee
Bodensee
Bregenz
Füssen
Rosenheim
Hallein
Bad Ischl
Garmisch-Partenkirchen
Wörgl
Kufstein
Bad Aussee
Dornbirn
Reutte
St. Johann in Tirol
Radstadt
Feldkirch
Ehrwald
Seefeld
AUS
Vaduz
Bludenz
Innsbruck
Schwaz
Zell am See
LIECHTENSTEIN
Landeck
Mauterndorf
Brunico
Lienz
Spittal an der Drau
SWITZERLAND
Drau
Villach
Cortina d'Ampezzo
Tolmezzo
ITALY
Belluno
Udine
Pordenone
Piave
Treviso
Lignano
Trieste
Mestre
Poreč
Venezia (Venice)
Adriatic
Sea
Pula
Croatia, Greece

Europe

North
Sea
SWEDEN
DENMARK
UNITED
KINGDOM
NETHERLANDS
POLAND
GERMANY
BELGIUM
CZECH
REPUBLIC
SLOVAKIA
Vienna
FRANCE
SWITZ.
AUSTRIA
HUNGARY
SLOVENIA
CROATIA
BOSNIA
HERZ.
SERBIA
MONTEN.
KOS
ITALY
MAC
SPAIN
ALBANIA
GREECE

For keys to symbols *see back flap*

Vienna and Environs

Floridsdorf

Nussdorf

Kagran

Raasdorf

Döbling

Brigittenau

Donaustadt

Leopoldstadt

Ottakring

Gross-
Enzersdorf

VIENNA

Hietzing

Favoriten

Simmering

Meidling

Mauer

Kaiserebersdorf

Mannswörth

Perchtoldsdorf

Schwechat

Zwölfaxing

Maria
Enzersdorf

Maria
Lanzendorf

Prague

Hradec
Kralove

R E P U B L I C

Havlíčkův Brod

Tábor

Jihlava

Třebíč

České Budějovice

Znojmo

Gmünd

Horn

Rastenfeld

Freistadt

Krems

SLOVAKIA

Linz

Mistelbach

Hollabrunn

Stockerau

Trnava

Zvolen

Melk

Tulln

Nitra

St. Pölten

See inset
map above

VIENNA

Bratislava

Haag

Amstetten

Bruck an der Leitha

Steyr

Waidhofen

Eisenstadt

Vác

Mitterbach

Wiener Neustadt

Neusiedler
See

Windischgarsten

Neuenkirchen

Győr

Hieflau

Bromberg

Budapest

Irdning

Oberpullendorf

Leoben

Bruck an der Mur

T R I A

Szombathely

Székesfenérvár

Murau

Judenburg

Veszprém

Friesach

Graz

Wolfsberg

Zalaegerszeg

H U N G A R Y

Leibnitz

Balaton
Lake

Klagenfurt

Dunaföldvár

Maribor

Kranj

Ptuj

Čakovec

Nagykanizsa

Szekszárd

Celje

Varaždin

Kaposvár

Ljubljana

Koprivnica

Pécs

S L O V E N I A

Vrbovec

Novo Mesto

Zagreb

Rijeka

C R O A T I A

Oločac

Nova
Gradiška

B O S N I A   A N D
H E R Z E G O V I N A

Bihać

Banja Luka

KEY

☐ Urban area

═══ Motorway

━━━ Major road

─── Railway

▬▬▬ Country boundary

┄┄┄ Minor road

0 kilometres   100

0 miles   50

Central Vienna

This book divides central Vienna into six areas and has further sections for sights on the outskirts, suggested walks and day trips, as well as practical information. Each of the six main areas has its own chapter, containing a selection of sights that convey some of that area's history and distinctive character, such as the Stephansdom in the Stephansdom Quarter and the imperial buildings in the Hofburg Quarter. Most of the city's famous sights are in or close to the centre and are easy to reach on foot or by public transport.

Michaelerplatz Fountain
The Michaelerplatz fountain, in the Hofburg Quarter (*see p94*), is formally titled *The Mastery of the Sea*. It was sculpted by Rudolf Weyr in 1895 and symbolizes Austria's naval power.

0 metres 500
0 yards 500

Vienna as seen from Stephansdom
Situated in the centre of Vienna, Stephansdom (see pp74–7) is surrounded by some of the oldest houses in the city, many of which date back to medieval times.

Rathauskeller Façade
The city has plenty of wine cellars – many associated with old vineyards – where wine, beer and simple food is served. This one is located beneath the city hall (see p132).

Pallas Athene Fountain
The figure of Pallas Athene by Carl Kundmann was placed on the fountain in front of the Parliament building in 1902 (see p123).

THE HISTORY OF VIENNA

Vienna was originally a Celtic settlement on the site of the present-day city. Under the Romans it became the garrison of Vindobona, but by the early 5th century, Barbarian invasions reduced the settlement to ruins. In the 10th century, the German Babenberg dynasty acquired Vienna, and during their reign of almost three centuries the city became a major trading centre. Later, in the 13th century, Vienna came under the control of the Habsburgs. In the 16th century, Turkish invasions threatened Vienna and devastated its outskirts. Only in 1683 were the Turks finally defeated, allowing Vienna to flourish. Immense palaces were built around the court within the city, and in the liberated outskirts, and by the 18th century Vienna was a major imperial and cultural centre. Napoleon's occupation of Vienna in 1809 shook the Habsburgs' confidence, as did the revolution of

1848 – the year Franz Joseph came to the throne. By 1914, Vienna's population had expanded to two million, as people from all over the Habsburg Empire flocked to this vibrant centre. After World War I, the Habsburg Empire collapsed and Vienna's role as the imperial capital ended. In the following years a strong municipal government – "Red Vienna"– tried to solve the social problems of the city. Austria was annexed by Nazi Germany in the Anschluss of 1938. The occupying powers after 1945 allowed the creation of a new independent state in 1955, at which time permanent neutrality was also agreed. Vienna hosted the USSR–USA superpower summit of Kennedy and Krushchev in 1961 and is now one of three official United Nations headquarters and home to many international organizations. In 1995, Austria joined the European Union.

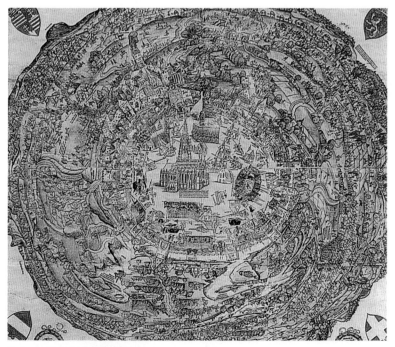

Circular map of the Turkish siege, from 1529

◀ Detail from *The Marriage of Joseph II to Isabella of Parma* (1760) by the Martin van Meytens School

Vienna's Rulers

Vienna emerged from the Dark Ages as a German outpost controlled by Babenberg dukes, who brought great prosperity to the city by the 12th century. There followed a period of social disorder and intermittent Bohemian rule known as the Interregnum. Vienna fell into Habsburg hands in the 13th century and remained the cornerstone of their domains until the dynasty's downfall in 1918. From 1452 until 1806, Habsburg rulers were almost invariably elected as Holy Roman Emperor, enabling Vienna to develop as an imperial capital on the grandest scale.

Duke Friedrich II with falconer

1278–82 Rudolf I of Germany is regent of Austria

1246–50 Interregnum under Margrave Hermann of Baden after death of Duke Friedrich II

900	1000	1100	1200	1300	1400
BABENBERG RULERS				**HABSBURG RULERS**	
900	1000	1100	1200	1300	1400

976 Leopold of Babenberg

1198–1230 Duke Leopold VI

1177–94 Duke Leopold V

1358–65 Duke Rudolf IV

1141–77 Duke Heinrich II Jasomirgott

1251–76 Interregnum under Přemysl Ottakar II

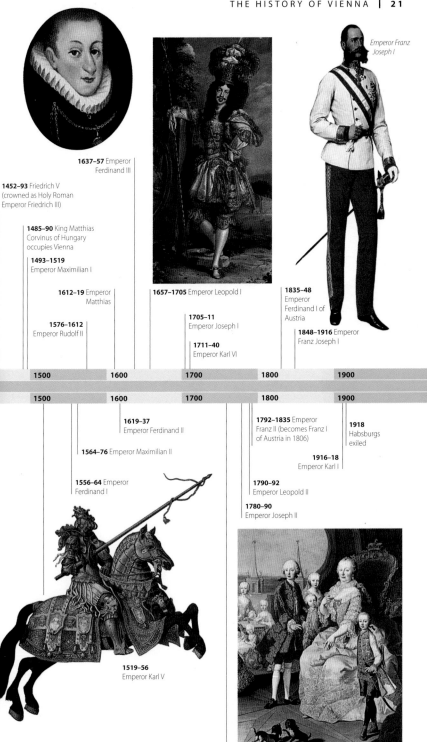

Emperor Franz Joseph I

1637–57 Emperor Ferdinand III

1452–93 Friedrich V (crowned as Holy Roman Emperor Friedrich III)

1485–90 King Matthias Corvinus of Hungary occupies Vienna

1493–1519 Emperor Maximilian I

1612–19 Emperor Matthias

1576–1612 Emperor Rudolf II

1657–1705 Emperor Leopold I

1705–11 Emperor Joseph I

1711–40 Emperor Karl VI

1835–48 Emperor Ferdinand I of Austria

1848–1916 Emperor Franz Joseph I

| 1500 | 1600 | 1700 | 1800 | 1900 |

| 1500 | 1600 | 1700 | 1800 | 1900 |

1619–37 Emperor Ferdinand II

1564–76 Emperor Maximilian II

1556–64 Emperor Ferdinand I

1792–1835 Emperor Franz II (becomes Franz I of Austria in 1806)

1918 Habsburgs exiled

1916–18 Emperor Karl I

1790–92 Emperor Leopold II

1780–90 Emperor Joseph II

1519–56 Emperor Karl V

1740–80 Empress Maria Theresa

Early Vienna

The region around Vienna was first inhabited in the late Stone Age, and Vienna itself was founded as a Bronze Age settlement around 800 BC. Settled by Celts from about 400 BC, it was incorporated by the Romans into the province of Pannonia in 15 BC, and the garrison of Vindobona was established by the 1st century AD. Later overrun by Barbarian tribes, Vindobona diminished in importance until the 8th century, when the Frankish Emperor Charlemagne made it part of his Eastern March and the Holy Roman Empire.

Extent of the City

▨ AD 150   ▢ Today

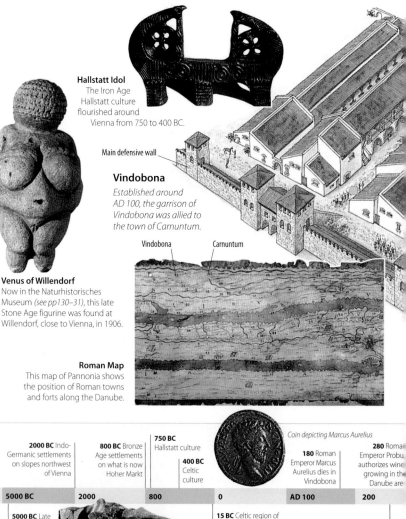

Hallstatt Idol
The Iron Age Hallstatt culture flourished around Vienna from 750 to 400 BC.

Main defensive wall

Vindobona
Established around AD 100, the garrison of Vindobona was allied to the town of Carnuntum.

Vindobona   Carnuntum

Venus of Willendorf
Now in the Naturhistorisches Museum *(see pp130–31)*, this late Stone Age figurine was found at Willendorf, close to Vienna, in 1906.

Roman Map
This map of Pannonia shows the position of Roman towns and forts along the Danube.

Coin depicting Marcus Aurelius

2000 BC Indo-Germanic settlements on slopes northwest of Vienna	**800 BC** Bronze Age settlements on what is now Hoher Markt	**750 BC** Hallstatt culture			**180** Roman Emperor Marcus Aurelius dies in Vindobona	**280** Roman Emperor Probu authorizes wine growing in the Danube are
			400 BC Celtic culture			
5000 BC	**2000**	**800**	**0**	**AD 100**	**200**	
5000 BC Late Stone Age culture			**15 BC** Celtic region of Noricum occupied by Romans		**250** Vindobona, developed as a garrison town, has a population of 20,000	

Preserved shoe from the Hallstatt culture

Marcus Aurelius
This great Roman emperor and philosopher came to Carnuntum to fight the Germanic tribes; he died in Vindobona in AD 180.

Gold Jewellery
The Romans were first attracted to the region around Vindobona for its valuable resources, among them gold.

Stables

Soldiers' quarters

Soldier's Tomb
This tomb, excavated at Carnuntum, dates from around the 1st century AD.

Where to See Early Vienna

Many of the Roman walls and ditches have left their mark on the layout of Vienna, but excavations have not been numerous. The most impressive are at Hoher Markt (see p86), at No. 10 Am Hof (p89), and in the Michaelerplatz (p94). The most extensive remains are not in Vienna itself but at Carnuntum, about 25 miles (40 km) to the east, where two amphitheatres and other ruins survive.

The Hoher Markt, in the very heart of Vienna, is the site of excavations of the Roman garrison of Vindobona.

This gorgon's head, a Roman relief of the mythical Medusa, was found at Hoher Markt.

395 First Barbarian invasions approach Vindobona

405 Romans withdraw from Vindobona

500–650 Repeated invasions by Langobards, Goths, Avars and Slav tribes

300	400	500	600	700	800

433 Vindobona destroyed by Huns

Barbarian horseman

883 First mention of Wenia (Vienna) on the borders of the Eastern March founded by Charlemagne

Medieval Vienna

In 955 the Holy Roman Emperor Otto I expelled Hungarian tribes from the Eastern March *(see p22)*. In 976 he made a gift of Vienna to the German Babenbergs, who, despite further incursions by the Hungarians, restored the city's importance as a centre of trade and culture. Following Friedrich II's death in 1246 and the ensuing Interregnum *(see p20)*, the Habsburgs began centuries of rule over Austria. Vienna became a major European city and hub of the Holy Roman Empire.

Extent of the City
1400   Today

St Ruprecht
St Ruprecht was the patron saint of salt merchants, who brought this precious commodity along the Danube from salt mines in western Austria. Today his statue overlooks the Danube canal.

Death of Friedrich II
Duke Friedrich II was the last of the Babenbergs to rule Vienna. He died in battle against invading Hungarian forces in 1246.

Stephansdom

The Nobility
Often elected as Holy Roman Emperors, the Habsburgs attracted nobility from all over their huge empire.

Duke Friedrich II

Coronation Robe
This magnificent medieval robe (1133), originally from Palermo, formed part of the Habsburg's imperial regalia.

955 Otto I of Germany defeats the Hungarians, restoring Christianity and re-establishing the Eastern March ("Ostmark", later renamed Ostarrichi)

1030 The Hungarians besiege Vienna

1147 Stephansdom consecrated

1136 Death of Margave Leopold III

900

1000

1100

909 Eastern March invaded by Hungarian forces

976 Otto II makes Leopold of Babenberg Margrave of the Eastern March, initiating Babenberg rule

1137 Vienna becomes a fortified city

1156 Heinrich II Jasomirgott moves his court to Vienna; builds Am Hof *(see p89)*

Richard the Lionheart
In 1192, Richard I of England, returning from the crusades in the Holy Land, was captured and held to ransom by Duke Leopold V.

Where to See Medieval Vienna

Gothic churches include the Stephansdom (see pp74–7), Maria am Gestade (p87), the Burgkapelle (p105), Minoritenkirche (p105), Ruprechtskirche (p83) and Augustinerkirche (p104). The Michaelerkirche (p94) includes some Gothic sculptures and the Schottenkirche medieval art (p112). Surviving medieval houses include the Basiliskenhaus in Schönlaterngasse (p80).

Tributary of the River Danube

Medieval city wall

Verduner Altar
This masterpiece forms part of the treasury of the huge abbey at Klosterneuburg (see p163). Its 51 panels were completed in 1181 by Nikolaus of Verdun. The abbey itself was consecrated in 1136.

Stained glass (c. 1340) in the Cathedral Museum (p80).

Hungarian encampment

University
Vienna's university was founded in 1365 by Duke Rudolf IV. This miniature (c. 1400) shows the medieval university building and some of the tutors and their students.

Seal of Przemysl Ottakar II

1278–82 Rudolf I becomes ruler of Austria after defeating Ottakar II; 640 years of Habsburg rule follow

1288 Viennese uprising against Habsburgs crushed

1359 Rudolf IV lays foundation stone of the Stephansdom tower

1365 University founded

1477 Friedrich III's son Maximilian I marries Mary of Burgundy, heiress to the Low Countries

1200

1300

1400

1221 Vienna granted a city charter

1246 Death of Friedrich II followed by Interregnum, during which Przemysl Ottakar II rules Vienna

1273 Count Rudolf of Habsburg crowned Rudolf I of Germany

1330 First Gothic section of Maria am Gestade built

1438 Albrecht V elected Holy Roman Emperor; Vienna made seat of Empire

1452 Friedrich V crowned as Holy Roman Emperor Friedrich III

1485 Vienna occupied by King Matthias Corvinus of Hungary

Renaissance Vienna

Under Maximilian I, Vienna was transformed into a centre for the arts. The Habsburgs were invariably elected Holy Roman Emperor, and by the 16th century their mighty empire had expanded into Spain, Holland, Burgundy, Bohemia and Hungary. But it was under constant threat: from Turkish attacks, the plague, and disputes between Protestants and Catholics that destabilized the city until the Jesuits spearheaded the Counter-Reformation.

Extent of the City

▓ 1600 ☐ Today

Book Illustration
This Renaissance war wagon (1512) is from Maximilian I's collection of books of engravings and illustrations.

Maximilian I married Mary of Burgundy in 1477 and acquired the Burgundian domains.

Viennese Enamel Casket
This ornate enamel and crystal casket is typical of the skilful craftsmanship practised in Vienna in the 16th century.

Imperial Crown
This beautiful crown was made by Bohemian craftsmen in 1610 for Rudolf II and can now be seen in the Hofburg Treasuries (see pp102–3).

Ferdinand I married Anna of Bohemia and Hungary, and inherited Bohemia in 1526. It was a Habsburg domain until 1918.

1516 Maximilian's grandson, Karl V, inherits Spain

1519 Karl V inherits Burgundy titles and is elected Holy Roman Emperor; his brother Ferdinand I becomes Austria's archduke

1533 Ferdinand I moves his court to the Hofburg in Vienna

1556 Karl V's son, Philip II, inherits Spain; Ferdinand I takes Bohemia, Austria, Hungary, and imperial title

1571 Protestant Maximilian II allows religious freedom; 80% of city is Protestant

1500	1520	1540	1560	1580

1498 Emperor Maximilian I founds Vienna Boys' Choir

1490 Hungarians expelled from Vienna

Suleiman the Magnificent

1541 Plague

1529 Graf Niklas Salm vanquishes Turkish army besieging Vienna

1551 Jesuits start Counter-Reformation

1572 Spanish Riding School founded

1577 Protestant services forbidden by Rudolf II

Triumphal Arch of Maximilian I

The German artist Albrecht Dürer (1471–1528) paid homage to Maximilian I in a famous volume of engravings, which included this design for a triumphal arch.

Philip I married Juana of Castile and Aragon in 1496 and acquired Spain.

The Family of Maximilian I

Painted by Bernhard Strigel around 1520, this portrait can be read as a document of how, by marrying into prominent European families, the Habsburg families were able to gain control of almost half of Europe.

Mary of Burgundy was married to Maximilian I and was Duchess of the Burgundian domains.

Karl V inherited Spain from his mother, Juana of Castile and Aragon, in 1516.

Where to See Renaissance Vienna

The Schweizertor (*see p99*) in the Hofburg is the most colourful surviving remnant of Renaissance Vienna, though the Salvatorkapelle portal (*p87*) surpasses it in elegance. Also in the Hofburg is the Renaissance Stallburg (*p95*). Some courtyards, such as those at No. 7 Bäckerstrasse (*p81*) and the Mollard-Clary Palace (*p96*), preserve a few Renaissance features.

The Schweizertor, built in the 16th century, forms the entrance to the Schweizerhof of the Hofburg (*p99*).

Alte Burg
The medieval core of the Hofburg was constantly being rebuilt. This engraving shows its appearance in the late 15th century, before Ferdinand I had it rebuilt in the 1550s.

Medallion commemorating Maximilian II

1618 Bohemian rebellion starts Thirty Years' War

1629 Plague claims 30,000 lives

1643 Swedish forces threaten Vienna

1673–9 War with France over the Low Countries

1600	1620	1640	1660

1598–1618 Protestantism is banned

1621 Jews expelled from inner city

1620 Ferdinand II defeats Protestant Bohemian aristocracy; Counter-Reformation spreads throughout Habsburg domains

17th-century French infantry

Baroque Vienna

The Turkish threat to Vienna ended in 1683 when Kara Mustapha's forces were repelled. Under Karl VI the city expanded and the Karlskirche and the Belvedere palaces were constructed. Around the Hofburg, mansions for noble families sprang up, built by architects such as Johann Bernhard Fischer von Erlach *(see p149)* and Johann Lukas von Hildebrandt *(see p154)*. Vienna was transformed into a resplendent imperial capital.

Extent of the City

▨ 1700   ▢ Today

Winter Palace of Prince Eugene

J B Fischer von Erlach and Johann Lukas von Hildebrandt designed the Winter Palace (see p82) for Prince Eugene, hero of the Turkish campaign.

Plague
This lithograph recalls the plague of 1679, which killed around 30,000 Viennese.

Turkish Bed
Ornamented with martial emblems, this bed was designed for Prince Eugene in 1707.

Coffee Houses
The first coffee houses opened in Vienna in the mid-17th century and they have been a prized institution ever since.

Baroque Architecture
Baroque architecture was at its most prolific in Vienna in the early 18th century.

Trautson Palace *(see p118)*

1679
Plague in Vienna

1680

1683 Turkish siege of Vienna by 200,000 soldiers, under Kara Mustapha, from 14 July to 12 September

1683–1736 Prince Eugene of Savoy wins more victories over Turks and French, restoring Austria's fortunes

1690

Kara Mustapha

The war of the Spanish Succession: Battle of Blenheim

1700–14 The war of the Spanish Succession

1700

Turkish Siege
The defeat of the Turks in 1683 was crucial, not only for Vienna, but for Central Europe, which was spared the prospect of Ottoman rule.

Baroque statues

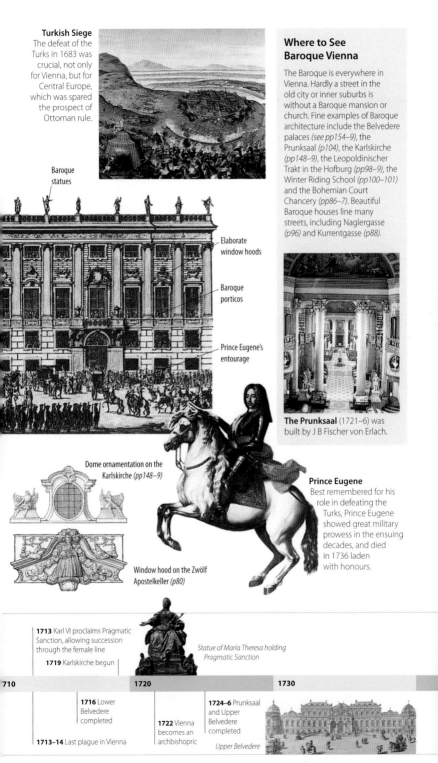

Elaborate window hoods

Baroque porticos

Prince Eugene's entourage

Where to See Baroque Vienna

The Baroque is everywhere in Vienna. Hardly a street in the old city or inner suburbs is without a Baroque mansion or church. Fine examples of Baroque architecture include the Belvedere palaces (see pp154–9), the Prunksaal (p104), the Karlskirche (pp148–9), the Leopoldinischer Trakt in the Hofburg (pp98–9), the Winter Riding School (pp100–101) and the Bohemian Court Chancery (pp86–7). Beautiful Baroque houses line many streets, including Naglergasse (p96) and Kurrentgasse (p88).

The Prunksaal (1721–6) was built by J B Fischer von Erlach.

Dome ornamentation on the Karlskirche (pp148–9)

Window hood on the Zwölf Apostelkeller (p80)

Prince Eugene
Best remembered for his role in defeating the Turks, Prince Eugene showed great military prowess in the ensuing decades, and died in 1736 laden with honours.

1713 Karl VI proclaims Pragmatic Sanction, allowing succession through the female line

1719 Karlskirche begun

Statue of Maria Theresa holding Pragmatic Sanction

710

1720

1730

1716 Lower Belvedere completed

1722 Vienna becomes an archbishopric

1724–6 Prunksaal and Upper Belvedere completed

1713–14 Last plague in Vienna

Upper Belvedere

Vienna under Maria Theresa

The long reign of Maria Theresa was a time of serenity, wealth and sensible administration, despite a background of frequent wars. The vast palace of Schönbrunn was completed by the Empress, who also presided over Vienna's development as the musical capital of Europe. She was succeeded by Joseph II, who introduced many reforms, including religious freedom and public health measures. However, these reforms made him unpopular with his subjects, including the nobility who were angered by the way he handed out titles to bankers and industrialists.

Extent of the City
1775   Today

Rococo Table
Wilhelm Martitz designed this Rococo table in 1769 for Maria Theresa, who employed artists committed to the elaborate Rococo style.

Karlskirche   Stephansdom

Young Mozart
Mozart often performed for the Habsburgs, who were highly receptive to his genius.

Burgtheater Programme
This programme was printed for the first performance of Mozart's *The Marriage of Figaro* in 1786, which took place in the original Burgtheater on Michaelerplatz.

Christoph Gluck

1744–9 Schönbrunn Palace is extensively altered by Maria Theresa's court architect, Nikolaus Pacassi

1754 Vienna's first census records a population of 175,000

1740   **1750**   **1760**

1740 Maria Theresa comes to the throne; war of the Austrian Succession

Schönbrunn Palace

1762 First performance of Christoph Gluck's *(see p40) Orpheus and Eurydice* in the Burgtheater

1766 Prater, formerly an imperial game reserve, opened to the public by Joseph II

Damenkarussell
This painting by Martin van Meytens depicts the Damenkarussell (1743), which was held at the Winter Riding School *(see pp100–101)* to celebrate the defeat of the French army at Prague.

Where to See Maria Theresa's Vienna

Schönbrunn Palace *(see pp174–7)* and the Theresianum *(p153)* date from the reign of Maria Theresa. Joseph II later commissioned the Josephinum *(p113)* and the Narrenturm *(p113)*, and opened the Augarten *(p166)* and Prater *(pp164–5)* to the public. There is a Rococo organ in the Michaelerkirche *(p94)*, and some of Maria Theresa's tableware is in the Hofburg Treasuries *(pp102–3)*.

Schönbrunn Palace is filled with Rococo interiors commissioned by Maria Theresa.

The Rococo high altar in the Michaelerkirche dates from around 1750.

Belvedere Gardens

View from the Belvedere
Under Maria Theresa, the Viennese were able to enjoy a prosperous city. This town-scape by Bernardo Bellotto (1759–61) shows them sauntering through the gardens of the Belvedere, with the palaces and churches of the city in the distance.

The Pope
In 1782 Pope Pius VI came to Vienna in an attempt to undo the religious reforms of Joseph II.

1775 Augarten opened to the public by Joseph II

1781 Joseph II's Edict of Toleration

Allgemeine Krankenhaus

1784 Joseph II founds the Allgemeine Krankenhaus and Narrenturm *(see p113)*

1770

1780

1790

1786 First performance of Mozart's *The Marriage of Figaro* in the Burgtheater

1790–2 Emperor Leopold II

1782 Pope Pius VI visits Vienna

1791 First performance of Mozart's *The Magic Flute*

Biedermeier Vienna

Napoleon's defeat of Austria was a humiliation for Emperor Franz I. The French conqueror briefly occupied Schönbrunn Palace, demolished part of the city walls, and married the emperor's daughter. After the Congress of Vienna, Franz I and his minister, Prince Metternich, imposed autocratic rule in Austria. The middle classes, excluded from political life, retreated into the artistic and domestic pursuits that characterized the Biedermeier age. Revolution in 1848 drove Metternich from power but led to a new period of conservative rule under Franz Joseph.

Extent of the City
▨ 1830   ☐ Today

Assembly of statesmen at the Congress of Vienna, 1814–15, by Engelbert Seibertz

The Congress of Vienna

After the defeat of Napoleon in 1814, the victorious European powers gathered in Vienna to restore the established order that had been severely disrupted by the French emperor. The crowned heads and elected rulers of Europe spent a year in the city, where the court and nobility entertained them with a succession of balls and other diversions. The outcome was the restoration of reactionary rule across Europe, which, although repressive in many countries, managed to maintain the peace until a series of revolutions swept across Europe in 1848.

Prince Metternich
The architect of the Congress of Vienna, Metternich exercised considerable political influence for four decades. In 1848 revolutionary mobs drove him from Vienna.

The singer Michael Vogl

Franz Schubert playing the piano

Napoleon Bonaparte

Franz Grillparzer

1800 Vienna's population 232,000

1806 The Holy Roman Empire ends after Franz II abdicates and becomes Emperor Franz I of Austria

1811 Austria suffers economic collapse and state bankruptcy

1812–14 Napoleon defeated by Russia, Prussia, England and Austria

1800

1810

1820

1805 First performance of Beethoven's *Eroica* Symphony and *Fidelio* in Theater an der Wien. Napoleon wins victory at Austerlitz

1809 Napoleon moves into Schönbrunn Palace and marries Franz I's daughter Maria Louisa

1815–48 Period of political suppression known as the Vormärz

1814–15 Congress of Vienna held; Austria loses Belgium but gains parts of Northern Italy

1825 Johann Strauss the Elder leads his first waltz orchestra

The 1848 Revolution
This painting from 1848 by Anton Ziegler shows the revolution in Vienna, when the middle classes and workers fought together against Metternich.

Biedermeier Chair
This style of furniture characterized the domestic aspirations of Vienna's middle classes in the 1820s.

Where to See Biedermeier Vienna

Napoleon's partial demolition of the city walls led to the creation of the Burggarten (see p104) and the Volksgarten (p106). Domestic architecture flourished – Biedermeier houses include the Geymüllerschlössel (p162) and the Dreimäderlhaus (p133) – as did the applied arts (pp84–5).

The Geymüllerschlössel, dating from 1802, is home to Vienna's Biedermeier museum.

Schubertiade

Franz Schubert (see p40) wrote over 600 vocal pieces. These were often performed at musical evenings such as the one shown in this painting, An Evening at Baron von Spaun's, *by Moritz von Schwind (1804–71).*

The Grand Gallop
Waltzes, popularized by Johann Strauss I (the Elder) (see p40), were extremely popular in the 1820s.

1827 Death of Beethoven

1828 Death of Schubert

1830 Vienna's population reaches 318,000

1831–2 Cholera epidemic

1831 The dramatist Franz Grillparzer completes *Des Meeres und der Liebe Wellen*

1830

1837 First railway constructed

1840

1845 Gas lighting introduced

1846 Johann Strauss the Younger becomes music director of the court balls until 1870

1848 Revolution in Vienna; Metternich forced from office, and Emperor Ferdinand I abdicates to be replaced by Franz Joseph

1850 City population reaches 431,000

Ringstrasse Vienna

Emperor Franz Joseph ushered in a new age of grandeur, despite the dwindling power of the Habsburgs. The city's defences were demolished and a circular boulevard, the Ringstrasse, was built, linking new cultural and political institutions. Vienna attracted gifted men and women from all over the empire, as well as traders from Eastern Europe. However, the resulting ethnic brew often resulted in overcrowding and social tension.

Extent of the City
◻ 1885   ◻ Today

Votivkirche *p113*
(Heinrich Ferstel, 1856–79)

Neues Rathaus *p132*
(Friedrich von Schmidt, 1872–83)

Parliament *p123*
(Theophil Hansen, 1874–84)

The Naturhistorisches Museum *pp130–3*
(Gottfried Semper, 1871–90)

Kunsthistorisches Museum *pp124–9*
(Gottfried Semper, 1871–90)

The Suicide of Archduke Rudolf at the Mayerling Hunting Lodge

In 1889 the 30-year-old heir to the throne was found dead alongside his mistress Mary Vetsera. The Archduke's suicide was more than a social scandal. It was a blow to the Habsburg regime, since he was a progressive and intelligent man. His despair may have been aggravated by court protocol that offered no outlet for his ideas.

Theophil Hansen
This Danish-born architect (1813–91) studied in Athens before settling in Vienna. A Greek influence is most evident in his Parliament building on the Ringstrasse.

Excavation for the Ringstrasse

1867 First performance of *The Blue Danube* by Strauss in Vienna. Hungary granted autonomy, leading to Dual Monarchy with separate governments

| 1850 | 1855 | 1860 | 1865 |

1868 Anton Bruckner *(see p41)* moves from Linz to Vienna

Anton Bruckner

1857–65 Demolition of fortifications and the building of the Ringstrasse

1869 The Opera House opens on Ringstrasse with a performance of Mozart's *Don Giovanni*

The Danube

The River Danube often flooded its banks, so its course was altered and regulated in the 1890s by a system of canals and locks.

Vienna Café Society

In the 19th century, Vienna's cafés became the haunts of literary and political cliques.

Horse-drawn Trams

Trams appeared on the Ringstrasse in the 1860s. Horseless trams ran along it by the end of the 19th century.

Museum of Applied Arts *pp84–5*
(Heinrich Ferstel, 1867–71)

Stadtpark

Opera House *pp140–41*
(Eduard van der Null and August Siccardsburg, 1861–9)

Ringstrasse

This great boulevard, built under Franz Joseph, separates the Stephansdom and Hofburg Quarters from the suburbs. Completed in the 1880s, the Ringstrasse is as grand now as it was then.

The Opening of the Stadtpark

Laid out on either side of the River Wien, the Stadtpark was inaugurated in 1862.

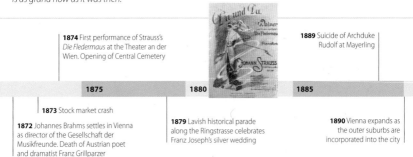

1874 First performance of Strauss's *Die Fledermaus* at the Theater an der Wien. Opening of Central Cemetery

1889 Suicide of Archduke Rudolf at Mayerling

870   1875   1880   1885

1873 Stock market crash

1872 Johannes Brahms settles in Vienna as director of the Gesellschaft der Musikfreunde. Death of Austrian poet and dramatist Franz Grillparzer

1879 Lavish historical parade along the Ringstrasse celebrates Franz Joseph's silver wedding

1890 Vienna expands as the outer suburbs are incorporated into the city

Vienna in the 1900s

The turn of the twentieth century was a time of intellectual ferment in Vienna. This was the age of Freud, of the writers Karl Kraus and Arthur Schnitzler, and of the Secession and Jugendstil movements *(see pp56–9)*. Artists such as Gustav Klimt and the architects Otto Wagner and Adolf Loos *(see p94)* created revolutionary new styles. This was all set against a decaying Habsburg empire, which Karl I's abdication in 1918 brought to an end. After World War I Austria became a republic.

Extent of the City
1912   Today

Wiener Werkstätte
Josef Hoffmann *(see p58)*, designer of this chair, was the principal artist and founder of this Viennese arts workshop *(see p85)*.

Kirche am Steinhof
This stupendous church was designed by Otto Wagner and decorated by Kolo Moser (see p59).

Looshaus
The restrained elegance of this former haberdashery is typical of Loos's style *(see p94)*.

The Secession
This poster by Kolo Moser *(see p59)* was used to publicize the Secession's exhibitions.

Angels by Othmar Schimkowitz

1899 First issue of Karl Kraus's periodical *Die Fackel*

1903 Wiener Werkstätte founded

1905 Franz Lehár's operetta *The Merry Widow* first performed. Anti-Semitic riots at the university

1895

1900

1905

1897 Secession established when 19 painters and architects break with the Künstlerhaus. Karl Lueger becomes mayor

1902 Gustav Klimt paints the *Beethoven Frieze*. Tramways are electrified

1907 Gustav Mahler resigns as director of Court Opera. Hitler studies art in Vienna

1896 Death of the composer Anton Bruckner

Gustav Klimt

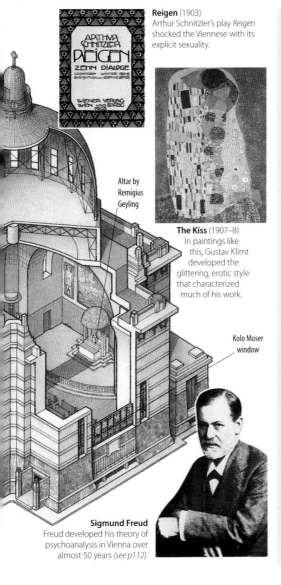

Reigen (1903)
Arthur Schnitzler's play *Reigen* shocked the Viennese with its explicit sexuality.

Altar by Remigius Geyling

The Kiss (1907–8)
In paintings like this, Gustav Klimt developed the glittering, erotic style that characterized much of his work.

Kolo Moser window

Sigmund Freud
Freud developed his theory of psychoanalysis in Vienna over almost 50 years *(see p112).*

Where to See 1900s Vienna

Otto Wagner designed the Karlsplatz Pavilions *(see p150),* the Wagner Apartments *(p143)* and the Kirche am Steinhof *(p162).* Adolf Loos designed the Looshaus *(p94)* and the American Bar *(p107).* Suburban architecture includes the Wagner Villas *(p162).* Works by Klimt, Schiele and Kokoschka are displayed at the Upper Belvedere *(pp156–7),* the Museum of Modern Art *(p122)* and the Leopold Museum *(p122).*

The Secession Building is where Gustav Klimt's *Beethoven Frieze* is exhibited *(p57).*

The Wagner Apartments are decorated with Jugendstil motifs *(p58)* by Kolo Moser *(p59).*

1911 Death of Gustav Mahler

1914 Archduke Ferdinand assassinated in Sarajevo; international crisis follows resulting in World War I

1910

1915

1910 Death of Karl Lueger

1913 Arnold Schönberg's *Chamber Symphony* and works by Anton von Webern and Alban Berg performed at the Musikverein, provoking a riot

1916 Death of Franz Joseph

1908 *The Kiss* by Klimt is first exhibited

1918 Declaration of Austrian Republic after abdication of Emperor Karl I. Austria shrinks from an empire of 50 million to a state of 6.5 million

Modern Vienna

Two decades of struggle between the left and right political parties followed World War I, ending with the union of Austria with Germany – the Anschluss – in 1938. After World War II Vienna was split among the Allies until 1955, when Austria regained its independence.

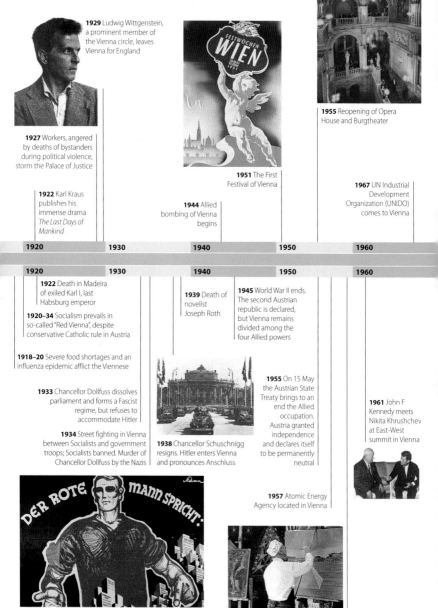

1929 Ludwig Wittgenstein, a prominent member of the Vienna circle, leaves Vienna for England

1955 Reopening of Opera House and Burgtheater

1927 Workers, angered by deaths of bystanders during political violence, storm the Palace of Justice

1951 The First Festival of Vienna

1967 UN Industrial Development Organization (UNIDO) comes to Vienna

1922 Karl Kraus publishes his immense drama *The Last Days of Mankind*

1944 Allied bombing of Vienna begins

1920	1930	1940	1950	1960

1920	1930	1940	1950	1960

1922 Death in Madeira of exiled Karl I, last Habsburg emperor

1939 Death of novelist Joseph Roth

1945 World War II ends. The second Austrian republic is declared, but Vienna remains divided among the four Allied powers

1920–34 Socialism prevails in so-called "Red Vienna", despite conservative Catholic rule in Austria

1918–20 Severe food shortages and an influenza epidemic afflict the Viennese

1933 Chancellor Dollfuss dissolves parliament and forms a Fascist regime, but refuses to accommodate Hitler

1955 On 15 May the Austrian State Treaty brings to an end the Allied occupation. Austria granted independence and declares itself to be permanently neutral

1961 John F Kennedy meets Nikita Khrushchev at East-West summit in Vienna

1934 Street fighting in Vienna between Socialists and government troops; Socialists banned. Murder of Chancellor Dollfuss by the Nazis

1938 Chancellor Schuschnigg resigns. Hitler enters Vienna and pronounces Anschluss

1957 Atomic Energy Agency located in Vienna

1959 Ernst Fuchs and Arik Brauer establish the school of fantastic realism

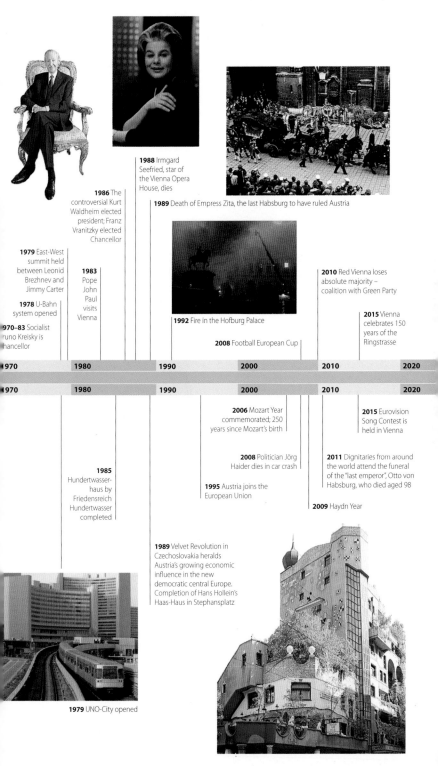

1988 Irmgard Seefried, star of the Vienna Opera House, dies

1986 The controversial Kurt Waldheim elected president; Franz Vranitzky elected Chancellor

1989 Death of Empress Zita, the last Habsburg to have ruled Austria

1979 East-West summit held between Leonid Brezhnev and Jimmy Carter

1983 Pope John Paul visits Vienna

1978 U-Bahn system opened

2010 Red Vienna loses absolute majority – coalition with Green Party

1970–83 Socialist Bruno Kreisky is Chancellor

2015 Vienna celebrates 150 years of the Ringstrasse

1992 Fire in the Hofburg Palace

2008 Football European Cup

| 1970 | 1980 | 1990 | 2000 | 2010 | 2020 |

| 1970 | 1980 | 1990 | 2000 | 2010 | 2020 |

2006 Mozart Year commemorated; 250 years since Mozart's birth

2015 Eurovision Song Contest is held in Vienna

1985 Hundertwasser-haus by Friedensreich Hundertwasser completed

2008 Politician Jörg Haider dies in car crash

1995 Austria joins the European Union

2011 Dignitaries from around the world attend the funeral of the "last emperor", Otto von Habsburg, who died aged 98

2009 Haydn Year

1989 Velvet Revolution in Czechoslovakia heralds Austria's growing economic influence in the new democratic central Europe. Completion of Hans Hollein's Haas-Haus in Stephansplatz

1979 UNO-City opened

Music in Vienna

From the late 18th to the mid 19th centuries Vienna was the music capital of Europe, and its musical heritage and magnificent venues remain one of the city's chief attractions. At first the Habsburgs and the aristocracy were the city's musical paymasters, but with the rise of the middle classes during the Biedermeier period *(see pp32–3)*, music became an important part of bourgeois life. Popular music also flourished as migration from all parts of the Habsburg Empire brought in richly diverse styles of music and dance.

Classicism

In the 18th century, Vienna's musical life was dominated by the imperial court. The composer Christoph Willibald Gluck (1714–87) was court *Kapellmeister* (in charge of the court orchestra) to Maria Theresa until 1770, and wrote 10 operas specially for Vienna, including *Orpheus and Eurydice* (1762). His contemporary Wolfgang Amadeus Mozart (1756–91) later built on these foundations.

Joseph Haydn (1732–1809) moved to Vienna in the 1790s from Prince Paul Esterházy's palace in Eisenstadt, where his house is now a museum *(see pp178–9)*, and wrote masterpieces such as his great oratorio *The Creation*.

Performance of *The Creation* (1808) on Haydn's birthday

Romanticism

With the arrival of Ludwig van Beethoven (1770–1827) in Vienna in the mid-1790s, the age of the composer as romantic hero was born. Beethoven was a controversial figure in his time, and many of his most innovative works were only successful outside Vienna. His funeral, however, was a state occasion, and was attended by more than 10,000 people.

The music of Franz Schubert (1797–1828) was little known in his short lifetime. He mostly performed chamber works, piano music and songs at Biedermeier *Schubertiaden* – evenings of music with friends. His music gained greater recognition following his death.

Both Johann Strauss I (1804–49) and Joseph Lanner (1801–43) created a number of pieces to accompany the hugely popular waltz. The waltz was a sensation, enjoyed by the peasant class and high society alike, not least because it was the first ballroom

Performance of *The Magic Flute* (1791) by Mozart

Biedermeier *Schubertiade* evening

dance in which couples danced clasped closely together. The ladies of Vienna gained renown throughout Europe for the grace and tireless energy of their waltzing.

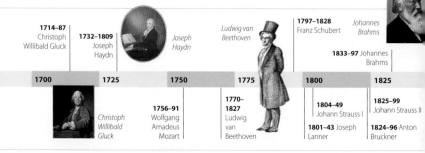

	1714–87 Christoph Willibald Gluck	1732–1809 Joseph Haydn	*Joseph Haydn*	*Ludwig van Beethoven*	1797–1828 Franz Schubert	*Johannes Brahms*
					1833–97 Johannes Brahms	
1700		**1725**	**1750**	**1775**	**1800**	**1825**
		Christoph Willibald Gluck	1756–91 Wolfgang Amadeus Mozart	1770–1827 Ludwig van Beethoven	1804–49 Johann Strauss I	1825–99 Johann Strauss II
					1801–43 Joseph Lanner	1824–96 Anton Bruckner

Age of Franz Joseph

The 1860s saw the emergence of a new era of music. Johannes Brahms (1833–97) came to Vienna in 1862, and incorporated popular musical styles into works such as his *Liebeslieder* waltzes and *Hungarian Dances*. The Romantic composer Anton Bruckner (1824–96) came to the city from Upper Austria in 1868. Johann Strauss II (1825–99) rose to the status of civic hero, composing nearly 400 waltzes, as well as his famous operetta *Die Fledermaus*. One popular offshoot of the period was *Schrammel* music, named after Joseph Schrammel (1852–95) and characterized by an

Jugendstil poster (1901) depicting Johann Strauss II

ensemble of guitars, violins and accordion. Popular music also influenced Gustav Mahler (1860–1911), director of the Vienna Opera for 10 years.

The Moderns

The early years of the 20th century saw the rise of the Second Viennese School: Alban Berg (1885–1935), Arnold Schönberg (1874–1951) and Anton von Webern (1883–1945). These composers were not well received in Vienna, and Schönberg found he had to start his own society to get his works, and those of his colleagues, heard. In 1933 he emigrated to the USA.

Since World War II no composers of comparable stature have arisen, though Kurt Schwertsik (born 1935) and H K Gruber (born 1943) now attract international attention. However, the Vienna Philharmonic, established in 1842, is still one of the finest orchestras in the world. The State Opera continues to enjoy a strong reputation, and Vienna also has an abundance of fine orchestras, opera and operetta venues, chamber ensembles and choirs, including the Vienna Boys' Choir.

The Johann Strauss II orchestra at a court ball

Concert poster (1913) for Arnold Schönberg

1860–1911 Gustav Mahler	1874–1951 Arnold Schönberg
	1875
1883–1945 Anton von Webern	1885–1935 Alban Berg
1852–95 Joseph Schrammel	

Vienna Boys' Choir

The world-famous Vienna Boys' Choir, the Wiener Sängerknaben, was founded in 1498 by that great patron of the arts, Maximilian I. Today the boys perform Masses by Mozart, Schubert or Haydn on Sundays and church holidays at the Burgkapelle *(see p105)*. To obtain a seat you need to book at least eight weeks in advance.

VIENNA AT A GLANCE

Vienna is a compact city and most of its sights are contained within a small area. The city boasts an astonishing array of monuments, palaces, parks and museums, which themselves house an impressive array of art and artifacts from all over the world and from all periods of history. Nearly 150 sights are listed in the *Area by Area* section of this book, but to help make the most of your stay, the next 20 pages offer a guide to the very best that Vienna has to offer. As well as churches, palaces, museums and galleries, there are sections on Jugendstil art and coffee houses. Many of the sights listed have a cross-reference to their own full entry. Pictured below are some of Vienna's top tourist attractions that no visitor should miss.

Vienna's Top Tourist Attractions

Opera House
See pp140–41.

Burgtheater
See pp134–5.

Prater
See pp164–5.

Karlskirche
See pp148–9.

Schönbrunn *See pp174–7.*

Spanish Riding School
See pp100–101.

Kunsthistorisches Museum
See pp124–9.

Stephansdom *See pp74–7.*

Café Central
See p63.

MuseumsQuartier
See p120–23.

Belvedere
See pp154–9.

◀ View across the decorative roof tiles of the Stephansdom

Vienna's Best: Historic Houses and Palaces

Baroque mansions dominate the streets of the Stephansdom Quarter, while outside the centre of Vienna are the grand summer palaces where the Habsburg emperors and aristocracy lived during warm Central European summers. The interiors of several of the houses can be visited, while others can only be admired from the outside or from their inner courtyards and staircases. Further details can be found on pages 46–7.

Freud Museum
The home – and office – of Sigmund Freud, who lived here from 1891 to 1938, is full of memorabilia of Freud's working and domestic life *(see p112)*.

Kinsky Palace
This mansion (1713–16) by Johann Lukas von Hildebrandt *(see p154)*, was built for the Daun family, and is sometimes called the Daun Kinsky Palace. Wirich Philipp von Daun was commander of the city garrison, and his son Leopold Joseph von Daun was Maria Theresa's field marshal.

Schottenring and Alsergrund

Hofburg
The apartments here are made up of over 20 rooms; among them are ceremonial halls and living quarters that were once occupied by Franz Joseph *(see pp34–5)* and the Empress Elisabeth.

Museum and Townhall Quarter

Hofburg Quarter

Opera and Naschmarkt

Schönbrunn Palace

0 kilometres 2
0 miles 1

Schönbrunn Palace
This palace, by J B Fischer von Erlach, was built on a scale to rival the palace of Versailles outside Paris. Parts of it were later redesigned by Maria Theresa's architect Nikolaus Pacassi *(see pp174–7)*.

Neidhart Fresco House
Frescoes dating from 1400, depicting the songs of the medieval minnesinger Neidhart van Reuenthal, decorate the dining room of this former house of a wealthy clockmaker.

```
0 metres        500
0 yards         500
```

Mozarthaus Vienna
Mozart lived in this Baroque building for three years between 1784 and 1787, and composed one of his most famous works, *The Marriage of Figaro*, here.

DANUBE CANAL

Stephansdom Quarter

Winter Palace of Prince Eugene
J B Fischer von Erlach and Johann Lukas von Hildebrandt designed this Baroque palace, with its spectacular staircase, for the war hero Prince Eugene *(see pp28–9)*.

Belvedere Quarter

Zum Blauen Karpfen
A stucco relief of a blue carp and a frieze of *putti* adorn the façade of this 17th-century house on Annagasse.

Belvedere
Designed by Johann Lukas von Hildebrandt, Prince Eugene's summer palaces were built on what were originally the southern outskirts of Vienna. The Upper Belvedere now houses the Museum of Austrian Art.

Exploring Vienna's Historic Houses and Palaces

A stroll around Vienna's streets provides the visitor an unparalleled view of beautifully preserved historic buildings, from former imperial residences to humbler burghers' dwellings. The majority date from the 17th and 18th centuries and illustrate the various phases of Baroque architecture. In most cases their original function as residences of the rich and famous has been superseded; a number have now been turned into museums and even hotels, and their interiors are open to the public.

Façade of the Schönborn-Batthyány Palace

Town Palaces

The most extensive town palace is the **Hofburg**, with its museums and imperial apartments. The staircase of the magnificent **Winter Palace of Prince Eugene** is on view to the public, as is the **Liechtenstein Palace** (1694–1706), the winter home of the Liechtenstein family. The Neo-Gothic **Ferstel Palace** (1860) houses the Café Central (see p60). The **Obizzi Palace** is home to the Clock Museum (see p88) and the **Lobkowitz Palace** to a theatre museum (see p106). Town palaces which can be admired from the outside only are the **Kinsky Palace** (1713–16), **Trautson Palace** and **Schönborn-Batthyány Palace**.

Garden Palaces

Although it seems strange that palaces within the city limits should be termed garden palaces, when they were built they were outside the city boundaries, and offered a cool refuge for their inhabitants during the hot summer months. The most famous example is **Schönbrunn Palace**, where the state apartments can be seen as part of a guided tour. The **Belvedere**, to the south of the city, houses the Museum of Austrian Art, and many rooms retain their original splendid decoration. The **Hermesvilla** (1884), a cross between a hunting lodge and a Viennese villa, was commissioned by Franz Joseph for his wife Elisabeth. The interior of the Neo-Classical **Rasumofsky Palace** (1806–7) can be seen only on special occasions. The **Liechtenstein Garden Palace** houses the private art collection of the Liechtenstein family (see p113). The pieces include Renaissance sculpture and Baroque paintings.

Frescoed ceiling of the Liechtenstein Garden Palace

Suburban Villas

The Döbling District Museum is housed in the Biedermeier **Villa Wertheimstein** (1834–5), whose interior is furnished in its original flamboyant and overcrowded manner. By contrast, the **Geymüller-schlössel**, containing the Sobek Collection of clocks and watches, is a model of taste and restraint. In Hietzing, the **Villa Primavesi** (1913–15) is a small Jugendstil masterpiece designed by Josef Hoffmann (see p58) for the banker Robert Primavesi.

Burghers' Houses

On Tuchlauben, the **Neidhart Fresco House** is decorated with secular frescoes from around 1400. Charming Baroque houses of modest dimensions can be seen on **Naglergasse** and **Kurrent-gasse** and in inner districts such as **Spittelberg** and **Josefstadt**. A particularly fine example of external decoration can be seen on the Baroque inn **Zum Blauen Karpfen** in Annagasse (see p82). The **Dreimäderlhaus** in Schreyvogelgasse, built in an intermediate style between Rococo and Neo-Classicism, is also worth visiting.

Façade and gardens of the Hermesvilla

Memorial Houses

Vienna abounds in the former residences of famous composers. They are not all of great architectural merit, and their interest resides mainly in the exhibits they contain. The **Pasqualatihaus** was one of Beethoven's many Viennese residences – it was here that he composed the opera *Fidelio* – and it now houses portraits and other mementoes of the great composer. The **Heiligenstadt Testament House** (at No. 6 Probusgasse, Heiligenstadt), where Beethoven stayed in an attempt to cure his deafness, is now a memorial.

The first-floor apartment of the **Haydn Museum** in Haydngasse is pleasantly furnished and filled with

Courtyard of the Heiligenstadt Testament House

letters, manuscripts, personal possessions and the composer's two pianos. Mozart and his family lived from 1784 to 1787 in the **Mozarthaus Vienna**. This is where Mozart wrote *The Marriage of Figaro*. The

Freud Museum houses furnishings, documents and photographs, and the consulting room is as it looked when Sigmund Freud used to see his patients. It is also used as a study centre.

Decorative Details

Many of the historic houses and palaces of Vienna were built during a period corresponding to the Baroque and late Baroque styles of architecture. Details such as window hoods and pediments over doorways were often extremely ornate.

Caryatid on the doorway of the Liechtenstein Palace

Decorative window hood on the façade of the Trautson Palace

Decorative urns on the Lobkowitz Palace

Decorative pediment with shield on the Schönborn-Batthyány Palace

Stucco *putti* on the façade of Zum Blauen Karpfen

Finding the Palaces and Houses

Vienna's Best: Museums and Galleries

Vienna boasts an astonishing number of museums, and many of the collections are housed in elegant former palaces or handsome buildings specially commissioned for the purpose. Some of the museums are of international importance, while others are of more local or specialist interest. Further details can be found on pages 50–51.

Sacred and Secular Treasuries
The Ainkurn sword (around 1450) can be seen in the Imperial Treasuries in the former imperial palace of the Hofburg.

Naturhistorisches Museum
This museum has displays on fossils, ethnography and mineralogy, and a much-visited dinosaur hall.

Schottenring and Alsergrund

Museum and Townhall Quarter

Kunsthistorisches Museum
Hans Holbein's portrait of Jane Seymour (1536) is one of hundreds of Old Masters displayed in this fine art museum.

Hofburg Quarter

Opera and Naschmarkt

MuseumsQuartier
Contained in this vast cultural centre is the largest Egon Schiele collection in the world, including this *Self-portrait with Lowered Head* (1912).

Albertina
This museum houses temporary exhibitions, mainly based on the Albertina's celebrated collection of prints and drawings (here, Albrecht Dürer's *The Hare*, dated 1502).

Wien Museum Karlsplatz
Stained-glass windows from the Stephansdom (around 1390) are among the many items here documenting Vienna's history.

Cathedral Museum
This St Andrew's cross reliquary (c. 1440) is one of many medieval religious treasures held by the cathedral.

DANUBE CANAL

Austrian Museum of Applied Arts
This early 19th-century beaker and Wiener Werkstätte furniture (see pp56–7) are among examples of decorative and applied arts on display in this museum.

Stephansdom Quarter

The Belvedere
The Upper Belvedere displays art from the Middle Ages onwards, including medieval painting and sculpture and Renaissance and Baroque works. Ferdinand Waldmüller's *Roses in the Window*, shown here, is part of this collection, as is Gustav Klimt's *The Kiss*. The Lower Belvedere and Orangery house temporary exhibitions.

Belvedere Quarter

Heeresgeschichtliches Museum
Paintings of battles and military commanders, such as Sigmund L'Allemand's portrait of Field Marshal Gideon-Ernst Freiherr von Laudon (1878), are part of this museum's collection.

0 metres	500
0 yards	500

Exploring Vienna's Museums and Galleries

Vienna's museums exhibit an amazing variety of fine, decorative and ethnic art from all periods of history and from different regions of the world. Visitors can enjoy ancient antiquities, Medieval religious art and a huge collection of 19th- and 20th-century paintings, including works by some of history's finest artists. There is also a range of museums dedicated to specialist subjects such as military history, music and crime.

Interior of Friedensreich Hundertwasser's Kunsthaus Wien

Ancient and Medieval Art

Vienna has marvellous collections of medieval art. The **Neidhart Fresco House** contains medieval secular frescoes, while a number of superb Gothic altarpieces can be seen in the historic Palace Stables at the **Belvedere**. Displayed in the **Cathedral Museum** are outstanding Gothic sculptures as well as masterpieces of applied art; the highlight is a 9th-century Carolingian Gospel. The **Sacred and Secular Treasuries** in the Hofburg are awash with precious medieval objects, including the insignia and crown of the Holy Roman Emperor, and a unique collection of medieval objects and Gothic paintings is on display in the treasury of the **Deutschordenskirche**. The splendours of the Verduner Altar at **Klosterneuburg** await those

prepared to make a short journey out from the centre of Vienna. The **Ephesos Museum** of the Hofburg houses ancient Roman and Greek antiquities unearthed at the turn of the century.

Old Masters

The picture gallery in the **Kunsthistorisches Museum** has one of the best collections of Old Masters in the world, reflecting the tastes of the many generations of Habsburg collectors who formed it. There are works by Flemish and Venetian artists, and the best collection of Bruegels on display in any art gallery, as well as Giuseppe Arcimboldo's (1527–93) curious portraits composed of fruit and vegetables. The **Academy of Fine Arts** houses some fine examples of Dutch and Flemish works, its prize exhibit being Hieronymus Bosch's triptych of The Last

Judgment, which contains some of the most horrifying images in Christan art. There are also paintings by Johannes Vermeer (1632–75) and Peter Paul Rubens (1577–1640). The ground floor of the **Upper Belvedere** focuses on Austrian painting and sculpture from the 17th and 18th centuries. The Belvedere itself is a master-piece of Baroque architecture.

19th- and 20th-Century Art

A permanent display of 19th- and 20th-century Austrian art is housed in the **Upper Belvedere**. The most famous works are by Gustav Klimt. *Beethoven Frieze* is regarded as one of the master-pieces of Viennese Art Nouveau and can be seen in the **Secession Building**.

The **Museum of Modern Art**, located in the Museums-Quartier *(see p122)*, shows the work of 20th- century European artists. Included are pieces by the Viennese avant-garde.

The **Leopold Museum** has an enormous Egon Schiele collection, as well as Expressionist and Austrian interwar paintings. The work of Friedensreich Hundertwasser, perhaps Vienna's best-known modern artist, is on show at the **Kunst Haus Wien**. Prints, drawings and photographs are housed in the **Albertina**.

Parthian monument (around AD 170) in the Ephesos Museum

The Applied Arts and Interiors

On display in the **Austrian Museum of Applied Arts** is a rich collection of the decorative arts, including Oriental carpets, medieval ecclesiastical garments, Biedermeier and Jugendstil furniture, and the archives of the Wiener Werkstätte. The **Wien Museum Karlsplatz** houses reconstructed versions of the poet Franz Grillparzer's apartment as well as Adolf Loos's *(see p94)* drawing room. In the **Silberkammer** of the Hofburg is a dazzling array of dinner services collected by the Habsburgs. The **Lobmeyr Museum** exhibits glassware designed by Josef Hoffmann.

Glass by Josef Hoffmann in the Lobmeyr Museum

Picture clock in the Clock Museum

Specialist Museums

Clock enthusiasts should visit the **Clock Museum** and the Sobek Clock and Watch Collection at the **Geymüller-schlössel**. Music is celebrated at the **Sammlung Alter Musik-instrumente**, while the darker side of life can be seen at the **Kriminalmuseum**, and at the **Bestattungsmuseum**, which is dedicated to funeral customs, burial rites and the Viennese perspective on death. The **Heeresgeschichtliches Museum** explores Austria's military past and the **Hofjagd und Rüstkammer** exhibits historical weaponry. Other specialist museums include the **Österreichisches Filmmuseum** and the **Haus der Musik**.

Natural History and Science

Still occupying the building constructed for it in the 19th century is the impressive **Naturhistorisches Museum**, which has mineralogy, zoology and dinosaur exhibits, and a planetarium. The **Josephinum** houses a range of wax anatomical models, while the **Technical Museum** documents the contribution Austria has made to developments in technology, ranging from homemade items such as an amateur wooden typewriter, to the invention of the car.

Ethnology and Folklore

Vienna's Museum of Ethnology in the Hofburg, the **Weltmuseum Wien**, contains objects from all over the world *(see p97)*. There are artifacts from Mexico, a collection of musical instruments, masks and textiles from the Far East, a collection from Benin in West Africa and a section dedicated to Eskimo culture. The **Volkskunde Museum**, housed in the Schönborn Palace in Josefstadt, explores traditional Austrian folk culture through a range of items, some dating from the 17th and 19th centuries.

Benin carving in the Weltmuseum Wien

Vienna's Best: Churches

Vienna's most potent symbol is its cathedral – the Stephansdom – a masterpiece of Gothic architecture which stands out in a city that is overwhelmingly Baroque. After the defeat of the Turks in 1683 *(see pp28–9)*, many churches were built or remodelled in the Baroque style, although it is often possible to detect the vestiges of older buildings beneath later additions. Many church interiors are lavishly furnished and several have fine frescoes. Churches are generally open during the day except when Mass is being held. Concerts or organ recitals are given in the evenings in some churches. A more detailed overview of Vienna's churches is on pages 54–5.

Peterskirche
The tall dome of this late Baroque church dominates the view as you approach from the Graben.

Schottenring and Alsergrund

Maria am Gestade

Hofburg Quarter

Museum and Townhall Quarter

Michaelerkirche
This church has one of the most impressive medieval interiors in Vienna. The Neo-Classical façade and this cascade of Baroque stucco angels over the high altar were later additions.

Opera and Naschmarkt

Maria-Treu-Kirche
A statue of Mary Immaculate graces the square in front of this Baroque church (1716). Its façade dates from 1860.

| 0 metres | | 500 |
| 0 yards | | 500 |

Augustinerkirche
Antonio Canova's (1753–1822) tomb for Archduchess Maria Christina is in the Gothic Augustinerkirche, which once served as the Habsburgs' parish church.

Maria am Gestade
Dating from the 14th century, this church was restored in the 19th century. This 15th-century Gothic panel shows *The Annunciation*.

Ruprechtskirche
Vienna's oldest church has a Romanesque nave and bell tower, a Gothic aisle and choir, and stained-glass windows dating back to the turn of the 14th century.

DANUBE CANAL

Stephansdom
The richly carved Wiener Neustädter Altar from 1447 was a gift from Friedrich III *(see p21)*.

Stephansdom Quarter

Jesuitenkirche
A series of twisted columns rises up to support the vault of the Jesuitenkirche (1623–31), which also features a *trompe l'oeil* dome.

Belvedere Quarter

Karlskirche
J B Fischer von Erlach's eclectic Baroque masterpiece (1714 –39) boasts a dome, minarets and two Chinese-inspired lateral pavilions.

Franziskanerkirche
The dramatic high altar (1707) by Andrea Pozzo features a Bohemian statue of the Virgin Mary as its centrepiece.

Exploring Vienna's Churches

Many of Vienna's churches have undergone modifications over the centuries, and they often present a fascinating mixture of styles, ranging from Romanesque to Baroque. The great era for church building in the city was in the 17th and 18th centuries, when the triumphant Catholic church, in a spate of Counter-Reformation fervour, remodelled several early churches and built new ones. A number of churches were also constructed after the Turks were defeated in 1683 *(see pp28–9)* and, as a result, the city was able to spread out beyond its earlier confines.

Medieval Churches

At the heart of the city is the **Stephansdom**. Parts date from the Romanesque period but most of the cathedral is Gothic; its collection of Gothic sculpture includes a pulpit by Anton Pilgram *(see p76)*. Vienna's oldest church is the **Ruprechtskirche**, which stands in its own square in the Bermuda Triangle *(see p86)*; its plain façade contrasts with the delicate Gothic tracery of **Maria am Gestade**, which has a filigree spire and a lofty, vaulted interior. The early interior of the **Deutschordens-kirche** contains a number of heraldic blazons. A late Romanesque basilica with Gothic modifications lurks behind the façade of the **Michaelerkirche**. The 14th-century

Madonna and Child in the Minoritenkirche

Augustinerkirche has superb Gothic interiors and contains the hearts of the Habsburg families *(see pp26–7)* down the centuries and Antonio Canova's tomb for Maria Christina *(see p104)*. The **Minoritenkirche** has a French Gothic façade and with an ornate interior; the same is true of the 13th-century **Burgkapelle**.

17th-Century Churches

There is little Renaissance architecture in Vienna, but a number of churches built before the Turkish siege survive. The **Franziskanerkirche**, with its gabled façade and theatrical high altar, and the **Jesuitenkirche** are fine examples of the architecture inspired by the Counter-Reformation *(see p26)*. The **Ursulinenkirche**, built between 1665 and 1675, has a high-galleried interior while the **Annakirche** is notable for its beautiful Baroque tower. The **Dominikanerkirche** has a majestic early Baroque façade, built in the 1630s by Antonio Caneval. Although it dates back

to the Romanesque period, the bulk of the rather squat **Schottenkirche** was built between 1638 and 1648. In the middle of the Baroque square of Am Hof is the impressive façade of the **Kirche am Hof**. It was founded by the Carmelites and is also known as "Church of the Nine Choir Angels".

Carving of St Anne (c. 1505) in Annakirche, attributed to Veit Stoss

Late Baroque and Neo-Classical Churches

After the Turkish defeat *(see pp28–9)*, a number of Viennese High Baroque churches were built. The most exotic is the **Karlskirche**, commissioned by Emperor Karl VI after the plague epidemic of 1713, and just off the Graben is the great **Peterskirche**. The tiny, ornate **Stanislaus-Kostka Chapel** was once the home of a Polish saint. Two graceful 18th-century churches are to be found on the edge of the inner city: the majestic **Maria-Treu-Kirche** and the **Ulrichskirche**.

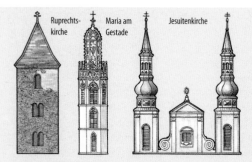

Towers, Domes and Spires

Vienna's skyline is punctuated by the domes, spires and towers of its fine churches. Topping **Maria am Gestade** is a delicate openwork lantern, while the **Ruprechtskirche** tower is characteristically squat. The towers of the **Jesuitenkirche** are Baroque and bulbous, and **Karlskirche** has freestanding columns. **Peterskirche** has an oval dome and small towers.

Ruprechts-kirche · Maria am Gestade · Jesuitenkirche

The frescoed interior of the late Baroque Stanislaus-Kostka Chapel

19th-Century Churches

During the 19th century the prevailing mood in Viennese architecture was one of Romantic historicism. Elements of past styles were adopted and recreated, in churches and many other municipal buildings, specifically on the Ringstrasse (see pp34–5). The **Griechische Kirche** on Fleischmarkt took its inspiration from Byzantine architecture, and the interior is replete with iconostases and frescoes. The **Votivkirche**, built just off the Ringstrasse as an expression of gratitude for Franz Joseph's escape from assassination, is based on French Gothic architecture; its richly coloured interior contains the marble tomb of Count Niklas Salm, who defended Vienna from the Turks during the siege of 1529 (see p26). On Lerchenfelder Strasse the red-brick **Altlerchenfelder Kirche** is a 19th-century architectural hodgepodge of Gothic and Italian Renaissance styles and the interior features colourful frescoes.

20th-Century Churches

A masterpiece of early 20th-century church architecture is Otto Wagner's (see p59) massive **Kirche am Steinhof**, built to serve a psychiatric hospital. The interior has a slightly clinical air, since it is tiled in white, but the austerity is relieved by Kolo Moser's (see p59) stained-glass windows and mosaics. The **Luegerkirche**, which is located in the

The haphazard, sculpted blocks of the modern Wotruba-Kirche

Central Cemetery, was built by Max Hegele, a protégé of Otto Wagner, and has the same monumental feel about it. For true devotees of modern art, there is the **Wotruba-Kirche** on Georgsgasse in the suburb of Mauer, designed by the sculptor Fritz Wotruba. A haphazard-looking assembly of large concrete blocks, its abstract form is not popular among everyone.

19th-century interior of the Altlerchenfelder Kirche

Finding the Churches

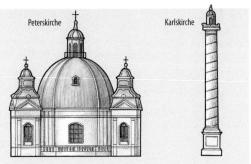

Peterskirche   Karlskirche

Vienna's Best: Jugendstil

A stroll around Vienna's streets will reveal the richness of the city's turn-of-the-century architecture. Some of the buildings are instantly recognizable, and a few of the public ones, such as the Secession building, are open to visitors. However, it can be just as rewarding to discover the lesser-known buildings and monuments of the period and to savour the wealth of finely crafted architectural details. Further details can be found on pages 58–9.

Strudlhof Steps
The setting for a famous novel of the same name by Heimato von Doderer (1896–1966), these magnificent steps were built by Theodore Jäger in 1910.

Schottenring and Alsergrund

0 metres 800
0 yards 800

Museum and Townhall Quarter

Wagner Apartments
Otto Wagner's two apartment blocks (1899) overlook the River Wien. No. 40, the Majolikahaus, is covered in ceramic decoration. No. 38 has gold Jugendstil motifs.

Opera and Naschmarkt

Kirche am Steinhof
Commissioned for the grounds of a lunatic asylum on the outskirts of the city, this church with its grand copper dome was designed by Otto Wagner in 1905. The stained-glass windows are by Kolo Moser.

0 kilometres 2
0 miles 1

Otto-Wagner-Hofpavillon
Otto Wagner's imperial station pavillon (1899) was built as a showcase for his work.

Anker Clock
This clock, created by the artist Franz Matsch in 1911, sits on a bridge spanning two buildings on the Hoher Markt. Every hour, on the hour, moving figures parade across the clock face.

Postsparkasse
One of Otto Wagner's masterpieces, the post office savings bank exhibits the finest workmanship inside and out. Even the interior ventilator shafts are by Wagner.

Stadtpark Portals
The city's municipal park is adorned with magnificent portals (1903–7), designed by Friedrich Ohmann as part of a project to regulate the flow of the River Wien.

Karlsplatz Pavilions
The two pavilions standing in Karlsplatz were built as part of Otto Wagner's scheme for Vienna's turn-of-the-century underground system.

Secession Building
Nicknamed the Golden Cabbage because of its golden filigree dome, the Secession Building was designed at the turn of the century by Joseph Maria Olbrich for exhibitions of avant-garde art. In the basement is Gustav Klimt's *Beethoven Frieze*.

DANUBE CANAL

Stephansdom Quarter

Hofburg Quarter

Belvedere Quarter

Exploring Viennese Jugendstil

The turn of the twentieth century saw a flowering of the visual arts in Vienna. A new generation of avant-garde artists formed the Secession in 1896 and, together with architects and designers, forged close ties between the fine and decorative arts and created new architectural styles.

Hoffmann tea service (1903) in the Austrian Museum of Applied Arts

Painting and Drawing

Viennese art at the turn of the century did not conform to one particular style, but there were common elements. These included an obsession with line and rich surface pattern, as well as themes such as the *femme fatale*, love, sex and death.

The finest collection of paintings from this period is in the **Belvedere**, where pictures by Gustav Klimt (1862–1918) and Egon Schiele (1890–1918) feature prominently. Paintings by both artists and their contemporaries also form part of the permanent display at the **Wien Museum Karlsplatz**. Further examples are at the **Museum of Modern Art** in the MuseumsQuartier. The **Albertina** sometimes shows Schiele drawings. Klimt's *Beethoven Frieze* is in the **Secession Building**, and the decorative schemes he produced for the **Burgtheater** and **Kunsthistorisches Museum** are still in situ.

Decoration (1891) by Gustav Klimt in the Kunsthistorisches Museum

Applied Arts

The Wiener Werkstätte – an arts and crafts studio – was founded by Josef Hoffmann (1870–1956) and others in 1903, and produced jewellery, fabrics, ceramics, metalwork, cutlery, bookbinding and fashion accessories with the same artistic consideration normally given to painting or sculpture. An outstanding collection is in the **Austrian Museum of Applied Arts**, which also houses a document archive open to researchers. Glass designed by Hoffmann for the Viennese firm of Lobmeyr is displayed in the **Lobmeyr Museum**.

Favourite Jugendstil Motifs

Jugendstil motifs were similar to those employed by the French Art Nouveau movement, but were generally more geometric in style. Decorations based on plant forms such as sunflowers were popular, as were female figures, heads and masks. Abstract designs made up of squares and triangles were also used to great effect. Such designs were showcased in the official magazine of the Vienna Secession, *Ver Sacrum*.

Sunflower motif from the Karlsplatz Pavilions by Otto Wagner

Design for a postcard by Joseph Maria Olbrich from *Ver Sacrum*

Furniture

The leading Secession designers, such as Hoffmann and Kolo Moser (1868–1918), wanted interior design to return to the simple lines of Biedermeier style *(see pp32–3)* after the excesses of the Ringstrasse era. The **Austrian Museum of Applied Arts** has several interesting displays of their work, as well as that of the Thonet firm, which made the bentwood furniture admired by the Wiener Werkstätte. Furniture was often conceived as just one element of interior design. Unfortunately, many interiors have disappeared or are not open to the public, but the **Wien Museum Karlsplatz**, which also has some pieces of Jugendstil furniture, has a recreation of Adolf Loos's *(see p94)* living room. This is a rare example of a progressive Viennese interior from the turn of the century, created before the architect finally broke with the Secession.

Writing desk and chair by Kolo Moser (1903) in the Austrian Museum of Applied Arts

Altar in the Kirche am Steinhof (1905–7)

Architecture

Anyone walking around Vienna will notice buildings with charming Jugendstil details. By the 1890s young architects were beginning to react against the structures of the Ringstrasse era, many of which were pastiches of earlier historical styles. The leading architects at this time were Otto Wagner (1841–1918) and Joseph Maria Olbrich (1867–1908), who collaborated on a number of projects, notably the design and installation of a new city railway and its stations, the most famous examples of which are the **Otto-Wagner-Hofpavillon** at Hietzing and the **Karlsplatz Pavilions**, as well as the **Wagner Apartments** on the Linke Wienzeile. Working independently, Wagner produced the extraordinary **Kirche am Steinhof** as well as the **Postsparkasse**, while Olbrich designed the **Secession Building** as an exhibition space

for radical artists and designers. Hoffmann created a number of houses for Secession artists in **Steinfeld-gasse**. There are also some Jugendstil houses in **Hietzing**, while the **Anker Clock** by Franz Matsch (1861–1942) is an example of the late flowering of the style. Other examples of street architecture are the **Strudlhof Steps** (1910) by Theodore Jäger and the **Stadtpark Portals** by Friedrich Ohmann (1858–1927) and Joseph Hackhofer (1863–1917).

Design for a postcard by Joseph Maria Olbrich from *Ver Sacrum*

Gold leaf detail from the Wagner Apartments

Lettering by Alfred Roller from *Ver Sacrum*

Abstract fabric design by Josef Hoffmann

Vienna's Best: Coffee Houses

Coffee houses have been an essential part of Viennese life for centuries. More than just a place to drink coffee, they are meeting places, somewhere to linger over a snack or a light lunch, and refuges from city life. Each attracts a particular clientele and has its own atmosphere. Further details of what coffee houses have to offer can be found on pages 62–3.

Landtmann
This formal but comfortable coffee house used to be frequented by Sigmund Freud. Today it is visited by theatregoers and actors from the nearby Burgtheater, and by journalists and politicians.

Schottenring and Alsergrund

Central
Once the meeting place of writers and free thinkers, the most splendid of all the coffee houses in Vienna has been restored to its former grandeur.

Museum and Townhall Quarter

Eiles
Its location near various government offices has made the Eiles a favourite haunt of officials and lawyers.

Hofburg Quarter

Sperl
Just outside the city centre, the Sperl has a faithful clientele, including many young people who come here for the billiard tables and hot strudels.

Opera and Naschmarkt

Café Museum
The Café Museum was built in 1899 with an interior by Adolf Loos (see p94), but was remodelled in the 1930s to designs by Josef Zotti that replaced Loos's stylish but spartan seating with comfortable banquettes.

Hawelka
This famous coffee house has long cultivated its bohemian image. The atmosphere is warm and theatrical, and no visit to Vienna is complete without a late-night cup of coffee or a drink here.

0 metres 500
0 yards 500

Prückel
The Prückel may not have the chic elegance of establishments like the Central, but it has become a mecca for locals, particularly bridge players, who crowd into its back room.

Stephansdom Quarter

DANUBE CANAL

Kleines
One of the smallest, quaintest coffee houses in Vienna, the Kleines attracts a loyal clientele of actors.

Belvedere Quarter

Frauenhuber
The oldest coffee house in Vienna, this is where Mozart once performed. Its location off Kärntner Strasse makes it handy for shoppers and for tourists visiting the nearby Stephansdom.

Exploring Vienna's Coffee Houses

A stalwart of Viennese culture, the coffee house has played many roles over the centuries and continues to attract a loyal clientele of locals and visitors alike. It is a place to relax with a newspaper or book, enjoy a simple lunch or check your email using the free Wi-Fi. Patrons can enjoy a traditional coffee, but most places also serve wine, beers and spirits. Though no longer unique to Vienna, it is here that the coffee house continues to flourish. Vienna also has many *Café-Konditoreien (see p201).*

The elegant wood-panelled interior of Café Schwarzenberg

The History of the Coffee House

Legend has it that the first coffee house opened its doors after the defeat of the Turks in 1683 *(see p28)*. However, historians insist that coffee was drunk in the city long before this date. Coffee houses took the form we know today in the late 18th century. They reached their heyday in the late 19th century, when they were patronized by cliques of like-minded politicians, artists, writers, composers, doctors or civil servants. In 1890, for instance, the

18th-century Viennese girl holding a coffee grinder

controversial literary group Jung Wien met regularly at the **Griensteidl**, while the essayist Peter Altenberg was reputed to have never been seen outside his favourite café, the **Central**.

Today, as in the past, the **Ministerium**, **Museum**, **Frauenhuber**, **Raimund**, **Eiles**, **Schwarzenberg** and **Zartl** continue to attract their own specific clientele.

Inside the Coffee House

Service inside the coffee house is simple yet formal. A waiter, formally dressed however shabby the coffee house, will take your order, which will often be served with a glass of water. Once you

have ordered you are free to occupy your table for as long as you like. A cup of coffee is not cheap, but entitles you to linger for an hour or two and to read the newspapers or use the free Wi-Fi. The grander coffee houses, such as the **Landtmann** and **Central**, will have a selection of foreign newspapers available for you to browse through.

Coffee House Entertainment

Coffee houses often function as local clubhouses. At the **Sperl** you can play billiards, at the **Prückel** there are bridge tables, and at the **Dommayer** you can

Types of Coffee

Just as the coffee house is a Viennese institution, so too are the extraordinary varieties of coffee that are available. Just asking for a cup of coffee in Vienna will not always guarantee a result, as the Viennese are exceedingly particular about how they take their coffee; over the centuries they have devised their own specific vocabulary to convey to the waiter precisely how they like their beverage served. The list that follows will cover most variations of the Viennese cup of coffee, although you may well find local ones.

Brauner: coffee with milk (small or large).
Melange: a blend of coffee and hot milk.
Kurz: extra strong.
Obers: with cream.
Mokka: strong black coffee.
Kapuziner: double Mokka with a hood of cream and a dusting of cocoa powder.
Schwarzer: black coffee (small or large).
Konsul: double Mokka with a dash of cream.
Koffeinfreier Kaffee: decaffeinated coffee.

Türkischer: plain, strong black Turkish coffee served in the traditional manner.

Espresso: strong black coffee made by machine. Ask for it *gestreckt* for a weak one.

attend literary readings. The **Central** and **Bräunerhof**, both in the Hofburg Quarter, have live piano music. The **Imperial** is part of the hotel of the same name and also has live music, as do the Prückel and Dommayer. The **Kleines** is, as its name suggests, too tiny to offer entertainment, but still draws a regular crowd.

Coffee house sign

What to Eat

Most coffee houses offer snacks throughout the day, simple lunches and occasional specialities, such as pastries, which are served at particular times of day. The **Hawelka** serves hot jam-filled buns (*Buchteln*) late at night, and the **Sperl** often has fresh strudel late morning. Larger coffee houses, such as **Diglas**, **Landtmann** and Bräunerhof, offer extensive lunchtime menus and a range of excellent pastries made on site.

Old Viennese coffee machine in Diglas

Coffee House Alternatives

There are times when you quite simply just want a good cup of coffee – when newspapers or a table of your own are luxuries you can dispense with. On such occasions you should keep an eye out for an Espresso bar, where you can lean informally against a counter and order coffee at a half or a third of the price you would normally expect to pay at a coffee house. Another alternative is to head to one of the plentiful *Konditoreien*, which are bakeries that serve cakes with coffee and other drinks.

DIRECTORY

Bräunerhof
Stallburggasse 2.
Map 5 C3. *Live music Sat & Sun afternoons.*

Central
Palais Ferstel, Herrengasse 14.
Map 2 D5 & 5 B2.

Diglas
Wollzeile 10. **Map** 6 D3.

Dommayer
Dommayergasse 1,
Hietzing. *Live music first Sat of month.*

Eiles
Josefstädter Strasse 2.
Map 1 B5.

Frauenhuber
Himmelpfortgasse 6.
Map 4 E1 & 6 D4.

Griensteidl
Michaelerplatz 2.
Map 2 D5 & 5 B3.

Hawelka
Dorotheergasse 6.
Map 2 D5 & 5 C3.

Imperial
Hotel Imperial, Kärntner
Ring 16. **Map** 4 E2 & 6 D5.
Live music.

Kleines
Franziskanerplatz 3.
Map 6 D4.

Landtmann
See p133.

Ministerium
Georg-Coch-Platz 4.
Map 2 F5 & 6 F3.

Museum
Friedrichstrasse 6.
Map 4 D2.

Prückel
Stubenring 24. **Map** 6 F3.
Live music evenings.

Raimund
Museumstrasse 6.
Map 3 B1.

Schwarzenberg
Kärntner Ring 17.
Map 6 D5.

Sperl
Gumpendorfer Strasse 11.
Map 3 A4.

Zartl
Rasumofskygasse 7,
Landstrasse.

Pharisäer: strong black, with whipped cream on top, served with a small liqueur glass of rum.

Schlagobers: strong black coffee served with either pouring or whipped cream.

Einspänner: large glass of coffee with whipped cream on top.

Kaisermelange: black coffee with an egg yolk and brandy.

VIENNA THROUGH THE YEAR

Spring often arrives unexpectedly, with a few days of sunshine and warmth. The climax of spring is the Wiener Festwochen in May–June. Summers are long and hot, and ideal for swimming and for river trips on the Danube *(see pp180–81)* during July and August, when some venues officially close. Vienna comes alive again in September when the most important theatres reopen, and more often than not, it is still warm enough to sit in the Stadtpark. As winter chills set in, chestnut sellers appear on the streets, and by the feast of St Nicholas on 6 December, snow has often fallen. Christmas is a family occasion, but the New Year is celebrated in style as it heralds the start of the Carnival season. The Wiener Tourismusverband *(see p239)* has details of important events.

Spring

Vienna is beautiful in spring, which is the time for the **Wiener Festwochen** *(see May)*. It is also a season that brings a few days of balmy weather, and when the parks and Prater woods burst into colour *(see pp164–5)*. This is the best time of the year to visit the Stadtpark *(see p167)* with its open-air bandstand and much-photographed resident peacock. The Volksgarten, Burggarten and the great parks of the Belvedere and Schönbrunn also come into their own. The Stephansdom tower offers splendid views of the city and its colourful parks.

A collection of life-sized dolls on display during the Wiener Festwochen

March

Easter Markets *(two weeks before Easter)*, held at the Freyung and in Schönbrunn. Arts, crafts and traditional food are all on sale.

 Schönbrunner Schlosskonzerte *(until end Oct)*, at the Orangery, Schönbrunn Palace *(see pp174–7)*. Performances of popular melodies by Johann Strauss.

Runners taking part in the annual City Marathon

April

Volksprater Funfair *(1 Apr–31 Oct)*, held in the Prater woods *(pp164–5)*.

City Marathon starts from UNO-City by Donaupark *(see p163)*, passing Schönbrunn Palace and around the inner city, ending at Heldenpaltz at the Hofburg.

Frühlingsfestival *(2nd week Apr to mid-May)*. Classical music festival alternating between the Musikverein *(p150)* and the Konzerthaus *(p229)*.

Spanish Riding School *(until Jun)*. Lipizzaner horse performances in the Winter Riding School *(pp100–101)*.

Hofburg Orchestra *(until Oct)*. Concerts at Musikverein *(p150)* and Hofburg *(pp98–9)*.

Kursalon *(until end Oct)*. Open-air concerts *(p229)*. Indoor concerts all year.

May

Tag der Arbeit *(1 May)*. An official public holiday, Labour Day is celebrated with parades on Rathausplatz and Ringstrasse.

Maifest *(1 May)* fills the Prater *(pp164–5)* with music and children's programmes.

Vienna Music Festival *(6 May–21 Jun)*, part of the Wiener Festwochen programme, which begins a few days earlier at the Wiener Konzerthaus *(p229)* and MuseumsQuartier *(pp120–23)*.

Dancing on the *Vindobona* *(15 May to end Sep)*. Board the boat at Schwedenplatz for a cruise on the Danube.

Wiener Festwochen *(mid-May to mid-Jun)*. Vienna's greatest festival features operas, plays and other performing arts.

Average Daily Hours of Sunshine

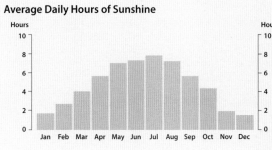

Hours

10
8
6
4
2
0
Jan Feb Mar Apr May Jun Jul Aug Sep Oct Nov Dec

Hours

10
8
6
4
2
0

Sunshine Chart
June, July and August are the sunniest months in Vienna, with between six and eight hours of sunshine each day, but summer can also be quite damp and humid. Although the clouds gather in September, Indian summers are quite common.

Summer

Summer can be both the busiest and most relaxing time in Vienna. The great theatres are officially closed, but the Jazz Festival is on at the Opera House and the Volkstheater in July. The Danube beaches are ideal for sunbathing, swimming and other watersports on sunny days. In the evenings, people frequent the Heuriger wine taverns on the outskirts of the city.

Summer outside the Votivkirche

June

Corpus Christi *(late May–Jun)*. Public holiday. Catholic festival held in honour of the Eucharist.
Vienna Pride and Regenbogen-parade *(mid-Jun)*. LGBT parade on the Ringstrasse.

Concordia Ball *(2nd Fri in Jun)* takes place at the Neues Rathaus *(p132)*.
Ball der Universität *(18 Jun)*. Popular ball held at the University *(p132)*.
Donauinselfest *(last weekend in Jun)*. Three-day pop concert on Danube island.

July

Outdoor films, operas and concerts *(until Sep)* shown on a giant screen in Rathausplatz. Admission is free.
Oper Klosterneuburg *(Jul)*. Performances are in the Kaiserhof courtyard of the palatial religious foundation, Klosterneuburg, a short way north of Vienna *(see p163)*.
Jazzfest *(1st two weeks Jul)*. Well-known artists perform at many venues, including the Opera House *(pp140–41)*, Porgy & Bess Jazz and Music Club *(p229)* and the arcaded courtyard of the Neues Rathaus *(p132)*.
Piber Meets Vienna *(Jul–Aug)*. Mares with their foals and young horses in training from the Piber Lipizzaner Stud come to the Spanish Riding School *(see pp100–101)* for summer shows that are less formal than the usual displays.

Sunbathing beside the Danube

Music in churches *(Jul–Aug)*. Many churches stage summer concerts while the big cultural venues take a summer break.
Impulstanz (International Dance Festival) *(end Jul–mid-Aug)* at the Volkstheater *(p230)* and Universitäts Sportzentrum at Schmelz.
Seefestspiele Mörbisch *(Thu–Sun mid-Jul to end Aug)*. An operetta festival, which takes place in Mörbisch, around 40 km (25 miles) outside Vienna.

August

Maria Himmelfahrt *(15 Aug)*. Public holiday. A Catholic festival, which celebrates the Assumption.

Seefestspiele Mörbisch, an annual operetta festival performed against the backdrop of Lake Neusiedl

Average Monthly Rainfall

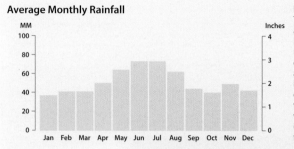

Autumn

In Vienna, autumn means a new start. The theatres, and particularly Vienna's great opera houses, reopen once again. Shops get ready to tempt buyers with their range of autumn fashions. Then, almost overnight, all the shop windows seem to be filled with figures of St Nicholas and his wicked companion Krampus. This cute little furry devil appears everywhere. It is only after 6 December that the shop windows are finally cleared for Christmas displays.

Krampus, the wicked furry devil who accompanies St Nicholas

September
Spanish Riding School performances *(until end Oct)* and training sessions of the Lipizzaner horses *(pp100–101)*.
Vienna Boys' Choir *(mid-Sep to Dec)* perform at Mass at the Burgkapelle *(p105)* on Sunday mornings.
Trotting in the Krieau *(until Jun)*. Trotting races at the Prater *(pp164–5)*.

October
National Day *(26 Oct)*. Public holiday to mark the passing of the Neutrality Act in 1955,

The Vienna Boys' Choir performing at the Konzerthaus

which was followed by the withdrawal of the Allied troops stationed in Austria since 1945.
Viennale *(end Oct)*. Austria's international film festival at Gartenbau, Parkring 12; Metro, Johannesgasse 4; Künstlerhaus, Akademiestrasse 13; and Stadtkino, Schwarzenbergplatz 7–8.
Wien Modern *(until end Nov)*. Modern music festival at the Konzerthaus *(p229)*.

November
Allerheiligen *(1 Nov)*. Public holiday. Catholic festival celebrating All Saints' Day.

KlezMore Festival Vienna *(2nd week Nov)*. Traditional Klezmer music at various city locations.
Vienna Art Week *(3rd week Nov)*. Contemporary art festival hosted by numerous galleries, studios and museums, with guided tours, lectures and performances.
Krippenschau *(until mid-Dec)*. Display of historic nativity scenes at Peterskirche *(p89)*.
Christkindlmarkt *(2nd Sat Nov to end Dec)*. Christmas market and children's workshop by the Rathaus *(p132)*.
Christmas markets *(from last Sat Nov)* held at the Freyung, Heiligenkreuzerhof, Schönbrunn, Karlsplatz, Spittelberg and Maria-Theresien-Platz.

Average Monthly Temperature

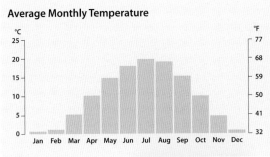

Temperature Chart
The chart shows the average temperatures each month. Top temperatures in July and August can reach 30° C (77° F) although May and September are also quite warm. Winters are icy, and temperatures can be as low as -1.4° C (29.5° F) in January.

Winter

Roasting chestnuts over hot coals is a regular winter sight on Vienna's streets. As Christmas draws near, stalls offer mulled wine and hot snacks and shops enter into the festive spirit, putting up lights and decorations.

The Viennese celebrate Christmas Eve with a traditional meal of *Fischbeuschelsuppe*, a creamy fish soup, followed by fresh fried carp. The usual dish eaten on Christmas Day is goose, although turkey is becoming more popular.

New Year also marks the start of Fasching, Vienna's famous Carnival season.

December

Christmas markets *(continue from November).*
Maria Empfängnis *(8 Dec).* Public holiday. Catholic festival

Public Holidays

New Year's Day (1 Jan)
Epiphany (6 Jan)
Easter Sunday
Easter Monday
Tag der Arbeit (1 May)
Ascension Day (6th Thu after Easter)
Whit Monday (6th Mon after Easter)
Corpus Christi (2 Jun)
Maria Himmelfahrt (15 Aug)
National Day (26 Oct)
Allerheiligen (1 Nov)
Maria Empfängnis (8 Dec)
Christmas Day (25 Dec)
Stefanitag (26 Dec)

Chestnut-roasting in winter

celebrating the Immaculate Conception.
Midnight Mass *(Christmas Eve)* held in the Stephansdom *(pp74–7)*. No tickets needed but arrive early for seats.
Stefanitag *(26 Dec).* Public holiday.
New Year's Eve performance of *Die Fledermaus* *(31 Dec)* at the Opera House *(pp140–41)* and Volksoper *(p229)*. It is also shown on a large screen in Stephansplatz *(p72)*.
New Year's Eve concerts at the Konzerthaus *(p229)* and Musikverein *(p150)*.
Kaiserball *(31 Dec)* at the Hofburg *(pp98–9)*.
New Year's Eve in the city centre: a street party with snacks and drink. Marquees provide music and cabaret.

January

New Year's Concert *(31 Dec & 1 Jan)* by the Vienna Philharmonic at the Musikverein *(p150)*. Requests for tickets for the next year's concert must arrive on 2 Jan *(p228)*.
Beethoven's Ninth Symphony *(31 Dec & 1 Jan)* is performed at the Konzerthaus *(p229)*.
Fasching *(6 Jan to Ash Wed)*, the Vienna Carnival includes the **Heringsschmaus** *(Ash Wed)*, a hot and cold buffet.
Holiday on Ice *(mid- to end Jan)*. This is held at the Stadthalle, Vogelweidplatz.
Resonanzen *(2nd to 3rd week Jan)*. Festival of ancient music at the Konzerthaus *(p229)*.
Vienna Ice Dream *(mid-Jan to mid-Mar)*. Ice-skating in front of the Neues Rathaus *(p132)*.

February

Opera Ball *(last Thu before Shrove Tue)*, one of the grandest balls of Fasching *(p141)*.
Johann Strauss Ball *(mid-Feb)*. The ball season waltzes on at the Kursalon *(see pp184–5)*.
Szene Bunte Wähne *(end Feb)*. International dance festival, featuring performances for a younger audience at the MuseumsQuartier *(pp120–23)* and the WUK cultural centre, Währinger Strasse 59.
Accordion Festival *(end Feb)*. Concerts at various venues.

The Christkindlmarkt, in front of the Neues Rathaus

Vienna's Old Town, with the domes of Michaelerplatz and the spire of Michaelerkirche ▶

VIENNA
AREA BY AREA

Splendid interior of the Stephansdom

Sights at a Glance

STEPHANSDOM QUARTER

The winding streets and spacious squares of this area form the ancient core of Vienna. Following World War II, excavations uncovered the remains of a Roman garrison from 2,000 years ago, and every succeeding age is represented here, from the Romanesque arches of the Ruprechtskirche to the steel and glass of the spectacular Haas-Haus in Stephansplatz. Many of the buildings in the area house government offices, businesses, taverns and stylish shops. Dominating the skyline is the Gothic Stephansdom, the focus of the city and its geographical centre.

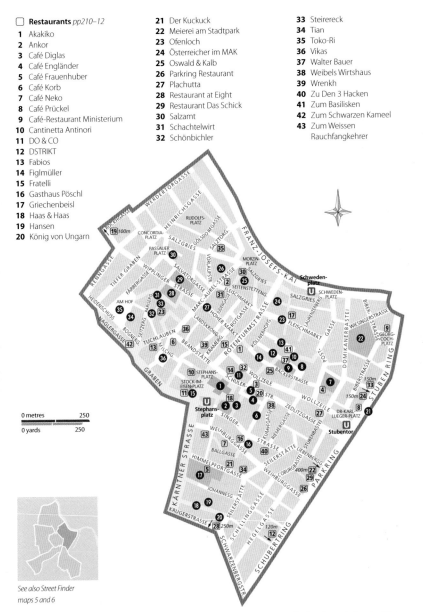

0 metres 250
0 yards 250

See also Street Finder maps 5 and 6

For keys to symbols *see back flap*

Street-by-Street: Old Vienna

This part of the inner city retains its medieval layout: lanes, alleys and spacious courtyards. The influence of the church is particularly evident. You can find remains of orders such as the Dominicans, the Teutonic Knights and the Jesuits. Yet there is nothing ossified about the area: the bars and restaurants on Bäckerstrasse and Schönlaterngasse are thronged with people until the early hours of the morning. Dominating the area is the 137-m (450-ft) spire of the Stephansdom cathedral, at the very centre of Vienna.

⓫ ★ Cathedral Museum
Much of this collection was donated by Duke Rudolf IV who is shown here.

❶ ★ Stephansdom
The cathedral took centuries to build and is rich in medieval and Renaissance monuments.

❷ Deutschordenskirche
A remarkable Treasury of objects collected by German aristocrats, lies alongside this Gothic church.

To Kärntner Strasse →

To Rotenturm- strasse

STEPHANS- PLATZ

STOBELGASSE

BLUTGASSE

GRÜNAN

The Haas & Haas Tea House is a charming, informal café and tea house.

SINGERSTRASSE

❺ Mozarthaus Vienna
Mozart lived in a suite of rooms here from 1784 to 1787. Here he wrote many of his great works.

❹ Domgasse
This pretty street includes a bookshop at No. 8, Buchhandlung 777.

❸ Blutgasse
Courtyards like this are typical of the tenement houses on Blutgasse.

7 Dominikaner-kirche
Originally consecrated on this site in 1237, the present Baroque church dates from the 1630s.

Locator Map
See Street Finder maps 2 and 6

10 Schönlaterngasse
The lantern at No. 6 gave this charming street its name.

SCHÖNLATERNGASSE

BACKERSTRASSE

DR-IGNAZ-SEIPELPLATZ

POSTGASSE

WOLLZEILE

SCHULERSTRASSE

KUMPFGASSE

8 Jesuitenkirche
This pulpit detail of the apostle Matthew is from the Baroque Jesuitenkirche. One of Vienna's most ornate churches, it was built by the Jesuits in the 1620s.

9 ★ Academy of Sciences
The ceiling of the Rococo hall is painted with frescoes depicting the four academic faculties.

6 Grünangergasse
This quiet lane is full of bookshops and galleries.

| 0 metres | 50 |
| 0 yards | 50 |

Key

— Suggested route

● Stephansdom

Situated in the centre of Vienna, the Stephansdom is the soul of the city, and its towers, crypt and altars are the number-one tourist attraction in Vienna. A church has stood on the site for over 800 years, but all that remains of the original 13th-century Romanesque church are the Giants' Doorway and Heathen Towers. The Gothic nave, choir and side chapels are the result of a rebuilding programme in the 14th and 15th centuries, while some of the outbuildings, such as the Lower Vestry, are Baroque additions. In a vault beneath the altar are urns containing the internal organs of some of the Habsburgs.

★ Giants' Doorway and Heathen Towers
The entrance and twin towers apparently stand on the site of an earlier heathen shrine.

KEY

① **Lower Vestry**

② **The symbolic number "05"** of the Austrian Resistance Movement was carved here in 1945.

③ **Main entrance**

④ **Pilgrim's Pulpit** *(see p76)*

⑤ **Entrance to the catacombs**

⑥ **The North Tower**, according to legend, was never completed because its master builder, Hans Puchsbaum, broke a pact he had made with the devil by speaking a holy name. The devil then caused him to fall to his death.

⑦ **Southeastern entrance**

★ Singer Gate
This was once the entrance for male visitors. A sculpted relief above the door depicts scenes from the life of St Paul.

★ Steffl or Spire
The 137-m high (450-ft) Gothic spire is a famous landmark. From the Sexton's Lodge (*see p77*), visitors can climb the stairs to a viewing platform.

VISITORS' CHECKLIST

Practical Information
Stephansplatz 1, A-1010. **Map** 2 E5 & 6 D3. **Tel** 515 52 30 54. **Open** 9–11:30am & 1–4:30pm Mon–Sat, 1pm–4:30pm Sun & hols. 🕆 High Mass: 10:15am Sun & hols (Jul & Aug: 9:30am). Guided tours in English: 10:30am Mon–Sat; Pummerin Bell (lift): 9am–5pm daily (to 6pm Jul & Aug). Catacomb tours daily. 🚻 📷 🔊 📷 🌐 **stephanskirche.at**

Transport
Ⓤ Stephansplatz. 🚌 1A, 2A, 3A.

★ Tiled Roof
Almost a quarter of a million glazed tiles cover the roof; they were meticulously restored after being damaged in the last days of World War II.

Johannes Capistranus

On the exterior northeastern wall of the choir is a pulpit built after the victory over the Turks at Belgrade in 1456. It was from here that the Italian Franciscan, Giovanni da Capestrano (1386–1456), is said to have preached against the Turkish invasion in 1451. The 18th-century Baroque statue above it depicts the triumphant saint – known in Austria as Johannes Capistranus – trampling on a defeated Turkish invader.

1147 The first Romanesque building on the site consecrated by the Bishop of Passau		**1304** Duke Rudolf IV initiates work on High Gothic Albertine Choir		**1515** Double wedding of grandchildren of Maximilian with children of the King of Hungary takes place		**1711** Pummerin bell cast from remains of guns left by Turks on their retreat from Vienna		**1948** Reconstruction and restoration carried out	

1100	1200	1300	1400	1500	1600	1700	1800	1900	2000

1230 Second Romanesque building erected on the same ground		**1359–1440** Main aisle, southern arches and southern tower built	**1515** Anton Pilgram carves his pulpit		**1556** North Tower is roofed over / **1783** Stephansdom graveyard closed after plague		**1916** Emperor Franz Joseph's funeral	**1945** Cathedral catches fire during bombing	

Inside the Stephansdom

The lofty vaulted interior of the Stephansdom contains an impressive collection of art spanning several centuries. Masterpieces of Gothic sculpture include the fabulously intricate pulpit, several figures of saints adorning the piers, and the canopies or baldachins over many of the side altars. To the left of the High Altar is the early 15th-century winged Wiener Neustädter Altar, bearing the painted images of 72 saints. The altar panels open out to reveal delicate sculptural groups. The most spectacular Renaissance work is the tomb of Friedrich III, while the High Altar adds a flamboyant Baroque note.

The Catacombs
A flight of steps leads down to the catacombs, which extend under the cathedral square.

Portrait of Pilgram
Master craftsman Anton Pilgram left a portrait of himself holding a square and compass below the corbel of the original organ.

★ Pilgram's Pulpit
Pilgram's intricate Gothic pulpit is decorated with portraits of the Four Fathers of the Church (theologians representing four physiognomic temperaments), while Pilgram himself looks out from a "window" below.

Organ Gallery and Case
In 1960 this modern organ was installed in the loft above the entrance. A more recent organ is in the south choir area.

The Pummerin Bell

The bell that hangs in the North Tower, known as the *Pummerin* or "Boomer", is a potent symbol of Vienna's turbulent past. The original bell was made from melted-down cannons abandoned when the Turks fled Vienna in 1683. The bell crashed down through the roof in 1945 when fire swept through the Stephansdom, and a new and even larger bell was cast using the remains of the old.

★ Wiener Neustädter Altar

Friedrich III commissioned the elaborate altarpiece in 1447. Painted panels open out to reveal an earlier carved interior showing scenes from the lives of the Virgin Mary and Christ. This panel portrays the *Adoration of the Magi* (1420).

★ High Altar

Tobias Pock's altarpiece shows the martyrdom of St Stephen. The sculptures were fashioned by Johann Jakob Pock in 1647.

KEY

① **The Canopy with the Pötsch Madonna** is a 16th-century canopy that shelters a 1697 icon of the Madonna, to which Prince Eugene's victory over the Turks at Zenta was attributed. It comes from Pöcs, a village in Hungary.

② **Main entrance**

③ **The Statue of Crucified Christ** above the altar has, according to legend, a beard of human hair that is still growing.

④ **The Tirna Chapel** houses

the grave of the military hero Prince Eugene.

⑤ **Bishop's Gate**

⑥ **Lift to the Pummerin Bell**

⑦ **Christ with Toothache** (1420) is the irreverent name of this figure; legend has it that Christ afflicts mockers with toothache.

⑧ **Exit from crypt**

⑨ **Albertine Choir**

⑩ **Emperor Friedrich III's tomb** is made from ornate red marble

and has a lid bearing a lifelike carved portrait of the emperor. It dates from the 15th century.

⑪ **The Sexton's Lodge** houses the stairs that lead up the steeple.

⑫ **Chapel of St Catherine**

⑬ **The Madonna of the Servants**

⑭ **The Füchsel Baldachin** is a fine Gothic canopy.

⑮ **The Trinity Altar** probably dates from around 1740.

❷ Deutschordens-kirche

Singerstrasse 7. **Map** 6 D3. **Tel** 5121065.
Ⓤ Stephansplatz. 🚌 1A, 2A, 3A.
Church: **Open** 7am–6pm daily.
Treasury: **Open** 10am–noon Tue, Thu &
Sat, 3–5pm Wed & Fri. **Closed** Sun, Mon
& pub hols. 🆆 **deutscher-orden.at**

This church belongs to the Order
of Teutonic Knights, a chivalric
order that was established in
the 12th century. It is 14th-
century Gothic, and though
restored in the 1720s in Baroque
style by Anton Erhard **Martinelli**,
it retains Gothic elements such
as pointed arched windows.
Numerous coats of arms of
Teutonic Knights and memorial
slabs are displayed on the walls.
The altarpiece from 1520 is
Flemish and incorporates panel
paintings and carvings of
scenes from the Passion
beneath some very delicate
traceried canopies.

The Order's Treasury is
situated off the church's
courtyard and now serves as
a museum, displaying various
collections acquired by its
Grand Masters over the
centuries. The starting point
is a room housing a large
collection of coins, medals and
a 13th-century enthronement
ring. A second room contains
chalices and Mass vessels
worked with silver filigree,
while a third displays maces,
daggers and ceremonial garb.
The museum also displays

Inner courtyard of No. 9 Blutgasse, the Fähnrichshof

some Gothic paintings and a
Carinthian carving of *St George
and the Dragon* (1457).

❸ Blutgasse

Map 6 D3. Ⓤ Stephansplatz.
🚌 1A, 2A, 3A.

A local legend relates that this
street acquired its gruesome
name – Blood Lane – after a
massacre in 1312 of the Knights
Templar (a religious military
order) in a skirmish so violent
that the streets flowed with
blood. But there is no evidence
to support this story and the
street's charm belies its name.

Its tall apartment buildings
date mostly from the 18th century. Walk into No. 3 and see how
the city's restorers have linked
up the buildings and their courtyards. No. 9, the Fähnrichshof, is
particularly impressive.

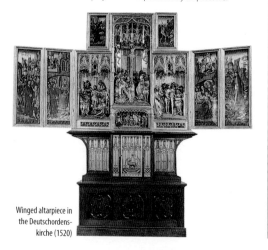
Winged altarpiece in
the Deutschordens-
kirche (1520)

❹ Domgasse

Map 6 D3. Ⓤ Stephansplatz.
🚌 1A, 2A, 3A.

Domgasse boasts some
interesting buildings, including
Mozarthaus Vienna *(see below)*
and the Trienter Hof, with its
airy courtyard. No. 6 is a house
of medieval origin called the
Kleiner Bischofshof (Small
Bishop's House): it has a 1761
Matthias Gerl façade. Next door
is the site of the house where
Georg Franz Kolschitzky lived
and, in 1694, died. It is said that
he claimed some Turkish coffee
beans as a reward for his
bravery in the 1683 Turkish
siege, and later opened Vienna's
first coffee house. The truth of
this story, however, is doubtful.

❺ Mozarthaus Vienna

Domgasse 5. **Map** 6 D3. **Tel** 5121791.
Ⓤ Stephansplatz. 🚌 1A, 2A, 3A.
Open 10am–7pm daily. 🚫
🆆 **mozarthausvienna.at**

Mozart and his family occupied
an apartment on the first floor
of this building from 1784 to
1787. Of Mozart's 11 Viennese
residences, this is the one
where he is said to have been
happiest. It is also where
he composed a significant
number of his masterworks:
the exquisite Haydn quartets, a
handful of piano concertos, and
The Marriage of Figaro. Restored
for the anniversary year 2006,
the Mozarthaus has exhibitions
on two upper floors as well as
the original apartment.

Elaborate nave of the Dominikanerkirche

➏ Grünangergasse

Map 6 D3 & D4. Ⓤ Stephansplatz.
🚌 1A, 2A, 3A.

This quiet lane takes its name from Zum Grünen Anker at No. 10, a former guesthouse that was frequented by Franz Schubert in the 19th century.

No. 8's doorway has carvings of rolls and pretzels. It is known as the Kipferlhaus after a Viennese crescent-shaped roll. The former Fürstenberg Palace, from 1720, has a Baroque doorway with carved hounds racing to the top of the keystone.

➐ Dominikaner- kirche

Postgasse 4. **Map** 2 E5 & 6 E3.
Tel 5129174. Ⓤ Stephansplatz, Schwedenplatz. 🚌 2A. **Open** 7am–6pm daily.

The Dominican order of monks came to Vienna in 1226, and by 1237 they had built a church here. In the 1630s Antonio

Canevale designed the present church, which boasts a majestic, rather handsome Baroque façade. The interior is equally imposing. The central chapel on the right has swirling Rococo grilles and candelabra, and there is a very beautiful gilt organ above the west door. Its casing dates from the mid-18th century. The frescoes by Tencalla and Rauchmiller are especially noteworthy, as is the high altar.

➑ Jesuitenkirche

Dr-Ignaz-Seipel-Platz 1. **Map** 2 E5 & 6 E3. **Tel** 512 523 20. Ⓤ Stubentor, Stephansplatz, Schwedenplatz.
🚌 2A. **Open** 7am–7pm Mon–Sat, 8am–7pm Sun & hols. 🖥 jesuiten.at

Andrea Pozzo, an Italian architect, redesigned the Jesuitenkirche between 1703 and 1705 and its broad, high façade dominates the Dr-Ignaz-Seipel-Platz. In the 1620s the Jesuits decided to move their

headquarters here in order to be near the Old University, which they controlled. The Jesuit order was the dominant force behind the Counter-Reformation and not afraid of making a statement. The grand redesign of the church highlighted their power.

The interior is gaudy, with plump marble columns screening the side chapels. Pozzo's ceiling frescoes are cleverly executed using a *trompe l'oeil* effect and the pews are richly carved.

➒ Academy of Sciences

Dr-Ignaz-Seipel-Platz 2. **Map** 2 E5 & 6 E3. Ⓤ Schwedenplatz, Stubentor. **Tel** 515810. **Open** 8am–5pm Mon–Fri. 🖥 oeaw.ac.at

Once the centrepiece of the Old University, the Akademie der Wissenschaften was designed in 1753 by Jean Nicolas Jadot de Ville-Issey as the *Aula*, or great hall. It boasts an impressive Baroque façade and fine rooms throughout. A double staircase leads up to a huge salon, one of the grandest in Vienna.

Elaborate frescoes adorn the ceilings of the Ceremonial Hall, the walls of which are made of marble embellished with Rococo plasterwork. Haydn's *Creation* was performed here in 1808 in the presence of the composer: it was the eve of his 76th birthday and his last public appearance.

Fountain by Franz Joseph Lenzbauer on the Academy of Sciences (c. 1755)

The Baroque Bernhardskapelle *(left)*, seen from Schönlaterngasse

⑩ Schönlaterngasse

Map 2 E5 & 6 E3. Ⓤ Stephansplatz,
Schwedenplatz. 🚌 1A, 2A, 3A.
Alte Schmiede: **Tel** 5128329.
Open 9am–5pm Mon–Fri.

This attractive curving lane
derives its name (Pretty Lantern
Lane) from the handsome
wrought-iron lantern clamped to
No. 6. The lantern is a copy of the
1610 original, now in the Wien
Museum Karlsplatz *(see p150)*. At
No. 4, a solid early 17th-century
house stands in the curve of the
street. No. 7, the Basiliskenhaus,
which is of medieval origin,
displays on its façade an artist's
impression of a basilisk, dating
from 1740. A serpent is reputed
to have been discovered in 1212
in a well by the house.
The composer Robert
Schumann lived at No. 7a from
1838 to 1839. No. 9 is the Alte
Schmiede – the smithy from
which it takes its name has been
reassembled in the basement.
This complex also contains an
art gallery and a hall where
poetry readings and music
workshops are held.

⑪ Cathedral Museum

Stephansplatz 6. **Map** 2 E5 & 6 D3.
Tel 515 52 33 00. Ⓤ Stephansplatz.
🚌 1A, 2A, 3A. **Open** 10am–6pm
Wed–Sun (to 8pm Thu).
🅦 dommuseum.at 🎨 ♿

The Cathedral Museum,
the Dom und Diözesan-
museum in German,
reopened in 2017 after four
years of renovation. All the
old treasures have been
returned, including 16th-
and 17th-century carvings
and personal gifts from
Duke Rudolf IV to the
cathedral. His shroud is
housed here, along with
a famous portrait of him by a
Bohemian master dating from
the 1360s *(see p72)*. Added to
the museum since renovation
are a number of modernist and
contemporary paintings and
sculptures. The museum now
includes an extensive collection
of modern pieces from Chagall,
Klimt and contemporary
Austrian artists. Creative displays
juxtapose the old with the new,
the purpose being to show a
continuity in underlying religious emotions across the ages,
expressed in changing styles
and in materials as varied as
paint, glass and metal.

⑫ Sonnenfelsgasse

Map 2 E5 & 6 E3. Ⓤ Stephansplatz,
Schwedenplatz.

Fine houses line this pleasant
street. Though by no means
uniform in style, most of the
dwellings on the north side of
the street are solid merchant
and patrician houses dating
from the late 16th century.
No. 19, which was built in 1628
and renovated in 1721, was
once part of the Old University
(see p79). No. 11 has an
impressive courtyard. Many of
the balconies overlooking the
courtyard have been glassed in
to their full height so as to
provide extra living space. No. 3
has the most elaborate façade,
and contains a *Stadtheuriger*
called the Zwölf Apostelkeller.
This is an urban equivalent of
the *Heuriger*, the wine growers'
inns found in the villages
outside Vienna *(see
pp200–201)*.
The street was
named after a soldier
called Joseph von
Sonnenfels. He
became Maria
Theresa's legal
adviser and under
his guidance
she reformed the
penal code and
abolished torture.

Gothic Madonna and
Child (1325) in the
Cathedral Museum

⑬ Heiligen-kreuzerhof

Schönlaterngasse 5. **Map** 2 E5 & 6 E3. **Tel** 5125896. Ⓤ Schwedenplatz. **Open** 6am–9pm Mon–Sat. ♿
Bernhardskapelle: **Open** on request

In the Middle Ages, rural monasteries expanded and established buildings in the cities. Secularization in the 1780s diminished such holdings, but this one, belonging to the abbey of Heiligenkreuz *(see p178)*, survived.

The buildings around the courtyard housing the city's Applied Arts College present a serene 18th-century face. On the south side of the courtyard is the Bernhardskapelle. Dating from 1662, but altered in the 1730s, the chapel is a Baroque gem. Across from the chapel a patch of wall from Babenberg times *(see pp24–5)* has been exposed: a reminder that, as so often in Vienna, the building is much older in origin than it at first appears.

Fresco at No. 12 Bäckerstrasse

⑭ Bäckerstrasse

Map 2 E5 & 6 D3. Ⓤ Stephansplatz. 🚌 1A, 2A, 3A.

Nowadays people visit this street, which used to house the city's bakers in medieval times, to sample its nightlife rather than its bread. The architecture here is also of considerable interest: No. 2 sits beneath a 17th-century tower and has a pretty courtyard. Opposite, at No. 1, is the site of the Alte Regensburgerhof, the outpost of Bavarian merchants who were given incentives to work in Vienna in the 15th century. No. 8 is the former palace of Count Seilern, dating from 1722, and No. 7 is famous for its arcaded Renaissance courtyard

and stables, the only surviving example in Vienna. Two other houses of Renaissance origin are located at Nos. 12 and 14.

⑮ Haas-Haus

Stephansplatz 12. **Map** 2 E5 & 6 D3. **Tel** 5356083. Ⓤ Stephansplatz. **Open** 8am–2am daily. ♿

Designing a modern building directly opposite the Stephansdom was a difficult task, and the city entrusted it to one of Austria's leading architects, Hans Hollein. The result is the 1990 Haas-Haus, a shining structure of glass and blue-green marble that curves elegantly into the Graben. The building has a very pleasing asymmetrical appearance, with decorative elements such as lopsided cubes of marble attached to the façade, a protruding structure high up resembling a diving board and a Japanese bridge inside. The atrium within is surrounded by cafés, shops, a restaurant, DO & CO *(see p197)* and offices.

⑯ Franziskaner-kirche

Franziskanerplatz 4. **Map** 4 E1 & 6 D4. **Tel** 662 84 36 29. Ⓤ Stephansplatz. 🚌 1A, 2A, 3A. **Open** 6:30am–noon & 2–5:30pm Mon–Sat, 7am–5:30pm Sun. ♿

In the 14th century, the Franciscans took over this church, originally built by wealthy citizens as a "house of the soul" for prostitutes wishing to reform. The present church was built in 1601–11.

The façade is in South German Renaissance style, and is topped by an elaborate scrolled gable with obelisks. The Moses Fountain in front of the church

Detail from Andrea Pozzo's altar (1707) in the Franziskanerkirche

was designed by the Neo-Classicist Johann Martin Fischer in 1798. The interior is in full-blown Baroque style and includes a finely modelled pulpit dating from 1726 and richly carved pews. A dramatic high altar by Andrea Pozzo rises to the full height of the church. Only the front part of the structure is three-dimensional – the rest is *trompe l'oeil*. Look out for a 1725 *Crucifixion* by Carlo Carlone among the paintings in the side altars.

You usually have to ask a passing monk for permission to see the church organ. It is worth being persistent, as this is the oldest organ in Vienna (1642), designed by Johann Wöckerl. It is beautifully painted, focusing on religious themes.

Gleaming façade of Haas-Haus (1990)

Statuary in the hall of the Winter Palace of Prince Eugene

⓱ Winter Palace of Prince Eugene

Himmelpfortgasse 4–8. **Map** 4 E1 & 6 D4. **Tel** 795 57 134. Ⓤ Stephansplatz. 🚌 1A, 2A, 3A. Vestibule: **Open** 10am–6pm daily. Ⓦ winterpalais.at

The Winter Palace (Winterpalais) was commissioned in 1694 by Prince Eugene of Savoy *(see p29)*, a brilliant military commander. The work was entrusted to Johann Bernhard Fischer von Erlach *(see p149)* and later by Johann Lukas von Hildebrandt *(see p154)* in 1702. The result is an imposing town mansion, one of the most magnificent Baroque edifices in Vienna. Maria Theresa bought it for the state in 1752 and it was home to the Ministry of Finance from 1848 until 2006. It is now an exhibition venue for the Belvedere *(see pp154–9)*, devoted to its Baroque collection.

⓲ Annagasse

Map 4 E1 & 6 D4. Ⓤ Stephansplatz. 🚌 1A, 2A, 3A. Zum Blauen Karpfen: **Closed** to the public.

Now splendidly Baroque, Annagasse dates from medieval times. It is pedestrianized and a pleasant place for browsing in the various bookshops.
Notable buildings include the luxurious Mailberger Hof and the stucco-decorated Römischer Kaiser hotels *(see p198)*. No. 14's lintel has a Baroque carving of cherubs making merry, while above this is a relief of the blue carp that gives the house, once a pub, its name: Zum Blauen Karpfen. No. 2 is the 17th-century Esterházy Palace, which is now a casino.

⓳ Annakirche

Annagasse 3b. **Map** 4 E1 & 6 D4. **Tel** 5124797. Ⓤ Stephansplatz. 🚌 1A, 2A, 3A. **Open** 7am–7pm daily.

There has been a chapel in Annagasse since 1320, but the present Annakirche was built between 1629 and 1634, and later renovated by the Jesuits during the early 18th century. Devotion to St Anne has deep roots in Vienna and this intimate church is often full of quiet worshippers.
The finest exterior feature of the church is the moulded copper cupola over the tower. The ceiling frescoes, painted by Daniel Gran, who was a leading painter of the Austrian Baroque period, are now fading but his richly coloured painting glorifying St Anne on the high altar is still striking. The first chapel on the left houses a copy of a carving of St Anne from about 1505 – the original is in the Cathedral Museum *(see p80)*. St Anne is portrayed as a powerfully maternal figure and shown with her daughter, the Virgin Mary, who in turn has the baby Jesus on her knee. The carving is attributed to the sculptor Veit Stoss.

⓴ Haus der Musik

Seilerstätte 30. **Map** 4 E1 & 6 D5. **Tel** 513 48 50. Ⓤ Stephansplatz, Stubenring. 🚌 1A, 2A, 3A. **Open** 10am–10pm daily. 🎨 🍴 on request. ☐ 🎧 Ⓦ hdm.at

The House of Music is a sound museum that delights adults and children alike. Its high-tech interactive displays include "experience zones" such as the Instrumentarium, with its giant instruments, and the Polyphonium, which is a collection of different sounds. The museum's staircase acts as a piano.

Moulded copper cupola over the tower of the Annakirche

Detail on the façade of the Griechische Kirche on Griechengasse

㉑ Austrian Museum of Applied Arts

See pp84–5.

㉒ Postsparkasse

Georg-Coch-Platz 2. **Map** 2 F5 & 6 F3. **Tel** 059905. Ⓤ Schwedenplatz. 🚌 3A. 🚋 1, 2. **Open** 10am–5pm Mon–Fri. Ⓦ **ottowagner.com**

This building, the Imperial-Royal Post Office Savings Bank, is a wonderful example of Secession architecture *(see pp56–9)*. Designed between 1904 and 1906 by Otto Wagner, it still looks unashamedly modern. It features the architect's characteristic overhanging eaves, spindly aluminium columns supporting a canopy, heroic sculptures of angels and ornament-like nailheads protruding from the surface of the building.

Wagner was a pioneer in incorporating many functional elements into his decorative schemes. Inside, the banking hall is circled by tubular heating ducts and the metal columns are clad in aluminium.

㉓ Fleischmarkt

Map 2 E5 & 6 D2–E3. Ⓤ Schwedenplatz. Griechische Kirche: **Tel** 5333889. **Open** 9am–4pm Mon–Fri.

Fleischmarkt, the former meat market, dates from 1220. The small cosy inn called the

Griechenbeisl *(see p210)* is its best-known landmark. On its façade is a woodcarving of a bagpiper known as *Der liebe Augustin* (Dear Augustin). Rumour has it that during the 1679 plague, this bagpiper slumped drunk into the gutter one night and, taken for dead, was put in the plague pit. He woke, attracted attention by playing his pipes and was rescued. Miraculously, he did not catch the plague.

Next to the Griechenbeisl is the beautiful Neo-Byzantine Griechische Kirche (Greek Church of the Holy Trinity). The versatile architect Theophil Hansen *(see p34)* created its rich, gilt structure in the 1850s. A passage links the Griechenbeisl to Griechengasse.

㉔ Griechengasse

Map 2 E5 & 6 E2. Ⓤ Schwedenplatz. Griechenkirche St Georg: **Tel** 5357882. **Open** by appt, 9am–4pm Mon–Fri, 10am–1pm for Mass only Sat & Sun.

The name of this street, leading up from Rotenturmstrasse, refers to the Greek merchants who settled here in the 18th century. The house on the right dates from 1611 but has since been altered. Opposite is the Greek Orthodox Griechenkirche St Georg, not to be confused with the Griechische Kirche in Fleischmarkt. This one was built in 1803 but the gable was added later, in 1898. No. 7 is a 17th-century house. whose façade was rebuilt in the late 18th century.

Ivy-clad façade of Ruprechtskirche

㉕ Ruprechtskirche

Ruprechtsplatz. **Map** 2 E5 & 6 D2. **Tel** 5356003. Ⓤ Schwedenplatz. **Open** 10am–noon Mon–Fri, 3–5pm Mon, Wed, Fri; for Mass 5pm Sat (6pm Jul & Aug). 🚶 Donation expected. Ⓦ **ruprechtskirche.at**

St Ruprecht *(see p24)* was the patron saint of Vienna's salt merchants and the church takes his name overlooks the merchants' landing stage on the Danube canal. There is a statue of the saint holding a tub of salt at the foot of the Romanesque tower. As salt was a valuable commodity in the Middle Ages, some historians suggests that the church dates back to the 11th century, making it the oldest church in Vienna. The interior is less interesting, having been restored at various times, but the chancel has two panes of Romanesque stained glass. The choir is 13th-century, the vaulted south aisle 15th-century.

Carving of the bagpiper on the façade of the Griechenbeisl, Fleischmarkt

㉑ Austrian Museum of Applied Arts

MAK (Museum für angewandte Kunst) acts both as a showcase for Austrian decorative arts and as a repository for fine objects from around the world. Originally founded in 1864 as a museum of art and industry, it expanded and diversified over the years to include objects representing new movements and contemporary design. The museum has a fine collection of furniture, including works of the German cabinet-maker David Roentgen, textiles, glass, carpets, East Asian art and fine Renaissance jewellery. In 2012, the museum was completely renovated and new multimedia exhibitions were added to the existing permanent collection.

★ **Josef Hoffmann, Tafelaufsatz**
Josef Hoffmann designed the centrepiece in silver and agate for the Vienna 1900 collection in 1905.

Stairs to second floor

First floor

First floor mezzanine

★ **Baroque Rococo Classicism**
A reassembly of a room (around 1724) in the Dubsky Palace at Brno, Czech Republic.

Entrance to MAK café (see p211)

MAK Permanent Collection Asia
One of the most remarkable collections of Asian art and applied arts in Europe.

Entrance hall

Stubenring entrance

Museum Guide

The basement houses the MAK Design Lab, MAK Forum and MAK Gallery. Most of the permanent collection is displayed in the ground-floor galleries, which include the MAK Permanent Collection Asia and the museum's collection of carpets. Stairs in the west wing lead to the MAK Exhibition Hall, which houses temporary exhibitions.

Basement

Key

- ☐ MAK Permanent Collection Asia
- ☐ Baroque, Rococo
- ☐ Vienna 1900
- ☐ Art Nouveau, Art Deco
- ☐ Biedermeier
- ☐ Contemporary Art
- ☐ Temporary exhibition space
- ☐ Carpets
- ☐ MAK Design Lab, MAK Forum and MAK Gallery

MAK Design Lab
Over 2,000 thematically arranged exhibits highlight the role of art, architecture and design in everyday life.

The Wiener Werkstätte

In 1903 Josef Hoffmann *(pictured)* and Kolo Moser founded a co-operative arts and crafts workshop, the Wiener Werkstätte. This promoted all aspects of design from postage stamps and book illustrations to fabric, furniture, jewellery and interiors. The museum houses its archives, which include sketches, fabric patterns and fine pieces.

VISITORS' CHECKLIST

Practical Information
Stubenring 5. **Map** 2 F5 & 6 F3.
Tel 711360. **Open** 10am–10pm
Tue, 10am–6pm Wed–Sun.
Closed 1 Jan, 25 Dec. 🚫 ♿ 🎫
📷 🏠 🅦 **mak.at**

Transport
Ⓤ Stubentor. 🚌 3A, 74A. 🚊 2.
Ⓢ Landstrasse.

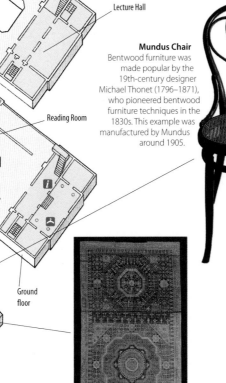

Lecture Hall

Reading Room

Ground floor

Mundus Chair
Bentwood furniture was made popular by the 19th-century designer Michael Thonet (1796–1871), who pioneered bentwood furniture techniques in the 1830s. This example was manufactured by Mundus around 1905.

Mamluk Carpet
This mid-15th-century knotted Egyptian rug features two octagonal medallions.

★ Biedermeier Room
This cherrywood sofa (1825–30), designed and manufactured by Danhauser'sche Möbelfabrik, is an outstanding example of Viennese Empire-style Biedermeier design *(see pp32–3)*. The original upholstery has been replaced.

❷ Jewish District

Map 2 E5 & 6 D2. Ⓤ Schwedenplatz.
Stadttempel: **Tel** 531040. **Open** Mon–
Thu for tours at 11:30am and 2pm
(take identification).

Vienna's Jewish District is more
famous today for its area of bars
and clubs called the Bermuda
Triangle than for its Jewish
community. Judengasse is now
a bustling lane lined with
clothes shops and bars. There
are some solid Biedermeier
apartment blocks and on
Ruprechtsplatz, in the former
town hall, a kosher restaurant,
the Arche Noah. Behind it is a
tower, the Kornhäusel-turm.
Named after Josef Kornhäusel,
an architect from the
Biedermeier period (see pp32–
3), it was apparently built as a
refuge from his wife.

The Neustädter-Hof, a
Baroque palace built by Anton
Ospel in 1734, can be found
on Sterngasse. A Turkish
cannonball, fired in 1683, is
embedded in the palace
façade. The English-language
bookshop Shakespeare & Co.
(see p225) is nearby.

Vienna's oldest surviving
synagogue, the Stadttempel,
designed by Kornhäusel in the
1820s, is on Seitenstettengasse.
It has been guarded by armed
police since an attack in 1983.

The Anker Clock in Hoher Markt

In 1895, the first Jewish
Museum was founded here
but it has since moved to
Dorotheergasse (see p95).

❷ Hoher Markt

Map 2 E5 & 6 D2. Ⓤ Stephansplatz,
Schwedenplatz. 🚌 1A, 2A, 3A.
Roman Museum: **Tel** 5355606.
Open 9am–6pm Tue–Sun & hols.
Closed 1 Jan, 1 May, 25 Dec 📷
Ⓦ wienmuseum.at

Hoher Markt is the oldest
square in Vienna. In medieval
times, fish and cloth markets
as well as executions were

held here. Today it is possible
to view the subterranean ruins
of a former Roman garrison
beneath the square (see p23).
Discovered after World War II,
the ancient foundations show
groups of houses bisected by
straight roads leading to the
town gates. It seems probable
that they were 2nd- and 3rd-
century officers' houses. The
excavations are well laid out
and exhibits of pottery, reliefs
and tiles supplement the ruins.

In the centre of the square
is the Vermählungsbrunnen
(Nuptial Fountain), also known
as the Josefsbrunnen. Emperor
Leopold I had vowed to
commemorate the safe return
of his son Joseph from the
Siege of Landau and commissioned Johann Bernhard Fischer
von Erlach to design this
monument, which was built
by von Erlach's son Joseph
Emanuel between 1729 and
1732. The fountain celebrates
the betrothal of Joseph and
Mary and bears figures of the
high priest and the couple, with
gilt urns, statues of angels and
fluted columns supporting an
elaborate canopy.

Linking two office buildings
on the square is the bronze
and copper Anker Clock.
Commissioned by the Anker
Insurance Company, and
designed by Franz Matsch, it
was completed in 1914. Every
hour a procession of cut-out
historical figures, ranging from
the Emperor Marcus Aurelius
and Duke Rudolf IV to Joseph
Haydn, glide from one side of
the clock to the other to the
sound of organ music. Noon is
the best time to see it, when all
the figures are on display.

❷ Bohemian Court Chancery

Judenplatz 11. **Map** 2 D5 & 5 C2.
Tel 531110. Ⓤ Stephansplatz. 🚌 1A,
2A, 3A. **Open** 8am–3:30pm Mon–Fri.

Vienna's Habsburg rulers were
also kings of Bohemia, which
was governed from this magnificent palace (1709–14). Its
architect was the finest of the
day: Johann Bernhard Fischer

Vienna's Jews – Past and Present

A Jewish community has existed in Vienna since at least the 12th
century, with Judenplatz and, later, the Stadttempel at its core.
During the early 15th century the Jews were persecuted and in
1421 almost the entire Jewish population was burned to death,
forcibly baptized or expelled. Thereafter Jewish fortunes fluctuated,
with periods of prosperity alternating with expulsions. The 1781
Edict of Tolerance lifted legal constraints that had applied to Jews
and by the late 19th century the city's cultural and intellectual life
was dominated by Jews. Anti-Semitism spread in the early 20th
century and burgeoning Nazism forced many Jews to leave. Of
those who remained, 65,000 were murdered. In 1938, 170,000 Jews
lived in the city; 50 years later there were 7,000. In the late 20th and

early 21st century,
immigration from
Eastern Europe has
seen the Jewish
population slowly
increase.

The interior of the
Stadttempel

von Erlach *(see p149)*. Matthias Gerl enlarged the Chancery between 1751 and 1754 to accommodate the Ministry of the Interior. The most spectacular parts of the building are the huge Baroque portals. The elegantly curved window frames on the first floor are also particularly noteworthy.

The building's interior, now a courthouse, and its two courtyards, are less impressive, partly due to reconstruction undertaken after serious bomb damage in World War II.

Ironwork at the Rathaus entrance

㉙ Altes Rathaus

Wipplinger Strasse 8. **Map** 2 D5 & 6 D2. Ⓤ Schwedenplatz. 🚋 1A, 3A. 🚈 1. Salvatorkapelle: **Tel** 3178394. **Open** 9am–5pm Mon–Wed, 9am–7pm Thu, or by appt. Austrian Resistance Archive: **Tel** 2289469 319. **Open** 9am–5pm Mon–Thu. Ⓦ doew.at

The building here at Wipplinger Strasse was once owned by the German brothers Otto and Haymo of Neuburg, who conspired to overthrow the Habsburgs *(see p24)* in 1309. The property was confiscated by Prince Friedrich the Fair and donated to the city. Over the centuries the site was expanded to form the complex of buildings that until 1883 served as the city hall or *Rathaus*.

The entrance of the Altes Rathaus is festooned with ornamental ironwork. Located in the main courtyard, is the Andromeda Fountain, the last work by sculptor Georg Raphael Donner who designed

Portal figure by Lorenzo Mattielli in the Bohemian Court Chancery

it in 1741. The fountain depicts Perseus rescuing Andromeda. A door leads from the courtyard to the Salvatorkapelle (St Saviour's chapel), the only surviving building of the original medieval town house and the former Neuburg family chapel. It has since been enlarged and renovated, but retains its fine Gothic vaults. The walls are lined with old marble tomb slabs, some from the 15th century. Its pretty organ dates from around 1740 and is sometimes used for recitals. The chapel has an exquisite Renaissance portal, facing Salvatorgasse. Dating from 1520 to 1530, it is a rare example of Italianate Renaissance style.

Today the Old Town Hall houses offices and shops, as well as the District Museum, which examines the first municipal district of Vienna (roughly covering the area within the Ring). Of much greater interest is the Museum of the Austrian Resistance Movement, devoted to the memory of those who risked their lives by opposing the Nazis during the Second World War.

㉚ Maria am Gestade

Salvatorgasse 12. **Map** 2 D4 & 5 C2. **Tel** 53395940. Ⓤ Schwedenplatz, Stephansplatz. 🚋 2A. **Open** 7am–7pm daily.

One of the city's oldest sights is this lofty, Gothic church with its 56-m high (180-ft) steeple and immense choir windows. There are recordings of the church from as early as 1158, but the present building dates from the late 14th century. It was restored in the 19th century. The church has had a chequered history and Napoleon's troops used it as an arsenal during their occupation of Vienna in 1809.

Inside, the nave piers are enlivened with Gothic canopies sheltering statues from various periods: medieval, Baroque and modern. The choir contains High Gothic panels (1460) depicting the Annunciation, the Crucifixion and the Coronation of the Virgin.

Behind the high altar the windows contain medieval stained glass, which is patched with surviving fragments.

Tucked away on the north side of the choir is a chapel with a painted stone altar from 1520. The main parts of the interior are visible from the front entrance, but to walk around inside you need to make an appointment.

Gothic canopies in the Maria am Gestade church

Holocaust memorial in Judenplatz

Whiteread's Holocaust memorial, the Museum Judenplatz at No. 8 and the excavated remains of the medieval synagogue that lie beneath the square. The museum celebrates the vibrant Jewish quarter that was centred on the square until the expulsion of the Jews in 1421, an event gleefully recorded in an inscription, *Zum Grossen Jordan*, on the façade of No. 2. It also houses a public database of the 65,000 Austrian Jews killed by the Nazis.

㉛ Judenplatz

Map 2 D5 & 5 C2. Ⓤ Stephansplatz, Herrengasse. 🚌 1A, 2A, 3A. Museum Judenplatz: **Tel** 535 04 31. **Open** 10am–6pm Sun–Thu, 10am–2pm Fri. **Closed** on main Jewish holidays. 🅿 🅰 except to synagogue. 🅰 free, 2pm & 5pm Thu & Sun (take identification). Ⓦ jmw.at

Judenplatz was the site of the Jewish ghetto in medieval times. At the centre of the square stands a statue of the German playwright and critic Ephraim Lessing by Siegfried Charoux. The Nazis did not like a tribute to a writer whose works plead for toleration towards Jews, and they destroyed it in 1939. It was later redesigned by the same sculptor and reinstated in the square in 1982.

In 1996 British artist Rachel Whiteread was the controversial winner of a competition to design a monument for the Jewish victims of the Nazi regime, to be unveiled in the square on 9 November 1999, the anniversary of Kristallnacht. A heated public debate ensued and, following many changes, including the repositioning of the monument by one metre, Judenplatz was reopened on 25 October 2000 as a place of remembrance. It now contains

㉜ Clock Museum

Schulhof 2. **Map** 2 D5 & 5 C2. **Tel** 5332265. Ⓤ Stephansplatz. 🚌 1A, 2A, 3A. **Open** 10am–6pm Tue–Sun. **Closed** 1 Jan, 1 May & 25 Dec. 🅰 (free for under-19s and 1st Sun of the month). 🅰 Ⓦ wienmuseum.at

You don't have to be a clock fanatic to enjoy a visit to this fascinating museum. Located in the beautiful former Obizzi Palace (1690), the museum contains a fine collection of clocks and gives visitors a comprehensive account of the history of chronometry through the ages, and of clock technology from the 15th century through to the present day.

There are more than 3,000 exhibits, some of which were accumulated by an

Lavish specimen in the Clock Museum

earlier curator, Rudolf Kaftan, while others belonged to the novelist Marie von Ebner-Eschenbach. On the first floor are displayed the mechanisms of tower clocks from the 16th century onwards, alongside painted clocks, grandfather clocks and pocket watches. On the other floors are huge astronomical clocks and a wide range of novelty timepieces.

A major highlight is the astronomical clock by David Cajetano, dating from the 18th century. It has over 30 readings and dials that show, among other things, the dates of solar and lunar eclipses. Other exhibits date from the Biedermeier and *belle époque* periods.

At every full hour the three floors of the museum resound to the incredible sound of clocks striking, chiming and playing. All are carefully maintained to keep the correct time.

㉝ Kurrentgasse

Map 2 D5 & 5 C2. Ⓤ Stephansplatz. 🚌 1A, 2A, 3A. Grimm bakery: **Open** 7am–6:30pm Mon–Fri, 8am–1pm Sat.

This narrow street is shaded by tall, elegant Baroque houses, their lower floors occupied by cosy bars and pricey Italian restaurants. It's a pleasant place to while away an afternoon. The Grimm bakery at No. 10 is one of the best in Vienna, selling an astonishing variety of breads. No. 12, a house dating from 1730, has an attractive pink cobbled courtyard filled with numerous plants and trees.

One of the many fascinating exhibits in the Clock Museum

Sculpture on top of No. 10 Am Hof

❹ Kirche am Hof

Schulhof 1. **Map** 2 D5 & 5 C2.
Tel 5338394. Ⓤ Herrengasse.
Open 7am–noon, 4–6pm daily. ♿

This Catholic church, which is dedicated to the Nine Choirs of Angels, was founded by Carmelite friars in the late 14th century. The façade was redesigned by the Italian architect Carlo Carlone in 1662 to provide space for a large balustraded balcony. The church is now used by Vienna's large Croatian community.

It is worth taking a walk behind the church into Schulhofplatz to look at the tiny restored shops which stand between the buttresses of the Gothic choir.

❺ Am Hof

Map 2 D5 & 5 C2. Ⓤ
Stephansplatz, Schottentor.
🚌 1A, 2A, 3A.

This is the largest enclosed square in Vienna, as well as the oldest. The Romans established a garrison here and, later, the Babenberg ruler Duke Heinrich II Jasomirgott built his castle close to where No. 2 Am Hof stands. At the centre of the square is the Mariensäule (Column of Our Lady), a monument that commemorates the

end of the threat of Swedish invasion during the Thirty Years' War *(see p27)*.

There are a number of interesting houses around the square. Opposite the church is the palatial Märkleinisches Haus, which was designed by Johann Lukas von Hildebrandt *(see p154)* in 1727. Its elegant façade was wrecked by the addition of a fire station on the ground floor in 1935 (it now houses the Vienna Fire Brigade Museum). The 16th-century red house next door is the headquarters of Johann Kattus, a producer of sparkling wine. No. 10, designed by Anton Ospel, is the Bürgerliche Zeughaus, the citizens' armoury, where the city's fire services are now based. The façade is dominated by the Habsburg coat of arms and military emblems. The allegorical statues above are by Lorenzo Mattielli.

At No. 12 the bay-windowed Urbanihaus, with its iron sign, dates from the 1730s. Next door is the Collalto Palace – where Mozart made his first public appearance aged just six *(see p40)*.

❻ Peterskirche

Petersplatz 6. **Map** 2 D5 & 5 C3.
Tel 53364330. Ⓤ Stephansplatz.
🚌 1A. **Open** 7am–8pm Mon–Fri,
9am–9pm Sat, Sun & hols.

A church has stood here since the 12th century, but the oval structure you see today dates from the early 18th century. It was modelled on St Peter's in Rome and a number of architects collaborated on the design, notably Gabriele Montani. The interior is amazingly lavish, culminating in an exuberant, eye-catching pulpit (1716) by the sculptor Matthias Steindl. The richly clothed skeletons on the right and beneath the altar are the remains of early Christian martyrs originally deposited in the catacombs in Rome. The frescoes inside the huge dome, depicting the Assumption of the Virgin, are by J M Rottmayr.

In 1729 Lorenzo Mattielli designed the sculpture of St John Nepomuk to the right of the choir. This priest earned his sainthood by being thrown into the River Vltava in Prague in 1393 after he refused to reveal the secrets of the confessional to King Wenceslas IV; his martyrdom by drowning later became a favourite subject of artists.

18th-century engraving of
Peterskirche

HOFBURG QUARTER

What began as a modest city fortress has grown over the centuries into a vast palace, the Hofburg. The palace was still expanding up until a few years before the Habsburgs fell from power in 1918. The presence of the court had a profound effect on the surrounding area. Streets such as Herrengasse and Bankgasse are lined with the palaces that the nobility built in their eagerness to be as close as possible to the centre of imperial power. The former gardens of the palace are now the Volksgarten and Burggarten, and some of the buildings are now splendid museums. This area is bustling with tourists by day, but at night it is almost deserted.

Sights at a Glance

Streets and Squares
- **1** Michaelerplatz
- **6** Josefsplatz
- **7** Dorotheergasse
- **8** Graben
- **10** Kohlmarkt
- **12** Naglergasse
- **13** Herrengasse
- **29** Minoritenplatz
- **31** Bankgasse
- **35** Neuer Markt
- **36** Kärntner Strasse
- **38** Stock-im-Eisen-Platz

Historic Buildings
- **2** Looshaus
- **3** Grosses und Kleines Michaelerhaus
- **5** Stallburg
- **11** Demel Konditorei
- **14** Mollard-Clary Palace
- **15** *Hofburg Complex pp98–9*
- **24** Prunksaal
- **26** *Spanish Riding School pp100–101*
- **28** Bundeskanzleramt
- **33** Lobkowitz Palace
- **37** American Bar

Churches and Cathedrals
- **4** Michaelerkirche
- **23** Augustinerkirche
- **25** Burgkapelle
- **30** Minoritenkirche
- **34** Kapuzinerkirche und Kaisergruft

Museums and Galleries
- **16** Neue Burg
- **17** Ephesos Museum
- **18** Sammlung Alter Musikinstrumente
- **19** Hofjagd und Rüstkammer
- **20** Weltmuseum Wien
- **22** Albertina
- **27** *State Apartments and Treasury pp102–3*

Parks and Gardens
- **21** Burggarten
- **32** Volksgarten

Monuments
- **9** Pestsäule

▢ Restaurants *pp212–14*
- **1** Beaulieu
- **2** Café Bräunerhof
- **3** Café Central
- **4** Café Demel
- **5** Café Hawelka
- **6** Café Hofburg
- **7** Café Mozart
- **8** Ilona Stüberl
- **9** Konditorei Gerstner
- **10** Konditorei Oberlaa
- **11** L'Osteria
- **12** Palmenhaus
- **13** Regina Margherita
- **14** Reinthaler's Beisl
- **15** Restaurant im Ambassador
- **16** Restaurant Kanzleramt
- **17** Restaurant Lohmann
- **18** Sapori Restaurant
- **19** Sky Restaurant
- **20** Trześniewski
- **21** YOHM

See also Street Finder maps 5 and 6

◀ Entrance to the Neue Burg on Heldenplatz, part of the Hofburg Complex

For keys to symbols *see back flap*

Street-by-Street: Imperial Vienna

The streets around the Hofburg are no longer filled with the carriages of the nobility. Most of the palaces have become offices, embassies or apartments. Yet this district remains the most fashionable in Vienna, crammed with elegant shops, art galleries and coffee houses, which offer enjoyable interludes between visits to the many museums and churches in the area.

⑬ Herrengasse
This was a prime site for the palaces of the nobility.

Herrengasse U-Bahn

⑪ Demel Konditorei
This Café-Konditorei offers delightful decor and exquisite pastries.

⑨ Grosses und Kleines Michaelerhaus
Joseph Haydn *(see p40)* once lived in rooms overlooking the handsome courtyard of the Grosses Michaelerhaus.

⑭ Mollard-Clary Palace
This mansion, built at the end of the 17th century, has a façade designed by J L Hildebrandt.

❷ ★ Looshaus
Built in 1912, this unadorned design outraged the conservative sensibilities of the ornament-loving Archduke Franz Ferdinand *(see p168)*.

❶ Michaelerplatz
Roman remains have been excavated here.

❹ ★ Michaelerkirche
The crypt of this church contains well-preserved corpses from the late 18th century.

❻ Josefsplatz
An equestrian statue of Joseph II stands at the centre of this elegant square.

Key

— Suggested route

0 metres	50
0 yards	50

⓬ **Naglergasse**
This lane has some of the finest Baroque façades in the city.

⑧ **Graben**
The Spar-Casse Bank, with its gilt bee on the pediment, is just one of many fine buildings on the pedestrianized Graben.

Locator Map
See Street Finder maps 2 and 5

⑩ **Kohlmarkt**
This street has a number of shops designed by Hans Hollein, one of Austria's finest architects.

⑨ ★ **Pestsäule**
Built after the plague of 1679, this is the most imposing of the Baroque plague columns.

⑦ **Dorotheergasse**
Lining this narrow lane are art galleries and auction houses, and the much-loved Café Hawelka *(see pp60–63)*.

⑤ **Stallburg**
Once a royal residence, the Stallburg now houses the Spanish Riding School stables and the Lipizzaner Museum.

The Pallavicini Palace is a late 18th-century aristocrats' palace, strategically located opposite the Hofburg.

The Palffy Palace
Built in the 16th century, this was the venue for a performance of Mozart's *The Marriage of Figaro*.

❶ Michaelerplatz

Map 5 C3. Ⓤ Herrengasse. 🚌 1A, 2A.

Michaelerplatz faces the impressive Neo-Baroque Michaelertor, which leads to the Hofburg's inner courtyard. On both sides of the doorway are 19th-century wall fountains, designed by Rudolf Weyer.

Opposite are the Michaelerkirche and Looshaus. On one side of Michaelerplatz is the domed Michaelertrakt, an extravagant wing of the imperial palace. An old design by Joseph Emanuel Fischer von Erlach (see p149) was used as the basis for a new design by Ferdinand Kirschner (1821–96). It was finished in 1893, complete with gilt-tasselled cupolas and statuary representing Austria's land and sea power.

At the centre is an excavation site that reveals remains of a Roman encampment, as well as some medieval foundations.

❷ Looshaus

Michaelerplatz 3. **Map** 2 D5 & 5 C3. **Tel** 517 00900. Ⓤ Herrengasse. 🚌 1A, 2A. **Open** 9am–3pm Mon–Wed & Fri, 9am–5:30pm Thu. ♿

Erected opposite the Michaelertor in 1910–12, and designed by Adolf Loos, this building so outraged Franz Ferdinand (see p168) that he declared he would never use the Michaelertor

again. Today it's hard to understand why: the outside is unexceptional but the inside is a lesson in stylish elegance.

❸ Grosses und Kleines Michaelerhaus

Kohlmarkt 11 & Michaelerplatz 6. **Map** 2 D5 & 5 C3. Ⓤ Herrengasse. 🚌 1A, 2A. **Closed** to the public.

At No. 6 Michaelerplatz a footpath leads to the Baroque Kleines Michaelerhaus (1735). Look out for a vivid painted relief of Christ on the Mount of Olives with a crucifixion in the background (1494) on the side of the Michaelerkirche. The Baroque façade of the Grosses Michaelerhaus

is at No. 11 Kohlmarkt. It has a handsome courtyard and coach house, with a fine view of the older parts of the Michaelerkirche. The buildings around the courtyard were erected in about 1720. The composer Joseph Haydn (see p40) is said to have lived in an unheated attic here in 1749.

Adolf Loos

Unlike his contemporary Otto Wagner (see p59), Adolf Loos (1870–1933) loathed ornament for its own sake. Instead, he used smooth lines and exquisite interior decoration; his buildings' lack of "eyebrows" (the window hoods on many of Vienna's buildings) scandalized Viennese society. Surviving interiors by Loos include Knize (see p95), the American Bar (see p107) and the Café Museum (see p139).

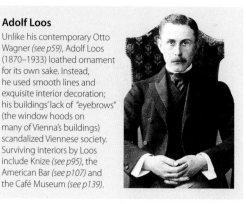

❹ Michaelerkirche

Michaelerplatz 1. **Map** 2 D5 & 5 C3. **Tel** 5338000. Ⓤ Herrengasse, Stephansplatz. 🚌 1A, 2A. **Open** 7am–10pm Mon–Sat, 8am–10pm Sun & hols. 🎧 ♿ 📷 Tours of the crypt: 11am & 1pm Mon–Sat.

The Michaelerkirche was once the parish church of the court. Its earliest parts were built in the 13th century; according to legend the church was built in 1221 but its present form dates from 1792. Its porch is topped by Baroque sculptures (1724–25) by Lorenzo Mattielli depicting the Fall of the Angels. Inside are Renaissance and 14th-century frescoes, and a vividly carved organ (1714) by Johann David Sieber. The main choir (1782), replete with cherubs and sunbursts, is by Karl Georg Merville.

Off the north choir is the crypt entrance. In the 17th and 18th centuries parishioners were frequently buried beneath their church. Corpses clothed in their burial finery, well preserved due to the constant temperature, can still be seen in open coffins.

Michaelerplatz fountain

Baroque organ (1714) in the Michaelerkirche

❺ Stallburg

Reitschulgasse 2. **Map** 4 D1 & 5 C3.
Ⓤ Stephansplatz, Herrengasse.
🚌 1A, 2A.

The Stallburg was built in the
mid-16th century for Emperor
Maximilian. This former royal
residence, which was ranged
around a large courtyard, was
later converted to stables for
the Hofburg. The Stallburg
houses the Spanish Riding
School stables (see pp100–101).

For much of the 18th century,
the Stallburg was the home
of the imperial art collection.
In 1776, the collection was
transferred to the Belvedere so
that it would be accessible to
the public, and in 1891 it was
moved to its present home, the
Kunsthistoriches Museum.

❻ Josefsplatz

Augustinerstrasse. **Map** 4 D1 & 5 C4.
Ⓤ Stephansplatz, Herrengasse.
🚌 1A, 2A.

At the centre of the Josefsplatz
is an equestrian statue (1807)
of Joseph II by Franz Anton von
Zauner. Despite his reforms,
Joseph II was a true monarchist,
and during the 1848 Revolution
(see p33) loyalists used the
square as a gathering place.

Facing the Hofburg are
two palaces. No. 5 is the
Pallavicini Palace (1783–
4), a blend of Baroque
and Neo-Classical styles
by Ferdinand von

Hohenberg. No. 6 is the 16th-
century Palffy Palace. On the
right of the Prunksaal (see p104)
is the Redoutensaal. Built in
1750–60, it was the venue for
balls in imperial times. To the
left is an extension to the library
which was built a few years
later. Both are by Nikolaus
Pacassi, a favourite architect of
Maria Theresa.

❼ Dorotheergasse

Map 4 D1 & 5 C4. Ⓤ Stephansplatz.
🚌 1A, 2A, 3A. Jewish Museum:
Tel 5350431. **Open** 10am–6pm
Sun–Fri. 🔳 **jmw.at**

At No. 11 on this street is the
Eskeles Palace, now home to
the Jewish Museum (Jüdisches
Museum) which, along with its
extension in Judenplatz (see
p88), chronicles the city's rich
Jewish heritage. At No. 17 is the
Dorotheum (see pp224–5), built in
the 17th century. A pawnbrokers
and an auction house, it has
branches all over Vienna.
Halfway along the street is the
Evangelical church (1783–4),
originally by Gottlieb Nigelli.
Close to where the street joins
Graben are two popular
Viennese gathering places, Café
Hawelka at No. 6 (see pp60–63)
and Trzesniewski sandwich
buffet at No. 1 (see p213).
There are many art and
antique dealers in this area.

The Pestsäule, a Baroque plague column

❽ Graben

Map 2 D5 & 5 C3. Ⓤ Stephansplatz.
🚌 1A, 2A. Neidhart Fresco House:
Tel 5359065. **Open** 1–6pm Tue–Sun.

Facing No. 16 on this pedestrianized street is the Joseph
Fountain by Johann Martin
Fischer. Further along is his
identical Leopold Fountain
(both 1804). No. 13, the
clothing shop Knize (see pp223–
5), is by Adolf Loos. No. 10, the
Anker-haus by Otto Wagner,
is topped by a studio used
by Wagner himself and, in
the 1980s, by Friedensreich
Hundertwasser (see p166).
Alois Pichl's Spar-Casse Bank
from the 1830s is at No. 21.
Just off the Graben at No. 19
Tuchlauben is the Neidhart
Fresco House, containing
medieval frescoes.

❾ Pestsäule

Graben. **Map** 2 D5 & 5 C3.
Ⓤ Stephansplatz. 🚌 1A, 2A.

During the plague of 1679,
Emperor Leopold I vowed to
commemorate Vienna's eventual
deliverance. The plague over,
he commissioned Matthias
Rauchmiller, Lodovico Burnacini
and the young Johann Bernhard
Fischer von Erlach (see p149) to
build this Baroque plague
column. Devised by the Jesuits,
its most striking image shows
a saintly figure and an angel
supervising the destruction of a
hag representing the plague,
while the Emperor prays above.

Statue in Josefsplatz of Joseph II by Franz Anton von Zauner (1746–1822)

The pedestrianized Kohlmarkt, home to many exclusive shops and beautiful shopfronts

❿ Kohlmarkt

Map 2 D5 & 5 C3. Ⓤ Herrengasse.
🚌 1A, 2A.

Leading directly up to the Imperial Palace, the Kohlmarkt is pedestrianized and lined with some of Vienna's most exclusive shops and remarkable shopfronts. No. 9, the Jugendstil Artaria Haus (1901), was the work of Max Fabiani (1865–1962), a protégé of Otto Wagner *(see p59)*. No.16, the bookshop and publisher Manz, boasts a characteristic portal from 1912 by Adolf Loos *(see p94)*. The striking abstract shopfront of jewellers Schullin (1982) was designed by the architect Hans Hollein *(see p93)*.

⓫ Demel Konditorei

Kohlmarkt 14. **Map** 2 D5 & 5 C3.
Tel 53517170. Ⓤ Stephansplatz.
🚌 1A, 2A. **Open** 9am–7pm daily. ♿

This famous pastry shop at No. 14 Kohlmarkt still bears its imperial patent – K.u.k. Hof-Zuckerbäcker – proudly lettered above the shopfront. The pastry shop was founded in Michaelerplatz in 1785 and acquired by the pâtissier Christoph Demel in 1857, before moving to its present site on Kohlmarkt in 1888. Its many small rooms are in an ornate late 19th-century style.

⓬ Naglergasse

Map 2 D5 & 5 C2. Ⓤ Herrengasse.
🚌 1A, 2A.

During the Middle Ages needle-makers had their shops here, which is how the street acquired

its name. This narrow lane follows the line of a wall that used to stand here in Roman times. Today Naglergasse is lined with a succession of gorgeous Baroque houses. The delightful Renaissance bay window of No. 19 is ornamented with carved cherubs. No. 13 dates from the 16th century but has been considerably altered since. No. 21 (1720) is now an inn with a particularly snug and cosy interior.

⓭ Herrengasse

Map 2 D5 & 5 B2. Ⓤ Herrengasse.
🚌 1A, 2A.

Flanking the Hofburg, this street was the prime location for the palaces of the Habsburg nobility. In 1843 a visiting writer, J G Kohl, wrote of the street's "silent palaces", and today little has changed.

The office of the provincial government of Lower Austria, the Landhaus, is at No. 13; the façade of the present building dates from the 1830s. In the courtyard

a tablet from 1571 warns visitors not to carry weapons or to fight here. The injunction was famously ignored when the 1848 Revolution *(see p33)* was ignited on this very spot.

The long, low Neo-Classical façade of No. 7 received its present appearance from Ludwig Pichl and Giacomo Quarenghi in 1811. At No. 5 Anton Ospel (1677–1756) gave the Wilczek Palace (built before 1737) an unusual façade, with angled pilasters lending the central bays an illusion of perspective.

⓮ Mollard-Clary Palace

Herrengasse 9. **Map** 2 D5 & 5 B3.
Tel 53410710. Ⓤ Herrengasse.
🚌 1A, 2A. Globe Museum:
Open 10am–6pm Tue–Sun (to 9pm Thu). 🌐 onb.ac.at

This magnificent Baroque palace, dating from 1686, owes its name to two aristocratic tenants, Mollard and Clary. It is famous for the reforming cultural soirées presided over there by Emperor Joseph II. Today it is home to the world's only museum devoted solely to globes and is part of the Austrian National Library. A special chamber houses the huge globes of Venetian Vincenzo Coronelli and the giant 16th-century globes by Gerard Mercator.

⓯ Hofburg Complex

See pp98–103.

People walking along Herrengasse, a street with a rich history

🔟 Neue Burg

Heldenplatz. **Map** 4 D1 & 5 B4.
Tel 52524484. 🔲 Volkstheater,
Herrengasse. 🚋 D, 1, 2, 71.
Open 10am–6pm Wed–Sun.
🅿 🔲 **hofburg-wien.at**

The Neue Burg, a massive curved
building situated on Heldenplatz,
was added to the Hofburg
Complex between 1881 and
1913. It embodies the last gasp
of the Habsburg Empire as it
strained under aspirations of
independence from its domains,
when the personal prestige of
Emperor Franz Joseph was all that
seemed able to keep it intact.
It was not the perfect moment
to embark on an extension to
the Hofburg, but the work was
undertaken nevertheless, and the
Neue Burg was built to designs
by the Ringstrasse architects Karl
von Hasenauer (1833–94) and
Gottfried Semper (1803–79). Five
years after its completion, the
Habsburg Empire ended.

In 1938, Adolf Hitler stood on
the terraced central bay to
proclaim the Anschluss – the
union of Austria and Germany
– to tens of thousands of
Viennese *(see p38)*.

The Neue Burg is home to the
reading room of the national
library, as well as a number of
museums *(see following entries)*
that are all under the direction
of the KHM-Museumsverband.

🔷 Ephesos Museum

As Neue Burg. **Tel** 525244902.
Open 10am–6pm Wed–Sun.
🔲 **khm.at**

For decades
Austrian
archaeologists
have been exca-
vating the Greek
and Roman site
of Ephesus in Turkey.
Since 1978 their discoveries
have been displayed in the main
block of the Neue Burg. Also on
show are finds from the Greek
island of Samothrace, excavated
in the 1870s. The main exhibits
include a huge frieze commemorating Lucius Verus's victory over
the Parthians in AD 165, and
many architectural fragments.

Suit of armour at Hofjagd und Rüstkammer

🔷 Sammlung Alter Musikinstrumente

As Neue Burg. **Tel** 525244602.
🔲 **khm.at**

Pianos that belonged to
Beethoven, Schubert and
Haydn, among countless other
items, are housed in the musical
instrument museum. More
impressive, however, is the
collection of Renaissance
instruments, widely believed to
be the finest in the world. The
claviorgan (1596), the oldest
surviving example of this
instrument, is particularly
interesting, and features stops
used to create special effects
such as birdsong.

Renaissance cittern from the
Sammlung Alter Musikinstrumente

🔟 Hofjagd und Rüstkammer

As Neue Burg. **Tel** 525244502.
🔲 **khm.at**

The Hofburg's weapons
collection is impressive both for
its size and for the workmanship
of its finest items: ivory and
filigree inlay on weapons,
medieval ceremonial saddles
and jewelled Turkish and Syrian
maces. Of note are the
16th-century ceremonial suits
worn by the Habsburgs for
tournaments and military
parades, and the decorative
fighting and hunting weapons.
The core of the collection is
the personal armouries of the
Habsburg emperors and, not
surprisingly, houses one of the
finest collections in Europe.

🔟 Weltmuseum Wien

As Neue Burg. **Tel** 534305052. **Open**
10am–6pm Tue–Sun (to 9pm Fri). 🅿
🅿 🖥 🔲 **weltmuseumwien.at**

Collecting for the Weltmuseum
began in 1806, and young
archdukes on their travels across
the globe were avid contributors. The "Museum of Man", as
Austria's foremost ethnological
institution is sometimes called,
has as its centrepiece the Italian
Renaissance-style Hall of
Columns. There is a café and
bistro and 14 galleries themed
by region or subject. There is a
permanent exhibition on the
English explorer James Cook.
But the most prized piece is the
500-year-old green quetzal-
feather Penacho tribal head-
dress from Mexico, sometimes
attributed to Montezuma. There
is also a rare collection from
Benin, but everyday items from
primitive cultures ranging from
the Arctic and Himalayas to
mud huts are equally evocative.

⓯ The Hofburg Complex

The vast Hofburg Complex contains the imperial apartments, several museums, a chapel, a church, the Austrian National Library, the Spanish Riding School and the President of Austria's offices. The seat of Austrian power since the 13th century, the complex has been developed over the years by successive rulers all anxious to leave their mark. The result is a range of architectural styles, from Gothic to late 19th-century historicism.

★ Prunksaal
The showpiece of the Austrian National Library (1722–35) is the flamboyant, wood-panelled Prunksaal, or Hall of Honour *(see pp104–5)*, which features this statue of Karl VI.

★ Michaelertrakt (1893)
The curved façade of the Michaelertrakt is surmounted by an imposing dome.

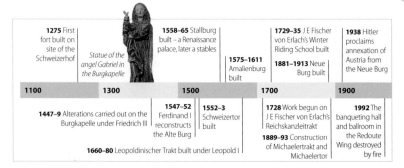

1100	1300	1500	1700	1900
1275 First fort built on site of the Schweizerhof	*Statue of the angel Gabriel in the Burgkapelle*	**1558–65** Stallburg built – a Renaissance palace, later as stables	**1729–35** J E Fischer von Erlach's Winter Riding School built	**1938** Hitler proclaims annexation of Austria from the Neue Burg
		1575–1611 Amalienburg built	**1881–1913** Neue Burg built	
	1447–9 Alterations carried out on the Burgkapelle under Friedrich III	**1547–52** Ferdinand I reconstructs the Alte Burg / **1552–3** Schweizertor built	**1728** Work begun on J E Fischer von Erlach's Reichskanzleitrakt	**1992** The banqueting hall and ballroom in the Redoute Wing destroyed by fire
	1660–80 Leopoldinischer Trakt built under Leopold I		**1889–93** Construction of Michaelertrakt and Michaelertor	

Mozart Memorial (1896)
Viktor Tilgner's statue of
the composer stands
just inside the
Ringstrasse entrance.

VISITORS' CHECKLIST

Practical Information
Michaelerplatz 1, A-1010.
Map 4 D1 & 5 B4. For opening
times of individual museums,
see pp94–107.

Transport
Ⓤ Stephansplatz, Herrengasse.
🚌 1A, 2A to Michaelerplatz.
🚊 D, 1, 2, 71.

★ **Prince Eugene Statue**
Anton Dominik von Fernkorn
designed this monument to
Prince Eugene (1865).
The pedestal is by
Eduard van der Nüll.

★ **Schweizertor**
This 16th-century
Renaissance
gateway leads to
the Schweizerhof,
the oldest part of
the Hofburg,
originally a
stronghold with
four towers.

KEY

① **Reichskanzleitrakt**

② **Michaelertor**

③ **Spanish Riding School**
(see pp100–101)

④ **Stallburg (Stables)** *(see p95)*

⑤ **Redoute Wing**

⑥ **Alte Burg**

⑦ **Burgkapelle** *(see p105)*

⑧ **Statue of Joseph II in Josefsplatz** *(see p95)*

⑨ **Augustinerkirche** *(see p104)*

⑩ **Albertina** *(see p104)*

⑪ **Burggarten** *(see p104)*

⑫ **Neue Burg** *(see p97)*

⑬ **Burgtor**, the outer gate, was
built to a design by Peter Nobile
in 1821–4.

⑭ **Heldenplatz**

⑮ **Leopoldinischer Trakt**

⑯ **Amalienburg** is an oddly
shaped building constructed in
1575 for Emperor Maximilian's
son Rudolf. It has a Renaissance
façade and an attractive Baroque
clock tower.

㉖ Spanish Riding School

The origins of the Spanish Riding School are obscure, but it is believed to have been founded in 1572 to cultivate the classic skills of *haute école* horsemanship. By breeding and training horses from Spain, the Habsburgs formed the Spanische Reitschule. Today, 80-minute shows take place in the building known as the Winter Riding School. Commissioned by Karl VI, it was built between 1729 and 1735 to a design by Josef Emanuel Fischer von Erlach. There are two entrances to the building – one from Josefsplatz, the other from the Michaelerkuppel.

Specially bred Lipizzaner stallions are trained from the age of three.

The black bicorn hat has a gold braid stripe from the upper left to the lower centre.

Jackets are coffee-coloured – waisted, double-breasted and with two rows of brass buttons.

Buckskin jodhpurs are worn.

Pale leather gloves are worn.

Long boots covering the knees are part of the uniform.

Tack
The elegant saddle with embroidered cloth differs from modern versions and complements the historical dress of the riders; the curb rein is generally used.

Stables
The three-storey-high Renaissance former palace of the Stallburg is across the road from the Winter Riding School. It now provides stabling for the horses.

The Horses' Steps

The steps made by the horses and riders are part of a carefully orchestrated ballet. Many derive from exercises that were developed during the Renaissance period by cavalrymen, who needed agile horses capable of special manoeuvres.

The Croupade: the horse leaps into the air with hind legs and forelegs bent under its belly.

Levade: the horse stands on its hind legs with hocks almost touching the ground.

Interior of the Winter Riding School

The gracious interior is lined with 46 columns and adorned with elaborate plasterwork, chandeliers and a coffered ceiling. At the head of the arena is the court box. Spectators sit here or watch from upper galleries.

VISITORS' CHECKLIST

Practical Information
Michaelerplatz 1, A-1010. **Map** 5 C3. **Tel** 5339031. **Open** 9am–4pm daily (visitor centre); performances at 11am Sat & Sun. **Closed** 1 Jan, 6 Jan, 1 May, Ascension Day, Corpus Christi, 15 Aug, 26 Oct, 1 Nov, 8 Dec, 25 & 26 Dec (dates may vary). some areas. **w srs.at**

Transport
Herrengasse. 1A, 2A to Michaelerplatz.

Portrait of Karl VI
An equestrian portrait of Emperor Karl VI, who commissioned the building, hangs in the royal box. Whenever a rider enters the hall, he must express his respect to the founder of the school by raising his bicorn hat to the portrait.

The Lipizzaner Horses

The stallions that perform their athletic feats on the sawdust of the Winter Riding School take their name from the stud at Lipizza near Trieste in Slovenia *(see below)*, which was founded by Archduke Karl in 1580. Today the horses are bred on the Austrian National Stud Farm at Piber near Graz. Lipizzaner horses were originally produced by crossing Arab, Berber and Spanish horses, and are renowned for their grace and stamina. You may be able to obtain a ticket without a reservation to see them at their morning training session.

Capriole: this is a leap into the air with a simultaneous kick of the hind legs.

The Piaffe: the horse trots on the spot, often between two pillars.

ⓧ State Apartments and Treasury

The state apartments in the Reichskanzleitrakt (1723–30) and the Amalienburg (1575) include rooms occupied by Franz Joseph from 1857 to 1916, the apartments of Empress Elisabeth from 1854 to 1898 and the rooms where Tsar Alexander I lived during the Congress of Vienna in 1815. The Imperial Treasury holds sacred and secular treasures amassed during centuries of Habsburg rule, including the crown of the Holy Roman Emperor, a "unicorn" horn and religious objects.

★ **10th-century Crown**
The insignia of the Holy Roman Empire includes this crown set with enamel plaques and cabochons.

Emperor Maximilian I
(c. 1500)
This portrait by Bernhard Strigel hangs in the room containing Burgundian treasure. Emperor Maximilian married Mary, Duchess of Burgundy in 1477.

Cradle of the King of Rome
Maria Louisa gave this cradle, designed by the French painter Prud'hon, to her son, the King of Rome (*see p177*).

KEY

① **Entrance through the Michaelerkuppel to State Apartments and Silberkammer**

② **Entrance to Treasuries**

③ **Passage to Neue Burg and Heldenplatz**

④ **Sisi Museum**

⑤ **Ticket office**

⑥ **Entrance through the Kaisertor to State Apartments and Silberkammer**

⑦ **Exit from apartments**

Crucifix after Giambologna
(c. 1590)
This type of crucifix, a Cristo Morto, can be traced back to a similar model by Giambologna which is in Florence.

Key

☐ Franz Joseph's State Apartments

☐ Elisabeth's State Apartments

☐ Alexander's State Apartments

▨ Sacred Treasury

▨ Secular Treasury

▨ Sisi Museum

☐ Non-exhibition space

The Silberkammer

On display in the ground-floor rooms is a dazzling array of items – gold, silver and the finest porcelain – that were once used at Habsburg state banquets. One of the highlights is a 33-m long (100-ft) gilded bronze centrepiece with accompanying candelabra from around 1800. Visitors can also admire the mid-18th-century Sèvres dinner service that was a diplomatic gift from Louis XV to Maria Theresa.

Goblet from the Laxenburg Service (c. 1821)

VISITORS' CHECKLIST

Practical Information
Map 4 D1 & 5 B3. State Apartments (Kaiserapparte-ments), Sisi Museum & Silberkammer: Michaelerkuppel. **Tel** 5337570. **Open** 9am–5:30pm daily (to 6pm Jul & Aug). 🖼 📷 Sat & Sun. 🔲 **hofburg-wien.at** Imperial Treasury (Kaiserliche Schatzkammer): Schweizerhof. **Tel** 525240. **Open** 9am–5:30pm Mon & Wed–Sun. 🖼 ♿ 📷 🔲 🔲 **kaiserliche-schatzkammer.at**

Elisabeth's Gymnastic Equipment
The Empress was a fitness enthusiast, and the bars at which she exercised are still in place in her dressing room.

★ **Imperial Dining Hall**
The table is laid as it would have been in Emperor Franz Joseph's day *(see p34–5),* in the room where the imperial family used to dine.

Guide to Treasury Rooms

Entering the Secular Treasury, Rooms 1–8 contain items from the Austrian Empire (with Room 5 commemorating Napoleon). Rooms 9–12 exhibit treasures from the Holy Roman Empire, while the Burgundian Inheritance is displayed in Rooms 13–16. Rooms I–V, furthest from the entrance, house the Sacred Treasury.

★ **Empress Elisabeth**
Winterhalter's portrait of the empress (1865) with stars in her hair hangs in the Sisi Museum.

Greenhouses in the Burggarten by Friedrich Ohmann (1858–1927)

㉑ Burggarten

Burgring/Opernring. **Map** 4 D1 & 5 B4.
Ⓤ Karlsplatz. ▥ D, 1, 2, 71. **Open**
Apr–Oct: 6am–10pm daily; Nov–Mar:
6:30am–7pm daily.

Before leaving Vienna, Napoleon showed his contempt for the Viennese by razing part of the city walls that had proved so ineffective at preventing his entry. Some of the space left around the Hofburg was later transformed by the Habsburgs into a landscaped garden, planted with a variety of trees. It was opened to the public in 1918.

Overlooking the garden are greenhouses (1901–7) by the Jugendstil architect Friedrich Ohmann, and near the Hofburg entrance is a small equestrian statue (1780) of Emperor Franz I by the sculptor Balthasar Moll. Closer to the Ringstrasse is the Mozart Memorial (1896) by Viktor Tilgner.

㉒ Albertina

Augustinerstrasse 1. **Map** 4 D1 &
5 C4. **Tel** 53483540. Ⓤ Karlsplatz,
Stephansplatz. **Open** 10am–6pm daily
(to 9pm Wed). ▨ ▥ ▨ ▥ ▨ ▥
Ⓦ albertina.at

Once hidden away at the Opera end of the Hofburg is the Albertina, now a distinctive, modern landmark. Its raised entrance boasts a controversial freestanding diving-board roof by architect Hans Hollein (see p93). The palace once belonged to Maria Theresa's daughter, Maria Christina, and her husband Duke Albert of

Sachsen-Teschen, after whom the gallery is named. Today the Albertina houses a collection of one million prints, over 65,000 watercolours and drawings, and some 70,000 photographs. Highlights include works by Dürer, with Michelangelo and Rubens also well represented. Picasso heads a fine 20th-century section.

Temporary exhibitions feature paintings on loan along with works owned by the Albertina. The Batliner Collection, which comprises over 500 works of art and is one of the most significant private collections in Europe, is on permanent loan.

The extension on the Burggarten side houses study facilities and the largest of the three exhibition halls. Renovation has restored a number of features of the Albertina to their former glory, including the façades and the central courtyard. The Habsburg State Rooms are open to the public and represent a remarkable example of Neo-Classical architecture and interior decoration.

㉓ Augustinerkirche

Augustinerstrasse 3. **Map** 4 D1 & 5 C4.
Tel 5337099. Ⓤ Stephansplatz.
▥ 1A, 2A. **Open** 7am–6pm Mon–Fri,
8am–7pm Sat & Sun. Ⓦ augustiner
kirche.at

The Augustinerkirche has one of the best-preserved 14th-century Gothic interiors in Vienna; only the modern chandeliers strike a jarring note. The church's Loreto Chapel, dating back to 1724, contains the silver urns that preserve the hearts of the Habsburg family (see pp26–7). In the church too is one of the most powerful works by the Italian Neo-Classical sculptor

Antonio Canova, and the tombs of Maria Christina, favourite daughter of Maria Theresa, and Leopold II. Both tombs are empty; the royal remains lie in the Kaisergruft (see p106).

The church is also celebrated for its music, including Masses by Schubert or Haydn held here on Sundays.

㉔ Prunksaal

Josefsplatz 1. **Map** 4 D1 & 5 C4.
Tel 53410394. Ⓤ Herrengasse.
▥ **Open** 10am–6pm Tue–
Sun, 10am–9pm Thu. ▨ ▥ ▥ ▥
Ⓦ onb.ac.at

Commissioned as the court library by Karl VI, the State Hall, or Prunksaal, of the National Library was designed by Johann Bernhard Fischer von Erlach (see p149) in 1719. After his death in 1723, the building was completed by his son. The collection consists of approximately 2.6 million books and includes the personal library of Prince Eugene (see pp28–9), as well as books that were taken from monastic libraries closed during the religious reforms of Joseph II (see pp30–31).

The Prunksaal is 77 m (252 ft) long and is the largest Baroque library in Europe. Paired marble columns frame the domed main room, and bookcases line the walls. Spanning the vaults are frescoes by the Baroque painter Daniel Gran (1730), which were

Domed interior of the Prunksaal in the National Library building

restored by Franz Anton Maulbertsch (1769). The fine statues, including the likeness of Karl VI in the hall, are the work of Paul Strudel (1648–1708) and his brother Peter (1660–1714).

㉕ Burgkapelle

Hofburg, Schweizerhof. **Map** 4 D1 & 5 B4. **Tel** 5339927. Ⓤ Herrengasse. **Open** 10am–2pm Mon & Tue, 11am– 1pm Fri. **Closed** Public holidays. 🎭 📷 📽 Vienna Boys' Choir: Jan–Jun & Sep– Dec: 9:15am Sun (book via website). 🎭 Ⓦ **hofmusikkapelle.gv.at**

From the Schweizerhof, steps lead up to the Burgkapelle, or Hofburg Chapel, originally constructed in 1296 but modified 150 years later. On Sundays, visitors can hear the Wiener Sängerknaben, the Vienna Boys' Choir (see p41). The chapel interior has Gothic carvings and statuary in canopied niches, and boasts a bronze crucifix (1720) by Johann Känischbauer.

㉖ Spanish Riding School

See pp100–101.

㉗ State Apartments and Treasury

See pp102–3.

㉘ Bundeskanzleramt

Ballhausplatz 2. **Map** 1 C5 & 5 B3. **Tel** 531150. Ⓤ Herrengasse. 🚌 1A, 2A. **Closed** to the public.

The Bundeskanzleramt (1717– 19), the Austrian Chancery and Foreign Ministry, was designed by Johann Lukas von Hildebrandt (see p154) and was expanded to its present size in 1766 by Nikolaus Pacassi. Major events that shaped Austria's history have taken place here, including meetings of the Congress of Vienna (see p32) in 1814–15, the final deliberations in 1914 that led to the outbreak of World War I, and the murder of Chancellor Dollfuss by Nazi terrorists in 1934 (see p38).

No. 4 Minoritenplatz

㉙ Minoritenplatz

Map 2 D5 & 5 B3. Ⓤ Herrengasse.

At No. 1 Minoritenplatz is the Baroque-style State Archives building (the archives are no longer housed here), built onto the back of the Bundes-kanzleramt in 1902. There are a number of palaces around the square. No. 3 is the former Dietrichstein Palace of 1755, an early building by Franz Hillebrand. It now contains the offices of the Federal Chancellor and the Foreign Office. No. 4 is the side of the Liechtenstein Palace on Bankgasse (see p106). The mid-17th-century Starhemberg Palace is at No. 5. Now housing ministry offices, it was the residence of Count Ernst Rüdiger von Starhemberg, a hero of the 1683 Turkish siege (see p29), when he led the Austrian forces within the city.

㉚ Minoritenkirche

Minoritenplatz 2. **Map** 1 C5 & 5 B3. **Tel** 676 6264113. Ⓤ Herrengasse. **Open** 9am–6pm daily.

This ancient church was established here by the Minor friars in around 1224, although the present structure dates from 1339. The tower was given its odd pyramidal shape during the Turkish siege of 1529, when shells sliced the top off the steeple. In the 1780s the Minoritenkirche was restored to its original Gothic style, when Maria Theresa's son, Joseph II (see p30), made a gift of the church to Vienna's Italian community. The church retains a fine west portal (1340) with statues beneath traceried canopies; the carvings above the doorway are modern.

The interior of the church is unexpectedly bright and large and contains a mosaic copy of Leonardo da Vinci's *Last Supper*. Napoleon Bonaparte commissioned Giacomo Raffaelli to execute this work as he proposed to substitute it for the original in Milan and remove the real painting to Paris. Following Napoleon's downfall at Waterloo in 1815, Raffaelli's version was bought by the Habsburgs. In the south aisle is a painted statue of the Madonna and Child (dating from around 1350), while at the same spot in the north aisle is a faded fragment of a 16th-century fresco of St Francis of Assisi.

Gothic statue (c. 1400) of Leopold III in the Burgkapelle

⑪ Bankgasse

Map 1 C5 & 5 B3. **Ⓤ** Herrengasse.

Few streets in Vienna are more crammed with the palaces of the nobility.

At Nos. 4–6 is the former Strattmann-Windischgrätz Palace (1692–1734), which was originally designed by Johann Bernhard Fischer von Erlach (see p149). The present façade (1783–4) was the work of Franz Hillebrand, who considerably increased the size of the building by incorporating the palace next door. Today, it houses the Hungarian Embassy.

Nos. 5–7 are at the back of the Starhemberg Palace. The Liechtenstein Palace, built as a town residence for the Liechtenstein family by Domenico Martinelli (1694–1706), is at No. 9. No. 2 is the Schönborn-Batthyány Palace (1695).

⑫ Volksgarten

Dr-Karl-Renner-Ring. **Map** 1 C5 & 5 A3. **Tel** 5339083. **Ⓤ** Herrengasse. **🚋** D, 1, 2, 71. **Open** Apr–Oct: 6am–10pm daily; Nov–Mar: 6:30am–7pm daily. **♿**

Like the Burggarten landscaped garden (see p104), the elegant Volksgarten was created after

Statuary above the portal to the Lobkowitz Palace

the destruction of the city walls by Napoleon, and opened up a space previously occupied by fortifications. Unlike the Burggarten, the Volksgarten was opened to the public soon after its completion in 1820. The formal gardens, especially the splendid rose gardens, are matched in grandeur by statuary and monuments, notably the Temple of Theseus (1823) by Peter von Nobile. It was built to house Canova's statue of the Greek god, which now graces the staircase of the Kunsthistorisches Museum. Other highlights include Karl von Hasenauer's monument to the poet Franz Grillparzer (see p35) and the fountain memorial to the assassinated Empress Elisabeth (1907) by Friedrich Ohmann (see p59) and the sculptor Hans Bitterlich.

⑬ Lobkowitz Palace

Lobkowitzplatz 2. **Map** 4 D1 & 5 C4. **Tel** 525243460. **Ⓤ** Karlsplatz, Stephansplatz. **Open** 10am–6pm Wed–Mon. **🏷** **♿** **Ⓦ** theatermuseum.at

This large palace was built for Count Dietrichstein in 1685–7 by Giovanni Pietro Tencala and altered by Johann Bernhard Fischer von Erlach (see p149) in 1710. In 1753 it was acquired by the Lobkowitz family. Balls were held here during the Congress of Vienna (see p32).

Since 1991 the palace has housed the Austrian Theatre Museum, which features a model of the first Hofburg theatre and the Eroica-Saal (1724–29) – where many first performances of Beethoven's work took place. The main exhibits chronicle Austrian theatre in the 1940s.

⑭ Kapuzinerkirche und Kaisergruft

Tegetthoffstrasse 2. **Map** 4 D1 & 5 C4. **Tel** 512685388. **Ⓤ** Stephansplatz. Kaisergruft: **Open** 10am–6pm daily. Kapuzinerkirche: **Open** 6am–6pm daily. **🏷** **♿** **Ⓦ** kaisergruft.at

Beneath the Kapuzinerkirche are the vaults of the Kaisergruft, the imperial crypt founded in 1619 by the Catholic Emperor Matthias. Here lie the remains of 138 Habsburgs, including Maria Theresa and her husband Franz Stephan in a large tomb by Balthasar Moll (1753). The most poignant tomb is that of Franz Joseph, flanked by his assassinated wife Elisabeth and their son Rudolf, who committed suicide (see p34).

Formal rose garden in the Volksgarten

Tomb of Karl VI by Balthasar Moll

The last reigning Habsburg, Empress Zita, died in 1989 and her remains are also buried in the crypt.

🕸 Neuer Markt

Map 4 D1 & 5 C4. Ⓤ Stephansplatz.

Known as the Mehlmarkt or flour market until around 1210, the Neuer Markt was also used as a jousting area. Of these origins nothing is left, though a few 18th-century houses remain. In the middle of the Neuer Markt is a replica of the Donner Fountain (1737–9) by Georg Raphael Donner, a symbolic celebration of the role played by rivers in the economic life of the Habsburg Empire. The four figures denote tributaries of the Danube, while the central figure represents Providence. The original figures are in the Lower Belvedere (see p159).

🕸 Kärntner Strasse

Map 4 D1 & 5 C5. Ⓤ Stephansplatz. Malteserkirche: **Open** 7am–7pm daily. Lobmeyr Museum: **Open** 9am–5pm Mon–Fri.

This pedestrianized street was the main road to Carinthia in medieval times. Now it is the old city's principal retail street. Day and night, it is packed with people shopping, buying fresh fruit juice from stands,

pausing in cafés, or listening to the street musicians.

No. 37 is the Malteserkirche. This church was founded by the Knights of Malta, who were invited to Vienna early in the 13th century by Leopold VI. The interior retains lofty Gothic windows and vaults.

At No. 1 is the Lobmeyr Museum, which houses glass designed by Josef Hoffmann (see p58), among others, for the Viennese firm of Lobmeyr.

Around the corner at No. 5 Johannesgasse is the superb Questenberg-Kaunitz Palace, which dates from the early 18th century. Its design has been attributed to the architect Johann Lukas von Hildebrandt (see p154).

🕸 American Bar

Kärntner Strasse 10. **Map** 4 D1 & 6 D3. **Tel** 5123283. Ⓤ Stephansplatz. **Open** noon–4am daily. Ⓦ **loosbar.at**

Beneath a garish depiction of the Stars and Stripes is this bar designed by Adolf Loos (see p94) in 1908. The interior, restored in 1990, is impressive. The bar is

The Donner Fountain in Neuer Markt

tiny, with every detail carefully constructed by Loos, such as the tables lit from below and the exquisite glass cabinets for storing glasses. One of his hallmarks is the use of mahogany panelling, and this bar is no exception. Mirrors give the impression that the interior is larger than it actually is, and onyx and marble panels reflect the soft lighting used throughout. The Loosbar is often cited as the first instance of rampant architectural modernism. Loos took his inspiration from a three-year sojourn studying the buildings of New York City, between 1893 and 1896. Today, it is a preferred hangout of movie stars, who come for the celebrated cocktails.

🕸 Stock-im-Eisen-Platz

Map 2 D5 & 5 C3. Ⓤ Stephansplatz.

This square is at the inter-section of Stephansplatz, Kärntner Strasse and Graben. Opposite Haas-Haus (see p81) is the Equitable Palace (1891), once headquarters of the Equitable Life Insurance Company. An old tree trunk, dotted with nails, stands in the square. Passing locksmiths' apprentices would bang in a nail to ensure a safe passage home.

SCHOTTENRING AND ALSERGRUND

This part of the city is dotted with sites of interest, such as the ornate Ferstel Palace and the glass-roofed Freyung Passage that runs through it. The Schottenring and the Schottentor are named after the Benedictine monks who came here in Babenberg times to found the Schottenkirche Monastery. Later rulers of Austria were responsible for the area's other monuments: Joseph II

built a huge public hospital, now the Josephinum, and Franz Joseph founded the Votivkirche as a way of giving thanks after escaping assassination in 1853. To the east, nearer the Danube Canal, quiet residential streets sit beside the imposing Liechtenstein Garden Palace, one of many summer palaces built beyond the city gates by Vienna's nobility.

Sights at a Glance

Streets and Squares
1 Freyung Passage
2 Freyung

Churches and Cathedrals
3 Schottenkirche
5 Servitenkirche
9 Votivkirche

Museums and Galleries
4 Freud Museum
6 Liechtenstein Garden Palace
7 Josephinum
8 Narrenturm

☐ Restaurants p214
1 Café Stein
2 CaffèCouture
3 I Vecchi Amici
4 Konzert-Café Weimar
5 Livingstone
6 Rembetiko
7 Restaurant Ragusa
8 Servitenwirt
9 Stomach
10 Trattoria Martinelli

See also Street Finder maps 1, 2 and 5

0 metres 250
0 yards 250

◀ The twin spires of the Votivkirche

For keys to symbols *see back flap*

Street-by-Street: Around the Freyung

At the core of this elegant part of the city is the former medieval complex of the Schottenkirche, courtyards and school. On the other side of the Freyung square are some beautiful Baroque palaces, including Hildebrandt's Kinsky Palace (1713–16), and the Palais Ferstel. The Freyung Passage links the Freyung with Herrengasse, which is lined with Baroque mansions and boasts the city's first skyscraper. Backing onto the Schottenring is the Italianate Börse.

❸ ★ Schottenkirche
Founded in 1177 and redecorated in the Baroque period, this fine church has a museum and there is a famous school alongside it.

❷ ★ Freyung
This square is overlooked by fine buildings, including the former Schottenkirche priory, originally founded in 1155, then rebuilt in 1744 and, due to its appearance, known by the Viennese as the "chest of drawers house".

Passageway leading from No. 2 Helferstorferstrasse to the Freyung

HELFERSTORFERSTRASSE

SCHOTTENGASSE

❶ ★ Freyung Passage
The Freyung and Herrengasse are connected by a luxury shopping arcade.

FREYUNG

HERRENGASSE

The Café Central has a papier-mâché statue of the poet Peter Altenberg next to the main entrance. Altenberg spent a great deal of time in various coffee houses around the city (*see pp60–63*).

To Herrengasse U-Bahn

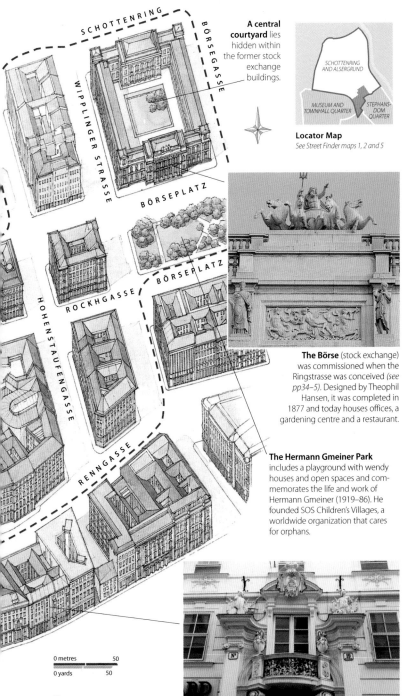

A central courtyard lies hidden within the former stock exchange buildings.

SCHOTTENRING AND ALSERGRUND

MUSEUM AND TOWNHALL QUARTER

STEPHANS-DOM QUARTER

Locator Map
See Street Finder maps 1, 2 and 5

The Börse (stock exchange) was commissioned when the Ringstrasse was conceived (*see pp34–5*). Designed by Theophil Hansen, it was completed in 1877 and today houses offices, a gardening centre and a restaurant.

The Hermann Gmeiner Park includes a playground with wendy houses and open spaces and commemorates the life and work of Hermann Gmeiner (1919–86). He founded SOS Children's Villages, a worldwide organization that cares for orphans.

The Schönborn-Batthyány Palace is a fine Baroque example that was built by Johann Bernhard Fischer von Erlach between 1699 and 1706.

0 metres 50
0 yards 50

Key

— Suggested route

❶ Freyung Passage

Map 2 D5 & 5 B2. **Ⓤ** Herrengasse.
🚌 1A, 2A.

Facing the Freyung is the Italian-style *palazzo* known as the Palais Ferstel, dating from 1860 and taking its name from the architect, Heinrich von Ferstel. The glass-roofed Freyung Passage, lined with elegant shops, converges on a small courtyard of which the centrepiece is a many-tiered statue portraying the lissome mermaid of the Danube holding a fish. It then emerges on Herrengasse. As an example of civilized urban amenities, the passage is a great success. It also has an entrance into one of Vienna's grandest coffee houses, the Café Central *(see pp60–63)*.

Danube Mermaid's Fountain (1861) in Freyung Passage

❷ Freyung

Map 2 D5 & 5 B2. **Ⓤ** Herrengasse.
Kinsky Palace: **Open** 10am–5pm Mon–Fri.

The Freyung is a curiously shaped "square". Its name derives from the right of sanctuary granted to the monks of the Schottenkirche. Fugitives from persecution who entered the area were safe from arrest. No. 4 is the Kinsky Palace (1713–16), by Johann Lukas von Hildebrandt *(see p154)*. Next door is the Porcia Palace of 1546, one of the oldest in Vienna, though much altered. At No. 3 is the Harrach Palace; the interior has some fine Rococo

Façade of the Schottenkirche

doors. Opposite is the Austria Fountain: its four figures symbolize the major rivers of the Habsburgs' lands. Behind is the former Schottenkirche priory, unkindly known as the chest-of-drawers house.

❸ Schottenkirche

Schottenstift, Freyung 6. **Map** 2 D5 & 5 B2. **Tel** 53498600. **Ⓤ** Schottentor, Herrengasse. 🚌 1A. Museum: **Open** 11am–5pm Tue–Sat. **Closed** Sun & hols. 🖼 ✉

Despite its name (Scottish church), this 1177 monastic foundation was established by Irish Benedictines. The adjoining buildings have a fine medieval art collection that includes the famous Schotten altarpiece (1475).

The church has been altered repeatedly and has undergone extensive renovation. Today it presents a rather drab Neo-Classical façade, but with a rich Baroque interior.

❹ Freud Museum

Berggasse 19. **Map** 1 C3. **Tel** 3191596. **Ⓤ** Schottentor. 🚌 40A. 🚊 D. **Open** 9am–6pm daily. 🖼 **W** freud-museum.at

No. 19 Berggasse differs little from any other 19th-century apartment building in Vienna, yet it is now one of the city's most famous addresses. The father of psychoanalysis, Sigmund Freud, lived, worked and received patients here from 1891 until his departure from Vienna in 1938.

The flat housed Freud's family as well as his practice. The catalogue lists 420 items of memorabilia on display, including letters and books, furnishings, photographs documenting Freud's long life, and various antiquities.

The flat was quickly abandoned when the Nazis forced Freud to leave the city where he had lived almost all his life, but, fortunately, it has been successfully preserved.

❺ Servitenkirche

Servitengasse 9. **Map** 1 C3. **Tel** 31761950. **Ⓤ** Rossauer Lände. **Open** 7–9am & 6–7pm Mon–Fri, 7–9am & 5–8pm Sat, 7am–noon & 5–8pm Sun. 🖼 ♿

Although off the beaten track, this church (1651–77) is well worth a visit. Inside, a riot of Baroque decoration includes elaborate stucco ornamentation, a fine wrought-iron screen near the entrance, and an exuberant pulpit (1739), partly by Balthasar Moll.

Freud's Theories

Sigmund Freud (1856–1939) was not only the founder of the techniques of psychoanalysis, but a theorist who wrote many essays and books expounding his contentious ideas. Modern concepts such as the subconscious, ego, sublimation and the Oedipus complex, evolved from Freudian theories. Freud posited different structural systems within the human psyche that, if seriously out of balance, result in emotional or mental disturbance.

❻ Liechtenstein Garden Palace

Fürstengasse 1. **Map** 1 C2.
Tel 3195767153. Ⓤ Friedensbrücke.
🚌 40A. 🚋 D. **Open** for guided tours only (call ahead for details). 🏛
🌐 **palaisliechtenstein.com**

Designed by Domenico Martinelli and completed in 1692, the summer palace of the Liechtenstein family now houses the art collection of Prince Hans-Adam II von und zu Liechtenstein. Behind the imposing Palladian exterior, notable features include the Neo-Classical library, and the Hercules Hall and grand staircase with their magnificent frescoes. The art collection centres on the Baroque, with a special focus on Rubens, and numerous paintings and sculptures by German, Dutch and Italian masters from the Renaissance through to the 19th century. The palace stands in an extensive English-style garden, designed in the 19th century.

❼ Josephinum

Währinger Strasse 25/1. **Map** 1 C4.
Tel 4016026001. Ⓤ Schottentor.
🚋 37, 38, 40, 41, 42. **Open** 10am–6pm Fri & Sat. **Closed** public hols.
♿ 🛗 🌐 **josephinum.ac.at**

The ardent reformer Joseph II *(see p30)* established this military surgical institute. Designed by Isidor Canevale in 1785, it is now a medical museum. Some rooms contain memorabilia from the 19th century, when Vienna was a leading centre for medical research, but the main attraction is the collection of wax anatomical models commissioned by the emperor from Tuscan artists.

❽ Narrenturm

Spitalgasse 2. **Map** 1 B3. **Tel** 52177606.
Ⓤ Schottentor. 🚋 5, 33. **Open** 10am–6pm Wed, 10am–1pm Sat. **Closed** public hols 🏛 🛗

What used to be the Allgemeines Krankenhaus, founded by Joseph II *(see p30)*

Detail on the Votivkirche façade

in 1784, the Narrenturm (Fools' Tower) is a former lunatic asylum designed by Isidor Canevale. The tower now houses the Museum for Pathological Anatomy, which includes a reconstruction of an apothecary's shop and wax models. The few ground-floor rooms open to the public only show a small part of what is one of the world's most comprehensive pathology and anatomy collections. Serious students can enrol on a guided tour of the corridors upstairs.

❾ Votivkirche

Rooseveltplatz 8. **Map** 1 C4 & 5 A1.
Tel 4061192. Ⓤ Schottentor. 🚋 D, 1, 71. **Open** 9am–1pm, 4–6pm Tue–Sat, 9am–1pm Sun. 🏛 🛗 side entrance.

After a deranged tailor tried to assassinate Emperor Franz Joseph on 18 February 1853, a collection was made to pay for a new church to be built opposite the Mölker-Bastei, where the attempt had been made. The architect was Heinrich von Ferstel, who began the church in 1856 though it was not dedicated until 1879. Many of the church's chapels are dedicated to Austrian regiments and military heroes. The finest monument is the Renaissance sarcophagus tomb of Niklas Salm, who commanded Austria's forces during the 1529 Turkish siege. It is located in the chapel just west of the north transept. Visitors should note the attractive lacy steeples and spire.

Wooden *Pietà* in Gothic style (1470) in the Servitenkirche

MUSEUM AND TOWNHALL QUARTER

It was Emperor Franz Joseph who commissioned the major institutional buildings of the Habsburg empire, and the city, along the Ringstrasse in the mid-19th century *(see pp34–5)*. Today these buildings remain a successful and imposing example of good urban planning. The districts that lie to the west of the Ringstrasse are untouched, including Josefstadt, which still retains an

18th-century atmosphere with its picturesque streets, modest palaces and Baroque churches. The area's cultural institutions are vibrant: the brilliant productions staged by the Burgtheater and the wide-ranging exhibits at the renowned Naturhistorisches Museum and the Kunsthistorisches Museum are hugely popular.

Sights at a Glance

Streets and Squares
6 Sankt-Ulrichs-Platz
7 Spittelberg Pedestrian Area
17 Mölker-Bastei

Historic Buildings
2 Alte Backstube
4 Theater in der Josefstadt
5 Trautson Palace
9 Parliament
12 Neues Rathaus
14 University
15 Café Landtmann
16 Dreimäderlhaus
18 Pasqualatihaus
19 Burgtheater pp134–5

Churches and Cathedrals
3 Maria-Treu-Kirche
13 Dreifaltigkeitskirche

Museums and Galleries
1 Volkskunde Museum
8 MuseumsQuartier Wien
10 Kunsthistorisches Museum pp124–9
11 Naturhistorisches Museum pp130–31

☐ **Restaurants** *pp214–15*
1 Amerlingbeisl
2 Café Bellaria
3 Café Eiles
4 Café Leopold
5 Café Maria Haag
6 Centimeter II am Spittelberg
7 Halle Café
8 Kunthistorisches Museum Café & Restaurant
9 Landtmann Café
10 Lebenbauer
11 Pizzeria-Osteria Da Giovanni
12 Prinz Ferdinand
13 Schnattl
14 Vestibül
15 Witwe Bolte
16 Zu ebener Erde und erster Stock

0 metres 250
0 yards 250

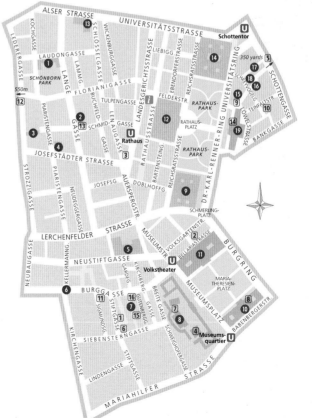

See also Street Finder maps 1, 3 and 5

◀ Statue of Pallas Athene on the Parliament building fountain   For keys to symbols *see back flap*

Street-by-Street: Josefstadt

Tucked behind the grand museums of the Ringstrasse is the 18th-century district known as Josefstadt, named after Emperor Joseph II. Although outside the inner city, Josefstadt has a vibrant cultural life, with a popular theatre, many good restaurants, and handsome churches and museums. Students from the university and lawyers from the courthouses provide a constantly changing clientele for the district's varied establishments.

③ ★ Maria-Treu-Kirche
Founded by the fathers of the Piarist order, this church was built from 1716.

The Plague Column here commemorates an epidemic that occurred in 1713.

④ Theater in der Josefstadt
Founded in 1788, Vienna's oldest theatre has kept its doors open continuously since it was rebuilt by Josef Kornhäusel (see p86) in 1822.

No. 29 Lange Gasse
Originally built for servants and workers in the 18th century, the cottages lining this courtyard have changed little over the years.

PIARISTENGASSE

MARIA TREU

JOSEFSTÄDTER STRASSE

To Lerchenfelder Strasse

ZELTGASSE

Key

— Suggested route

② Alte Backstube
A working bakery from 1701 to 1963.

Locator Map
See Street Finder maps 1, 3 and 5

❶ ★ Volkskunde Museum
The Schönborn Palace houses exhibits examining folklore and rural life in Austria.

Schönborn Park
is a secluded, leafy retreat. Among the sculptures is a bust (1974) of the composer Edmund Eysler by Leo Gruber.

No. 53 Lange Gasse has handsome statuary on its gates. It was built in the early 18th century when Vienna was expanding beyond the old city walls.

The Schnattl Restaurant, occupying the spacious ground floor and courtyard of an old house on Lange Gasse, is one of Vienna's finest *(see p215)*.

0 metres	50
0 yards	50

❶ Volkskunde Museum

Laudongasse 15–19. **Map** 1 B4.
Tel 4068905. Ⓤ Rathaus. 🚌 13A.
🚋 3, 33. **Open** 10am–5pm Tue–Sun. **Closed** 1 Jan, Easter Mon, 1 May, 1 Nov, 25 Dec. 📷 ♿ ✎
🌐 **volkskundemuseum.at**

The charming Museum of Austrian Folklore is a reminder that Vienna has a history beyond imperialism. Here you will find artifacts reflecting the culture and daily life of people in Austria and neighbouring countries. Exhibits include objects dating from the 17th to 19th centuries. The museum is housed in the 18th-century Schönborn Palace, designed by Johann Lukas von Hildebrandt as a two-storey mansion and altered in 1760 by Isidor Canevale. Today it has a rather imposing façade with statuary running along its top. It has a popular, reasonably priced restaurant that serves dishes made with organic produce There is a pleasant park behind the palace.

❷ Alte Backstube

Lange Gasse 34. **Map** 1 B5. Ⓤ Rathaus.
🚌 13A. **Closed** to the public.

One of the finest middle-class houses in Vienna was built at No. 34 Lange Gasse in 1697 by the jeweller Hans Bernhard Leopold. The sandstone sculpture above the doorway symbolizes the Holy Trinity. Inside is an old bakery, the Alte Backstube, which was in continuous use from 1701 to 1963. Since then the building served as a restaurant and museum. The original baking ovens were never removed, but ceased to be used for baking. Today, the former musuem awaits renovation and the interior is closed to the public, though visitors still come to see the fine exterior.

A few doors away, at No. 29, glance into the courtyard to see the rows of single-storey houses facing each other – a rare slice of working-class Vienna that is more than 200 years old.

❸ Maria-Treu-Kirche

Jodok-Fink-Platz. **Map** 1 B5. **Tel** 40504 25. Ⓤ Rathaus. 🚌 13A. 🚋 2.
Open for services and by appointment. Ⓦ **mariatreu.at**

Overlooking Jodok-Fink-Platz and flanked by monastic buildings stands the Church of Maria Treu. Originally designed by Johann Lukas von Hildebrandt in 1716, and later altered by Matthias Gerl in the 1750s, the church didn't acquire its present form until the 19th century, when the elegant twin towers were added.

Inside, there is a splendid, vibrant Baroque frescoed ceiling (1752–3) by the great Austrian painter Franz Anton Maulbertsch. A chapel immediately to the left of the choir contains an altarpiece with a Crucifixion dating from about 1774, also painted by Maulbertsch.

Directly in front of the church and rising up from the square is a Baroque pillar topped with a statue of the Madonna, attended beneath by statues of saints and angels. Like many such columns in Vienna, it commemorates delivery from a plague, in this case the epidemic of 1713.

Ceiling frescoes above the altar in the Maria-Treu-Kirche

❹ Theater in der Josefstadt

Josefstädter Strasse 26. **Map** 1 B5. **Tel** 427000-300. Ⓤ Rathaus. 🚌 13A. 🚋 2. **Open** for performances. Ⓦ **josefstadt.org**

This intimate theatre *(see p230)*, one of the oldest still standing in Vienna, has enjoyed an

The façade of the Theater in der Josefstadt

illustrious history. Founded in 1788, it was rebuilt by Joseph Kornhäusel *(see p86)* in 1822, and has been in operation ever since, accommodating ballet, opera and theatre performances. Beethoven composed his overture *The Consecration of the House* for the reopening of the theatre after its renovation, conducting it himself at the reopening gala. In 1924, the director Max Reinhardt supervised its further restoration, and introduced an ambitious modern repertoire of comedy, classic plays and musicals.

❺ Trautson Palace

Museumstrasse 7. **Map** 3 B1. Ⓤ Volkstheater. **Closed** to the public.

Set back from the street next to the Volkstheater is this elegant Baroque palace, designed in 1710 by Johann Bernhard Fischer von Erlach *(see p149)*. Most Viennese palaces have flat fronts but on this one the central bays of the façade jut out. Nor is there anything restrained about the ornamentation: above the cornice and pediment is one of the largest collections of statuary atop any palace in the whole of Vienna. This includes a large statue of Apollo playing the lyre.

Passing through the entrance you will see on the left an immense staircase, with carvings of bearded giants bearing its weight, by the Italian sculptor Giovanni Giuliani. This leads to the ceremonial hall.

Originally built for Count Johann Leopold Donat Trautson, who was in the service of Joseph I, the palace was acquired in 1760 by Maria Theresa *(see pp30–31)*. She donated it to the Royal Hungarian Bodyguard that she had founded. It has housed the Ministry of Justice since 1961, so there is no public access to the interior.

❻ Sankt-Ulrichs-Platz

Between Neustiftgasse and Burggasse. **Map** 3 B1. Ⓤ Volkstheater. 🚌 48A. Ulrichskirche (St Ulrich's Church): **Tel** 523124610. **Open** for services only. Ⓦ **stulrich.com**

This tiny sloping square is an exquisite remnant of early Vienna. The dainty Baroque house at No. 27 is worth taking the time to see, and adjoining it is a Renaissance house that escaped destruction by the Turks during the sieges, most probably because the Turkish commander Kara Mustafa pitched his own tent nearby.

This house partly obscures the façade of the Baroque Ulrichskirche, built by Josef Reymund in 1721–4. The composer Christoph Willibald Gluck was married here and Johann Strauss the Younger was christened.

Handsome patrician houses encircle it, of which the prettiest is No. 2, the Schulhaus. Elaborately decorated, it dates from the mid-18th century.

❼ Spittelberg Pedestrian Area

Map 3 B1. Ⓤ Volkstheater. Amerlinghaus: **Open** 2–10pm Mon–Fri. Market: **Open** Apr–Jun & Sep–Nov: 10am–6pm Sat; Jul & Aug: 2–9pm Sat. ♿

Spittelberg is the oldest and most colourful part of the district. In the 17th century, the cluster of streets between Siebensterngasse and Burggasse, and around Spittelberggasse, was Vienna's first immigrant worker district. Its inhabitants were mainly craftsmen, merchants and servants from Croatia and Hungary, brought to work in the court.

Façade detail at No. 20 Spittelberggasse

The charming area was rediscovered in the 1970s and the city authorities restored the buildings. Today, it is a district of restaurants, cafés and boutiques, all of which keep the cobbled streets buzzing into the early hours. It hosts a Christmas market, and a regular arts and crafts market from April to November. The Amerlinghaus theatre at No. 8 Stiftgasse serves as the area's cultural and community centre and provides a venue for exhibitions and events.

The Amerlinghaus at No. 8 Stiftgasse was the birthplace of the painter Friedrich Amerling. Today it is a cultural centre, theatre and *Beisl (see p201)*.

No. 10 Stiftgasse has a handsome façade, decorated with statues.

Nos. 18 and 20 Spittelberggasse are fine examples of Baroque houses.

BURGGASSE

SCHRANKGASSE

SPITTELBERGGASSE

GUTENBERGGASSE

KIRCHBERGGASSE

SIEBENSTERNGASSE

No. 29 Gutenberggasse is a delightfully pretty Biedermeier building.

Spittelberggasse is the venue for an arts and crafts market held every Saturday from April to November, and daily during Easter and Christmas.

The Witwe Bolte restaurant used to be an inn in the 18th century; legend has it that Emperor Joseph II was thrown out of here in 1778.

No. 9 Spittelberggasse is a beautifully decorated house, with skilfully painted *trompe l'oeil* windows, dating from the 18th century.

❽ MuseumsQuartier Wien

Once home to the imperial stables, the Museums-Quartier Wien is one of the largest cultural centres in the world. Developed in the 1980s, it houses a diverse range of facilities from classical art museums to venues for film, theatre, architecture, dance, new media, and a children's creativity centre, as well as a variety of shops, cafés and restaurants. The Baroque architecture of the imperial stables is blended with bold modern buildings. The white limestone façade of the Leopold Museum and the dark grey basalt of the Museum of Modern Art Ludwig Foundation create an impressive and diverse complex.

★ **Leopold Museum**
Self-Portrait with Chinese Lantern (1912) by Egon Schiele is part of the world's largest collection of Schiele's works, housed in this museum.

★ **ZOOM Kindermuseum**
Providing an exciting place to learn, children are encouraged to explore in the ZOOM Lab, play in ZOOM Ocean, be creative in ZOOM Atelier and have fun throughout the ZOOM exhibitions.

Q21
Vienna's centre for contemporary applied art, Q21 provides a range of frequently changing exhibitions, as well as numerous fashion, design, book and music shops.

KEY

① Tanzquartier Wien

② math.space

③ Architekturzentrum Wien

④ Q21 (alternate entrance)

⑤ Main entrance in the Fischer von Erlach Wing

Halls E + G
This foyer leads to the former Winter Riding Hall, now Halls E + G, hosting a variety of concert, theatre and dance performances. The foyer is also the entrance to the Kunsthalle Wien which exhibits international modern art.

Main Courtyard
Known as "Vienna's living room" and serving both as an outdoor festival venue and social meeting point, the courtyard is open day and night.

★ Museum of Modern Art Ludwig Foundation Vienna
Homme accroupi (1907) by André Derain is part of the collection of European contemporary and modern art in this museum, otherwise known as MUMOK.

Exploring the MuseumsQuartier Wien

More than 60 different cultural institutions are gathered together in the MuseumsQuartier Wien, together with restaurants, cafés and shops. This is an ideal starting point for any trip to Vienna, since many other attractions are also nearby. It is advisable to stop off first at the MQ Point Info-Tickets-Shop in the Fischer von Erlach Wing, to obtain a programme detailing all events and exhibitions currently taking place throughout the complex.

Die Quelle (1923), Leopold Museum

Architekturzentrum Wien
Tel 5223115. **Open** 10am–7pm daily. ✏ W azw.at

The permanent exhibition here is concerned with thematic and structural diversity in 20th-century architecture, and the centre is committed to showcasing new architectural work to the public. The four to six temporary exhibitions a year examine links between modern architecture and architecture throughout history.

Museum of Modern Art Ludwig Foundation Vienna (MUMOK)
Tel 52500. **Open** 2–7pm Mon, 10am–7pm Tue–Sun (to 9pm Thu). W mumok.at

This museum contains one of the largest European collections of modern and contemporary art, from American Pop Art, Photo Realism, Fluxus and Nouveau Réalism to Viennese Actionism, Arte Povera, Conceptual and Minimal Art. The galleries are split chronologically over five levels, two underground. There is also a cinema, library and studio.

Q21
Tel 52358810. **Open** Courtyard: 24 hrs; attractions: 10am–8pm daily.

Over 50 cultural initiatives have turned Q21 into Vienna's centre for contemporary applied art. The attractions for the public, which are on the ground floor, include fashion, design, book and music shops, an exhibition space for art schools, and large event halls.

Leopold Museum
Tel 525700. **Open** 10am–6pm daily (to 9pm Thu; Oct–May: Wed–Mon). W leopoldmuseum.org

Home to over 5,000 works, the Leopold Collection of Austrian Art was compiled over five decades by Rudolf Leopold. The exhibition space spans five floors. One of the museum's highlights is the world's largest Egon Schiele collection (on the second floor), along with Expressionist paintings and Austrian interwar paintings.

Paintings after 1945 and works by Albin Egger-Lienz, including *Die Quelle,* are on the first floor, while an exhibition on Secessionism and Art Nouveau on the ground level includes major works by Gustav Klimt, Richard

Gerstl and Oskar Kokoschka. The lower two levels display works by other 19th- and early 20th-century Austrian artists.

Tanzquartier Wien
Tel 5813591. W tqw.at

The Tanzquartier Wien offers facilities for dancers and hosts dance and other performances for the public.

ZOOM Kindermuseum
Tel 5247908. **Open** 8:30am–4pm Tue–Fri, 10am–4pm Sat, Sun, school hols & public hols. W kindermuseum.at

This lively centre offers an unconventional approach to the world of the museum for children, from babies up to the age of 12. The aim is to encourage learning about exhibition subjects through play and exploration, such as the ZOOM Lab for older children, while younger ones can have a dip in the ZOOM Ocean with their parents.

KUNSTHALLE Wien
Tel 5218933. **Open** 11am–7pm daily (to 9pm Thu). W kunsthallewien.at

This striking red-brick building is a home for innovation and creativity, showing international and contemporary art. The exhibitions emphasize cross-genre and cross-border trends in the arts, and include displays on experimental architecture, video, photography and film, and new media.

math.space
Tel 5235881/1730. **Open** 9am–5pm daily. W math.space.or.at

Linking maths to the arts, this centre for the popularization of maths is aimed at people of all ages, with interactive workshops for children and many programmes for adults.

The Red Horseman (1974) by Roy Lichtenstein in MUMOK

❾ Parliament

Dr-Karl-Renner-Ring 3. **Map** 1 C5 & 5
A3. **Tel** 401100. Ⓤ Volkstheater.
🚋 D, 1, 2, 71. **Open** for 🎧 except
when parliament is in session: mid-
Sep–mid-Jul: 11am, 2pm, 3pm, 4pm
Mon–Thu; 11am, 1pm, 2pm, 3pm,
4pm Fri; 11am, noon, 1pm, 2pm, 3pm,
4pm Sat; mid-Jul–mid-Sep: 11am,
noon, 1pm, 2pm, 3pm, 4pm Mon–Sat.
♿ Ⓦ **parliament.gv.at**

Façade of the Parliament building and the Athenebrunnen fountain

The architect Theophil Hansen
(see p34) chose a strict Neo-
Classical style when he
designed the Parliament
building (and the neighbouring
Palais Epstein). The building
was originally constructed as
part of the Ringstrasse
development to act as the
Reichsrat building (the
Parliament of the Austrian
part of the Habsburg Empire).
Construction began in 1874
and finished in 1884.

The Parliament's entrance is
raised above street level and
approached up a broad ramp.
At the foot of the ramp are the
bronze *Horse Tamers* (1901) by
sculptor Josef Lax; the ramp
itself is decorated with marble
figures of Greek and Roman
historians. On the roof there
are chariots and impressive
statues of ancient scholars
and statesmen.

In front of the central portico is
the Athenebrunnen, a fountain
dominated by the figure of
Pallas Athene, Greek goddess
of wisdom. It was designed by
Carl Kundmann and placed
here in 1902. In this splendid,
if chilly, setting on 11 November
1918, after the collapse of the
Habsburg Empire, the
parliamentary deputies

proclaimed the formation of the
republic of Deutsch-Österreich.
It was renamed the Republic
of Austria in 1919.

During World War II, half of
the Parliament building was
destroyed. Reconstruction was
eventually completed by June
1956, but the restoration of
some of the damaged artwork
began only in the 1990s.

The Austrian Parliament

The Austrian parliament is composed of two houses:
the Lower House, or *Nationalrat*, and the Upper House,
or *Bundesrat*. The Lower House has 183 seats and its
members are elected for a four-year term by proportional
representation. It comprises the governing party and the
opposition. The Upper House is composed of elected
representatives from Austria's nine provinces, and its
function is to approve legislation
passed by the Lower House.
Bills may also be presented
to parliament by the general
public or by the Chambers of
Labour (representing consumers
and employees) and the
Chambers of the Economy
(representing employers and
industry). The federal President
is elected for a six-year term
and is largely a figurehead.
Theoretically, he or she has the
power to veto bills and dissolve
parliament, though this has
never occurred.

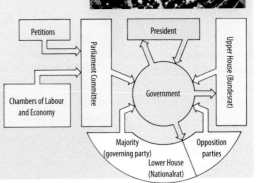

❿ Kunsthistorisches Museum

More than one and a half million people visit the Museum of the History of Art every year. Its collections are based largely on those built up over the centuries by generations of Habsburg monarchs. Originally the works of art were housed in the Hofburg and the Belvedere, but when the Ringstrasse was built *(see pp34–5)*, two magnificent buildings were erected to house the collections of imperial art and natural history. The former are on display in this museum, where lavish internal decoration complements the exhibits.

Second floor

Coin collection

★ **Hunters in the Snow** (1565)
The last painting in Pieter Bruegel the Elder's series of the seasons shows hunters returning to the village on a winter's day.

★ **The Artist's Studio**
In this 1665 allegory of art, Johannes Vermeer shows an artist in decorative dress painting a model posing as Clio, the Muse of History.

First floor

★ **Salt Cellar** (1540–3)
Benvenuto Cellini's sumptuous gold *Saliera* shows the sea and earth united, represented by a female earth goddess and the sea god Neptune.

Key to Floorplan

- ☐ Egyptian and Near Eastern collection
- ▦ Collection of Greek and Roman antiquities
- ☐ Kunstkammer (chamber of curiosities)
- ☐ Picture gallery
- ☐ Coin cabinets
- ▦ Non-exhibition space

Portrait of the Infanta Margarita Teresa (1659)
Diego Velázquez captures the fragility of the eight-year-old Spanish princess in all her finery in this official portrait.

VISITORS' CHECKLIST

Practical Information
Maria-Theresien-Platz, A-1010.
Map 3 C1 & 5 B5. **Tel** 525240.
Open 10am–6pm Tue–Sun (to 9pm Thu); Jun–Aug daily.
Closed 1 Nov, 25 Dec. 🅿 🅲 🄰 ♿ ♻ Ⓦ khm.at

Transport
Ⓤ Museumsquartier, Volkstheater.
🚌 57A. 🚊 D, 1, 2, 71.

Gemma Augustea
The Emperor Augustus dressed as Jupiter sits next to Roma, the personification of Rome, in this Roman cameo carved from onyx.

Ground floor

Museum Guide

The museum displays are spread over three floors. On the ground floor are the Egyptian, Near Eastern and Greek, Roman antiquities and Kunstkammer collections. The first floor holds the painting collections, and on the second floor is one of the largest and greatest coin collections in the world.

King Thutmosis III
Sculpted around 1460 BC, Thutmosis III is depicted in the style typical of the Late Kingdom period.

Main entrance from Maria-Theresien-Platz

Rotunda

The Apotheosis of the Renaissance

Many prominent artists were employed to decorate the museum's interior. As part of an extravagant decorative scheme, the Hungarian painter Michael Munkácsy contributed a fabulous *trompe l'oeil* ceiling painting for the main staircase, depicting *The Apotheosis of the Renaissance* (1890). It features Leonardo, Raphael, Michelangelo, Veronese, Titian and their models, all presided over by Pope Julius II.

Exploring the Kunsthistorisches' Picture Collection

The collection focuses on Old Masters from the 15th to the 18th centuries and largely reflects the personal tastes of its Habsburg founders. Venetian and 17th-century Flemish paintings are particularly well represented, and there is an excellent display of works by earlier Netherlandish and German artists. Broadly speaking, the pictures are hung following regional schools or styles of painting, although there is considerable overlap between the various categories.

The Fur (c. 1635–40) by Peter Paul Rubens

XIV and XX) are devoted to Rubens and include large-scale religious works, such as the *Ildefonso Altarpiece* (1630–32) and *The Fur*, an intimate portrait of his wife. Rubens' collaborator and pupil Anthony Van Dyck is also represented here by some outstanding works in which his sensitivity to human emotion is fully portrayed.

Dutch Painting

Protestant Holland's newly rich merchants of the 17th century delighted in pictures that reflected their own world rather than the hereafter. The Dutch genre scenes include works of great domestic charm, such as Pieter de Hooch's lovely *Woman with Child at her Breast* (1663–5) and Gerard ter Borch's *Woman Peeling Apples* (1661), while Jacob van Ruisdael's *Great Forest* (1655–60) shows the advances made by Dutch painters in their observations of the natural world. All the Rembrandts on show in Room XV are portraits; there is

Flemish Painting

The gallery has a vast collection of work from Flanders (now Belgium), an area that produced some of the finest painters of the 15th to 17th centuries. The works of the early Flemish masters, who pioneered the development of oil painting, are characterized by their luminous colours and close attention to detail. This can be seen in the triptychs by Rogier van der Weyden and Hans Memling, and Jan van Eyck's *Cardinal Niccolo Albergati* (1435). The highlight for many is Room X, in which about half of all Pieter Bruegel the Elder's surviving works are displayed, including his *Tower of Babel* and most of the cycle of *The Seasons*, all from the mid-16th century. Three rooms (XIII,

Large Self-Portrait (1652) by Rembrandt van Rijn

the picture of his mother as the prophetess Hannah (1639) and, in contrast to earlier works, the *Large Self-Portrait* shows the artist wearing a plain smock, with the emphasis on his face. The only painting by Johannes Vermeer is the enigmatic *The Artist's Studio* (Room 24). It is a complicated work with layers of symbolism; whether it is a self-portrait or not has never been resolved.

Italian Painting

The Italian galleries have a strong collection of 16th-century paintings from Venice and the Veneto. In Room I the broad chronological and stylistic sweep of Titian's work, from his early *Gypsy Madonna* (1510) to the late *Nymph and Shepherd* (1570–5), can be seen. Other Venetian

Susanna and the Elders (1555) by Tintoretto

highlights include Giovanni Bellini's graceful *Young Woman at her Toilette* (1515) and Tintoretto's *Susanna and the Elders*. This is considered to be one of the major works of Venetian Mannerism. Giuseppe Arcimboldo's series of allegorical portrait heads representing the elements and the seasons are usually on show in Room 19, together with other works commissioned by Emperor Rudolf II. Italian Baroque paintings include works by Annibale Carracci and Michelangelo Merisi da Caravaggio, notably the huge *Madonna of the Rosary*. Painted between 1606 and 1607, it depicts an intensely realistic Madonna advising St Dominic to distribute rosaries.

French Painting

Although the number of French paintings on show is relatively small, there are some minor masterpieces. The minutely detailed and highly original portrait of *The Court Jester Gonella* (1440–45) is thought to be the work of Jean Fouquet. It depicts a wily old man, seemingly squeezed into the picture, believed to be a famous court jester of the time. A more formal court portrait from 1569 is that of the youthful Charles IX of France by François Clouet. *The Destruction of the Temple in Jerusalem*, a monumental work painted by Nicolas Poussin in 1638, depicts the Emperor Titus watching the Old Testament prophecy of the

Summer (1563) by Giuseppe Arcimboldo

destruction of the Temple of Solomon come true. It combines agitated movement with thorough archaeological research. Joseph Duplessis' *Christopher Willibald Ritter von Gluck at the Spinet* shows the famous composer gazing into the heavens for inspiration.

British and German Painting

There are few British works. Perhaps the most appealing is the *Landscape of Suffolk*

(around 1750) by Thomas Gainsborough. There are also portraits by Gainsborough, Reynolds and Lawrence.

The German collection is rich in 16th-century paintings. There are several Albrecht Dürer pieces, including his *Madonna with the Pear* (1512). Other works include the *Stag Hunt of Elector Friedrich the Wise* (1529) by Lucas Cranach the Elder and seven portraits by Hans Holbein the Younger.

Spanish Painting

Room 10 houses several fine portraits of the Spanish royal family by Diego Velázquez. The artist lived from 1599 to 1660 and was the court painter to Philip IV. His works include three portraits of Philip IV's daughter, the Infanta Margarita Teresa (in one aged three, another aged five and in a third aged eight), as well as a portrait of her sickly infant brother, Philip Prosper. Other Spanish works include paintings by Alonso Sánchez Coello and Antonio de Pereda.

Stag Hunt of Elector Friedrich the Wise (1529) by Lucas Cranach the Elder

Exploring the Kunsthistorisches' Other Collections

As well as the picture gallery, the art history museum contains a "museum within a museum" within the 20 galleries of its Kunstkammer Wien, or Viennese chamber of curiosities, said to be the most magnificent in the world. The ancient civilizations of Egypt, Greece and Rome are chronicled in all their full splendour. Additionally, the museum has one of the world's largest, and most important, medal and coin collections.

to contain deceased souls. Other rooms house mummified animals, Egyptian scripts, and artifacts such as pots, clothing and jewellery.

Also on show are a glazed brick relief of a lion from Babylon and items from Arabia.

Egyptian and Near Eastern Collection

Five specially decorated rooms adorned with Egyptian friezes and motifs provide the perfect setting for the bulk of the museum's collection of Egyptian and Near Eastern antiquities. The collection was founded by the Habsburg monarchs though most of the items were either bought in the 19th century, after Napoleon's Egyptian expedition had increased interest in the area, or added early in the 20th century, when Austrian archaeologists excavated at the Pyramid district of Giza; an outstanding example is the so-called *Reserve Head* (around 2600 BC). The entire Fifth dynasty Tomb Chapel of Ka-Ni-Nisut, from Giza, and its well-preserved hieroglyphics (from around 2400 BC) are on display in Room II.

Blue ceramic hippopotamus from Middle Kingdom Egypt (around 2000 BC)

This collection contains more than 17,000 objects, with the oldest dating back to around 3500 BC. There is a bust of King Thutmosis III *(see p125)* and portraits of Egyptian gods and goddesses. In Rooms I and V, where the decorative scheme incorporates Egyptian columns from Aswan, there are items associated with the mortuary cult in Ancient Egypt, including sarcophagi, canopic jars (which used to contain the entrails of mummified corpses), scarabs, mummy cases and papyrus books of the dead. In Room VIII there is a small blue ceramic statue of a hippopotamus. These were often found in Middle Kingdom tombs, as hippopotamus hunting was a royal privilege given to citizens who had won the king's favour. Many of the small-scale sculptures on display were made

Room I from the Egyptian galleries, with papyrus stalk columns from Aswan (c. 1410 BC)

Greek and Roman Antiquities

Only part of the museum's Greek and Roman collection is housed in the main building; the finds from Ephesus and Samothrace are displayed in the Neue Burg *(see p97)* in the Hofburg.

If you approach the collection from the Egyptian galleries, the first room you come to (Room X) is devoted to early Greek sculpture. Rooms 6–7 house the Austria Romana collection which includes the *Youth from Magdalensberg*, a 16th-century cast of a lost Roman statue, found buried in an Austrian field. The main gallery (Room XI), decorated in the style of an imperial Roman villa, includes a mosaic of Theseus and the Minotaur, a Roman marble statue of Isis, Greek sculpture and a sarcophagus with fine relief decoration. Rooms XII and XIII house numerous portraits.

Visitors can also see figurines and bronzes from Greece and Rome, vases from Tanagra (a town in Ancient Greece) and a large collection of Roman cameos, jewellery, busts of

Roman emperors and Roman glass. Etruscan and Cypriot art are in rooms 1–3. Coptic, Byzantine and Germanic items are shown in the rest of the rooms, where pride of place goes to the Treasure of Nagyszentmiklós, a late 9th-century collection of golden vessels found in Romania in 1799.

Medal of Ulrich II Molitor (1581)

by artists such as Tilman Riemenschneider, some medieval ivories, drinking horns and communion vessels. The highlights of the Italian Renaissance rooms are a marble bust of a laughing boy by Desiderio da Settignano, a marble relief of Bacchus and Ariadne, and a fine bronze and gilt figurine called Venus Felix. Included in the large German Renaissance collection are early playing cards and a table centrepiece incorporating "vipers' tongues" (in fact, fossilized sharks' teeth), said to ward off poison. Other gems include Benvenuto Cellini's Salt Cellar (see p124), made for the French king François I, and some statuettes by Giambologna.

forms of money such as stones used on Yap Island in Micronesia.

Rooms II and III house an extensive collection of 19th- and 20th-century medals. The portrait medallions are often miniature works of art in themselves. Particularly noteworthy are the unusual silver and gilt medals belonging to Ulrich Molitor, the Abbot of Heiligenkreuz, and the silver medallion which was engraved by Bertrand Andrieu and minted to commemorate the baptism of Napoleon's son. This shows the emperor as a proud father, lifting aloft his baby, the King of Rome (see p177).

Kunstkammer Wien

The curators call this "the cradle of the museum". Here, the personal prizes of Habsburg collectors Rudolf II and Archduke Leopold William are housed in their "wonder rooms". These were originally chambers of artifacts and natural wonders that were intended to represent the sum total of human knowledge of the day. In addition to sculpture, these princely treasuries contained precious items of high craftsmanship, exotic, highly unusual novelties, and scientific instruments. Among the most intriguing are some intricate automata, including a musical box in the form of a ship, and a moving clock. Some of the royal patrons worked in the studio themselves; on display is some glass blown by the Archduke Ferdinand II and also embroidery hand-sewn by Maria Theresa. As in the Picture Gallery, the main emphasis is on the Renaissance and Baroque, although there is a great display of medieval items. These include fine, late Gothic religious carved statues

Youth from Magdalensberg, 16th-century cast of a Roman original

Coins and Medals

Tucked away on the second floor is one of the most extensive coin and medal collections in the world. Once again, the nucleus of the collection came from the former possessions of the Habsburgs, but it has been added to by modern curators and now includes many 20th-century items. Only a fraction of the museum's 600,000 pieces can be seen in the three exhibition rooms.

Room I gives an overview of the development of money. It includes coins from Ancient Greece and Rome, examples of Egyptian, Celtic and Byzantine money, and medieval, Renaissance and European coins, as well as Austrian currency from its origins to the present.

Also on display is a collection of primitive

Virgin with Child (c. 1495) by Tilman Riemenschneider

⓫ Naturhistorisches Museum

Around 700,000 visitors every year come to see the frescoed ceilings and 39 grand halls of the Natural History Museum Vienna, which dates back to 1889. It also houses 30 million fascinating objects – from fossils of the very first life on Earth, to meteorites and a display on interstellar travel plotted in the digital planetarium. Particularly noteworthy are the replicas of huge dinosaur skeletons, an almost complete skeleton of Steller's sea cow, the full-size preservations of extinct animals, and the collections of butterflies, birds, gems and prehistoric sculptures.

★ **Salt Bag**
This Bronze Age cowhide bag was used to carry salt in the Hallstatt mines.

Digital Planetarium

Lecturehall

★ **Venus of Willendorf**
Made about 29,500 years ago, this tiny limestone figure is one of the most important examples of Stone Age art work. The purpose of the figurine is unknown.

Key to Floorplan

- ☐ Mineralogy
- ☐ Geology, Palaeontology
- ☐ Prehistory
- ☐ Anthropology
- ☐ Zoology
- ☐ Temporary exhibition space
- ☐ Non-exhibition space

Main entrance from
Maria-Theresien-Platz

★ **Cast of Iguanodon bernissartensis**
This is just one of the replica dinosaur skeletons that are on display. The collection includes some of the largest casts in the world.

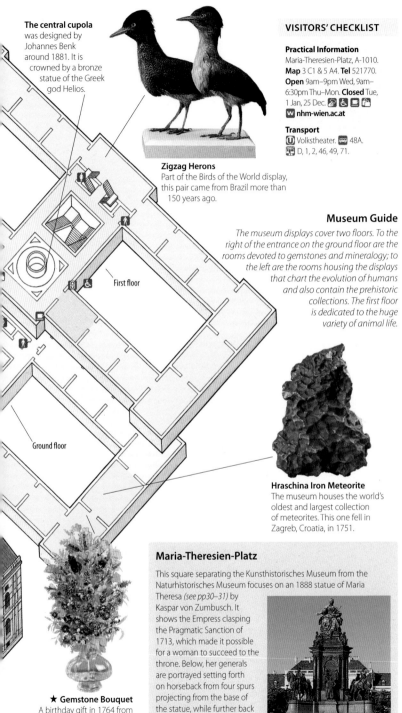

The central cupola was designed by Johannes Benk around 1881. It is crowned by a bronze statue of the Greek god Helios.

Zigzag Herons
Part of the Birds of the World display, this pair came from Brazil more than 150 years ago.

First floor

Ground floor

Museum Guide

The museum displays cover two floors. To the right of the entrance on the ground floor are the rooms devoted to gemstones and mineralogy; to the left are the rooms housing the displays that chart the evolution of humans and also contain the prehistoric collections. The first floor is dedicated to the huge variety of animal life.

Hraschina Iron Meteorite
The museum houses the world's oldest and largest collection of meteorites. This one fell in Zagreb, Croatia, in 1751.

Maria-Theresien-Platz

This square separating the Kunsthistorisches Museum from the Naturhistorisches Museum focuses on an 1888 statue of Maria Theresa *(see pp30–31)* by Kaspar von Zumbusch. It shows the Empress clasping the Pragmatic Sanction of 1713, which made it possible for a woman to succeed to the throne. Below, her generals are portrayed setting forth on horseback from four spurs projecting from the base of the statue, while further back against the plinth stand her principal nobles and advisors.

★ Gemstone Bouquet
A birthday gift in 1764 from Maria Theresa to her husband Franz Stephen of Lorraine, this piece contains 2,102 diamonds.

⑫ Neues Rathaus

Friedrich-Schmidt-Platz 1. **Map** 1 B5 & 5 A2. **Tel** 52550. Ⓤ Rathaus. 🚋 D, 1, 71. **Open** for 🅰 1pm Mon, Wed & Fri & through phone bookings for groups. 🔳 **wien.gv.at**

The new town hall is the seat of the Vienna City and Provincial Assembly. Built from 1872 to 1883 to replace the Altes Rathaus (see p87), it is unashamedly Neo-Gothic in style. The architect, Friedrich von Schmidt, was chosen by the authorities in a competition for the best design.

A huge central tower, 100 m (325 ft) high and topped by the 3-m (11-ft) statue of a knight in armour with a lance, dominates the front façade. Known affectionately as the Rathausmann, the figure was designed by Franz Gastell and made by the wrought-iron craftsman Alexander Nehr. The building's most attractive feature is the lofty loggia with its delicate tracery and curved balconies. Around all four sides are Neo-Gothic arcades and statues of Austrian worthies. Inside, at the top of the first of two grand staircases is the *Festsaal*, a ceremonial hall that stretches the length of the building. In front is the wide Rathausplatz Park and there are also several courtyards, one of which is the venue for concerts.

⑬ Dreifaltigkeits-kirche

Alser Strasse 17. **Map** 1 B4. **Tel** 4057225. Ⓤ Rathaus. 🚋 43, 44. **Open** 8–11:30am Mon–Sat, 8am–noon Sun. ♿ entrance on Schlösselgasse for services.

Built between 1685 and 1727, the Church of the Holy Trinity contains an altarpiece (1708) in the north aisle by the painter

The 16th-century Crucifix that hangs in the Dreifaltigkeitskirche

Martino Altomonte, and a graphic Crucifix from the workshop of Veit Stoss in the south aisle. It was to this church that Beethoven's body was brought after he died in 1827. Following the funeral service, which was attended by many of his contemporaries, including Schubert and the poet Franz Grillparzer, the cortege bore his coffin to the cemetery at Währing on the city's outskirts.

⑭ University

Universitätsring 1. **Map** 1 C4 & 5 A2. **Tel** 42770. Ⓤ Schottentor. **Open** 6:30am–8:30pm Mon–Fri, 8am–1pm Sat. ♿ 🅰 6pm Thu (in German), 11:30am Sat (in English). 🔳 **univie.ac.at**

Founded in 1365 by Duke Rudolf IV, the University of Vienna now has over 90,000 students. The versatile architect Heinrich Ferstel designed its present home in 1883, adopting an Italian Renaissance style.

From the entrance hall, huge staircases lead up to the university's ceremonial halls. In 1895 Gustav Klimt was commissioned to decorate the hall with frescoes, but the degree of nudity portrayed in some panels proved unacceptable to the authorities. Eventually, when no agreement could be reached, Klimt returned his fee to the government and took back the paintings; they were destroyed during World War II.

Front elevation of the Neues Rathaus, showing the Rathausmann on his tower some 98 m (320 ft) above the ground

A spacious arcaded courtyard, lined with busts of the university's most distinguished professors, is located in the centre of the building. Among the figures on display include the founder of psychoanalysis Sigmund Freud *(see p112)* and the philosopher Franz Brentano. Nearby are the smoke-filled and poster-daubed corridors of today's university students.

One of the arcades surrounding the university courtyard

⓯ Café Landtmann

Universitätsring 4. **Map** 1 C5 & 5 B2. **Tel** 24100100. Ⓤ Schottentor, Herrengasse. 🚋 D, 1, 71. **Open** 7am– midnight daily. ♿ 🖿 **landtmann.at**

If the Café Central *(see p60)* is the coffee house of Vienna's intelligentsia, this café *(see p60)* is surely the coffee house of the affluent middle classes. Established in 1873 by coffee-maker Franz Landtmann, it was Sigmund Freud's *(see p112)* favourite coffee house, and is still very popular. The walls are adorned with mirrors and elegant panelling, creating an attractive setting for a cup of coffee.

The attractive Dreimäderlhaus *(left)* on Schreyvogelgasse

⓰ Dreimäderlhaus

Schreyvogelgasse 10. **Map** 1 C5 & 5 B2. Ⓤ Schottentor.

Houses on one side of the cobbled Schreyvogelgasse are a reminder of Biedermeier Vienna and the prettiest of all is the Dreimäderlhaus (1803). There is a legend that Schubert had three sweethearts *(drei Mäderl)* ensconced here, but it is more likely that the house was named after the 1920s operetta *Dreimäderlhaus*, which uses his melodies.

⓱ Mölker-Bastei

Map 1 C5 & 5 B2. Ⓤ Schottentor. 🚋 D, 1, 71.

A few paces away from the bustling Schottentor is the quiet street of Mölker-Bastei, built on a former bastion of the city walls. It boasts some beautiful late 18th-century houses. Beethoven lived here, and the Emperor Franz Joseph nearly met his death on the bastion in 1853 when a tailor attempted to assassinate him. No. 10 is the house where the Belgian Prince Charles de Ligne lived during the Congress of Vienna in 1815 *(see p32)*. De Ligne wrote several cynical commentaries on the activities of the crowned heads of Europe who came to Vienna at that time. A ladies' man, he caught a fatal chill while waiting for an assignation on the bastion.

Plaque on the front of the Pasqualatihaus

⓲ Pasqualatihaus

Mölker-Bastei 8. **Map** 1 C5 & 5 B2. **Tel** 5358905. Ⓤ Schottentor. Museum: **Open** 10am–1pm & 2–6pm Tue–Sun. 📷 ♿

The Pasqualatihaus is no different in appearance from any of the other houses along this lane, but it is the most famous of more than 30 places where Ludwig van Beethoven resided in Vienna. Named after its original owner, Baron Johann von Pasqualati, it was Beethoven's home between 1804 and 1808, and from 1810 to 1815. He composed many of his best-loved works here, including Symphonies 4, 5, 7 and 8, the opera *Fidelio*, Piano Concerto No. 4, and string quartets. Today, the rooms on the fourth floor which the composer occupied house a small museum. Various memorabilia, such as a lock of Beethoven's hair, a photograph of his grave at Währing cemetery, a deathbed engraving and early editions of his scores are on display. The museum also contains busts and paintings of Beethoven and his patron Prince Rasumofsky, the Russian ambassador to Vienna.

Liebenberg monument (1890) below the Mölker-Bastei

⑲ The Burgtheater

The Burgtheater is the most prestigious stage in the German-speaking world *(see also p230)*. The original theatre built in Maria Theresa's reign was replaced in 1888 by today's Italian Renaissance-style building by Karl von Hasenauer and Gottfried Semper. It closed for refurbishment in 1897 after the discovery that the auditorium had several seats with no view of the stage. Forty-eight years later a bomb devastated the building, leaving only the side wings containing the Grand Staircases intact. Subsequent restoration was so seamless that today its extent is hard to assess.

Busts of playwrights
Lining the walls of the Grand Staircases are busts of playwrights whose works are still performed here, including this one of Johann Nestroy by Hans Knesl.

JOHANN NESTROY 1801 – 1862

Entrance for tours

★ Grand Staircases in North and South Wings
Two imposing staircases lead up from the side entrances to the foyer. Each is a mirror image of the other.

Main entrance on Universitätsring

KEY

① **Candelabra lining the staircase**

② **Ceiling frescoes** by Gustav and Ernst Klimt and Franz Matsch cover the north and south wings.

③ **Two statues of the Muses** of music and dramatic art adorn the roof.

④ **Sculpted cherubs on the balustrade** (1880–83)

Foyer
The 60-m long (200-ft) curving foyer serves as a waiting area during intervals. Portraits of famous actors and actresses line its walls.

Auditorium

The central part of the Burgtheater was rebuilt in 1952–5 after war damage, but the auditorium is still decorated in the imperial colours of cream, red and gold.

★ Der Thespiskarren

This ceiling fresco (1886–8) by Gustav Klimt, part of the series *The History of the Theatre*, depicts Thespis, the first performer of a Greek tragedy.

④

Front Façade

A statue of Apollo (about 1883) seated between Melpomene and Thalia presides over a frieze of Bacchus and Ariadne by Rudolf Weyr.

1741 Maria Theresa founds the Burgtheater in an empty ballroom at the Hofburg

The Old Burgtheater in the mid-18th century

1897 The auditorium is adapted

1945 World War II fire destroys the auditorium

1700	1750	1800	1850	1900	1950

1750–76 Joseph II reorganizes the theatre and promotes it to the status of a national theatre

1874 Work on the presentbuilding begins

1888 The Burgtheater opens on 14 October in the presence of the Emperor Franz Joseph and his family

1955 Theatre reopens with Grillparzer's *King Ottokar*

OPERA AND NASCHMARKT

This is an area of huge contrasts, ranging from the stateliness of the Opera House and the opulence of the Opernring shops to the raucous modernity of Mariahilfer Strasse. The long street is lined with cinemas and department stores, drawing shoppers not just from Vienna but from parts of eastern Europe. The other major thoroughfare in the area is the Linke Wienzeile, which runs parallel to the Rechte Wienzeile. Both roads stretch from just beyond the Ringstrasse to

the city's outskirts, following the curving and sometimes subterranean River Wien. Between these roads is the bustling Naschmarkt, overlooked by Otto Wagner's Jugendstil apartments on the Linke Wienzeile. Visitors needing a break can seek refuge in the celebrated Café Museum, located near the three great cultural institutions of the area – the Academy of Fine Arts, the Opera House and the Secession Building.

Sights at a Glance

Streets and Squares
8 Mariahilfer Strasse

Historic Buildings
1 State Opera House pp140–41
2 Hotel Sacher
5 Theater an der Wien
7 Wagner Apartments

Museums and Galleries
3 Academy of Fine Arts
4 Secession Building
9 Kaiserliches Hofmobiliendepot
10 Haydn Museum

Markets
6 Naschmarkt

☐ **Restaurants** pp215–16

1 Aux Gazelles
2 Café Drechsler
3 Café Ritter
4 Café Sacher
5 Café Sperl
6 Café Westend
7 Kostas
8 Mama Liu & Sons
9 Neni
10 Restaurant Anna Sacher
11 Restaurant Hofbräu
12 Saint Charles Alimentary
13 Tewa

See also Street Finder maps 3, 4 and 5

0 metres 250
0 yards 250

◀ Pretty flower pattens on the façade of Majolikahaus, one of the Wagner Apartments   **For keys to symbols** see back flap

Street-by-Street: Opernring

Between the Opera House and the Karlskirche, two of the great landmarks of Vienna, lies an area that typifies the varied culture of the city. Here visitors can find an 18th-century theatre, a 19th-century art academy, and the Secession Building. Mixed in with these cultural monuments are emblems of the Viennese devotion to good living: the Hotel Sacher, as sumptuous today as it was a century ago; the Café Museum *(see p60)*, still as popular as it was in the 1900s; and the hurly-burly of the colourful Naschmarkt, where you can buy everything from oysters and exotic fruits to second-hand clothes.

❸ ★ Academy of Fine Arts
This Italianate building is home to one of the best collections of Old Masters in Vienna.

The Goethe Statue was designed by Edmund Hellmer in 1890.

The Schiller Statue dominates the park in front of the Academy of Fine Arts.

❹ ★ Secession Building
This delightful structure, built in 1898 as a showroom for the Secession artists, houses the *Beethoven Frieze* by Gustav Klimt *(see p57)*.

❺ Theater an der Wien
Today this 18th-century theatre is used as an opera house. It has been the venue for many premieres, among them Beethoven's *Fidelio*.

❻ Naschmarkt
This market sells everything from fresh farm produce to bric-a-brac. It is liveliest on Saturday mornings.

② Hotel Sacher
The famous Sacher-torte *(see p206)* originated here.

To Albertina-platz

MUSEUM AND TOWNHALL QUARTER

HOFBURG QUARTER

OPERA AND NASCHMARKT

Locator Map
See Street Finder maps 3, 4 and 5

To Kärntner Strasse

❶ ★ State Opera House
This stately building, opened on this site in 1869, is still the hub of Vienna's glorious cultural life.

The Café Museum, built in 1899, has served many of Vienna's artistic and literary figures, including Gustav Klimt, Egon Schiele, Joseph Roth and Robert Musil.

The Mark Anthony Statue (1899), alongside the Secession Building, is a decadent bronze statue by Arthur Strasser.

0 metres   50
0 yards   50

Key
— Suggested route

❶ State Opera House

Vienna's State Opera House, or Staatsoper, was the first of the grand Ringstrasse buildings to be completed *(see pp34–5)*; it opened on 25 May 1869 to the strains of Mozart's *Don Giovanni*. Built in Neo-Renaissance style, it initially failed to impress the Viennese. Yet when it was hit by a bomb in 1945 and largely destroyed, the event was seen as a symbolic blow to the city. With a brand new auditorium and stage incorporating the latest technology, the State Opera House reopened on 5 November 1955 with a performance of Beethoven's *Fidelio*.

Reliefs of Opera and Ballet (1861–9)
Painted allegorical lunettes by Johann Preleuthner represent ballet, tragic opera and comic opera *(above)*.

★ Grand Staircase
A splendid marble staircase sweeps up from the main entrance to the first floor. It is embellished with statues by Josef Gasser of the seven liberal arts and reliefs of opera and ballet.

★ Schwind Foyer
The foyer is decorated with scenes from operas painted by Moritz von Schwind. Among the busts of famous composers and conductors is Rodin's bronze bust of Mahler (1909).

Main entrance

KEY

① **One of the five bronze statues** by Ernst Julius Hähnel, depicting Heroism, Drama, Fantasy, Humour and Love, stands under the arches of the loggia.

② **The Auditorium**

★ Tea Room
Franz Joseph and his entourage used to spend the intervals in this graceful room, which is decorated with silk hangings bearing the emperor's initials.

The Vienna Opera Ball

On the last Thursday of the Vienna Carnival the stage is extended to cover the seats in the auditorium, creating space for the Opera Ball *(see p231)*. This is Vienna's most extravagant social event, opened by debutantes in white dresses and attended by around 5,000 guests, including international celebrities.

VISITORS' CHECKLIST

Practical Information
Opernring 2, A-1010.
Map 4 D1 & 5 C5. **Tel** 514442250.
Open for performances and guided tours. call 514442606 for tour details.
w wiener-staatsoper.at

Transport
U Karlsplatz. D, 1, 2, 71.

The Architects
The architects of the Opera House, August Sicard von Sicardsburg *(right)* and Eduard van der Null *(left)*.

Fountain
On either side of the Opera House stand two graceful fountains. Designed by Josef Gasser, this one depicts the legendary siren Lorelei supported by figures representing Grief, Love and Vengeance.

The Magic Flute Tapestries
One of the two side salons, the Gustav Mahler Saal, is hung with modern tapestries by Rudolf Eisenmenger illustrating scenes from *The Magic Flute*.

❷ Hotel Sacher

Philharmonikerstrasse 4. **Map** 4 D1 & 5 C5. **Tel** 514560. Ⓤ Karlsplatz. **Open** 8am–1am daily. ♿
Ⓦ **sacher.com**

Founded by the son of Franz Sacher, who, according to some, was the creator of the *Sachertorte* in 1840 *(see p206)*, this hotel *(see p199)* came into its own under Anna Sacher. The cigar-smoking daughter-in-law of the founder ran the hotel from 1892 until her death in 1930. During her time the Sacher became a venue for the extra-marital affairs of the rich and noble. It is still a discreetly sumptuous hotel.

❸ Academy of Fine Arts

Schillerplatz 3. **Map** 4 D2 & 5 B5. **Tel** 588162222. Ⓤ Karlsplatz. 🚋 D, 1, 2, 71. **Open** 10am–6pm Tue–Sun & public hols. 🏛 ♿ Ⓦ **akademiegalerie.at**

Theophil Hansen built the Academy of Fine Arts in Italian Renaissance style between 1872 and 1876. In 1907 Adolf Hitler was barred from entrance on the grounds that he lacked talent.

The Academy is an arts college and also has a gallery showing changing exhibitions. These include late Gothic and early Renaissance works, some

Façade of the Secession Building, an example of Jugenstil style

Rubens pieces, and 17th-century Dutch and Flemish landscapes, as well as a 19th-century Austrian collection.

❹ Secession Building

Friedrichstrasse 12. **Map** 4 D2. **Tel** 5875307. Ⓤ Karlsplatz. **Open** 10am–6pm Tue–Sun. **Closed** 1 May, 1 Nov, 25 Dec. 🏛 🎫 11am Sat. ♿
Ⓦ **secession.at**

Joseph Maria Olbrich designed the unusual Secession Building in Jugendstil style *(see pp56–9)* as a showcase for the Secession movement's artists *(see pp36–7)*. The almost windowless building, with its filigree globe of entwined laurel leaves on the roof, is a squat cube with four towers. The motto of the founders, emblazoned in gold on the façade, states, *"Der Zeit ihre Kunst, der Kunst ihre Freiheit"*, which translates as: "To every age its art, to art its freedom". Alongside the building stands a marvellous statue of Mark Antony in his chariot being drawn by lions (1899) by Arthur Strasser. Gustav Klimt's *Beethoven*

Frieze is the Secession's best-known exhibit. Designed in 1902, it covers three walls and is 34 m (110 ft) long. It shows interrelated groups of figures and is thought to be a commentary on Beethoven's Ninth Symphony.

❺ Theater an der Wien

Linke Wienzeile 6. **Map** 3 C2. **Tel** 58885. Ⓤ Karlsplatz. 🚌 59A. **Open** for performances and occasional guided tours. 🎫 twice a month; call 588302015 for details. Ⓦ **theater-wien.at**

Emanuel Schikaneder founded this theatre *(see p226)* in 1801; a statue above the entrance shows him playing Papageno in Mozart's *The Magic Flute*. The premiere of Beethoven's *Fidelio* was staged here in 1805. Today it hosts popular opera performances.

❻ Naschmarkt

Map 3 C2–C3. Ⓤ Kettenbrücken-gasse. Market: **Open** 6am–6:30pm Mon–Fri, 6am–6pm Sat. Schubert Museum: **Tel** 5816730. **Open** 10am–1pm, 2–6pm Wed & Thu. Ⓦ **naschmarkt-vienna.at**

The Naschmarkt is Vienna's liveliest market. It has a huge variety of market stalls and some of the best snack bars in the city *(see pp215–16)*. Walking west sees a profusion of stalls selling flowers, farm produce and wine, as well as cakes, bread and meats. The Saturday flea market, rated as one of Vienna's top ten fun things to do, mixes professional antique dealers with pure junk. Bargains can be had, but it also pays to be aware. No returns are accepted.

At No. 6 Kettenbrückengasse, by the U-Bahn, is the simple flat where Franz Schubert died in 1828. It is signposted Schubert Sterbewohnung. This tiny two-room flat with music studio, housing an elaborate grand piano and a meagre scattering of personal effects, is perhaps the most haunting of all memorials to the composer.

Columned entrance to the Theater an der Wien

The Majolikahaus, one of the Wagner Apartments

❼ Wagner Apartments

Linke Wienzeile 38 & 40. **Map** 3 C2.
Ⓤ Kettenbrückengasse.

Overlooking the Naschmarkt are two remarkable apartment buildings. Designed by Otto Wagner in 1899, they represent the apex of Jugendstil *(see pp56–9)*. No. 38 has sparkling gilt ornament, mostly by Kolo Moser. No. 40, which is called the Majolikahaus after the glazed pottery used for the weather-resistant surface decoration, is the more striking. The façade has subtle flower patterns in pink, blue and green. Even the sills are moulded and decorated. No. 42 next door, in historicist style *(see pp34–5)*, shows what the Secession was reacting against.

❽ Mariahilfer Strasse

Map 3 A3 & 5 A5. Ⓤ Zieglergasse, Neubaugasse. Stiftkirche: **Open** 7:30am–6pm Mon–Fri, 7am–11pm Sat, 8:30am–9:30pm Sun. Mariahilfer Kirche: **Open** 8am–7pm Mon–Sat, 8:30am–7pm Sun.

This is one of Vienna's busiest, pedestrianized shopping streets. On the corner of Stiftgasse is the Stiftkirche. The architect is

unknown, but the church dates from 1739. The façade is an austere pyramidal structure, rising to a bulbous steeple, and has some lively Rococo reliefs set into the walls.

Across the street at No. 45 is the house where the playwright Ferdinand Raimund was born in 1790. Its cobbled courtyard is lined with shops.

Mariahilfer Kirche is named after a 16th-century cult of the Virgin Mary which was founded at the Mariahilfer Kirche at Passau. The Viennese church is in the Baroque style and is dominated by two towers with large steeples.

❾ Kaiserliches Hofmobiliendepot

Andreasgasse 7. **Map** 3 A2.
Tel 5243357. Ⓤ Zieglergasse.
Open 10am–6pm Tue–Sun. 🅟
Ⓦ hofmobiliendepot.at

The imperial furniture collection, founded by Maria Theresa in 1747, gives an intimate portrait of the Habsburg way of life, as well as a detailed historical record of Viennese interior decoration and cabinet-making in the 18th and 19th centuries. Also included in the collection are pieces created

by artists and designers of the early 20th century. Room after room is filled with outstanding furnishings and royal domestic objects, ranging from a faithful recreation of Empress Elisabeth's Schönbrunn Palace apartments to a simple folding throne that was used while travelling. The exhibits, which range from the mundane to the priceless and often eccentric, provide a fascinating and evocative insight into the everyday lives of the imperial family.

❿ Haydn Museum

Haydngasse 19. **Map** 3 A3.
Tel 5961307. Ⓤ Zieglergasse.
Open 10am–1pm & 2–6pm Tue–Sun.
Closed Mon, public hols. 🅟
Ⓦ wienmuseum.at

As with many of the museums dedicated to composers, the Haydn Museum does not have a very comprehensive collection of exhibits: only a few copies of documents and scores, a piano and clavichord.

Haydn built this house in what was then a new suburb of Vienna with money he had earned from his successful visits to London between 1791 and 1795. He lived here from 1797 until his death in 1809 and it was here that he composed many of his major works, including *The Creation* and *The Seasons*. There is also a room that contains some furniture and mementoes belonging to Johannes Brahms.

Antique wheelchair in the Kaiserliches Hofmobiliendepot

BELVEDERE QUARTER

The Belvedere Quarter is a grandiose and extravagant district. From the Karlsplatz, with its gardens and statues, there is a lovely view of Johann Bernhard Fischer von Erlach's Baroque Karlskirche. East of this great church, visitors can see two palaces of the Belvedere, now public galleries, and the Schwarzenberg Palace. The palaces and beautiful gardens were designed by Johann Lukas von Hildebrandt, following the crucial defeat of the Turks

in 1683. Only after the Turkish threat had been removed was it possible for Vienna to expand. The turbulent history of the city is excellently documented in the Wien Museum Karlsplatz. Just a few paces away is the Musikverein, home to the Vienna Philharmonic. The Arnold Schönberg Center contains a wealth of material relating to the great innovator's compositions, as well as some of his paintings.

Sights at a Glance

Streets and Squares
7 Schwarzenbergplatz
10 Rennweg

Historic Buildings
3 Musikverein
4 Karlsplatz Pavilions
6 Imperial Hotel
9 Schwarzenberg Palace
13 Theresianum

Museums and Galleries
2 Wien Museum Karlsplatz
5 Künstlerhaus
8 Arnold Schönberg Center
11 Palaces and Gardens of the Belvedere pp154–9

Parks and Gardens
12 Botanical Gardens

Churches
1 Karlskirche pp148–9

☐ **Restaurants** pp216–17
1 Bistro Menagerie
2 Bristol Lounge
3 Café Dialog
4 Café Museum
5 Café Schwarzenberg
6 Entler
7 Heuer am Karlsplatz
8 Opus Restaurant im Imperial
9 Salm Bräu
10 Shiki
11 Wiener Wirtschaft

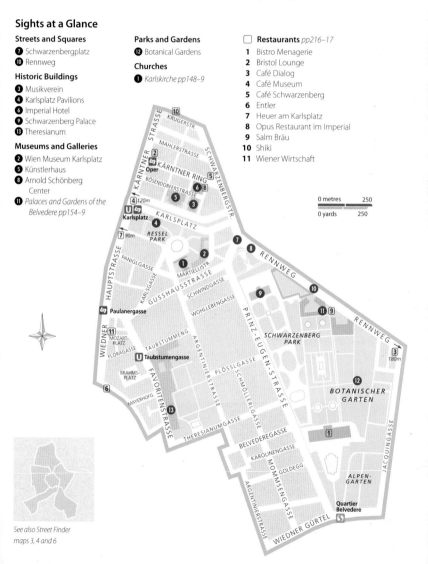

See also Street Finder maps 3, 4 and 6

◀ Interior view of the domes of the Karlskirche

For keys to symbols *see back flap*

Street-by-Street: Karlsplatz

This part of the city became ripe for development once the threat of Turkish invasion had receded for good in 1683 *(see pp28–9)*. The Ressel Park, in front of the Karlskirche, gives an unobstructed view of this grandiose church, built on the orders of Karl VI. The park itself has a variety of cultural institutions, notably the Wien Museum Karlsplatz and, across the road, the Musikverein.

❹ ★ Karlsplatz Pavilions
These pavilions were built as part of the underground system of 1899.

Underpass

To Karlsplatz U-Bahn

Ressel Park café

KARLPL

The Technical University with its Neo-Classical façade (1816) fronts onto Ressel Park, which contains busts and statues of famous 19th-century Austrian scientists and engineers.

Ressel Statue

Key

— Suggested route

Henry Moore's Hill Arches were presented to Vienna by the artist himself in 1978.

❸ Musikverein
This Ringstrasse-style concert hall (see p150), home of the Vienna Philharmonic Orchestra, is renowned for its superb acoustics.

Locator Map
See Street Finder maps 4 and 6

❷ ★ Wien Museum Karlsplatz
This museum chronicles Vienna's history from Neolithic times to the present, with weapons, paintings and reconstructed rooms from each period.

KARLSPLATZ

DUMBASTRASSE

STRASSE

LOTHRINGER

MADERSTRASSE

MATTIELLISTRASSE

TECHNIKERSTR

GUSSHAUSSTRASSE

❶ ★ Karlskirche
Promised to the people during the 1713 plague, this is Vienna's finest Baroque church.

French Embassy

The Art Nouveau French Embassy

Built in 1904–12 by the French architect Georges Chédanne, the Embassy is typical of French Art Nouveau, resembling houses along Rue Victor Hugo in Paris. Unaccustomed to this foreign style, some thought the building was oriental, giving rise to a rumour that its plans had been mixed up with those of the French Embassy in Istanbul.

Art Nouveau façade of the French Embassy

0 metres 50
0 yards 50

❶ Karlskirche

During Vienna's plague epidemic in 1713, Emperor Karl VI vowed that as soon as the city was delivered from its plight he would build a church dedicated to St Charles Borromeo (1538–84), a former Archbishop of Milan who was celebrated for the help he gave plague sufferers. The following year he announced a competition to design the church, which was won by the architect Johann Bernhard Fischer von Erlach. The result was a richly eclectic Baroque masterpiece: the gigantic dome and portico are borrowed from the architecture of ancient Greece and Rome, while there are Oriental echoes in the gatehouses and minaret-like columns. Building took almost 25 years, and the interior was richly embellished with carvings and altarpieces by the foremost artists of the day, including Daniel Gran and Martino Altomonte.

The Pulpit
Two *putti* surmount the canopy of the richly gilded pulpit, decorated with rocailles and flower garlands.

★ High Altar
The high altar features a stucco relief by Albert Camesina showing St Charles Borromeo being assumed into heaven on a cloud laden with angels and *putti*.

KEY

① **Angel representing the Old Testament**

② **Pediment** *reliefs* by Giovanni Stanetti show the suffering of the Viennese during the 1713 plague.

③ **The two gatehouses** leading into the side entrances of the church are reminiscent of Chinese pavilions.

④ **Stairway** (closed to public)

⑤ **Cupola Cross**

⑥ **Angel representing the New Testament**

Main entrance

★ Frescoes in the Cupola
Johann Michael Rottmayr's fresco, painted between 1725 and 1730, depicts the Apotheosis of St Charles Borromeo. It was the painter's last commission.

VISITORS' CHECKLIST

Karlsplatz, A-1040.
Map 4 E2. **Tel** 5056294.
4A. **Open** 9am–6pm Mon–Sat, noon–7pm Sun & hols.
6pm Mon–Sat, 11am & 6pm Sun & hols.
to cupola.
W karlskirche.at

Transport
U Karlsplatz.

Johann Bernhard Fischer von Erlach

Many of Vienna's finest buildings, including the Trautson and Schönbrunn Palaces, were designed by Fischer von Erlach (1656–1723). He died before he finished the Karlskirche and his son completed it in 1737.

★ The Two Columns
Inspired by Trajan's Column in Rome, they are decorated with spiralling scenes of St Charles Borromeo's life. Qualities of Steadfastness are illustrated on the left, and Courage on the right.

Visitor entrance and tickets

⑥

St Charles Borromeo
Lorenzo Mattielli's statue of the saint crowns the pediment.

❷ Wien Museum Karlsplatz

Karlsplatz 8. **Map** 4 E2. **Tel** 5058747.
Ⓤ Karlsplatz. **Open** 10am–6pm Tue–
Sun & hols. **Closed** 1 Jan, 1 May,
25 Dec. 🚻 ♿ 🌐 **wienmuseum.at**

Permanent highlights at this
museum include the large 3D
scale models of city buildings
and paintings by Gustav Klimt
and Egon Schiele, most notably
his celebrated self-portrait.
In terms of historical periods,
the museum is strongest
on the 19th century – not only
paintings but also furniture,
clothing and household items.
There are several reconstructed
apartments to show period life,
including the flats of radical
architect Adolf Loos (see p94)
and local poet Franz Grillparzer.
The oldest reconstructed room
is decorated with painted silks
and comes from 1798, in the
Caprara-Geymüller Palace.

Visitors quickly get an overview
of the entirety of Vienna's history
by strolling through the rooms.
Neolithic shards and spears lead
onto the Roman military encampment of Vindobona. In later
periods, the planning of today's
monuments and palaces is preserved, as are Johann Bernhard
Fischer von Erlach's original plans
for the Schönbrunn Palace (see
pp174–7) and original stained-

The monumental, historicist façade of the Musikverein

glass windows and sculptures
from the Stephansdom, among
them the famous *Fürstenfiguren*,
or figures of royalty.

Everything from the plague to
celebrations of victory over the
Turks is portrayed. Many objects
are not just of historical interest
but are art works in their own
right, such as glassware by
Josef Hoffmann, designs from
the Wiener Werkstätte (see p58)
and 14th- and 15th-century
gargoyles. Weapons and war
are represented in each period,
including armour and weapons
from Turkish invaders. Vienna's
fascination with music is also
well covered, with papers and
paintings chronicling opera,
ballet and operetta.

The museum has a wealth
of paintings. There is a room
dedicated to Baroque painting
in Vienna that includes works
by Franz Anton Maulbertsch,
Johann Michael Rottmayr and
Paul Troger.

An exciting plan to build a
modernistic museum on top of
the existing three-storey structure has been announced, and
the museum may soon close for
several years, starting sometime
in 2019 or 2020. It will continue
to schedule themed special exhibitions on Viennese citizens and
phases of Vienna history, such
as construction of the Ring and
removal of the medieval walls.

❸ Musikverein

Bösendorferstrasse 12. **Map** 4 E2.
Tel 5058190. Ⓤ Karlsplatz. **Open** for
concerts and guided tours (1pm
Mon–Sat). ✉ ♿ 🌐 **musikverein.at**

The Musikverein building – the
headquarters of the Society of
the Friends of Music – was
designed from 1867 to 1869
by Theophil Hansen, in a mixture
of styles employing terracotta
statues, capitals and balustrades.
It is the home of the great
Vienna Philharmonic Orchestra
(see p229), which gives regular
performances here and in the
Opera House. The concert hall
seats almost 2,000. Tickets are
sold on a subscription basis to
Viennese music lovers, but some
are also available on the day of
the performance. The most
famous annual event here is the
New Year's Day concert (see p67).

Sunflower motifs on the façade of the Karlsplatz Pavilions

The enormous Hochstrahlbrunnen in Schwarzenbergplatz

❹ Karlsplatz Pavilions

Karlsplatz. **Map** 4 D2. **Tel** 5058747-85177. Ⓤ Karlsplatz. **Open** Apr–Oct: 10am–6pm Tue–Sun & hols. **Closed** 1 May. Ⓦ **wienmuseum.at**

Otto Wagner *(see pp56–9)* was responsible for many aspects of Vienna's underground system in the late 1800s. Some of these bridges and tunnels are remarkable, but they cannot match his stylish pair of underground railway exit pavilions (1898–9) next to the Karlsplatz. The green copper of the roofs and the ornamentation complement the Karlskirche beyond. Gilt patterns are stamped on the white marble cladding and eaves, with repetitions of Wagner's sunflower motif. But the greatest impact is made by the buildings' curving rooflines. The two pavilions face each other: one is now a café; the other is used for exhibitions.

❺ Künstlerhaus

Karlsplatz 5. **Map** 4 D2 & 6 D5. **Tel** 587 9663. Ⓤ Karlsplatz. **Open** 2–6pm Mon–Sat (to 9pm Thu, from 11am Sat). ✉ Ⓖ Ⓦ **k-haus.at**

The Vienna Artists' Society's HQ, this 1868 Renaissance palazzo-style hall is due to reopen at the end of 2018 with a theatre and space for lectures and art shows.

❻ Imperial Hotel

Kärntner Ring 16. **Map** 4 E2 & 6 D5. **Tel** 501100. Ⓤ Karlsplatz. Ⓖ Ⓦ **imperialvienna.com**

Along with the Hotel Sacher *(see p142)*, this is the best-known of Vienna's sumptuous 19th-century hotels. You can sip tea to the sound of a pianist playing in the background or stay in the same room Richard Wagner occupied. Adolf Hitler made the Imperial Hotel his headquarters after the Anschluss *(see p38)*.

❼ Schwarzenberg-platz

Map 4 E2. Ⓤ Karlsplatz. 🚋 D, 71.

At the centre of this grand square is an equestrian statue (1867) of Prince Schwarzenberg, who led the Austrian and allied armies against Napoleon at the Battle of Leipzig (1813). The square comprises huge office blocks, the Ringstrasse and the Baroque splendours of the Schwarzenberg and Belvedere palaces. Behind the fountain of Hochstrahlbrunnen (1873), at the intersection of Prinz-Eugen-Strasse and Gusshausstrasse, is a monument commemorating the Red Army's liberation of the city. It is none too popular with older Viennese, who still recall the brutalities endured in the Russian zone until 1955.

The Arnold Schönberg Center *(see p152)* lies at the eastern end of the square.

Palazzo-style façade of the Künstlerhaus (1868)

Schwarzenberg Palace and Joseph Fischer von Ehrlach's fountain

⑧ Arnold Schönberg Center

Schwarzenbergplatz 6 (entrance at Zaunergasse 1–3). **Map** 4 E2. **Tel** 7121888. Ⓤ Karlsplatz. 🚌 4A. 🚋 D, 71. **Open** 9am–5pm Mon–Fri. **Closed** public hols, 24 & 31 Dec. 🅦 schoenberg.at

Vienna's Arnold Schönberg Center, established in 1998, is both a unique archive for music scholars and a cultural centre that is open to the general public. Schönberg – composer, painter, teacher, music theoretician and innovator – was born in Vienna in 1874 and died in Los Angeles in 1951. Something of a prodigy, he began composing at the age of 9. However, he later dismissed much of his early work as "imitative", gradually developing a more experimental and, for the times, daring approach to composition. This was to culminate in his highly influential twelve-tone composition technique.

Although Schönberg's work was much admired by fellow musicians, it baffled the general public. In 1913 he famously conducted what became known as the "Skandalkonzert" at Vienna's Musikverein (see p150). This featured a programme of modern music so provocative that the audience rioted, bringing the concert to a halt.

The Center contains fascinating artifacts relating to Schönberg's life and work, a gallery of his paintings, a replica of his Los Angeles study and a library on topics relating to the Viennese School. It also stages concerts, lectures, workshops and symposia. Visitors with an academic interest may be able to arrange access to Schönberg's music manuscripts, writings and correspondence.

Schönberg is buried in the Central Cemetery (see pp170–71). His grave has a striking Modernist monument by Fritz Wotruba.

⑨ Schwarzenberg Palace

Schwarzenbergplatz 9. **Map** 4 E2.

The Palais Schwarzenberg was built by Johann Lukas von Hildebrandt (see p154) in 1697 and then altered by the Fischer von Erlachs (see p149) in the 1720s. The main salon has a domed hall with a magnificent chandelier. Behind the palace are the lawns and shady paths of the park, focused around a pool and fountain designed by Joseph Emanuel Fischer von Erlach. In the past the main reception rooms were used as a venue for concerts and balls.

One wing is occupied by the Swiss Embassy. The present head of the Schwarzenberg family served as an advisor to President Havel after the Velvet Revolution in Czechoslovakia in 1989 and was Czech foreign minister in 2007–2009 and 2010–2013.

⑩ Rennweg

Map 4 E2. Ⓤ Karlsplatz. Gardekirche. **Open** 8am–8pm daily.

Rennweg runs from the Schwarzenbergplatz along the edges of the Belvedere palaces. At No. 3, a house built by Otto Wagner (see p59) in 1890 is now the (former) Yugoslav Embassy. Though the façade is in shabby condition, the building remains an interesting example of Wagner's work just as he was making the transition from Ringstrasse pomp to his later Jugendstil phase.

Detail of the façade of the Salesianerinnenkirche in Rennweg

Next door at No. 5 is where Gustav Mahler (see p41) lived from 1898 to 1909. No. 5a is the Gardekirche (1755–63) by Nikolaus Pacassi (1716–99), Maria Theresa's court architect. It was originally built as the church of the Imperial Hospital and since 1897 has been Vienna's Polish church. A huge dome covers the entire interior, which adds to its spaciousness. One feature of interest is the gilt Rococo embellishment over the side chapels and between the ribs of the dome. Just beyond the Belvedere palace gates at No. 6a stands a Baroque mansion. The forecourt at No. 8 has formed part of the Hochschule für Musik since 1988.

At No. 10, behind splendid wrought-iron gates, stands the Salesianerinnenkirche of 1717–30. Its Baroque façade is flanked by monastic buildings in the same style. The upper storey has scrolled projections that serve as the base for statues. Like the Gardekirche, this church is domed, its design partly attributed to Joseph Emanuel Fischer von Erlach (see p149). Apart from the pulpit, the interior is of little interest.

At No. 27, the present-day Italian Embassy occupies the palace where Prince Metternich (see p32) lived until he was forced to flee the city in 1848.

⓫ Palaces and Gardens of the Belvedere

See pp154–9.

⓬ Botanical Gardens

Rennweg 14. **Map** 4 F3. **Tel** 4277 54100. 🚋 71. **Open** 10am–dusk. ♿
🌐 botanik.univie.ac.at

The Botanical Gardens were created in 1754 by Maria Theresa and her physician, Van Swieten, for cultivating medicinal herbs. Expanded to their present shape in the 19th

The Botanical Gardens created by Maria Theresa in 1754

century, they remain a centre for the study of plant sciences as part of the University of Vienna's Institute of Botany and contain more than 9,000 plant species. Of equal interest to amateurs, the gardens offer a quiet spot to sit and relax after sightseeing.

The main entrance to the Botanical Gardens is on the corner of Prätoriusgasse and Mechelgasse. Other entrances are on Jacquingasse, and via a small gate at the rear of the Upper Belvedere, which leads to the Alpine Garden and the Botanical Gardens.

⓭ Theresianum

Favoritenstrasse 15. **Map** 4 E3. Ⓤ Taubstummengasse. **Closed** to public.

The original buildings of this former imperial summer palace date from the early 17th century, but were essentially rebuilt in a Baroque

style after the Turkish siege of 1683 by the architect and theatre designer Lodovico Burnacini (1636–1707) and others. Known at the time as the Favorita, it became a favourite residence of emperors Leopold I, Joseph I and Karl VI. In 1746 Maria Theresa, who had moved into Schönbrunn (see pp174–9), her summer palace, handed it over to the Jesuits. They established a college here for the education of children from less well-off aristocratic families – the sons of these families were trained to be officials.

Today, the Theresianum is still a school and, since 1964, has also been a college for diplomats and civil servants. In the Theresianum park on Argentinierstrasse stands Radio House. It has a beautiful entrance hall, which was designed by Clemens Holzmeister in 1935.

Theresianum, housing a school and a college for diplomats

⑩ Palaces and Gardens of the Belvedere

The Belvedere was built by Johann Lukas von Hildebrandt as the summer residence of Prince Eugene of Savoy, the brilliant military commander whose strategies helped vanquish the Turks in 1683. Situated on a gently sloping hill, the Belvedere consists of two palaces linked by a formal garden laid out in the French style by Dominique Girard. The garden is sited on three levels, each conveying a complicated programme of Classical allusions: the lower part of the garden represents the domain of the Four Elements, the centre is Parnassus and the upper section is Olympus.

★ **Upper Cascade**
Water flows from the upper basin over five shallow steps into the pool below.

Putti on the Steps (1852)
Children and cherubs representing the 12 months adorn the steps to the left and right in the middle area of the gardens.

Johann Lukas von Hildebrandt

Hildebrandt became the court architect in Vienna in 1700 and was one of J B Fischer von Erlach's greatest rivals. In addition to the Belvedere, he designed the Schönborn Palace (see p117), the Kinsky Palace (see p112) and the Maria-Treu-Kirche (see p118).

The magnificent 18th-century Upper Belvedere palace, with its striking copper roofs

Entrance to Lower Belvedere from Rennweg

④
③
②
①

1700	1750	1800	1850	1900	1950

1717–19 Dominique Girard landscapes the gardens

1720 Orangery built

1721–3 Upper Belvedere built

1714–16 Lower Belvedere built

1752 Habsburgs acquire the Belvedere

1765 Lower Belvedere becomes the barracks for the military guard

1781–1891 Belvedere houses the Imperial Picture Gallery, which opens to the public

1779 Belvedere gardens open to the public

1897 Archduke Franz Ferdinand, heir to the throne, moves to the Upper Belvedere

1923–9 The Baroque Museum, the 19th-Century Gallery and the 20th-Century Gallery open to the public

1953 Museum of Medieval Austrian Art opens to the public

1955 The Austrian State Treaty signed in the Marble Hall

Detail on Upper Cascade

VISITORS' CHECKLIST

Practical Information
Map 4 F3. Upper Belvedere:
see pp156–7. Lower Belvedere
and Orangery: *see pp158–9*.
Gardens: **Open** 6:30am–dusk
all year round. ♿

★ **Main Gate of the Upper Belvedere**
The Baroque iron gate (1728) by Arnold and Konrad
Küffner, with an "S" for Savoy and the cross of Savoy,
leads to the south façade of the Upper Belvedere.

★ **Upper Belvedere Façade**
The lively façade dominates the
sweeping entrance to the palace
(*see pp156–7*). The domed copper
roofs of the end pavilions
resemble the shape of Turkish
tents – an allusion to Prince
Eugene's victories over the Turks.

Entrance to Upper
Belvedere (*see
pp156–7*) and
gardens from
Prinz-Eugen-
Strasse

Statues of Sphinxes
With their lion bodies
and human heads, the
imposing sphinx
statues represent
strength and
intelligence.

KEY

① **Triumphal gate to Lower Belvedere**

② **Lower Belvedere** (*see pp158–9*)

③ **Statues of the Eight Muses**

④ ***Bosquet*** or hedge garden

⑤ **Lower Cascade**

⑥ **Orangery** (*see p158*)

⑦ **Palace Stables**

Entrance to
Orangery

Upper Belvedere

Standing at the highest point of the garden, the Upper Belvedere has a more elaborate façade than the Lower Belvedere: it was intended to be a symbolic reflection of Prince Eugene's glory. In addition to the impressive interiors of the Sala Terrena with its sweeping staircase, the chapel and the Marble Hall, the building now houses an Austrian art collection with works ranging from the Middle Ages to the present day.

★ Chapel
The centrepiece of this brown, white and gold interior is an altarpiece, *The Resurrection* by Francesco Solimena (1723), set among statues of angels. Prince Eugene could enter the chapel directly from his apartments.

Viewing balcony for chapel

Laughing Self-Portrait
(1908)
This picture is by Richard Gerstl, the Viennese artist who was developing his own Expressionist style when he killed himself in his twenties.

Gallery Guide
The ground floor houses masterpieces of medieval and modern art. Baroque art and art from the fin-de-siècle to World War I is on the first floor. Nineteenth-century and Biedermeier art is on the second floor.

Main entrance from gardens

★ Sala Terrena
Four Herculean figures by Lorenzo Mattielli support the ceiling vault of the Sala Terrena, while white stuccowork by Santino Bussi covers the walls and ceiling.

Key
- Neo-Classicism, Romanticism and Biedermeier
- Realism and Impressionism
- Baroque and early 19th-century art
- Vienna 1880–1914
- Medieval art
- Modern art: interwar period
- Non-exhibition space

★ Gustav Klimt Collection
This marvellous Jugendstil collection by Gustav Klimt is considered by some to be the Belvedere's highlight. In the work here, *Judith I* (1901), Klimt depicts the Old Testament heroine as a Viennese *femme fatale*.

The Tiger Lion (1926)
This savage beast from the interwar period was painted by Oskar Kokoschka, a leading figure in Austrian Expressionism.

Second floor

Marble Hall

First floor

Stairs to

Ground floor

The Plain of Auvers (1890)
Van Gogh's airy landscape is part of a series inspired by the wheat fields around Auvers-sur-Oise, where the artist spent the last few months of his life.

Corpus Christi Morning (1857)
This bright genre scene is typical of the work of Biedermeier painter Ferdinand Georg Waldmüller.

Lower Belvedere and Orangery

The architect Johann Lukas von Hildebrandt (1668–1745) was commissioned by Prince Eugene of Savoy to build the Lower Belvedere in 1714, and it was completed in 1716. It previously housed the Museum of Austrian Baroque Art but now displays temporary exhibitions only. Attractions include the Marble Hall, the state bedroom of Prince Eugene of Savoy, the Hall of Grotesques and the Marble Gallery. The Lower Belvedere also incorporates the Orangery and the palace stables.

Exit to
Orangery and
stables

★ **Golden Cabinet**
A statue of Prince Eugene (1721) by Balthasar Permoser stands in this room. The walls are covered with huge gilt-framed mirrors.

Hall of Grotesques
The hall is decorated with paintings of grotesques inspired by ancient Roman frescoes of fantastical creatures. They were created by the German painter Jonas Drentwett.

★ **The Marble Gallery**
This room features a stucco ceiling relief honouring Prince Eugene and a number of dynamic sculptures by the Baroque artist Domenico Parodi.

Lower Belvedere Palace
This impressive Baroque palace is set in beautiful landscaped gardens. The façade is adorned with Ionic columns and statues.

Gallery Guide

All works on display in the Lower Belvedere and Orangery are temporary. Exhibitions include traditional and contemporary painting and sculpture. Pieces are often loaned from galleries and museums worldwide, supplemented by the Belvedere's own collection.

VISITORS' CHECKLIST

Practical Information
Rennweg 6, A-1030. **Map** 4 E3.
Tel 795 57 134. **Open** 10am–6pm daily (to 9pm Wed). Palace Stables: **Open** 10am–6pm daily (to 9pm Wed). 🅿 ♿ 📷
W belvedere.at

Transport
🚊 D, 71.

The Orangery

Next door to the Lower Belvedere is the handsome Orangery building, originally used to shelter tender garden plants in winter and now transformed into an exhibition hall retaining its original character. It previously housed the Museum of Austrian Medieval Art but now has regularly changing temporary exhibitions. Next to the "White Cube", the southern side gallery corridor offers a spectacular view of the Privy Garden and the Upper Belvedere.

The Palace Stables
Collected here are some 150 items of medieval art, including masterpieces of panel painting and sculpture.

Key
🔲 Temporary Exhibitions

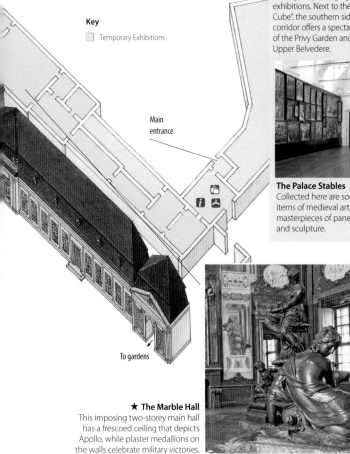

Main entrance

To gardens

★ The Marble Hall
This imposing two-storey main hall has a frescoed ceiling that depicts Apollo, while plaster medallions on the walls celebrate military victories.

FURTHER AFIELD

For a city of almost 2 million inhabitants, Vienna is surprisingly compact. It is less than 8 km (5 miles) from Stephensplatz to Schönbrunn. At Schönbrunn sprawls the immense palace and gardens so loved by Maria Theresa. The monastery at

Klosterneuburg houses some of Austria's great ecclesiastical art treasures. Many parks and gardens, including the Prater, the Augarten and the Lainzer Tiergarten, all formerly private Habsburg land, are now open to the public.

Sights at a Glance

Historic Buildings
1 Wagner Villas
7 Karl-Marx-Hof
9 Augarten Palace and Park
11 Hundertwasserhaus
16 Favoriten Water Tower
17 Amalienbad
20 Schönbrunn Palace and Gardens pp174–7
21 Otto-Wagner-Hofpavillon Hietzing
22 Werkbundsiedlung

Churches and Monasteries
2 Kirche am Steinhof
6 Klosterneuburg
24 Wotruba-Kirche

Museums and Galleries
3 Geymüllerschlössel
10 Kriminalmuseum
14 Heeresgeschichtliches Museum pp168–9
19 Technical Museum

Parks and Gardens
8 Donaupark
12 Prater pp164–5
13 Stadtpark
23 Lainzer Tiergarten

Historic Districts
4 Grinzing
5 Kahlenberg

Monuments
18 Spinnerin am Kreuz

Cemeteries
15 Central Cemetery pp170–71

Key
- Central Vienna
- Greater Vienna
- Motorway
- Motorway tunnel
- Major road
- Minor road

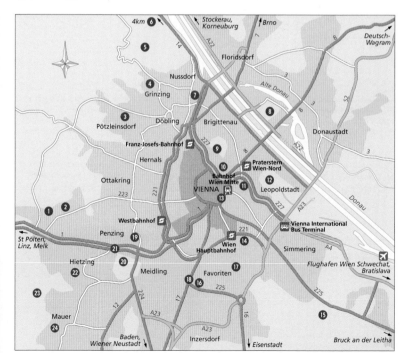

◄ The Expressionist architecture of the iconic Hundertwasserhaus   **For keys to symbols** *see back flap*

Detail of Ernst Fuchs' Brunnenhaus, next to Wagner Villas

with nailhead ornament and has spindly screw-shaped pillars, topped by wreaths, supporting the porch. Four stone columns on the façade are adorned with angels by Othmar Schimkowitz (1864–1947). The statues at each end of the façade are of St Leopold and St Severin to the left and right respectively. They were designed by Richard Luksch and are seated in chairs by Josef Hoffmann (see p58).

Inside is a single space with shallow side chapels, decorated with gold and white friezes and square roof panels ornamented with gilt nailhead. Illumination is provided by daylight shining through lovely blue glass windows by Kolo Moser (see p59).

❸ Geymüller-schlössel

Khevenhüllerstrasse 2, Währing.
Tel 71136231. 🚌 41A. 🚋 41.
Open May–Nov: 11am–6pm Sun.
🎫 📷 by reservation. 🅆 mak.at

The Geymüllerschlössel in Pötzleinsdorf, northwest of the city, is a temple to Biedermeier style (see pp32–3). Dating from 1808, the house was built for Johann Heinrich von Geymüller, a rich banker. Now a branch of the Austrian Museum of Applied Arts (see pp84–5), it has a collection of intricate Biedermeier and Empire furniture, such as an apparently simple desk that combines a writing desk with a water-colour cabinet. There are also spittoons, still-lifes painted on porcelain, bowls, as well as 200 clocks dating from 1780 to about 1850, the heyday of Viennese clock manufacture.

❶ Wagner Villas

Hüttelbergstrasse 26, Penzing. **Tel** 9148575. 🄿 Hütteldorf. 🚌 52A & 52B to Camping Platz Wien West. **Open** 10am–4pm Tue–Sat, by appointment Sun & Mon. 🎫
🅆 ernstfuchsmuseum.at

The Villa Otto Wagner, designed by Wagner from 1886 to 1888 as his own residence, is stylistically midway between his earlier Ringstrasse architecture and the decorative elements of Jugendstil (see pp56–9). The house is built on a grand scale, incorporating Classical elements such as Ionic columns, and seems more suited to a north Italian hillside than to Austria. The present owner, the painter Ernst Fuchs (see p38), has imposed his own personality on the villa, adding a fertility statue and garish colours.

The simpler villa next door was built more than 20 years later. Completed in 1913, Brunnenhaus is of steel and concrete rather than brick. It is lightly decorated in a geometrical style with deep blue panels and a glass nailhead ornament by Kolo Moser (see p59).

❷ Kirche am Steinhof

Baumgartner Höhe 1, Penzing.
Tel 9106011007. 🚋 48A.
Open 4–5pm Sat, noon–4pm Sun.
📷 by appointment. 🎫

Completed in 1907, this astonishing church was Otto Wagner's (see pp56–9) last commission. It is set within the grounds of the Psychiatrisches Krankenhaus, a large mental hospital. The exterior is marble-clad

Jugendstil angels by Othmar Schimkowitz adorning the façade of the Kirche am Steinhof

❹ Grinzing

ⓊHeiligenstadt. 🚌 38A. 🚋 38.

Grinzing is the most famous *Heuriger* village *(see pp188–9)*, but it is also the most touristy, with many of the inns here catering to very large groups. It is nonetheless very pretty.

It is divided into the Oberer Ort and Unterer Ort (upper and lower towns), the lower town being where you will find more authentic *Heurigen* along lanes such as Sandgasse.

Grinzing was repeatedly attacked by Turkish troops during the many sieges of Vienna *(see pp28–9)*, and was later damaged by Napoleon's forces in 1809 *(see p32)*.

❺ Kahlenberg

🚌 38A.

Kahlenberg, at 484 m (1,585 ft), is the highest point in the Vienna Woods *(see pp178–9)*. It has a television mast at the top, as well as a church, an observation terrace and a restaurant. The views over the vineyards below and the city beyond are fabulous, with the Danube bridges to the left and the Vienna Woods to the right. The Kahlenberg played a crucial part in the city's history in 1683, when the Polish king, Jan Sobieski, led his troops down from this spot to rescue the Viennese forces who were fighting for the city.

❻ Klosterneuburg

Stift Klosterneuburg. **Tel** 022434110. ⓊHeiligenstadt. Ⓢ Franz-Josefs-Bahnhof to Klosterneuburg-Kierling. 🚌 238, 239. **Open** 9am–5pm daily. 🎫 Daily tours include the Monastery Museum and Imperial Apartments. 🛗 ⓦ **stift-klosterneuburg.at**

Above the Danube, 13 km (8 miles) north of Vienna, stands the vast monastery and fortress of Klosterneuburg. Dating originally from the 12th century, it houses the

The peach- and salmon-coloured façade of the Karl-Marx-Hof

astonishing Verduner Altar, whose 51 panels were completed in 1181 *(see p25)*. In the 18th century it was expanded by Karl VI, who intended to build a complex on the same grand scale as the Escorial palace near Madrid. The work was halted after his death in 1740.

Statue in Grinzing

❼ Karl-Marx-Hof

Heiligenstädterstrasse 82–92, Döbling. ⓊHeiligenstadt. 🚋 D. **Closed** to the public.

The Karl-Marx-Hof, dating from 1927 to 1930, is an immense social housing project, containing 1,382 flats. It is the most celebrated of the municipal housing developments built during the period of Red Vienna

(see p38), when 63,000 new dwellings went up across the city between 1919 and 1934. The architect of the Karl-Marx-Hof was Karl Ehn, a pupil of Otto Wagner *(see pp56–9)*.

❽ Donaupark

ⓊKaisermühlen. 🚌 20B. **Open** 24 hours. Donauturm: **Tel** 4000 8042. **Open** 10am–11:30pm daily. ♿

Adjoining UNO-City *(see p39)*, the complex of United Nations agencies, is the Donaupark. Developed in 1964, the park features a variety of beautiful gardens, cycle lanes and cafés. Its landmark is the Donauturm, which rises 252 m (827 ft) above the park and has two revolving restaurants and an observation platform. The park and the surrounding area are incorporated into Donau City, a vast urban project.

The Klosterneuburg monastery with its Baroque dome

⑫ Prater

Originally an imperial hunting ground, these woods and meadows between the Danube and its canal were opened to the public by Joseph II in 1766. The central avenue, or Hauptallee, was for a long time the preserve of the nobility and their footmen. During the 19th century the western end of the Prater became a massive funfair with booths, sideshows, beer gardens and *Wurst* stands catering for Viennese workers.

Miniature Railway
The Liliputbahn travels a 4-km (2.5-mile) circuit.

To Praterstern station

★ **Ferris Wheel**
The huge wheel circulates very slowly at a speed of about 75 cm (2.5 ft) per second, allowing riders spectacular views over the park and funfair.

★ **Volksprater Funfair**
An amusement park has existed here since the 19th century. Today the enormous funfair is full of rides ranging from dodgem cars to ghost trains.

KEY

① *Tennisplätze* (tennis courts)
② Planetarium
③ Messegelände exhibition centre
④ *Stadion* (stadium)
⑤ *Stadionbad* (swimming pool),
⑥ Cycle paths
⑦ Maria Grun Kirche
⑧ *Golfplatz* (golf course)

The Trotting Stadium
Built in 1913, the Krieau Stadium is the scene of regional and international trotting races from September to June (*see p231*).

The History of the Ferris Wheel

One of Vienna's most famous landmarks, the giant Ferris Wheel was immortalized in the film of Graham Greene's *The Third Man*. It was built in 1896 by the English engineer Walter Basset, but it has only half the original number of cabins, since a fire destroyed many of them in 1945.

0 metres   800
0 yards   800

★ **Hauptallee**
The avenue lined with chestnut trees stretches for 5 km (3 miles) through the centre of the Prater.

Lusthaus
The 18th-century octagonal pavilion, formerly a hunting lodge, now houses a restaurant.

Baroque façade of the Augarten Palace, set amid 18th-century parkland

❾ Augarten Palace and Park

Obere Augartenstrasse 1. **Map** 2 E2.
Tel 21124201. Ⓤ Taborstrasse. 🚌 5A,
5B. 🚃 5, 31. Park: **Open** 6am–9pm
daily. Porcelain Museum: **Open** 10am–
6pm Mon–Sat. Thyssen-Bornemisza Art
Contemporary: **Open** noon–5pm
Wed–Thu, noon–7pm Fri–Sun. ♿

There has been a palace on this
site since the days of Leopold I,
when it was known as the Alte
Favorita, but it was destroyed
by the Turks in 1683 and later
rebuilt around 1700 to a design
attributed to Johann Bernhard
Fischer von Erlach (see p149).
The palace was used for royal
receptions and gatherings while
the Congress of Vienna (see p32)
was taking place in 1815. Since
1948 it has been the home of
the Vienna Boys' Choir (see p41)
and for the most part it is
inaccessible to the public.
Visitors can explore the Porcelain
Museum housed in the palace,
which examines the history of
porcelain and displays pieces
from the Rococo, Classical and
Biedermeier periods, as well as
the 20th and 21st century.

The park was planted in the
second half of the 17th century,
renewed in 1712, and opened to
the public in 1775 by Joseph II.
The handsome gates by which
the public now enters the
gardens were designed by
Isidor Canevale in 1775. Mozart,
Beethoven and Johann Strauss I
all gave concerts in the park
pavilion. Behind the pavilion
is the studio of the early
20th-century sculptor Gustinus
Ambrosi, now home to the
Thyssen-Bornemisza Art
Contemporary, a large space
devoted to, as its name
suggests, contemporary art.

The Augarten has the oldest
Baroque garden in Vienna. In the
distance, you can see two huge
flakturms, immovable reminders
of World War II. Built by German
forces in 1942 as defence towers
and anti-aircraft batteries, these
enormous concrete monoliths
could house thousands of troops.
So thick are their walls that any
explosives powerful enough to
destroy them would have a
similar effect on the surrounding
residential areas. There are four
other such flakturms still standing in other parts of the city.

❿ Kriminalmuseum

Grosse Sperlgasse 24. **Map** 6 E1.
Tel 06643005677. Ⓤ Taborstrasse. 🚌
5A. 🚃 2. **Open** 10am–5pm Tue–Sun.
🅦 kriminalmuseum.at

Once known as the *Seifensieder-
haus* (the soap boiler's house),
this house of medieval origin
has been the home of Vienna's
Museum of Crime since 1991.
Its 20 rooms mostly chronicle
violent crime, charting the
murderous impulses of Vienna's
citizens from the Middle Ages

⓫ Hundert-wasserhaus

Löwengasse Kegelgasse. Ⓤ
Landstrasse. 🚌 4A Löwengasse.
🚃 1 Hetzgasse. **Closed** to the public.
🅦 hundertwasserhaus.at

The Hundertwasserhaus is a
municipal apartment block
created in 1985 by the artist
Friedensreich Hundertwasser
(see p39), who wished to strike
a blow against what he saw as
soulless modern architecture.
The resulting building, with its
irregular bands of colour and
onion dome cupolas, has been
controversial since its construction. While it is loved by some,
others think it is more like a
stage set than a block of flats.

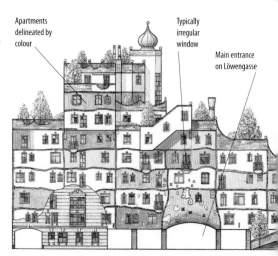

Apartments delineated by colour

Typically irregular window

Main entrance on Löwengasse

through to the 20th century, as well as the various methods of capital punishment used on some of them. The museum also examines the development of the police force and its approach to tackling crime.

Many of the exhibits come from the archives of the Viennese police force and are distinctly gruesome; there is a wide selection of murder weapons, mummified heads of executed criminals, death masks and case histories illustrated with photographs and prints. Political criminality, from failed coup attempts to the rather more grisly lynching of a government minister during the revolution of 1848 *(see p32)*, is well covered.

Though not for the faint-hearted, the museum provides visitors with a unique take on Vienna's social history.

⓬ Prater

See pp164–5.

⓭ Stadtpark

Parkring. **Map** 6 E4. **Tel** 40008042. Ⓤ Stadtpark, Stubentor. 🚌 74A. 🚋 2. **Open** 24 hours.

Stadtpark, Vienna's first and largest public park, opened when the old city walls were demolished. Among many monuments – to Schubert and Bruckner among others – is the single most photographed memorial in Vienna: Edmund Heller's "golden" (actually gilded bronze) statue of Johann Strauss playing a violin. English park design was the inspiration. There is a large playground for children featuring swings, slides, climbing frames, a sand pit and a skate park. The Italian Renaissance-style Kursalon has summer open-air concerts and costume balls. The restaurant is a popular meeting place.

⓮ Heeresgeschicht-liches Museum

See pp168–9.

⓯ Central Cemetery

See pp170–71.

⓰ Favoriten Water Tower

Windtenstrasse 3, Favoriten. **Tel** 5995931070. Ⓤ Reumannplatz. 🚌 15A, 65A. 🚋 1. **Open** for guided tours (phone to arrange).

The Favoriten pumping station was constructed in 1889 by Franz Borkowitz as part of a municipal scheme for the transportation of drinking water from the Alpine foothills to the rapidly growing city. By 1910 the construction of other installations around Vienna meant that the operations of the complex had to be scaled down, and of the seven original buildings only the highly decorative yellow- and red-brick water tower, with its ornate turrets and pinnacles, remains. The restored interior, in contrast with the attractive exterior, comprises a vast steel structure, ready to store and pump water. Guided tours are available to the public and visitors who make the climb up the spiral staircase are rewarded with impressive views of the city, including the nearby Prater funfair, which is pinpointed by its striking Ferris wheel *(see p234)*.

Favoriten Water Tower

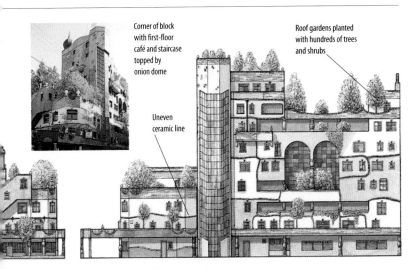

Corner of block with first-floor café and staircase topped by onion dome

Roof gardens planted with hundreds of trees and shrubs

Uneven ceramic line

⑭ Heeresgeschichtliches Museum

This impressive museum of army history is housed in a single block of the military complex called the Arsenal, which was built as a fortress in 1856. Theophil Hansen designed the museum itself, which chronicles Austria's military history from the 16th to the mid-20th century. Exhibits relate to the Turkish siege of 1683, the French Revolution and the Napoleonic wars. Visitors should not miss seeing the car in which Archduke Franz Ferdinand was assassinated, or the modern armaments used in the war that the murder precipitated.

Radetzky
1848–66

Façade of Heeresgeschichtliches Museum

Ground floor

Sea Power Austria

Republic and Dictatorship 1918–45

Tank Park
Situated behind the museum are armoured vehicles used by the Austrian army from 1955, as well as some that belonged to the German army that occupied Austria.

Main entrance from Ghegastrasse

The Assassination of Franz Ferdinand

On 28 June 1914 the heir to the throne, Archduke Franz Ferdinand, and his wife Sophie von Hohenberg paid a visit to Sarajevo. Gavrilo Princip, a Serbian nationalist, assassinated the couple, provoking an international crisis that later resulted in World War I. The museum houses the car in which the couple were killed.

Museum Guide

The museum is housed on two floors. To view it in chronological order, begin on the first floor on the left, where exhibits relating to the Turkish siege are displayed. Other rooms chronicle the various 18th-century wars and Napoleon's victory over Austria. The 19th- and 20th-century displays, including heavy artillery used in World War I, are on the ground floor. There is also a "tank garden" located behind the museum.

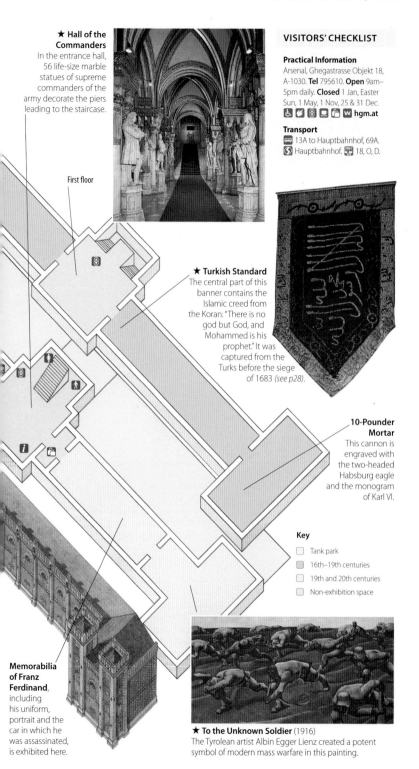

★ **Hall of the Commanders**
In the entrance hall, 56 life-size marble statues of supreme commanders of the army decorate the piers leading to the staircase.

First floor

VISITORS' CHECKLIST

Practical Information
Arsenal, Ghegastrasse Objekt 18, A-1030. **Tel** 795610. **Open** 9am–5pm daily. **Closed** 1 Jan, Easter Sun, 1 May, 1 Nov, 25 & 31 Dec.
⬤ 🅿 🅰 💻 📷 W hgm.at

Transport
🚌 13A to Hauptbahnhof, 69A.
Ⓢ Hauptbahnhof. 🚊 18, O, D.

★ **Turkish Standard**
The central part of this banner contains the Islamic creed from the Koran: "There is no god but God, and Mohammed is his prophet." It was captured from the Turks before the siege of 1683 *(see p28)*.

10-Pounder Mortar
This cannon is engraved with the two-headed Habsburg eagle and the monogram of Karl VI.

Key
- ☐ Tank park
- ▨ 16th–19th centuries
- ☐ 19th and 20th centuries
- ☐ Non-exhibition space

Memorabilia of Franz Ferdinand, including his uniform, portrait and the car in which he was assassinated, is exhibited here.

★ **To the Unknown Soldier** (1916)
The Tyrolean artist Albin Egger Lienz created a potent symbol of modern mass warfare in this painting.

⑮ Central Cemetery

Austria's largest cemetery, opened in 1874, contains 300,000 graves inside an area of 2.5 sq km (1 sq mile). Funerals are usually quite lavish affairs, as the Viennese like to be buried in style, with the pomp appropriate to their station in life. The underground funeral museum plays popular funeral dirges and shows rare footage of the interment of Franz Josef I.

★ **Luegerkirche**
Max Hegele, a pupil of Otto Wagner, designed this church dedicated to Vienna's mayor in 1907–10.

Presidential Vault
This contains the remains of Dr Karl Renner, the first president of the Austrian Republic after World War II.

Cemetery Layout

The cemetery is divided into specific numbered sections: as well as the central garden of honour where VIPs are buried, there are old and new Jewish cemeteries; a Protestant cemetery; a Russian Orthodox section; and various war graves and memorials. It is easier to take the circulating bus that covers the whole area than to walk.

The Monument to the Dead of World War I is a powerful depiction of a mother lamenting by Anton Hanak.

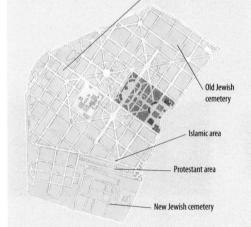

Old Jewish cemetery

Islamic area

Protestant area

New Jewish cemetery

Arnold Schönberg's Cube
The grave of the modernist Viennese composer Arnold Schönberg is marked with this bold cube by Fritz Wotruba.

Key

① Arcades around the Luegerkirche

② Fritz Wotruba's grave *(see p173)*

③ Monument to Dr Johann Nepomuk Prix by Viktor Tilgner (1894)

④ **Bestattungsmuseum**, the Undertakers' Museum, gives a fascinating insight into the history of Vienna's love affair with stylish burials.

Theophil Hansen's Grave
The architect of Vienna's Parliament building
(*see p123*) rests near other artists and
architects. Hansen died in 1891.

VISITORS' CHECKLIST

Practical Information
Simmeringer Hauptstrasse 234,
Tor 2, A-1110. **Tel** 534690. **Open**
daily; Nov–Feb: 8am–5pm; Mar,
Oct: 7am–6pm; Apr–Sep: 7am–
7pm (May–Aug: to 8pm Thu). 🅿 ♿ 🅆 friedhoefewien.at
Museum: **Tel** 76067. **Open**
9am–4:30pm Mon–Fri.
🅆 bestattungsmuseum.at

Transport
Ⓢ Zentralfriedhof, Kledering.
🚋 6, 71.

The Arcades
Some spectacular monuments
are carved in the semicircular
arcades facing the main entrance,
including this 1848 memorial to
the miner August Zang.

Main entrance
from Simmeringer
Hauptstrasse

**★ Musicians'
Graves**
Among the city's musicians
buried in this area are
Johann Strauss I and II
(grave pictured left),
Beethoven, Brahms and
Schubert. There is a monu-
ment to Mozart, who is
buried in St Marx cemetery.

Russian Orthodox Chapel
Built in traditional Russian
Orthodox style and completed
in 1894, this chapel is used by
Vienna's Russian community.

⑰ Amalienbad

Reumannplatz 23, Favoriten.
Tel 6074747. Ⓤ Reumannplatz.
🚌 7A, 14A, 66A, 67A, 68A. 🚊 6, 67.
Swimming pool: **Open** 12:30–3pm
Mon, 9am–6pm Tue, 9am–9:30pm
Wed–Fri, 7am–8pm Sat, 7am–6pm
Sun. Sauna: **Open** 1–9:30pm Tue,
9am–9:30pm Wed–Fri, 7am–8pm Sat,
7am–6pm Sun. ♿

Public baths may not seem like
an obvious tourist destination,
but the Jugendstil Amalienbad
(1923–6) shows how the
municipal administration in
the 1920s not only provided
essential public facilities, but
did so with stylistic vigour and
conviction. The two designers,
Otto Nadel and Karl Schmalhofer,
were employees of the city's
architectural department.

The magnificent main pool
is covered by a glass roof that
can be opened in minutes and
is surrounded by galleries
overlooking the pool. Elsewhere
in the building are saunas and
smaller baths and pools used
for therapeutic purposes.
The interior throughout is
enlivened by imaginative
mosaic and tile decoration.

When first opened, the
baths were one of the largest
of their kind in Europe,
designed to accommodate
1,300 people. The baths were
damaged in World War II
but were impeccably restored
in 1986.

Spinnerin am Kreuz

⑱ Spinnerin am Kreuz

Triesterstrasse 10, Meidling.
Ⓤ Meidling. 🚌 15A, 65A. 🚊 1.

A medieval column marks the
southernmost boundary of
Vienna's inner suburbs. Built in
1452 and carved on all sides, it
stands on the spot where,
according to legend, a woman
sat spinning for years awaiting
her husband's return from the
Crusades. Known as the Spinner
at the Cross, it was designed by
Hans Puchsbaum. Pinnacled
canopies shelter groups of
statuary, including a Crucifixion
and a grotesque figure placing
the crown of thorns on the
head of Christ.

⑲ Technical Museum

Mariahilfer Strasse 212, Penzing.
Tel 899980. 🚌 10A 🚊 52, 58.
Open 9am–6pm Mon–Fri, 10am–
6pm Sat, Sun & public hols. 🎦 (free
for under-19s). ♿ (free admission).
🖥 Ⓦ tmw.ac.at

Franz Joseph founded the
Technisches Museum Wien
in 1908, using the Habsburgs'
personal collections as core
material, but it only opened
its doors to the public 10 years
later. It documents all aspects
of technical progress, from
domestic appliances to
large turbines, and includes
exhibitions on heavy industry,
energy, physics and musical
instruments.

A major section of the
museum features interactive
displays on computer
technology and oil and gas
drilling and refining, as well
as a reconstruction of a
coal mine.

The Railway Museum
forms an integral part of the
Technical Museum. It houses
an extensive collection of
imperial railway carriages
and engines.

⑳ Schönbrunn Palace and Gardens

See pp174–7.

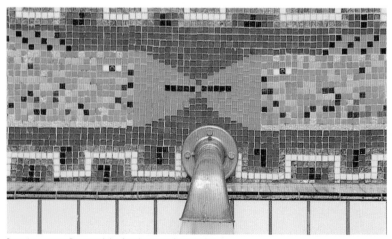

Decorative, geometrically patterned tiling from the 1920s in the Amalienbad

㉑ Otto-Wagner-Hofpavillon Hietzing

Schönbrunner Schlosstrasse 13, Hietzing. **Tel** 8771571. Ⓤ Hietzing. 🚌 51A, 56B. 🚉 10, 58, 60. **Open** 10am–6pm Sat & Sun. **Closed** 1 Jan, 1 May & 25 Dec. 🚻 (free 1st Sun of month). 🏛

Otto Wagner *(see pp56–9)* designed and built this railway station for the imperial family and royal guests in 1899. The lovely building is in the shape of a white cube with green ironwork and a copper dome. Its waiting room is decorated with wood and glass panelling, a peach and russet asymmetrical carpet and a marble and brass fireplace. The cupola is decorated with glass and gilt flower and leaf motifs.

Wagner built the pavilion without a commission from the emperor in an attempt to showcase his work. Unfortunately, Franz Joseph used the station only twice.

The Hofpavillon Hietzing

㉒ Werkbund-siedlung

Jagdschlossgasse, Veitingergasse and Woinovichgasse, Hietzing. 🚌 54B, 55B. 🚉 62.

In the 13th district you can find the 30 or so fascinating "model" houses of the *Werkbundsiedlung* (housing estate) built in the early 1930s for the municipality by some of Europe's leading architects. They are neither beautiful nor lavish, since the idea was to produce a formula for cheap two-bedroom homes that were plain and functional. No. 19 Woinovichgasse is by Adolf Loos *(see p94)* and Nos. 83–5 Veitingergasse are by Josef Hoffmann *(see p58)*. Each architect had to design a single building, placed side by side with the rest in order to evaluate the different qualities of each. Although intended to be temporary, they have luckily survived.

㉓ Lainzer Tiergarten

Lainzer Tiergarten, Hietzing. Tiergarten: **Tel** 400049200. 🚌 55A. 🚉 60. **Open** mid-Feb–mid-Nov 8am–dusk daily. 🏛 Hermesvilla: **Closed** to the public.

The Lainzer Tiergarten is a former Habsburg hunting ground which has been converted into an immense nature reserve in the Vienna Woods *(see p178)*. The Tiergarten was opened to the public in 1923 and is still encircled by its 24-km (15-mile) stone wall, protecting its herds of deer and wild boar. There are three restaurants in the park and scenic viewing posts overlooking the favourite feeding areas for the wild boar, bighorn sheep, deer and elk. There is also a large bat habitat. From the entrance, a 15-minute walk along paths through woods

Hermesvilla in the grounds of the Lainzer Tiergarten

and meadows brings you to the Hermesvilla, a favourite summer retreat of the imperial family. The interior of the Hermesvilla is currently closed to the public.

㉔ Wotruba-Kirche

Georgsgasse/Rysergasse, Mauer. **Tel** 8885003. 🚌 60A. **Open** 2–8pm Sat, 9am–4:30pm Sun & hols **Tel** 0650 3324833 to make an appointment to see the church.

Built between 1965 and 1976 in uncompromisingly modern style, this church stands on a hillside very close to the Vienna Woods. It consists of a pile of uneven rectangular concrete slabs and glass panels, some of the latter rising to the full height of the church. They provide its principal lighting and views for the congregation out on to the woods and hills. The building is raw in style, but powerful and compact. Designed by the sculptor Fritz Wotruba (1907–75), the church looks different from every angle and has a strong sculptural quality. It accommodates a congregation of up to 250.

The exterior of the Wotruba-Kirche by Fritz Wotruba, not unlike a modern sculpture

㉑ Schönbrunn Palace and Gardens

The former summer residence of the imperial family is named for a beautiful spring that was found on this site. An earlier hunting lodge was destroyed by the Turks, so Leopold I asked Johann Bernhard Fischer von Erlach to design a grand Baroque residence here in 1695. However, it was not until Maria Theresa employed Nikolaus Pacassi in the mid-18th century that the project was completed. The strict symmetry of the architecture is complemented by the gardens, with their fountains and statues framed by trees and alleyways.

KEY

① Theatre
② Orangery
③ Obelisk Cascade
④ Public swimming pool
⑤ Japanese Gardens
⑥ Hietzing Gate

Main entrance

Maze
The maze was a favourite element of many European stately gardens and this one at Schönbrunn provides a fun detour for visitors.

★ Coach Museum
The former Winter Riding School houses the coaches, sleighs and sedan chairs that were used to transport the imperial family.

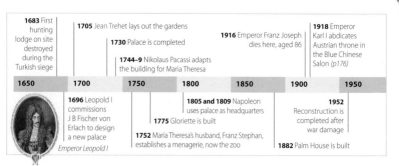

1650	1700	1750	1800	1850	1900	1950

1683 First hunting lodge on site destroyed during the Turkish siege

1705 Jean Trehet lays out the gardens

1730 Palace is completed

1744–9 Nikolaus Pacassi adapts the building for Maria Theresa

1916 Emperor Franz Joseph dies here, aged 86

1918 Emperor Karl I abdicates Austrian throne in the Blue Chinese Salon (p176)

1696 Leopold I commissions J B Fischer von Erlach to design a new palace
Emperor Leopold I

1805 and 1809 Napoleon uses palace as headquarters

1775 Gloriette is built

1752 Maria Theresa's husband, Franz Stephan, establishes a menagerie, now the zoo

1952 Reconstruction is completed after war damage

1882 Palm House is built

Neptune Fountain
This exuberant fountain and basin, at the foot of the hill, was sculpted in 1780 by Franz Anton Zauner.

★ **Gloriette**
This Neo-Classical arcade, designed by Ferdinand von Hohenberg and built in 1775, is the crowning glory of the hill behind the palace.

Schönbrunn Zoo
Founded in 1752 by Franz Stephan, the historic zoo has an octagonal pavilion.

★ **Palm House**
A vast collection of exotic plants flourishes in the magnificent tropical greenhouse erected in 1882.

Façade of Schönbrunn Palace seen from the gardens

Inside Schönbrunn Palace

The Rococo decorative schemes devised by Nikolaus Pacassi dominate the Schönbrunn state rooms, where white panelling, often adorned with gilded ornamental framework, tends to prevail. The rooms vary from extremely sumptuous – such as the Millionenzimmer, panelled with fig wood inlaid with Persian miniatures – to the quite plain apartments occupied by Franz Joseph and Empress Elisabeth.

★ Round Chinese Cabinet
Maria Theresa used this room for private discussions with her State Chancellor. The walls are adorned with lacquered panels and vases.

★ Great Gallery
Once the venue for imperial banquets, the gallery was used for state receptions until 1994.

Hidden staircase which leads to the apartment of the State Chancellor on the floor above and was used for access to secret conferences.

Blue Chinese Salon
The room where Karl I abdicated in 1918 has hand-painted wallpaper with blue insets showing Chinese scenes.

Napoleon Room

Millionenzimmer

Memorial Room

First floor

★ Vieux-Lacque Room
During her widowhood, Maria Theresa lived in this room, which is decorated with exquisite oriental lacquered panels.

Main entrance

Large Rosa Room
Landscape scenes of Switzerland and northern Italy by Joseph Rosa give this room its name. The paintings are surrounded by Rococo gilded panels.

Breakfast Room
The imperial family's breakfast room has white wood panelling inlaid with appliqué floral designs worked by Maria Theresa and her daughters.

The Blue Staircase (so-called due to its original decorative scheme) leads to the entrance for guided tours of state rooms.

Room Guide

The state rooms open to the public are on the first floor. The suite of rooms to the right of the Blue Staircase were occupied by Franz Joseph and Elisabeth. Two galleries divide these from rooms in the east wing, which include Maria Theresa's bedroom and rooms used by Grand Duke Karl. Two guided tours, the Imperial and the Grand Tour, take visitors through several rooms.

Key

- ☐ Franz Joseph's apartments
- ▦ Empress Elisabeth's apartments
- ☐ Ceremonial and reception rooms
- ▦ Maria Theresa's rooms
- ☐ Grand Duke Karl's rooms
- ▦ Non-exhibition space

Portrait of Napoleon

Portrait of Maria Louisa

Maria Louisa and the King of Rome

After Napoleon's fall from power, his young son by his Austrian wife Maria Louisa was kept a virtual prisoner in Schönbrunn Palace. In 1832 at the age of 21, after a lonely childhood, he died of consumption in what is known as the Napoleon Room. He was called the Duke of Reichstadt, or the King of Rome, and the Memorial Room contains his portrait as a five-year-old and his effigy. There is also a stuffed crested larch under a glass dome; the unhappy boy claimed that he never had a single friend in the palace apart from this bird.

Day Trips from Vienna

Within an hour or two's journey from Vienna there is an astonishing range of countryside, from Hungarian-style plains to Alpine mountains, majestic rivers and idyllic lakes. Vienna is at the centre of Austria's wine-growing country and is surrounded by picturesque towns and villages, among which stand historic castles and churches. All the sights are accessible by bus or train and visits to Baden and Mayerling can easily be combined on one trip.

Vienna Woods, a popular recreation area and great place for long walks

❶ Mayerling and the Vienna Woods

Vienna Sightseeing organizes trips *(see p251)*. 🚌 360 from Opera to Baden, then 459 to Mayerling Altes Jagdschloss and Heiligenkreuz. Ⓢ R2249 from Hauptbahnhof to Baden, then bus 459 to Mayerling. Mayerling Chapel: **Tel** 02258 2275. **Open** 2 Jan–31 Mar: 9am–5pm Sat, Sun & hols; Apr–1 Jan: 9am–5pm daily. **Closed** Good Fri & Holy Sat. Heiligenkreuz Abbey: **Tel** 0225 887030. **Open** daily for tours. 10am, 11am, 2pm, 3pm & 4pm Mon–Sat, 11am, 2pm, 3pm & 4pm Sun & hols. **Closed** Good Fri & 24 Dec. **W stift-heiligenkreuz.org**

The Vienna Woods extend from the western bounds of the city towards the lower slopes of the Alps. The woods make excellent walking country: a turn around the Lainzer Tiergarten *(see p173)* makes a convenient half- or full-day outing from Vienna.

The Mayerling hunting lodge, now the site of a chapel, was the scene in 1889 of the double suicide of Archduke Rudolf *(see p34)* and his 17-year-old lover Mary Vetsera, daughter of the diplomat Baron Albin Vetsera. Their tragic deaths shook the Austro-Hungarian empire. After his son's death, the Emperor Franz Joseph gave the hunting lodge to a Carmelite convent and it was completely rebuilt.

A few miles north of Mayerling is the medieval Cistercian abbey of Heiligenkreuz. It is the oldest continuously inhabited Cistercian monastery in the world. Inside is a 12th-century nave and a 13th-century chapter house. Fine Baroque features include the bell tower and Trinity Column. The abbey houses the tombs of 13 of the Babenbergs who ruled in Austria during the medieval period *(see pp24–5)*.

❷ Baden

🚌 360 from Karlsplatz/Oper. Ⓢ S2 or R2335 or 2337 from Hauptbahnhof. Badner Bahn (WLB) from Karlsplatz/Oper. **Tel** 02252 22600600. **W badenonline.at**

South of Vienna are several spas and wine-growing towns in the southern Vienna Woods. The most famous is Baden (or Baden bei Wien), a spa with curative hot springs dating from Roman times. As well as bathing in sulphurous water and mud to treat rheumatism, you can enjoy hot pools of 36°C (97°F).

In the early 19th century Baden was popular with the Imperial Court of Vienna. Then many elegant Biedermeier villas, baths, town houses and a square were built, and the gardens of the Kurpark laid out. The park extends from the town centre to the Vienna Woods and has a rose garden and a memorial museum to Beethoven and Mozart. Today you can sample local wines in Baden's restaurants.

❸ Schloss Hof

🚌 Shuttle bus Sat, Sun & hols from Marchegg station, Hop-on, Hop-off Sat, Sun & hols from Vienna Hilton or Wien Mitte. **W viennasightseeing.at** Schloss Hof: **Open** Apr–Oct: 10am–6pm daily; Nov–Mar: 10am–4pm Sat, Sun & hols. **Tel** 02285 20000. **W schlosshof.at**

Now restored, Schloss Hof is well worth a visit. In 1725 Prince Eugene made it his principal country seat and laid out the present formal garden. Extended a generation later under Empress Maria Theresa, the palace contains private and state rooms from both periods.

Schloss Esterházy, the 17th-century residence of the Esterházy princes

Day Trips from Vienna

1. Mayerling and the Vienna Woods
2. Baden
3. Schloss Hof
4. Eisenstadt
5. Rust and Lake Neusiedl
6. Mariazell
7. River Trip from Krems to Melk

Key

- City centre
- Greater Vienna
- Motorway
- Major road
- Minor road
- Railway
- International border

0 kilometres 25

0 miles 25

❹ Eisenstadt

🚌 566 from Hauptbahnhof. 🚆 REX 2627. ℹ️ 02682 630040. Schloss Esterházy: **Tel** 02682 630047600. **Open** 15 Mar–11 Nov: 10am– 6pm daily; 15 Nov–30 Dec: 10am–5pm Fri– Sun & hols. 📷 only. Haydn Haus: **Tel** 02682 7196000. **Open** Mar–May & Oct–mid-Nov: 9am–5pm Tue–Sat, 10am–5pm Sun & hols; Jun–Sep: 9am– 5pm Mon–Sat, 10am–5pm Sun & hols. Jewish Museum: **Tel** 02682 65145. **Open** 2 May–26 Oct: 10am–5pm Tue– Sun; 27 Oct–1 May: 9am–4pm Mon– Thu & 9am–1pm Fri (for groups only by appt). **Closed** 21 Dec–3 Jan. 🌐 **eisenstadt-tourismus.at**

Schloss Esterházy, built for Prince Paul Esterházy in 1663–73, lies in Eisenstadt. It contains the Haydn-saal, a great hall of state in which Joseph Haydn (see pp40–41) conducted the prince's orchestra. His former home (Haydn Haus) on Haydngasse is now a museum. Also nearby is a Jewish Museum.

❺ Rust and Lake Neusiedl

🚌 566 from Hauptbahnhof; 566 from Eisenstadt. ℹ️ 07909100.

Lake Neusiedl, part of which is in Hungary, is surrounded by reeds, the home of dozens of species of wild birds. The reeds are used locally for crafts from thatching to basketwork. Around the lake are several wine villages and resorts; the prettiest is Rust, known for its storks' nests.

❻ Mariazell

🚌 552 or 1130 from Hauptbahnhof. 🚆 from Westbahnhof, change at St Pölten to Mariazell alpine railway. ℹ️ 03882 3945. Basilica: **Open** Nov–Apr: 7:30am–7:15pm daily; May–Oct: 6am–8pm Sun–Fri, 7am–9:30pm Sat. 📷 **Tel** 03882 25950 for tours. Steam tram: **Tel** 03882 3014. **Open** May–Oct 9:30am–4:30pm hourly Sat, Sun & hols.

The Mariazell alpine railway takes visitors from St Pölten to Mariazell. The town has long been the main Catholic pilgrim site of Central Europe, to which a Gothic and Baroque basilica bear witness. Inside the basilica, which was enlarged in the 17th century, is a wealth of Baroque stucco, painting and decoration. The treasury also forms part of the church.

A cable car up the mountain leaves every 20 minutes from the town centre. An additional attraction in summer is to ride the world's oldest steam tram. It was built in 1884, and runs between Mariazell railway station and a nearby lake.

❼ River Trip from Krems to Melk

See pp180–81.

The town of Mariazell, an important Marian shrine since 1377, located in the northern Alps

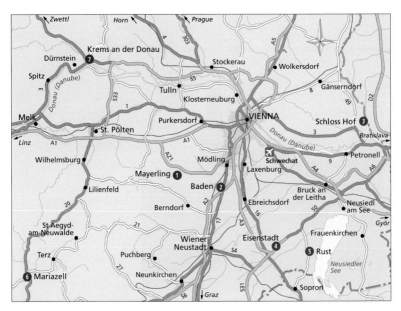

❼ River Trip from Krems to Melk

Some 80 km (50 miles) west of Vienna is one of the most magnificent stretches of river scenery in Europe. Castles, churches and wine-producing villages rise up on either side of the Danube valley and breathtaking views unfold. Redolent with history (it has been settled for over 30,000 years), this stretch from Krems to Melk is called the Wachau. A river trip is the best way to take in the landmarks and scenery, either with one of the organized tours, or independently *(see box)*.

④ The perfectly preserved medieval town of Dürnstein

Krems to Dürnstein

The beautiful Renaissance town of Stein has in modern times merged into one with Krems, which has a medieval centre ①. At the end of Steinerstrasse is the house of the Baroque artist Kremser Schmidt. Climb one of the narrow hillside streets and look across the Danube for a fine view of Göttweig Abbey ②, an excellent example of Austrian Baroque, and in the 17th century a centre of the Counter-Reformation. You can also see the small town of Mautern ③, which developed

from a 1st-century Roman fortification, and now boasts the gourmet restaurant Landhaus Bacher in Südtirolerplatz.

Board a river boat in Krems. After about 8 km (5 miles) you pass the medieval town of Dürnstein ④, with a Baroque church overlooked by the ruins of a castle. From 1192 to 1193, after his return from the Third Crusade, England's King Richard the Lionheart was held prisoner in the castle by Duke Leopold V of Babenberg *(see p24)*. He was released only on payment of a huge ransom. Dürnstein has conserved much of its medieval and Baroque character and has splendid river views. Side streets lead to charming river walks. A separate visit is advisable if you want to see the town at leisure.

Wine-producing towns from Rossatz to Wösendorf

On the bank opposite Dürnstein lies Rossatz ⑤, a former busy port that has been making wine for centuries. Neolithic and Roman remains found here testify to early settlement. In the 10th century the town belonged to a Bavarian convent, but passed to the Babenbergs and became part of

⑦ The church at Weissenkirchen, which was fortified to hold off the Turks

0 km   5

0 miles   3

Key

— Railway line

〜 River

▬ Major road

▭ Minor road

their Austrian domain. The Renaissance castle and Gothic church were redeveloped in the Baroque style around 1700.

At Weissenkirchen ⑥ the church dates mainly from the 15th and 16th centuries. The town is known for its wine, as are Joching ⑦ and Wösendorf ⑧.

⑳ The Benedictine abbey of Melk dominates the river and town

Spitz to Aggsbachdorf

Spitz ⑫ is another pretty wine town and was a Protestant stronghold during the Reformation. It lies at the foot of the 1,000-Eimer Berg (1,000-Bucket Mountain), so called because it is claimed that in a good year the vine-clad hills can produce enough wine to fill 1,000 buckets. Further on is a wall-like rocky precipice jutting out from the bank, the Teufelsmauer or Devil's Wall ⑬, which has given rise to a number of legends. At Schwallenbach ⑭ the church was rebuilt after the Bohemians devastated the village in 1463. Although you cannot see it from the boat, you will pass very close to the village of Willendorf ⑮, famous for the prehistoric findings made nearby, including the statue Venus of Willendorf *(see pp22 and 130)*.

Aggstein ⑯ has a ruined castle high above the river. Jörg Scheck von Wald, follower of Duke Albrecht I, rebuilt and enlarged the original castle in 1429. Legend has it that he referred to a rock, placed at the highest point of the castle, as his rose garden. He would force his imprisoned enemies to leap to their deaths if the ransom he demanded failed to arrive. Aggsbachdorf ⑰ was settled by the Romans in the 2nd century and owned by the Kuenringer robber-barons during the Middle Ages.

Schönbühel Castle to Melk

The picturesque castle of Schönbühel ⑱ stands on a rocky outcrop overlooking the Danube. Although early records date it to the 9th century, its present form is early 19th-century. Further on, at the mouth of the 70-km long

(43-mile) River Pielach ⑲, 30 Bronze Age tombs and the foundations of a Roman tower have been excavated.

The high point of the trip is the Benedictine abbey of Melk ⑳. The pretty town has Renaissance houses, little streets, old towers and the remnants of a city wall built in the Middle Ages. The Baroque abbey, where Umberto Eco's novel *The Name of the Rose* begins and ends, is a treasure trove of paintings, sculptures and decorative art. The great library contains 2,000 volumes from the 9th to the 15th centuries alone. The church has a magnificent organ and an odd display of skeletons dressed in luxurious materials inside glass coffins.

⑯ The ruined castle above the river at Aggstein

Churches and ruins

Clearly visible on top of a hill, the fortified Church of St Michael ⑨ was built between 1500 and 1523. An unusual architectural detail is the stone hares on its tower. Local folklore tells how so much snow fell here once that hares were able to leap onto the roof.

On the same side of the river is a ruined arch on a hill, Das Rote Tor ⑩, a fragment of a 14th-century gate through which Swedish soldiers walked on their way to Spitz in 1645 during the Thirty Years' War *(see p27)*. The town of Mitterarnsdorf ⑪ has Roman remains.

Tips for Independent Travellers

Starting points: Krems, Dürnstein, Melk or any river trip boarding point. River trip tickets are on sale at these points.

W ddsg-blue-danube.at

Getting there: Take the train from Franz-Josefs-Bahnhof to Krems or Dürnstein. For Melk, depart from Westbahnhof.

Stopping-off points: Dürnstein has restaurants and shops.

Melk Abbey Tel 02752 5550.

Open Palm Sunday–1st Sun after All Souls: 9am–4:30pm (May–Sep: 9am–5:30pm). ☑ in English: May–Oct 10:55am & 2:55pm.

Cycling: A cycle path runs along the Danube. Hire bikes at Krems, Melk, Spitz or Dürnstein train stations (reduction with train ticket), or from river trip boarding points. Take your passport for identification. W stiftmelk.at

THREE GUIDED WALKS

Vienna is a comparatively small city, with most main attractions within walking distance of each other. All six sightseeing areas in this guide have a suggested short walk marked on a Street-by-Street map. Yet the city's suburbs are also worth exploring on foot. The following guided walks take you through some of the best walking areas in and around the city, all easily accessible by public transport. The first walk meanders through the city itself. Starting in the Stadtpark, it continues past the Karlskirche to the elegant Wagner Apartments and the colourful Naschmarkt on the Linke Wienzeile. Hietzing, on the western edge of the grounds of Schönbrunn Palace, is our second walk.

The former village's quiet streets are lined with an interesting mix of Biedermeier and Jugendstil villas. Towards the end of the walk is Schönbrunn Palace Park, with an area of woodland and the more formally planted Botanical Garden. The third walk takes you to the old wine village of Grinzing, with its many *Heurigen*. The route goes through Heiligenstadt, where there are a number of buildings by well-known 20th-century architects. In addition to the walks that are suggested on these pages, there are signposted routes through the Vienna Woods and the Prater, marked *Stadtwanderwege*. For details of these, visit or contact the Vienna Tourist Board offices *(see p238)*.

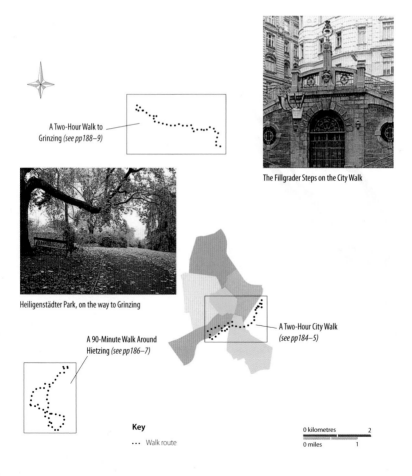

A Two-Hour Walk to Grinzing *(see pp188–9)*

The Fillgrader Steps on the City Walk

Heiligenstädter Park, on the way to Grinzing

A 90-Minute Walk Around Hietzing *(see pp186–7)*

A Two-Hour City Walk *(see pp184–5)*

Key

··· Walk route

0 kilometres 2

0 miles 1

◀ The Strauss Monument, the most photographed sight in Vienna

A Two-Hour City Walk

This walk skirts the southwestern perimeter of the inner city, following part of the course of the River Wien. It begins with a leisurely stroll through the Stadtpark, which was laid out in English landscape style when the Ringstrasse was built (*see p34*). Continuing past Schwarzenbergplatz and Karlsplatz through the lively Naschmarkt, it ends with a glance at some masterpieces of Jugendstil architecture on the Linke Wienzeile.

The Stadtpark

Begin the walk at the entrance to the Stadtpark (*see p167*) opposite Weihburggasse. Almost facing you is an impressive side entrance ① with sculpted portals, which was designed between 1857 and 1862.

On the city side, the park contains many monuments to musicians and artists. The first is the gilded statue of Johann Strauss II (*see p41*) playing his violin (1921). The most popular spot in Vienna for selfies, the bronze statue has twice been regilded ②. Go left past this monument, and left again, into a paved circular seating area with a fountain dedicated to the Sprite of the Danube ③. Turn right out of this area and you come to an iron bridge across the River Wien, from the middle of which you get a view of the embankments ④.

Walk back to the nearby lake ⑤. On its southern side a statue of the Viennese landscape painter Emil Jakob Schindler (1895) ⑥ sits in the bushes. Follow the path until it peters out into a culvert then go left across the bridge. Turn left again until you come

to a monument to Franz Schubert (1872) by Carl Kundmann ⑦. Take the path past the lake and turn right at the clocktower. The painter Hans Makart, who dominated the visual arts in Vienna in the 1870s and 1880s, strikes a rhetorical pose in Viktor Tilgner's 1898 statue ⑧. Walk on past the entrance to the park. On the right is the bust of Franz Lehár, composer of *The Merry Widow* ⑨. Walk towards the Kursalon ⑩, which opened for concerts, balls and waltzes in the 1860s.

⑪ Jugendstil gate in the Stadtpark, built in 1903–4 as part of the flood defences along the river

Continue past the Kursalon, leaving the park through one of the Jugendstil gates (*see p59*) ⑪.

⑯ Statue of Johannes Brahms (1908) by Rudolf Weyr, in the Ressel Park

Tips for Walkers

Starting point: Weihburggasse Tram 2 (on Parkring).
Length: 3 km (1½ miles).
Getting there: Tram 2; Stubentor U-Bahn; or bus 3A, then walk.
Stopping-off points: The Kursalon in the Stadtpark serves tea, coffee and cakes on the terrace and has a beer garden to one side. There are also many benches where you can rest. There are cafés in Ressel Park and the Naschmarkt; towards the end of the walk you will find Café Sperl on Gumpendorfer Strasse.

Schwarzenbergplatz

Walk straight ahead, crossing the road into Lothringerstrasse. A monument to Beethoven (1880), showing the composer surrounded by figures alluding to the Ninth Symphony, stands on the right ⑫. Cross the road to the Konzerthaus (1912–13), home to the Vienna Symphony Orchestra *(see p228)* ⑬.

Cross the busy intersection to get a striking vista of Schwarzenbergplatz to your left. At the end of it is a fountain, erected in 1873 to celebrate the city's supply of pure drinking water, which comes from the mountains. Behind it is the Memorial to the Red Army, which liberated Austria in 1945 ⑭.

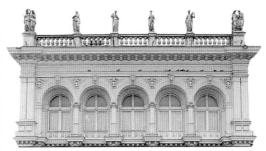

⑩ The Neo-Renaissance Kursalon

road to look at Otto Wagner's Apartments *(see p143)* with golden medallions by Kolo Moser at No. 38 ㉑, and the Majolikahaus at No. 40, so called because of its floral tiles ㉒. As you turn into Köstlergasse alongside No. 38 it is worth pausing to admire the entrance.

⑰ Confession box, Karlskirche

Ressel Park

Continue along Lothringerstrasse, past the Wien Museum Karlsplatz *(see p150)* ⑮, into Ressel Park. On the left is a statue by Rudolf Weyr of Brahms with his muse at his feet (1908) ⑯. Look left past Brahms to the Karlskirche *(see pp148–9)* ⑰. Continue, noting Otto Wagner's pavilions *(see p150)* at road level ⑱. Pass the Neo-Classical Technical High School ⑲ to leave the park. Cross Wiedner Hauptstrasse, go straight ahead then left into Operngasse, crossing the road. Walk through Bärenmühlendurchgang

passage in the building facing you and cross the road into the Naschmarkt ⑳.

Naschmarkt

A lively food market *(see p142)*, originally held in the Karlsplatz, moved here after this part of the river was paved over in the late 19th century. It is a good vantage point from which to admire the elegant 19th-century buildings along the left bank, or Linke Wienzeile. Leave the market and cross the

㉕ Papageno Gate of the Theater an der Wien

Gumpendorfer Strasse

Turn right at the end of Köstlergasse and walk up Gumpendorfer Strasse. Look left up Fillgradergasse for a glimpse of the Fillgrader Steps ㉓. Continue past the historic Café Sperl *(see p60)*, once the haunt of the composer Lehár ㉔. Turn right into Millöcker-gasse to see the famous Papageno Gate of the Theater an der Wien *(see p142)* ㉕. The sculpture above the entrance shows the theatre's first owner, Emanuel Schikaneder, in the character of Papageno from Mozart's *The Magic Flute*. Continue down Millöckergasse to the Linke Wienzeile. Bear left, passing the Secession Building *(see p142)* ㉖, and go on to Karlsplatz U-Bahn.

Key

• • • Walk route

A 90-Minute Walk Around Hietzing

The former village of Hietzing runs along the western edge of the extensive grounds of Schönbrunn Palace (see pp174–7). In Maria Theresa's time this was a fashionable area where the nobility spent their summers; later it became a suburb for the wealthy middle classes. The quiet streets contain a marvellous mix of Biedermeier and Jugendstil villas, while the square around the parish church retains an intimate small-town atmosphere.

⑥ The Kaiserstöckl opposite the Park Hotel, now a post office

From the station to Am Platz

Take the Hadikgasse exit from Hietzing U-Bahn ① and cross the tram tracks and road to Kennedybrücke. Turn right down Hadikgasse and after a minute you arrive at Otto-Wagner-Hofpavillon Hietzing (see p173) ②, a former station designed for the use of the imperial family when they were at Schönbrunn. Retrace your steps to the U-Bahn and cross the road into Hietzinger Hauptstrasse. Notice the attic of No. 6 with cherubs hugging the columns. The building dates from 1901–2, but the lower storey has been altered to accommodate shops ③. On your left through

the railings are long avenues of trees at the side of Schönbrunn ④. Just across the road is the Park Hotel, its ochre façade echoing that of the palace buildings ⑤. Facing it is the Kaiserstöckl (1770) or Emperor's Pavilion ⑥. Today it is a post office, but it used to be the holiday home of Maria Theresa's foreign ministers. Continue to Am Platz with its plague column dating from 1730 ⑦. Nearby is the parish church of Maria Geburt ⑧, originally built in the 13th century and remodelled in the 17th century. The Baroque interior contains altars by the sculptor Matthias Steindl and ceiling frescoes by Georg Greiner. The church was used by Maria Theresa when she was in residence at Schönbrunn, and her box can be seen in the right-hand wall of the choir. In front of the church stands a statue of Franz Joseph's brother Maximilian, the Emperor of Mexico, who

⑤ Façade of the Park Hotel

Key

• • • Walk route

| 0 metres | 250 |
| 0 yards | 250 |

⑧ Elaborate altar by Matthias Steindl in the Maria-Geburt-Kirche

Tips for Walkers

Starting point: Hietzing U-Bahn.
Length: 5 km (3 miles).
Getting there: U-Bahn U4; tram 10, 58, 60; bus 51A, 56B, 58B, 156B. **Note:** On Sundays you may need to retrace your steps a short distance if the Maxing Gate is locked. **Stopping-off points:** the Café am Platz in Hietzing is a pleasant place for a coffee. Bezirksmuseum Hietzing: **Open** 2–6pm Wed, 2–5pm Sat. **Closed** Jul–Aug. Schönbrunn Palace and Park: see pp174–7. Villa Primavesi: **Closed** to public.

was executed in 1867 ⑨. Nearby is a Neo-Classical building housing the Bezirksmuseum Hietzing ⑩; outside it is Vienna's last gas lamp.

Trauttmansdorffgasse and Gloriettegasse

Turn left into Maxingstrasse, named after Maximilian, then right into Altgasse. Almost facing Fasholdgasse is an old *Heuriger*, a Biedermeier building with ochre walls ⑪.

⑲ Detail from the majolica façade of the Lebkuchenhaus

road, at No. 27 is a house where the composer Alban Berg *(see p41)* once lived ⑬. Nos. 48 and 50 are contrasting examples of Viennese turn-of-the-century architecture ⑭. More examples of Biedermeier style can be seen at Nos. 54 and 56 ⑮. At the end of the road, turn right into Gloriettegasse. On the right at Nos. 14 and 16 is a villa with monumental sculpted figures resting in the pediments, built in 1913–15 by Josef Hoffmann for the financier Robert Primavesi ⑯. Cross the road to pass a terrace of Biedermeier houses – Nos. 38 and 40 have lunettes above the windows ⑰. No. 21 is the Villa Schopp, designed by Friedrich Ohmann in 1901–2 ⑱. Turn left down Wattmanngasse to see No. 29, the extraordinary Lebkuchenhaus (Gingerbread House) ⑲, so-called because of its dark brown majolica decoration. It was built in 1914 to designs by a pupil of Otto Wagner *(see pp56–9)*. Turn back into Gloriettegasse. At its southern junction with Wattmann-gasse, at No. 9, is the house that

Turn down Fasholdgasse into Trautt-mansdorffgasse, a street full of interesting houses. No. 40 is a beautifully restored, long and low Biedermeier villa ⑫, while across the

belonged to Katharina Schratt, an actress and confidante of Emperor Franz Joseph during his later years. It is said that the Emperor was in the habit of arriving here for breakfast ⑳.

Maxing Park and Schönbrunn Park

Walk to the end of Gloriette-gasse, then turn right up Maxingstrasse and cross the road at Maxing Park. A half-hour detour a little further up the hill takes you to Hietzing cemetery, which contains the graves of Otto Wagner, Gustav Klimt, Kolo Moser and Franz Grillparzer, among others. Alternatively, enter Maxing Park ㉑ and follow the main path upwards to the right. At the top, go through the gates marked *Zum Tiergarten Schönbrunn*, passing the forestry research institute on your left. Although you are actually in the grounds of Schönbrunn, this heavily wooded area feels very remote from the formal gardens and you may catch a glimpse of deer. At the crossroads in the path turn left, signposted to the Botanical Garden. You soon arrive at a little wooden hut, which was Crown Prince Rudolf's playhouse ㉒.

The path eventually leads to the formally planted Botanical Garden ㉓, which was laid out in 1848 under Emperor Franz I. Take the path through the garden, keeping to the boundary wall with Hietzing. Exit into Maxingstrasse (this gate may be locked on Sundays) and continue north. At No. 18 is the house where Johann Strauss II wrote *Die Fledermaus* in 1874 ㉔. Carry on north along Maxingstrasse and retrace your steps to Hietzing U-Bahn.

⑯ Sculpted figure in a pediment of the Villa Primavesi

For keys to symbols *see back flap*

A Two-Hour Walk to Grinzing

This walk through part of Vienna's 19th district begins at the site of one of the most important monuments of 20th-century Vienna, the public housing development of the Karl-Marx-Hof. It then takes you through a pretty 19th-century park to the old wine village of Grinzing. Although the village suffered destruction at the hands of the Turks in 1529 and 1683 and from Napoleon's army in 1809, and is now facing changes as a result of modern tourism, its main street preserves its charm.

⑮ Façade of the 16th-century Reinprecht *Heuriger*

Karl-Marx-Hof to Heiligenstädter Park

Facing you as you step out of Heiligenstadt station is the long ochre, terracotta and mauve façade of the Karl-Marx-Hof *(see p163)*, a huge housing project designed by the city architect Karl Ehn and built from 1927 to 1930 during the Red Vienna period ①. It sprawls for 1.2 km (3/4 mile) and contains 1,272 flats.

Cross the road and pass through one of the four arches into 12 Februar Platz to see the main façade from the other side. On the keystone of each arch stands a large figure sculpted by Joseph Riedl (1928) ②.

① Figure on the Karl-Marx-Hof

Continue through the square, past a statue (1928) by Otto Hofner of a man sowing seeds ③, and you come to Heiligenstädter Strasse. Turn right, cross the road at the second pedestrian crossing and walk through the square opening in the building facing you. Go up the steps and take the path on the left into Heiligenstädter Park. When you come to a fork, take the left path that winds up a hill, going through woods. Turn right at the top into the formal part of the park ④. From here, you get a good view of the vine-clad slopes of the Kahlenberg ⑤.

Steinfeldgasse

Take the second small path on the right, which descends gradually into Steinfeldgasse,

where there is a cluster of houses built by the Secessionist designer Josef Hoffmann. The first one you come to is the Villa Moser-Moll at Nos. 6–8, designed for Carl Moll and Kolo Moser ⑥. Next to it is the Villa Spitzer ⑦, then the more classical Villa Ast, built in 1909–11 ⑧. Where Steinfeldgasse meets Wollergasse is the Villa Henneberg of 1901 ⑨, and at

No. 10 Wollergasse ⑩ is the Moll House II of 1906–7, with charming timber detail.

Steinfeldgasse to Grinzinger Strasse

At the point where Steinfeldgasse and Wollergasse meet, there is a path leading

④ Views of Kahlenberg can be enjoyed from the top of Heiligenstädter Park

down through some woods. Follow this and descend the steps to the Church of St Michael, Heiligenstadt ⑪, which has striking modern stained-glass windows. Walk past the church, cross Hohe Warte and go up Grinzinger Strasse. You quickly arrive at No. 70, a house visited by Albert Einstein several times ⑫. On the same side of the road is No. 64, the late 18th-century house where Beethoven and the Viennese playwright Franz Grillparzer lodged during the summer of 1808 while Beethoven was composing the Pastoral Symphony ⑬. Continue up Grinzinger Strasse, passing a number of attractive Biedermeier houses, until you arrive at Grinzinger Allee. Turn right past a series of wine gardens and immediately right again to get a quick glimpse of the upper part of Sandgasse, where there are a number of less touristy *Heurigen* ⑭.

Grinzing

Turning back on yourself, towards the centre of Grinzing, climb

Cobenzlgasse, Grinzing's main street

Himmelstrasse ⑲. Continue down Himmelstrasse to No. 35, another *Heuriger*, Das Alte Haus, which has a charming plaque of the Virgin Mary above its door ⑳. There is another such painting at No. 31, which shows a holy man carrying various items ㉑. No. 29 ㉒ is another *Heuriger*, with a tablet to Sepp Fellner, a *Schrammel* musician (see p41) described as "The Schubert of Grinzing". Ironically, at No. 25, a grand building with shields above the doorway, there is a memorial to the real Schubert, described as "The Prince of Song, who loved to tarry in Grinzing" ㉓. Grinzing also has an attractive late Gothic church with a copper cupola and much-restored interior ㉔. Continue down the road to the tram terminus, from where the No. 38 tram goes back to town.

⑰ Courtyard at the Passauer Hof, formerly home to a wine press

Tips for Walkers

Starting point: Heiligenstadt station. **Length:** 3.5 km (2 miles). **Getting there:** Heiligenstadt station is served by U-Bahn line U4, trains S40 and S45 and buses 10A, 11A, 38A and 39A. Tram D stops on Heiligenstädter Strasse. **Stopping-off points:** There are numerous *Heurigen* (usually open from 4pm), coffee shops and restaurants in Grinzing. Avoid the larger *Heurigen* – the smaller ones sell their own wine. Those at the top of Sandgasse are good.

Key

••• Walk route

==== Railway line

Cobenzlgasse, the upper fork of Grinzing's main street. The Reinprecht *Heuriger* at No. 22 Cobenzlgasse is a 16th-century house, the façade of which has a tablet commemorating the composer Robert Stolz ⑮. No. 30 Cobenzlgasse is the Baroque Trummelhof, standing on the site of an 1835 brewery ⑯. Further up on the left, at No. 9, is the Passauer Hof, which contains fragments of a far older, Romanesque building ⑰. It used to house a wine press. On the corner of Cobenzlgasse and Feilergasse is the Altes Presshaus, whose cellar contains an old wine press ⑱.

Turn left into Feilergasse, and you soon come face to face with the impressive white Jugendstil façade of Nos. 41–3

㉑ Plaque of a holy man on the façade of No. 31 Himmelstrasse

TRAVELLERS' NEEDS

WHERE TO STAY

With more than 500 hotels and pensions, Vienna offers accommodation to suit travellers on every budget. From palaces to simple lodgings, it has some of the grandest European city hotels as well as numerous small boarding-houses and self-catering establishments. Hotels are generally larger and better equipped to cater to a mix of business and leisure clientele while Vienna's numerous pensions offer simple bed-and-breakfast accommodation. The hotels on pages 196–9 include a selection of the best boutique, contemporary, family-friendly, luxury and pension accommodation, listed by area and by price category.

Baroque façade of the Mailberger Hof in Stephansdom Quarter *(see p197)*

Where to Look

One of the perks of visiting Vienna is that guests can stay in either grand or modest accommodation right in the city centre. Many of the most famous historic hotels, such as the **Sacher**, **Bristol** and **Imperial** *(see p199)*, are on or just off the Ringstrasse, as are many of the large chain hotels.

There are also a number of less expensive, comfortable hotels and pensions in the city centre, most on fairly quiet side streets. The Museum and Townhall Quarter has some good small hotels and offers affordable lodgings for budget travellers. A few hotels on Vienna's outskirts are also included in the listings.

The **Österreich Werbung** (Austrian Tourist Board) publishes information on over 500 hotels and pensions.

Hotel Prices

As in other cities, Vienna accommodation prices vary according to centrality of location and opulence. Hotels without air conditioning or swimming pools will always be less expensive, as are those even a short tram ride away from the Ring and, most particularly, across the Danube.

Upmarket hotels offer luxurious suites, some taking an entire floor and including a private butler. In general, there are ranges of rooms dubbed "standard" or "deluxe", with size and opulence, as well as a view, determining the prices. Family rooms, some with cooking facilities, are available in price-conscious hotels.

Vienna's low season is November–March (excluding Christmas and New Year) and July–August. Few hotels drop prices in summer, although some lower their winter rates by 25 per cent. Most of the large chain hotels reduce the room tariff during quiet periods and offer weekend specials.

Penthouse suite No. 663 in the Hotel Bristol in Belvedere Quarter *(see p199)*

Hidden Extras

Apart from some five-star hotels, breakfast is included in the tariff for most establishments. Rates will always include taxes such as VAT (or MWSt). Hotels near the airport offer free shuttle service.

Some hotels have private garages and most will suggest a nearby underground car park. It is impossible for guests in central hotels to find parking on the street. Many hotels offer valet parking. Underground hotel parking can easily cost €40 a night.

Opulent lobby of the Imperial in Belvedere Quarter *(see p199)*

Room with contemporary design at Hollmann Beletage, a boutique hotel in Stephansdom Quarter *(see p196)*

With the widespread use of VOIP apps like Skype, few guests make use of in-room phones for international calls, and such calls are expensive. Many hotels offer free Wi-Fi, but others charge by the day.

Many hotels allow pet dogs to stay in the rooms – for a fee.

Facilities

Hotels are rated one to five stars and pensions have a four-star system; a three-star hotel corresponds to a four-star pension. The rating also attempts to cover the quality and ambience of the hotel or pension. Five-star hotels are upmarket and well-run. Some three- and four-star hotels refer to themselves as *Palais*, which equates to a fine town house. At the cheaper end of the scale, small pensions above two stars are often more salubrious than cheap hotels. One- or two-star hotels and pensions are generally very basic and are a good choice for travellers on a budget.

Large hotels have the full range of public rooms – restaurant, bar, coffee shop and lounge. Smaller establishments usually have lounge seating in the foyer. Even if there is no bar, drinks are often served. Almost all hotels and pensions have a breakfast room, with lower-priced establishments serving a continental breakfast and pricier hotels offering hot and cold breakfast buffets.

Hotels that are located in old buildings tend to have a touch of character, and no two bedrooms are the same. The rooms almost always have a phone and usually a TV. Mid-range hotel rooms often have cable TV, a mini-bar and a bathroom with either a shower or bathtub. Many Viennese buildings look onto quiet courtyards so you can select a peaceful room or one with a view.

In the 19th century there was a restriction on building heights. To circumvent the regulation, lower floors were (and still are) called *Hochparterre* and *Mezzanin*. Consequently, guests may find that the "first floor" is actually up three flights of stairs. Additionally, in pensions a communal lift serves the whole building.

The quality of service in the best luxury hotels is as good as anywhere in the world. Wherever you stay, it could be well worth befriending the concierge (an early tip may help) as their local knowledge and contacts are invaluable – from helping guests find interesting restaurants and bars or conjuring tickets for the opera. Most hotel staff speak good English.

How to Book

Easter, May, June, September, October, Christmas and New Year are considered peak season, when accommodation may be fully booked as early as three months in advance – especially if an opera, ballet or conference draws in more than the usual number of foreign visitors.

Vienna hotels offer price incentives to those who book early using the hotel website. Such direct booking saves the hotel commissions on travel websites. There are many general travel websites and hotel websites that will find hotels according to location or price – or for smokers or those with pets or children. **Wiener Tourismusverband** (Vienna Tourist Board), which is located on the corner of Albertinaplatz, Tegethoffstrasse and Meysedergasse, can reserve hotel rooms in advance on your behalf.

The comfortable bar are of the famous Hotel Bristol *(see p199)*

Imposing lobby at Sans Souci in Museum and Townhall Quarter (see p198)

Travelling with Children

An increasing number of hotels in Vienna are family friendly and offer facilities such as bottle sterilizers, cots (some hotels charge extra) and baby-sitting services, as well as family-sized rooms. See pages 197–8 for a selection of family-friendly hotels.

Travellers with Disabilities

"Barrier-free" access has become a major concern for the entire tourist industry in Austria, and hotels make every allowance. A comprehensive booklet on accommodation for the disabled can be downloaded at wien.info/en/travel-info/accessible-vienna

Hostels

Youth hostel organizations such as **Österreichischer Jugendherbergsverband** have premises in Vienna and the **Wiener Tourismusverband**'s youth hostel and camping brochure lists their facilities. Another type of hostel has evolved to appeal to back-packer clients. These newer hostels offer more comfort and amenities like PlayStations and also serve as meeting places

with bars and discos. They often go by the name "city hostel" and only accept online bookings.

Summer Hotels

More expensive than a hostel, but with central locations and of a good standard, are summer rooms in student accommo-dation. About a dozen Vienna "summer hotels" take advantage of empty student rooms from June to September. Prices are about €40–80 per night. **The Wieden** is a popular example.

Camping

Five well-equipped campsites can be found within a radius of 8–15 km (5–9 miles) from the city centre. Sites are equipped with water and electricity connecti-vity. All offer quick transportation into the city centre. Basic shop-ping supplies, as well as bars and restaurants, are on site. For more camping information, contact **Wiener Tourismusverband**, **Camping und Caravaning Club Austria**, and **Österreichischer Camping Club**.

Self-Catering

For those who are keen to "go it alone" there are plenty of self-catering options. **Ferienwoh-nungen Wien** has a range of apartments of various sizes for rent in and around Vienna. It also puts clients directly in touch with the landlord of the property and does not charge commission fees. Some apartments have a combined living and sleeping space. Expect to pay less than the price of a pension.

Private Homes

Staying in private homes is easy with internet-based services such as **Airbnb**. Vienna locations are expanding every day, with single rooms to whole houses available at attractive rates. Renters should exercise all the cautions required of any internet transaction.

Bed-and-breakfast bookings of rooms in private homes can also be done directly online, with photos and virtual tours of the property and rooms.

The entrance of the Westend City Hostel

Chain Hotels

Almost all of the major hotel chains are well represented in Vienna. Marriott hotels include the **Vienna Marriott** *(see p197)*, **Imperial Riding School Renaissance Vienna** *(see p199)* and **Renaissance Wien Hotel**. Other familiar names are **InterContinental** *(see p198)*, **Hilton** and **Hotel Novotel City**, all of which are centrally located.

Chain hotels are often geared up for executive travellers and offer the best range of business services. Room rates tend to vary according to their level of occupancy rather than the season. Examples of chains are **Lindner Hotel Am Belvedere** *(see p197)* and **Radisson Blu Style Hotel** *(see p197)*.

Recommended Hotels

The hotels listed on pages 196–9 are among the best in the historic centre of Vienna and its more bohemian

Elegantly furnished room at the luxurious Hotel Sacher in Opera and Naschmarkt *(see p199)*

outlying districts. They cover a variety of accommodation types in several price categories, ranging from simple pensions and family-friendly hotels to luxury palaces, characterful boutique hotels and contemporary options with minimalist decor and the latest high-tech gadgets. Hotels are listed first by theme, then area and then price.

Throughout the listings some establishments have been highlighted as DK Choice. These offer something particularly special for a memorable stay, such as a historic landmark location, exceptional art or design features, superlative service and amenities, a fantastic spa, outstanding city views, eco-friendly credentials or any combination of these qualities.

DIRECTORY

Where to Look

Österreich Werbung
Zollamtsstrasse 13, 1030.
Tel 588 66 0.
ⓦ austriatourism.com

How to Book

Wiener Tourismusverband
Albertinaplatz 1/ Meysedergasse, 1010.
Map 5 C4. **Tel** 245 55.
ⓦ wien.info

Hostels

Backpacker Hostels
ⓦ back-packer.org
ⓦ gobackpacking.com
ⓦ hostelworld.com

Österreichischer Jugendherbergs-verband
Zelinkagasse 12, 1010.
Map 2 D4.
Tel 533 53 53.
ⓦ oejhv.at

Summer Hotels

Summer Hotels Booking
ⓦ universityrooms. com

The Wieden
Schelleingasse 36, 1040.
Map 4 E1. **Tel** 576 66 76.
ⓦ sommerhotel wieden.at

Camping

Camping und Caravaning Club Austria
Donaustadtstrasse 34, 1220. **Tel** 123 22 22.
ⓦ cca-camping.at

Camping Wien West
Hüttelbergstrasse 80, 1140. **Tel** 9142314.
ⓦ wiencamping.at

Österreichischer Camping Club
Schubertring 1–3, 1010. **Map** 6 D5.
Tel 713 61 51.
ⓦ campingclub.at

Self-Catering

Ferienwohnungen Wien
Schubertgasse 11, 1090.
Map 1 B2.
Tel 699 122 65 721
ⓦ ferienwohnungen wien.com

Private Homes

Airbnb
ⓦ airbnb.com

Bed and Breakfast
ⓦ bedandbreakfast. com

Chain Hotels

Hilton
Am Stadtpark, 1030.
Map 6 F4.
Tel 717 00 0.
ⓦ hilton.com

Hotel Novotel City
Aspernbrückenstrasse 1, 1020. **Map** 1 B5.
Tel 903 03 0.
ⓦ accorhotels.com

Imperial Riding School Reinaissance Vienna
Ungargasse 60, 1030.
Map 4 F1. **Tel** 711 75 0.
ⓦ marriott.com

InterContinental
Johannesgasse 28, 1037.
Map 6 E5. **Tel** 711 22 0.
ⓦ intercontinental.com

Lindner Hotel Am Belvedere
Rennweg 12, 1030.
Map 4 E2. **Tel** 794 77 0.
ⓦ lindnerhotels.com

Radisson Blu Style Hotel
Herrengasse 12, 1010.
Map 5 C3. **Tel** 227 80 0.
ⓦ radissonblu.com

Renaissance Wien Hotel
Ullmannstrasse 71, 1150.
Tel 891 02 0.
ⓦ marriott.com

Vienna Marriott
Parkring 12A, 1010.
Map 6 E4. **Tel** 515 18 0.
ⓦ marriott.com

Where to Stay

Boutique

Stephansdom Quarter

Alma Boutique Hotel €
Hafnersteig 7, 1010
Tel *533 29 61* **Map** 6 E2
W hotel-alma.com
This elegant Art Nouveau hotel is just steps away from the cathedral, in a pedestrian zone.

Hotel Kärntnerhof €
Grashofgasse 4, 1010
Tel *512 19 23* **Map** 6 E3
W karntnerhof.com
Each room has its own style in this 19th-century hotel with an old-fashioned birdcage lift, roof garden and parquet floors. Non-smoking throughout.

Aviano Boutique Hotel €€
Marco-d'Aviano-Gasse 1, 1010
Tel *512 83 30* **Map** 5 C4
W secrethomes.at
This is a good-value B&B in a smart building with traditional Viennese decor.

DK Choice

Hollmann Beletage €€
Köllnerhofgasse 6, 1010
Tel *961 19 60* **Map** 6 E2
W hollmann-beletage.at
With its sleek tangerine and granite decor, and 25 spacious rooms with an array of gadgets, this family-run hotel in a 19th-century building is a true gem. The rooms feature large en-suite bathrooms.

Hotel Lamée €€
Rotenturmstrasse 15, 1010
Tel *532 22 40* **Map** 6 D3
W hotellamee.com
The stark white, uninteresting modern exterior hides spacious and old-world rooms inside, all non-smoking. There's also a roof terrace and a lively bar scene.

DK Choice

The Ring €€€
Kärntner Ring 8, 1010
Tel *221 22* **Map** 6 D5
W theringhotel.com
Behind this hotel's 19th-century façade is a warm interior with sensual fabrics, bold designs and luxurious touches. Individually styled rooms blend historic details with contemporary design. The superb spa offers great views.

Hofburg Quarter

Graben Hotel €€
Dorotheergasse 3, 1010
Tel *512 15 31 0* **Map** 5 C4
W kremslehnerhotels.at
This hotel is very popular and is good value, so book early. The rooms are not overly large, but each has period furniture.

Schottering and Alsergrund

DK Choice

Hotel Boltzmann €
Boltzmanngasse 8, 1090
Tel *354 50 0* **Map** 1 C3
W hotelboltzmann.at
Hotel Boltzmann is in an ideal location for exploring the city on foot. Pleasant courtyard garden, underground parking and attractive prices booking early is advisable. Children friendly.

Museum and Townhall Quarter

Fleming's Deluxe Hotel €€
Josefstädter Strasse 10–12, 1080
Tel *205 99 0* **Map** 1 B5
W flemings-hotels.com
State-of-the-art gadgets and excellent service are found at this up-scale yet child-friendly hotel with sleek and elegant decor.

Hotel Rathaus €€
Lange Gasse 13, 1080
Tel *400 11 22* **Map** 1 B5
W hotel-rathaus-wien.at
This is a design hotel with a wine theme, which is evident in

Artistically furnished room at the Boutique Hotel Stadthalle

everything from the paintings to the cosmetics in the rooms. Rooms are large and quiet. There is a small spa.

The Levante Parliament €€
Auerspergstrasse 9, 1080
Tel *228 28 0* **Map** 1 B5
W thelevante.com
Glass sculptures and photos of dancers prevail here. There are high ceilings, a large courtyard and a small spa that all make for a comfortable stay.

Belvedere Quarter

Hotel Am Konzerthaus €€
Am Heumarkt 35–37, 1030
Tel *716 16 0* **Map** 4 F2
W hotelamkonzerthaus.com
Located amongst Jugendstil landmarks, this arty hotel attracts a sophisticated clientele.

Further Afield

Art Hotel Vienna €
Brandmaygergasse 7–9, 1050
Tel *544 51 08* **Map** 3 B5
W thearthotelvienna.at
The exterior is somewhat dingy, but once inside there is art everywhere. There is no air conditioning, but there is a courtyard, and rooms are a good size.

Hein Boutique Hotel €
Mannswörther Strasse 94, 2320
Tel *707 19 50*
W heinhotel.at
Free shuttles to the nearby airport, fitness rooms and functional, modern design make this hotel popular with those looking for peace and quiet.

DK Choice

Boutique Hotel Stadthalle €€
Hackengasse 20, 1150
Tel *982 4272*
W hotelstadthalle.at
An ivy-clad early 20th-century building in the multicultural 15th district. Some rooms are small, but suites offer garden views. Each room is unique, with colourful accents. Amenities include oils, lotions and candles.

Elegant interior of a deluxe suite at the DO & CO Hotel

Contemporary

Stephansdom Quarter

Hotel Am Stephansplatz €€
Stephansplatz 9, 1010
Tel *534 05 0*   **Map** 6 D3
Ⓦ hotelamstephansplatz.at
Two minutes from the cathedral, this hotel has an uninspiring exterior, however the hip, casual atmosphere, spa, fitness centre and generously sized bathrooms make up for it.

Schick Hotel Am Parkring €€
Parkring 12, 1010
Tel *514 80 0*   **Map** 6 E4
Ⓦ schick-hotels.com
Renowned for its high-quality, the rooms at this hotel have views of Veinna's rooftops. Many rooms also have balconies. All the amenities of a four-star hotel are provided.

DO & CO Hotel €€€
Stephansplatz 12, 1010
Tel *241 88*   **Map** 6 D3
Ⓦ docohotel.com
A stunning curved glass exterior houses superior design and comfort. This place has all the amenities of a luxury hotel, plus a highly rated restaurant on site.

Hofburg Quarter

Pension A und A €
Habsburgergasse 3 Floor M, 1010
Tel *890 51 28*   **Map** 5 C3
Ⓦ pensionaunda.at
A family-run guesthouse offering eight rooms and a deluxe apartment decorated and furnished in minimalist black-and-white.

Das Tigra €€
Tiefer Graben 14–20, 1010
Tel *533 96 41 0*   **Map** 5 C2
Ⓦ hotel-tigra.at
Location is the main attraction at this hotel, which offers friendly service and cycle rental. Reasonably priced for the area.

Museum and Townhall Quarter

Altstadt Vienna €
Kirchengasse 41, 1070
Tel *522 66 66*   **Map** 3 B1
Ⓦ altstadt.at
Art is literally all over the walls here – all 20th century and some collectors' pieces. Young, vibrant staff and excellent location.

Cordial Theaterhotel €
Josefstädter Strasse 22, 1080
Tel *405 36 48*   **Map** 1 B5
Ⓦ cordial.at/wien
The chic, comfortable, but slightly dated, rooms here are inexpensive. Kids are welcome. No smoking.

Hotel Korotan €
Albertgasse 48, 1080
Tel *403 41 93*   **Map** 1 A5
Ⓦ korotan.com
Bright artworks adorn the walls here and a glass front provides a "window" on the city. There are baby-sitting services and a library.

Mercure Josefhof Wien €€
Josefsgasse 4–6, 1080
Tel *404 19*   **Map** 1 B5
Ⓦ josefshof.com
A chain hotel with modern facilities, but also has pure Vienna period charm. Popular with business travellers.

Radisson Blu Style Hotel €€
Herrengasse 12, 1010
Tel *227 80 0*   **Map** 5 C3
Ⓦ radissonblu.com
Luxury chain hotel with a great location and an impressive fusion of modern style and old-world comfort. Ample amenities.

Opera and Naschmarkt

Le Meridien Vienna €€
Robert-Stolz-Platz 1, 1010
Tel *588 90 0*   **Map** 4 D1
Ⓦ lemeridienvienna.com
Luxury chain hotel with large rooms and amenities including

a spa, a swimming pool and a gourmet restaurant. Charming furnishings and wood floors, too.

Belvedere Quarter

Clima Cityhotel €
Theresianumgasse 21A, 1040
Tel *505 16 96*   **Map** 4 E4
Ⓦ climacity-hotel.com
This is a stylish hotel that also contains a gallery displaying contemporary art.

Hotel Daniel €€
Landstrasser Gürtel 5, 1030
Tel *901 31 0*   **Map** 4 F4
Ⓦ hoteldaniel.com/vienna
This smart, minimalist hotel has its own bakery on site. Facilities include iPad and Vespa hire.

Lindner Hotel Am Belvedere €€
Rennweg 12, 1030
Tel *794 77 0*   **Map** 4 E2
Ⓦ lindnerhotels.com
There are high-tech lounges and a small sauna and workout room here, just 4 minutes from Rennweg train station.

Further Afield

Hotel Fabrik €
Gaudenzdorfer Gürtel 73, 1120
Tel *813 28 00*   **Map** 3 A5
Ⓦ hotel-fabrik.at
Once a 19th-century linen factory, this family-run hotel has large rooms with high windows.

Family-Friendly

Stephansdom Quarter

Marc Aurel €
Marc-Aurel Strasse 8, 1010
Tel *533 36 40 0*   **Map** 6 D2
Ⓦ hotel-marcaurel.com
There are extra beds for children in some rooms here, and all have modern bathrooms. Free breakfast.

Hotel Capricorno €€
Schwedenplatz 3–4, 1010
Tel *533 31 04 0*   **Map** 6 E2
Ⓦ schick-hotels.com
One of a handful of Schick Hotels around the city, Capricorno has vibrant, welcoming rooms and communal spaces. Helpful staff.

Mailberger Hof €€
Annagasse 7, 1010
Tel *512 06 41 0*   **Map** 4 E1
Ⓦ mailbergerhof.at
House in a large Baroque house, once the HQ of the Knights of Malta, the Mailberger retains great charm. It is a short walk from the cathedral.

For more information on types of hotels *see pages 192–5*

Individually designed suite at the fashionable Sans Souci

Schottering and Alsergrund

Harmonie €€
Harmoniegasse 5–7, 1090
Tel *317 66 04*   **Map** 1 C3
Ⓦ harmonie-vienna.at
This Best Western chain hotel, a stroll from the Freud museum, has a dance art theme. Family rooms available.

Hotel Mozart €
Julius-Tandler-Platz 4, 1090
Tel *317 15 37*   **Map** 1 C2
Ⓦ hotelmozart-vienna.at
Families are attracted here by the low prices, the generous breakfast spread and the large rooms, where comfort reigns over style.

Opera and Naschmarkt

Hotel Beethoven €€
Papagenogasse 6, 1060
Tel *587 44 82 0*   **Map** 3 C2
Ⓦ hotel-beethoven.at
Reopened in 2017 with wooden floors and sparkling bathrooms, this hotel retains its early 20th-century charm and offers a warm welcome to families.

Belvedere Quarter

Schick Hotel Erzherzog Rainer €€€
Wiedner Hauptstrasse 27–29, 1040
Tel *221 11*   **Map** 4 D3
Ⓦ schick-hotels.com
One of five Vienna Schick family hotels, this one is situated in a fashionable bohemian area in a century-old traditional building. Children are warmly welcomed.

Further Afield

Hotel Jäger €
Hernalser Hauptstrasse 187, 1170
Tel *486 66 20 0*
Ⓦ hoteljaeger.at
This large Art Nouveau villa welcomes children and offers babysitting services. Breakfast is free for kids under 6. Dog friendly.

Das Capri €€
Praterstrasse 44–46, 1020
Tel *214 84 04*   **Map** 2 F4
Ⓦ dascapri.at
A family-friendly hotel, the Das Capri issues each child with a free tablet to use while in residence. Stuffed toys can also be borrowed. It's just a short walk to the Ferris wheel. Dog friendly.

Luxury

Stephansdom Quarter

Kaiserin Elisabeth €€
Weihburggasse 3, 1010
Tel *515 26 0*   **Map** 6 D4
Ⓦ kaiserinelisabeth.at
Although this place is missing the spa and gourmet amenities of some of Vienna's most luxurious hotels, the helpful staff and period furnishings make for a comfortable stay.

König von Ungarn €€
Schulerstrasse 10, 1010
Tel *515 84 0*   **Map** 6 D3
Ⓦ kvu.at
Despite its imposing exterior, this hotel is described as a small family-run inn. Its history is palpable, and the luxury is undeniable and at good value.

Grand, Neo-Renaissance façade of Hotel Beethoven

Hotel Ambassador €€€
Karntner Strasse 22, 1010
Tel *961 61 0*   **Map** 5 C4
Ⓦ ambassador.at
Rich in tradition and dripping in silk, the Ambassador offers rooms in classic Viennese style, as well as more modern decorated rooms.

InterContinental €€€
Johannesgasse 28, 1037
Tel *711 22 0*   **Map** 6 E5
Ⓦ ihg.com
Everything you would expect of an international hotel, with business-class rooms and suites, and great views from the top. No pool, but there is an exercise room.

Palais Coburg Residenz €€€
Coburgbastei 4, 1010
Tel *518 18 0*   **Map** 6 E4
Ⓦ palais-coburg.com
This is real luxury: a 19th-century palace where there are no rooms, only suites, a special steel vault room for valuables and a beauty spa offering a wine massage.

Ritz-Carlton Vienna €€€
Schubertring 5–7, 1010
Tel *311 88*   **Map** 6 D5
Ⓦ ritzcarlton.com
Housed in four 19th-century palaces, this hotel indulges every whim, with sumptuous furnishings and the most elaborate beauty spa, as well as fitness facilities, including a swimming pool.

Schlosshotel Römischer Kaiser €€€
Annagasse 16, 1010
Tel *512 77 51 0*   **Map** 6 D4
Ⓦ hotel-roemischer-kaiser.at
This is like a museum, or palace, which the hotel was in its heyday. Opulent, with 24 rooms and the best concierge service in Vienna.

Hofburg Quarter

Steigenberger Hotel Herrenhof €€
Herrengasse 10, 1010
Tel *534 04 0*   **Map** 5 B3
Ⓦ steigenberger.com
There are almost 200 rooms in this five-star palace of luxury. A fitness area is available, but no beauty spa. It is, however, competitively priced.

Museum and Townhall Quarter

Palais Hansen Kempinski €€€
Schottenring 24, 1010
Tel *236 10 00*   **Map** 2 D4
Ⓦ kempinski.com/wien
One of the city's most prestigious hotels, the glamorous Palais

Hansen Kempinski features opulent rooms, high-tech facilities and a ballroom.

Sans Souci €€€
Burggasse 2, 1070
Tel *522 25 20*   **Map** 3 B1
W sanssouci-wien.com
With all the features of a luxury hotel, plus a spa and a gourmet restaurant, this is often rated Vienna's number-one hotel.

Opera and Naschmarkt

DK Choice

Hotel Sacher €€€
Philharmonikerstrasse 4, 1010
Tel *514 56 0*   **Map** 4 D1
W sacher.com
The Sacher is Vienna. Tradition, taste and luxury, without neglecting the kids, who have their own concierge, their own spa treatments and complimentary toys. This is one of the city's most sumptuous places to stay, with prices to match.

Belvedere Quarter

Imperial Riding School Renaissance Vienna €€
Ungargasse 60, 1030
Tel *711 75 0*   **Map** 4 F1
W imperialrenaissance.at
A large historic hotel with several lounges, bars, gardens and an indoor pool. The opulent rooms have all modern conveniences.

Hotel Bristol €€€
Kärntner Ring 1, 1010
Tel *515 16 0*   **Map** 4 D2
W bristolvienna.com
One of Vienna's grandest hotels, the Bristol features both Art Deco and Biedermeir rooms. The antique lift and the two romantic tower rooms are delights.

Imperial €€€
Kärntner Ring 16, 1015
Tel *501 10 0*   **Map** 4 D2
W imperialvienna.com
Sumptuous accommodation in this palatial 1863 building. Each suite has its own personal butler.

Further Afield

Landhaus Fuhrgassl-Huber €€
Rathstrasse 24, 1190
Tel *440 30 33*
W landhaus-fuhrgassl-huber.at
Located in a quaint village in the vineyards, with many wine taverns, this magnificent country house has a quirky character, oriental rugs and huge old cabinets.

Pension

Stephansdom Quarter

Domizil €
Schulerstrasse 14, 1010
Tel *513 31 99*   **Map** 6 D3
W hoteldomizil.at
Enjoy high comfort at a low price at the Domizil. The rooms have homely touches.

Hofburg Quarter

Pension Nossek €
Graben 17, 1010
Tel *533 70 41 0*   **Map** 5 C3
W pension-nossek.at
Mozart stayed here. There are parquet floors, high ceilings, and Art Deco design. All rooms are non-smoking. Very homey.

Pertschy Palais Hotel €
Habsburgergasse 5, 1010
Tel *534 49 0*   **Map** 5 C3
W pertschy.com
Far from palatial, this place does have bags of charm. Rooms have a bath, TV and minibar, and many have old wood floors.

Schottering and Alsergrund

Pension Liechtenstein €
Hörlgasse 9, 1090
Tel *319 66 75*   **Map** 1 C4
W pension-liechtenstein.at
With a range of well-equipped apartments and rooms, this B&B is ideal for longer stays.

Museum and Townhall Quarter

Academia €
Pfeilgasse 3A, 1080
Tel *401 76*   **Map** 1 A5
W academia.wienhotel.net
These 280 small student rooms are available in the summer. All have bathrooms and balconies, but no air conditioning.

Arpi €
Kochgasse 15/9, 1080
Tel *405 00 33*   **Map** 1 B4
W hotelarpi.com
The small but clean rooms at Arpi are comfortable and have Wi-Fi and TVs. A buffet breakfast is included in the price.

Hotel-Pension Museum €€
Museumstrasse 3
Tel *523 44 26*   **Map** 3 B1
W hotelmuseum.at
Here, a range of accommodation is offered in two faded-glory buildings with authentic furnishings.

Opera and Naschmarkt

Pension Mariahilf €
Mariahilfer Strasse 49, 1060
Tel *586 17 81*   **Map** 3 B2
W mariahilf-hotel.at
Quiet rooms of various sizes with private bathrooms, plus apartments, are offered at this popular guesthouse. Free continental breakfast.

DK Choice

Pension Suzanne €
Walfischgasse 4, 1010
Tel *513 25 07*   **Map** 4 D1
W pension-suzanne.at
This family-owned, upmarket guesthouse boasts an impressive collection of antiques and works of art, including Freud's couch, Klimt's bench and Mahler's chair. The rooms are lovely, and some of them face a quiet, open courtyard. The service is warm and friendly.

Further Afield

A&O Wien Stadthalle €
Lerchenfelder Gürtel 9–11, 1160
Tel *4930 480 3900*
W aohostels.com
Rooms are clean and comfortable at this hostel. There is a stylish bar, a library and a lovely beer garden. Located close to an underground station.

The Rooms B&B €
Schlenthergasse 17, 1220
Tel *431 68 30*
W therooms.at
On the old Danube across from the United Nations Office, this bed and breakfast has four individually decorated rooms, each with wood floors, designer furniture and a different theme. There is one shared bathroom.

Luxuriously furnished room at the historic Hotel Sacher

For more information on types of hotels *see pages 192–5*

WHERE TO EAT AND DRINK

The Viennese know how to eat well. The staples of Vienna's cuisine are assimilated from cooking styles across the Habsburg Empire, and include *Schnitzels*, originating as North Italian escalopes; dumplings that are a speciality of Bohemia; Hungarian goulash; and even *cevapcici* – Balkan grills and sausages. Vienna's tastes range around the world, including everything from Asian influences to American burger bars. The range of gastronomy is vast, from gourmet nouvelle cuisine down to the *Würstelstände* (booths selling sausages and beer on street corners). Diners can take their pick from old-fashioned sumptuous splendour to tavern gardens or Baroque wine cellars. Mealtimes are also flexible and in the city centre plenty of places serve hot meals between 11:30am and midnight. The restaurants on pages 210–19 are listed by area and by price, with the emphasis being on local cuisine, though there is also a range of alternatives for visitors wanting something a bit different.

Types of Eating Place

Open until 4am in many instances, *Würstelstände* sell sausages and *Leberkäse* – a type of meat loaf made from finely ground corned beef or pork and bacon, with onions. Also inexpensive are the numerous small eateries selling sandwiches, filled rolls, pastries and soft drinks. Mouth-watering open sandwiches are the speciality at the celebrated Austrian institution Trześniewski *(see p213)*. Order these with a glass of wine or a miniature Pfiff (200ml) of beer to accompany them.

If something a little more substantial is required then the *Stehbeisln* (stand-up counters) at some butchers and food stores offer fresh dishes and

Wine cellar sign

sometimes a welcome bowl of hot soup, perfect on a winter's day. Upmarket restaurants are great for a *Gabelfrühstück* (fork breakfast), and many serve brunch-style hot delicacies mid-morning. Another snack enjoyed by the Viennese is the *Jause* (cold meats and cheese, typically eaten between regular mealtimes). All these options are useful alternatives to the museum restaurants and cafés which, however good, tend to be on the expensive side.

Vienna's self-service restaurants offer a range of cold and hot dishes, including grills made to order, as well as pastas and salads. The ubiquitous coffee houses and wine cellars are good evening options, whether for a meal or just a drink.

Café-Restaurant Dunkelbunt *(see p218)*

Wine Cellars and Heurigen

Wine cellars represent good value, with cold buffets and a limited range of hot dishes to accompany local wines from the barrel. The atmosphere is informal, and even more so in the gardens of the *Heurigen* (taverns) on the periphery of the city, at Neustift am Walde, Grinzing and elsewhere. *Heuriger* has two meanings: it refers to the youngest available vintage of the local wine and it also refers to the venues that sell such wines by the glass. In theory, *Heurigen* serve only the wine from their own vineyards and of the current vintage. According to regulations laid down by Emperor Joseph II, pine twigs placed over or by the door *(ausg'steckt)* remained as long as the vintage lasted,

Open sandwiches at Zum Schwarzen Kameel *(see p212)*

An array of tasty pastries and cakes at Café Mozart *(see p213)*

after which they were removed and the tavern closed for the year. Visitors will still see such taverns, but in practice the larger ones are open all year and serve an extensive buffet with hot and cold cuts of meat. The wine is mostly white, often a blend of the *gemischter Satz* or local grapes, and is a true *Heuriger* until 11th November of the year after harvest. To sample a genuine local product, look for *Eigenbau* (meaning that the grower serves their own wine) by the entrance.

The Viennese Beisl

The French have their bistros, and Vienna has its *Beisl*. As befits the Austrian ethos of cosy comfort, *gemütlichkeit*, the *Beisl* is a meeting place. It is as close as you can get to sitting down in a real Viennese home, with grandmother's cooking. But before the cooking comes the bar. A *Beisl* is a place to drink – both wine and beer. Simple wood tables and wooden floors define the interior. It is not uncommon to find waitresses dressed in traditional folk costume, though that is not required. The name is thought to be of Jewish origin – in the 18th century, many innkeepers

were Jewish. The top end of the *Beisln* merge with what Austrians somewhat misleadingly call *"gutbürgerliche Küche"*, "good plain cooking", where the food is not just good but rather sophisticated as well. Many *Beisln* have gone upmarket and their prices have risen accordingly. All serve typical Viennese specialities such as *Tafelspitz* (boiled beef), *Vanillerostbraten* (beef cutlets with garlic), *Kalbsbeuschel* (calf's lung and heart), and of course *Wiener Schnitzel*, often in dauntingly large portions.

To follow are some stodgy but enticingly named desserts: *Powidltascherln* (pasta envelopes with plum jam) or *Zwetschkenknödel* (plums in potato dumpling). Viennese cooking also features some delicious soups. A popular soup is *Eierschwammerlsuppe*, made with chanterelle mushrooms.

Coffee Houses and Konditoreien

The Viennese are particular about their legendary coffee houses *(see pp60–63)*: politicians, for example, favour Landtmann Café *(see p215)*, while the literati swap ideas in Café Hawelka *(see p212)*. Coffee is served in different ways

varying in strength and the addition of hot milk or cream.

Prices vary according to location and type: a Ringstrasse café is more expensive than a smoke-filled den with a billiard table at the rear, or somewhere like the Café-Restaurant Ministerium *(see p210)*, patronized by bureaucrats from the nearby ministries. While coffee houses serve a small range of simple hot dishes, *Konditoreien* (confectioners) concentrate on pastries and cakes, though a few also do a good light lunch.

Café Sacher, known for its exquisite coffee and the *Sachertorte (see p216)*

The 7th-floor DO & CO restaurant *(see p212)*, with a splendid view of the Stephansdom

Luxury Restaurants

Gourmet eating in Vienna generally retains a local flavour. Seriously good cuisine may be found at luxury hotels such as the Hotel Sacher *(see p216)*, the Opus Restaurant in the Imperial Hotel *(see p217)* and the Bristol Lounge *(see p217)*. Steirereck *(see p212)*, located in the leafy surroundings of the Stadtpark, is considered one of the city's best fine-dining venues. The restaurant's menu has a strong Austrian slant. Trattoria Martinelli *(see p214)* serves traditional Tuscan specialities, which can be enjoyed in the Baroque ambience of the Harrach Palace.

International Cuisines

Away from the traditional Viennese eateries, the city offers a great variety of cuisines from all over the world, and these places are often very good value. Authentic Greek restaurants, such as Kostas *(see p216)*, tend to be inexpensive and there are a number of Asian restaurants offering great meals for a nominal fee, such as Sri Thai Imbiss *(see p218)*, as well as several pricier, more upmarket Asian and Japanese venues.

Italian food is easy to find in Vienna and ranges from pizza slices to authentic dishes from the Lombardy or Tuscany regions.

Vegetarians

Even traditional meat-oriented eateries now offer at least some vegetarian options. Dedicated vegan and vegetarian establishments such as the Wrenkh *(see p211)* and organic Lebenbauer *(see p215)* are especially well known for their offerings.

Reading the Menu

Generally, there tend to be three main parts to the Austrian menu: *kalte* or *warme Vorspeisen* (cold or hot hors d'oeuvres), *Hauptspeisen* (main course) and *Mehlspeisen* (desserts). There may be separate entries for *Suppen* (soups), *Fisch* (fish), *Rindfleisch* (beef) and *Schweinefleisch* (pork). Menus vary seasonally, particularly in asparagus and game seasons. Many give details of where beef or fish came from, as well as allergy information about ingredients such as nuts. Menus for children are common and there are also great-value daily specials called *Tagesangebot*. The phrase *Fertige Speisen* refers to dishes not on the fixed-price menu. *Schmankerln* indicates regional delicacies. Portions tend to be on the generous side, although there is a trend towards lighter eating in the more upmarket establishments serving nouvelle cuisine.

Tables settings at the acclaimed fine-dining Restaurant at Eight *(see p212)*

House wines are usually served in glasses, which hold exactly a quarter of a litre, though smaller glasses may also be served, and half a litre may come in a carafe. Most restaurants, at least in the city centre, have menus in English, but if this is not the case, there is usually a member of staff who can help.

Food and Drink Costs

Per calorie, Vienna's pastries are a bargain. But the coffee-house culture of lingering for hours comes at a cost, seldom less than €3 per cup. Add a dash of schnapps, and the price doubles. Pastry shops, *Konditorieien*, are much cheaper than famous-name coffee houses. Fast food and takeaways are everywhere, and a snack or a sausage from a stand costs about €5. Daily specials in modest restaurants can cost as little as €15 for a generous meal. An evening meal is easily more than double that, without wine. A reasonably priced *Beisl* might cost €20 a head with a glass of wine, but sticking to the fixed-price menu will probably reduce that significantly. Gourmet restaurants in hotels are more expensive than equally rated establishments tucked away in small streets. There is also a premium paid for dining in

Outdoor terrace of Vestibül, in the Burgtheater *(see p215)*

opulent period restaurants. Foodies will appreciate fixed "tasting menus" in gourmet restaurants, with prices graduated according to the number of courses, starting at around €100. Ethnic restaurants – Croatian, Asian and Italian, among others – often offer very good value. Credit cards are now widely accepted but not in small family restaurants or snack establishments.

Booking and Service

Booking ahead is essential at Vienna's most famous eateries. Most offer online booking on the restaurant website, or you can book by email or SMS. Some tourist restaurants include service in the final bill; elsewhere and in coffee houses it is customary to leave a tip, in the region of 5–15 per cent. Local practice dictates that you do not leave the gratuity on the table; instead, give it directly to your waiter, often with the remark *"Stimmt so"* ("Keep the change").

Recommended Restaurants

The restaurants on pages 210–19 are listed by area and by price and represent a wide choice of establishments. They range from *Beisln* and coffee houses serving traditional Viennese cuisine, both sweet

and savoury delicacies *(see pp204–7)*, and restaurants with regional Austrian dishes from various provinces *(see pp204–5)*, to modern Austrian fusion cooking and international gourmet nouvelle cuisine. Asian and Japanese restaurants are popular in Vienna, and a number of these are listed, as are some Italian and Mediterranean options.

The restaurants highlighted as DK Choice have been chosen for one or more exceptional quality. This could be the historical setting, outstanding food, impeccable service, unique atmosphere or celebrated chefs. These special places come highly recommended and are particularly worth seeking out.

Cosy decor of Griechenbeisl, Vienna's oldest inn *(see p210)*

Bright, airy interiors of the trendy Dellago *(see p218)*

The Flavours of Vienna: Savoury Dishes

Austrian cuisine is a direct legacy of the country's imperial past, when culinary traditions from many parts of Europe influenced Viennese cooks. As a result, it is far more varied and flavoursome than most people realize. There are Italian and Adriatic influences, Polish- and Hungarian- inspired dishes, and even a rich seam of Balkan flavours running through much of the Austrian kitchen repertoire. *Schnitzel*, for example, may have come to Austria via Milan, which was once under Austrian control, while *Gulasch* is the Austrian version of a Hungarian dish that became popular in Vienna in the 19th century.

Chanterelle mushrooms

An array of cheeses on sale at a local farmers' market

Meat, Poultry and Dairy

Beef is narrowly ahead of pork as the nation's favourite meat. Austrian cattle farmers have a long and proud heritage of producing fine beef, which is used in many dishes, such as paprika-rich *Gulasch*. That most famous of Austrian dishes, *Wiener Schnitzel*, is traditionally made with veal. Pork is used primarily to make hams and sausages. The classic Austrian way with pork is to cure it, smoke it and leave it to mature for months in the clean air of the high Alpine pastures. The result is called *Speck*. Lean *Speck* is similar to Italian *prosciutto*, though with a distinctive smoky tang, while fattier cuts are more like *pancetta* or streaky bacon.

Bratwurst, made with beef, pork and veal, are Austria's preferred sausages, but other types, such as *Frankfurters*, are also common. Chicken is almost always served breaded (*Backhendl*), but *Grillhendl* is a whole chicken roasted over an open fire, or on a spit. Duck (*Ente*) is often served with sweet sauces, but sometimes with

Beef frankfurters

Bierwurst

Bratwurst

Pork frankfurters

Lean Speck

Speck

Selection of typical Austrian cured pork, sausages and salami

Austrian Dishes and Specialities

Tafelspitz is silverside of beef, boiled with root vegetables and served thickly sliced with roasted potatoes and minced horseradish.

While most classic Austrian dishes (especially those originating in Vienna) are found all over the country, there are some regional differences. *Knödel* are more popular in the east, as are carp, game and pork, while beef and lamb appear more often the further west (and higher up the mountains) you travel. Beef is essential for *Tafelspitz*, often called the national dish. *Speck* is used to make *Speck Knödel*, small, dense dumplings; the one part of the pig that Austrians love to eat uncured is the knuckle, called *Stelze*, roasted and served chopped with heaps of sauerkraut. *Fischgröstl* is a mix of fish and seafood, fried together with onion, potato and mince (usually leftovers). It is rarely found on menus, but you may be lucky enough to try it in an Austrian home.

Paprika

Spectacular array of vegetables on display in a Viennese market

sour accompaniments, such as pickled red cabbage. Roast goose *(Gänsebraten)* is also popular, as are goose livers. The milk of Austrian dairy cows, grazed on sweet Alpine pastures, makes some excellent artisan cheeses, such as fruity *Wälder*.

Fish

Though traditionally meat lovers, Austrians do enjoy a good piece of fish. Trout *(Forelle)* is the most popular, usually served grilled with boiled potatoes. Herring *(Hering)* is pickled and eaten as an appetizer. *Heringsschmaus*, a smoked herring and apple salad, is hugely popular at Easter. Carp *(Karpfen)* is a favourite Christmas dish, but is eaten all year, as is plaice *(Scholle* or *Goldbutt)*, which is often served with a rich vegetable-based sauce.

Vegetables

Vegetables in Austria are of the highest quality and, though imported produce is available all year round, Austrians favour homegrown, seasonal, vegetables. That is truest of all for the nation's favourite, asparagus *(Spargel)*.

Bunches of pale spears of Austrian *Spargel* (asparagus)

Austrians only use local produce so asparagus is found on menus only during the harvesting season, from the end of April to early July. Austrians use asparagus in every way imaginable at this time of year. Wild mushrooms are another seasonal prize, especially chanterelles *(Eierschwammerl)*. Potatoes *(Erdäpfel)* feature widely, often in the form of *Knödel*. These are dumplings made of potatoes or stale white bread and served with venison or pork dishes. White cabbage is often pickled *(Sauerkraut)*; red cabbage is served with venison and most game dishes.

SAVOURY SNACKS

Liptauer: Goat's or sheep's milk cheese is mixed with paprika, caraway seeds, capers, mustard, chives and onions to create this paste, a staple of Austrian wine bars.

Maroni: Roast chestnuts are a winter treat; the aroma of them, toasting over a brazier on a snowy day, is somehow quintessentially Vienna.

Blunzen: Blood sausage is marinated in vinegar, thinly sliced and served with brown bread. A popular "beer snack".

Schmalzbrot: Brown bread spread thickly with beef or pork dripping, and eaten with onions and pickles.

Wiener Schnitzel should classically be veal, breaded and fried. In Austria is is never served with sauce.

Rindsgulasch is the beef version of Hungarian goulash, a rich stew flavoured with paprika and caraway.

Forelle Blau, literally "blue trout", is made by poaching an unscaled fish in stock, which gives it a blueish hue.

The Flavours of Vienna: Sweet Foods

Few cities in the world rival Vienna's devotion to all things sweet. The Viennese enjoy cakes mid-morning or afternoon, and set aside time for between-meal snacks. The finest *torten* (gâteaux), pastries and cakes tend to be found in *Konditoreien (see p201)* and are usually consumed with a cup of coffee. Traditional Viennese desserts can be found in all good restaurants, and are typically rich. From the classic Viennese *Apfelstrudel* to *Gugelhupf* from the Tirol, Austrian desserts all carry a regional influence. In Vienna, pastries take pride of place while, to the west, the Italian influence is strong and cakes, ice creams and meringues are preferred.

Poppy seeds

Relaxing over coffee and cake in an elegant Viennese café

Cakes

The Austrian tradition of cake-baking goes back centuries, with competition fierce between towns and cities to produce the finest. Even in small villages, bakeries would try to outdo each other with their sweet creations. Almost every Austrian city now has its trademark cake, with its citizens quick to boast that theirs is the best. The most famous Austrian cake is a Viennese creation, the *Sachertorte*, a rich chocolate cake invented by chef Franz Sacher for Chancellor Metternich in 1832. The signature dish of many an Austrian chef, it should be the first cake the visitor tries – with so much choice on offer, it will be difficult to decide on the second. While the Viennese rave about *Sachertorte*, over in Linz the locals insist their own *Linzertorte* – an almond-based cake usually topped with raspberries – is superior. The people of Linz also say that the *Linzertorte* is older, dating back – legend has it – to the 17th century. Around the Hungarian border, they are proud of their *Dobostorte*,

Linzertorte Stollen Sachertorte Dobostorte Esterházytorte
Some of the many mouthwatering Austrian cakes available

Viennese Desserts

From *Topfentascherl* (curd cheese envelopes) to *Kastaniereis* (chestnut purée), Vienna's dessert cuisine uses rich and varied ingredients. The term *Mehlspeisen* is used to cover a broad range of puddings and pastries, including some that use ground hazelnuts or almonds in place of flour. Fruits such as plums and apples fill featherlight dumplings, pancakes, fritters and strudels. Whole or chopped nuts play a key role, especially hazelnuts and pine nuts, the latter often featuring in *Apfelstrudel*. More unusual desserts include sweet "pasta" served with poppy seeds to create *Mohnnudeln*, and *Böhmische Palatschinken* (Bohemian crêpes) served with whipped cream and prune sauce. *Palatschinken* may also be a savoury snack.

Hazelnuts

Mohr im Hemd, a hazelnut and chocolate pudding, is served with chocolate sauce and whipped cream.

Display of traditional pastries and cakes in a *Konditorei*

named for the Budapest chef who created it in the 19th century. Its layers of sponge and chocolate butter cream are topped with a caramel glaze. From Salzburg, the cake of choice is baked meringue, known as *Salzburger Nockerl*, or Salzburg Soufflé. *Esterházytorte* also features meringue, layered with a rich hazelnut cream. Stollen is a marzipan-filled fruit bread originally from Germany and now an integral part of the Austrian Christmas. Regional or not, you'll now find all these classic cakes in Vienna and across the country.

Pastries

In the perfect global village, a place on the main street would always be reserved for an Austrian pastry and coffee shop. That the French collective name for sweet pastry is *Viennoiserie*

underlines the noble Viennese tradition of sweet baking. Austrian legend has it that the nation's café habit began when the Turks left all their coffee behind as they abandoned Vienna after the failed siege of 1529. The *Kipferl*, a light, crescent-shaped pastry (which later became famous as the croissant), also dates from the time of the

Entrance to one of the world-famous Mozart chocolate shops

Turkish siege, its shape being based on the crescent moon of the Ottoman flag. While such symbolism is often lost today, the importance of the café in Austrian society is not. Modern-day Austrians view cafés as extensions of their home, and spend hours reading, chatting and even watching television in them. Treats on offer in cafés will generally include a classic *Apfelstrudel*, *Cremeschnitte* (slices of puff pastry filled with custard and glazed with strawberry fondant), and *Punschkrapfen*, a calorie-packed, pink-fondant-topped pastry laced with rum.

Mozartkugel

Fine chocolates, presented in colourfully decorated boxes carrying the portrait of Mozart, are probably the quintessential Austrian souvenir. Known in Austria as *Mozartkugel*, the chocolates originated in Salzburg, where Mozart lived while composing *Cosi fan tutte*, the opera in which he worships chocolate. In 1890, master confectioner Paul Fürst made the first Mozart chocolates by forming small balls of marzipan which he coated in a praline cream and then dipped in warm chocolate. Viennese confectioners soon adopted the technique and even today producers vie with one another as to whose *Mozartkugel* are the best and most authentic.

Apfelstrudel rolls paper-thin pastry with apple, sultanas, cinnamon and sometimes pine nuts or poppy seeds.

Palatschinken are fat, fluffy crêpes that may be filled with fruit or jam, or served with vanilla or chocolate sauce.

Topfenknödel are light curd cheese dumplings rolled in breadcrumbs and served with fruit compôte.

What to Drink in Vienna

Austria is a source of excellent wine and good rich beers. Vienna itself is in a wine-growing region surrounded by vineyards which supply the *Heurigen (see p200–201)* in villages on the edge of the city with young local wines. Fine Austrian wines are found in good restaurants. Austrian wine is mainly white but there are some fantastic local red wines, especially from the Burgenland and Carnuntum districts. Sweet *Eiswein* is made from grapes left on the vines until the first frosts arrive, concentrating their juices. Fruit brandies and schnapps, many of them first class, are also produced.

Beyond the villages north and west of Vienna lie vineyards producing wines sold in *Heurigen*

Chardonnay from Styria and sparkling wine from Lower Austria

Austrian Wines

The most popular wine in Austria is Grüner Veltliner *(see below)*. Other wines include superb dry Rieslings, especially from the Wachau, and rich Weissburgunder (Pinot Blanc) from Burgenland. Red wines tend to be soft and lush – robust reds come from the Blaufränkisch grape *(see below)*.

Riesling from the Wachau can be light, or full bodied like the Smaragd style.

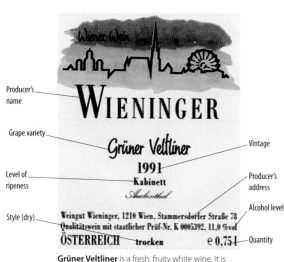

Producer's name
Grape variety
Level of ripeness
Style (dry)
Vintage
Producer's address
Alcohol level
Quantity

Grüner Veltliner is a fresh, fruity white wine. It is widely grown in Austria and is usually made in a dry style. It also makes excellent *Eiswein*.

St Laurent is a soft red wine; at its best it is rich and stylish.

Blaufränkisch is a quality local red – the best comes from Burgenland.

Krügel or half-litre tankard

Seidl or standard third-litre measure

Krügel or half-litre of pale beer

Pfiff or eighth-litre beer glass

Kaiser beer, a light beer

Weizengold wheat beer

The rich *Gösser Spezial*

Austrian Beers

Vienna has been producing great beers for centuries. Viennese lagers are bronze in colour and sweet in flavour. They make an excellent accompaniment to the hearty soups and stews found in *Beisln (see p201)*. The local Ottakring brewery's *Gold Fassl* is typical of the style, although lighter Bavarian-type beers such as *Weizengold* are also commonly available. One of Austria's most popular beers is *Gösser*, produced in Styria and found in the pubs and restaurants of Vienna. Speciality beers include the Styrian *Eggenberger Urbock 23°*, one of the strongest beers in the world. It is made by the Schloss Eggenberg brewery founded in the 17th century.

Bierhof beer mat advertising a pub in the Haarhof.

Null Komma Josef is a local alcohol-free beer.

Other Austrian Drinks

Austria offers a good range of non-alcoholic fruit juices such as *Himbeersaft* (raspberry juice) or *Johannisbeersaft* (blackcurrant juice). *Almdudler* (herbal lemonade) is also a speciality. Fruit is also the basis of many types of schnapps (sometimes called *Brand*). This powerful eau de vie is distilled from berries such as juniper and rowan, as well as apricots *(Marillen)* and quince *(Quitten)*. It's worth paying the extra to sample the exquisite fruit schnapps produced by dedicated specialists. For a few weeks in autumn, fermenting grape juice, *Sturm*, is available. Milky in colour and quite sweet, it is more alcoholic than its grape flavour suggests.

Apricot schnaps

The Wiener Rathauskeller is a popular restaurant with a variety of beers on the menu

Where to Eat and Drink

Stephansdom Quarter

Akakiko €
Japanese   Map 6 D3
Rotenturmstrasse 6, 1010
Tel *057 33 31 97*
This is the flagship restaurant of a Japanese chain that has various locations in Vienna. Reliable for soups and sushi at modest prices.

Café Diglas €
Coffee House   Map 6 E3
Wollzeile 10, 1010
Tel *512 57 65*
Regulars descend on this friendly café for the hearty goulash and warm bread pudding, as well as salads, *Schnitzel* and wine – all at a decent price.

Café Engländer €
Café   Map 6 E3
Postgasse 2, 1010
Tel *966 86 65*
From breakfast until 1am, this unpretentious café is open for coffee and snacks throughout the day and offers reasonably priced Angus beef tartare and other main dishes in the evening.

Café Frauenhuber €
Coffee House   Map 6 D4
Himmelpfortgasse 6, 1010
Tel *512 53 53*
Both Beethoven and Mozart performed in this former medieval bathhouse. Come here for traditional dishes, tasty cakes and good coffee.

Café Korb €
Traditional Austrian   Map 6 D3
Brandstätte 9, 1010
Tel *533 72 15*
Art displays, a bowling alley in the basement and a distinct air of the 1960s make this place popular with arty types. Don't miss the strudel.

Café Neko €
Japanese/Teashop   Map 6 D4
Blumenstockgasse 5, 1010
Tel *512 14 66*
Cat lovers will enjoy this small café. Rescue cats roam freely, sleeping on seats or purring under tables as guests sip tea and eat the "cake of the day".

Café Prückel €
Coffee House   Map 6 F3
Stubenring 24, 1010
Tel *512 61 15*
Head to this much-loved café for excellent coffee, fresh pastries

and meals served by waiters in bow-ties. With its 1950s-style decor of velvet banquettes, it attracts a cool and arty crowd.

Café-Restaurant Ministerium €
Coffee House   Map 6 F3
Georg Coch-Platz 4, 1010
Tel *512 92 25*   **Closed** *Sun & hols*
This former ministerial dining room offers a good-value *Tageskarte* (daily changing menu) featuring dishes such as pork with stuffed cabbage, plus teas, coffee and snacks.

Gasthaus Pöschl €
Traditional Austrian   Map 6 D4
Weihburggasse 17, 1010
Tel *513 52 88*
Less expensive, less crowded and less impressive glass-walled eatery in the park, Pöschl is the little sister restaurant to the acclaimed Steirereck (*see p212*). Open until 11:30pm.

Schachtelwirt €
Modern Austrian   Map 6 D2
Judengasse 5, 1010
Tel *532 07 07*   **Closed** *Sun & Mon*
There are only five choices on the weekly changing menu here. The artichoke and beetroot dumplings are highly praised. Inexpensive but innovative.

Vikas €
Seafood   Map 6 D3
Wildpretmarkt 3, 1010
Tel *533 21 93*   **Closed** *Mon*
One of the best seafood restaurants in Vienna, Umar1 serves a wide variety of exquisite fish dishes as well as caviar, oysters and scallops. The menu

Signed photographs of famous guests on the walls at Griechenbeisl

also includes succulent beef and lamb steaks. Reservations are recommended.

Ankor €€
Seafood   Map 6 D2
Marc-Aurel-Strasse 8, 1010
Tel *535 65 18*
Everybody agrees that the fish here is first class, but the service can be indifferent. Lobster with pasta is the signature dish.

Cantinetta Antinori €€
Italian   Map 6 D3
Jasomirgottstrasse 3–5, 1010
Tel *533 77 22*
This is an outpost of the famed restaurant in Florence, with wines from the family estate and crowds of devoted Austrian fans. Steak Florentine is a speciality.

Figlmüller €€
Traditional Viennese   Map 2 E5
Wollzeile 5, 1010
Tel *512 61 77*
Open since 1905, this restaurant is popular with locals and visitors alike. Flavourful dishes include *Schnitzel*, rabbit casseroles, veal goulash and roast boar. The *Powidltascherl* (dumplings filled with plum jam) are delicious.

Fratelli €€
Tuscan   Map 6 D3
Rotentormstrasse 11, 1010
Tel *533 87 45*
Italian cuisine is served with northern Italian flavours in an atmospheric space with frescoed ceilings. In winter, the outdoor terrace is heated.

Griechenbeisl €€
Beisl   Map 6 D2
Fleischmarkt 11, 1010
Tel *533 19 77*
Vienna's oldest inn (dating from 1447) has signed, framed photos of famous guests, including politicians, artists, writers and musicians, lining the walls. It serves classic dishes.

Haas & Haas €€
Teashop   Map 6 D3
Stephansplatz 4, 1010
Tel *512 26 66*
A Vienna institution, this friendly teahouse is renowned for its

lovely courtyard. It offers a wide-ranging menu for brunch, lunch and afternoon tea.

Hansen   €€
Austro-Mediterranean   Map 5 C2
Wipplingerstrasse 34
Tel *532 05 42*   **Closed** *Sun*
In the arched hall of a former Stock Exchange basement, traditional Viennese dishes are given a Mediterranean flavor. Try the risotto of the day.

König von Ungarn   €€
Traditional Viennese   Map 6 D3
Schulerstrasse 10, 1010
Tel *515 84*
The restaurant in Vienna's oldest hotel, founded in 1746, serves hearty cuisine and is popular with families. The highlight is the beef trolley.

Der Kuckuck   €€
Traditional Austrian   Map 6 D4
Himmelpfortgasse 15, 1010
Tel *512 84 70*
"The Cuckoo" is one of Vienna's most traditional restaurants. It is set in a medieval room with arched ceilings and pristine white linen. Order a classic *Schnitzel*.

Meierei am Stadtpark   €€
Traditional Viennese   Map 6 F4
Am Heumarkt 2A, 1030
Tel *713 31 6810*
This is the sister restaurant of the much acclaimed Steiereck *(see p212)*. Although less expensive, the food here is equally good. It offers the perfect setting for breakfast, lunch or dinner.

Ofenloch   €€
Traditional Austrian   Map 5 C2
Kurrentgasse 8,1010
Tel *533 88 44*   **Closed** *Sun*
The service here is impeccable, with traditionally attired waiters serving classic dishes in an elegant arched hall.

Tables on the terrace for alfresco dining at Ofenloch

Dining room and bar area of Wrenkh, which specializes in vegetarian dishes

Österreicher im MAK   €€
Modern Austrian   Map 6 F3
Stubenring 5, 1010
Tel *226 00 46*
This hip dining room in the museum of applied arts offers ambitious health-conscious cuisine. Open until midnight.

Salzamt   €€
Traditional Austrian   Map 6 D2
Ruprechtsplatz 1,1010
Tel *533 53 32*
Ideal for night owls, Salzamt serves tasty Austrian comfort food until 2am in an old-fashioned setting.

Schönbichler   €€
Teashop   Map 6 D3
Wollzeile 4, 1010
Tel *512 18 16*   **Closed** *Sun*
Enjoy a selection of fine teas from all over the world, plus scones and sandwiches, at the tea gallery inside this shop. Regulars rave about the service and the care with which the tea is made.

Tian   €€
Vegetarian   Map 6 D4
Himmelpfortgasse 23, 1010
Tel *890 46 65*   **Closed** *Sun & Mon*
This pretty diner is a meat-free oasis in the city's carnivorous dining scene. All dishes make use of produce grown in the restaurant's own organic garden.

Toko-Ri   €€
Japanese   Map 6 D2
Salztorgasse 4, 1010
Tel *532 77 77*
Sizzling-hot plates of spicy noodles, tempura prawns and large trays of sushi to share are served at this restaurant with sleek minimalist decor.

Weibels Wirtshaus   €€
Beisl   Map 6 E3
Kumpfgasse 2, 1010
Tel *512 39 86*
Tucked away down a cobbled street, this quaint restaurant

serves high-quality, wholesome sausage and *Schnitzel* dishes that never fall short on taste.

Wrenkh   €€
Vegetarian   Map 6 D3
Bauernmarkt 10, 1010
Tel *533 15 26*   **Closed** *Sun*
Anything that can be done with a vegetable, in any cooking style, can be ordered here at Wrenkh. It is also a vegetarian chef school, with a pleasant terrace.

Zu Den 3 Hacken   €€
Traditional Austrian   Map 6 D4
Singerstrasse 28, 1010
Tel *512 58 95*   **Closed** *Sun*
Schubert used to eat here regularly and, although the menu has changed, the food is still good. Specialities include berry-topped game stew and platters of roast meats.

Zum Basilisken   €€
Traditional Austrian   Map 6 E5
Schönlaterngasse 3
Tel *5133123*
This restaurant with low lighting is filled with oversized furniture from a bygone age. Savour the pork belly with red cabbage – old-style comfort food at its finest.

Zum Weissen Rauchfangkehrer   €€
Traditional Viennese   Map 6 D4
Weihburggasse 4, 1010
Tel *512 34 71*   **Closed** *Sun & hols*
"The White Chimneysweep" is popular with locals for its piano music and traditional cooking, using ingredients from regional farms. A *Schnitzel* paradise.

DO & CO   €€€
Modern Austrian   Map 6 D3
Stephansplatz 12, 1010
Tel *535 39 69*
On the top floor of the upscale DO & CO hotel, this place serves fine dishes prepared with care and creativity. Try the gourmet *Schnitzel* or the delicate sashimi.

For more information on types of restaurants *see pages 200–203*

Outside seating at the Zum Schwarzen Kameel

DSTRIKT   €€€
Modern Austrian   **Map** 6 D5
Schubertring 5–7, 1010
Tel *311 88 15 0*
Award-winning chef here
delivers the best in local cuisine
mixed with international flair at
this upmarket diner in the Ritz-
Carlton Vienna. Reservations
recommended.

Fabios   €€€
Mediterranean   **Map** 5 C3
Tuchlauben 4–6, 1010
Tel *532 22 22*   **Closed** *Sun*
Stunning architecture, dramatic
glass and orange-tinted lighting
all help create the mood here at
Fabios. But the food is also
outstanding – try the venison
with sage gnocchi or the sole
fillet with asparagus.

Oswald & Kalb   €€€
Traditional Austrian   **Map** 6 D3
Bäckerstrasse 14, 1010
Tel *512 13 71*
A firm favourite with locals,
Oswald & Kolb serves some of
the best *Schnitzel* anywhere in
the city. The changing menu also
boasts classic regional dishes
prepared with innovative,
creative touches.

Parkring Restaurant   €€€
Austrian/French   **Map** 6 E4
Parkring 12A, 1010
Tel *515 18 68 00*
This is the gourmet dining room
of the massive Marriott Hotel,
which also houses a sports
bar and eatery with a waterfall.
The tasting menus here
range from classic Viennese
to Asian fusion.

Plachutta   €€€
Traditional Viennese   **Map** 6 E3
Wollzeile 38, 1010
Tel *512 15 77*
Known throughout the city for
its *Tafelspitz* (boiled beef), this
restaurant is frequented by
numerous Austrian politicians
and celebrities.

DK Choice

Restaurant at Eight   €€€
Modern Austrian   **Map** 6 D5
Kärntner Ring 8, 1010
Tel *221 22 38 30*
Restaurant at Eight is the highly
praised dining room of the
Palace Ring Hotel. During the
daytime, it is light and airy, but
for the evening the room is
transformed, and guests are
requested to dress appropriately. The menu is completely
rewritten each month, and
classic dishes prevail.

Restaurant Das Schick   €€€
Austro-Spanish   **Map** 6 E4
Parkring 12, 1010
Tel *514 80 41 7*
There are rooftop views of Vienna
from this 12th-floor dining room of
the Schick Parkring Hotel. The food
is a fusion of Austrian cooking and
Spanish fish and spice influences.
Varied selection of Spanish wines.

Steirereck   €€€
Modern Austrian   **Map** 6 F5
Am Heumarkt 2A/ Stadtpark, 1030
Tel *713 31 68*   **Closed** *Sat & Sun*
Steirereck offers an incredible
seven-course tasting menu – a
luxurious feast of seafood, game
and poultry accompanied by
honey, rye and lavender bread.

Walter Bauer   €€€
Modern Austrian   **Map** 6 E3
Sonnenfelsgasse 17, 1010
Tel *512 98 71*   **Closed** *Sat & Sun*
Exuding old Viennese charm,
this award-winning restaurant
is famed for its modern
interpretation of local culinary
classics. The smoked eel and
venison dishes are a must.

Zum Schwarzen Kameel   €€€
Traditional Viennese   **Map** 5 C3
Bognergasse 5, 1010
Tel *533 81 25 11*   **Closed** *Sun*
This impressive Jugendstil dining
room serves Viennese favourites

---

including game such as wild
boar. There is an extensive wine
selection and impeccable old-
world service.

Hofburg Quarter

Café Bräunerhof   €
Coffee House   **Map** 5 C4
Stallburggasse 2, 1010
Tel *512 38 93*
This coffee house offers all the
typical local delicacies. The
1920s furnishings and a
fascinating clientele of
intellectuals and academics
bolsters its appeal.

Café Hawelka   €
Coffee House   **Map** 5 C4
Dorotheergasse 6, 1010
Tel *512 82 30*
Opened by Leopold Hawelka in
1939, this family-run café was
a meeting point for postwar
writers and critics. It is popular for
its desserts, especially *Buchteln*
(Austrian sweet rolls).

Café Hofburg   €
Coffee House   **Map** 5 B4
Michaelerkuppel, Hofburg, 1010
Tel *24 100 400*
This charming grand café is a
great stop-off point for coffee,
snacks or lunch before or after
a visit to the Hofburg palace.
There are "emperor's pancakes"
on the menu and classical piano
music every afternoon.

Konditorei Gerstner   €
Konditorei   **Map** 5 C5
Kärntner Strasse 13–15, 1010
Tel *512 49 63*
One of the city's greatest pastry
makers and chocolatiers, Gerstner
is a favourite with locals and

Tables on the terrace at the fine-dining
Restaurant at Eight

For key to prices *see page 210*

visitors. Indulge your tastebuds with heavenly macaroons, cupcakes or a slice of *Sachertorte*.

Konditorei Oberlaa €
Konditorei **Map** 5 C4
Neuer Markt 16, 1010
Tel *513 29 36 0*
A treasure trove for the sweet-toothed, this charming confectioners sells deliciouscakes and fruit-topped pastries. Do not miss delights such as *Dobostorte* and *Apfelstrudel (see pp206–7)*. It has a an excellent outdoor terrace.

L'Osteria €
Italian **Map** 5 C3
Bräunerstrasse 11, 1010
Tel *512 25 36 10*
This lovely restaurant offers a wide variety of antipasti and salads, as well as classic pasta dishes. Open every evening until midnight.

Reinthaler's Beisl €
Beisl **Map** 2 D5
Dorotheergasse 2–4, 1010
Tel *5131249*
Expect a reliable menu of typically hearty food in generous portions at this informal restaurant. The classic dishes such as *Wiener Schnitzel* and goulash are superb.

Trześniewski €
Deli **Map** 5 C3
Dorotheergasse 1, 1010
Tel *512 32 91* **Closed** *Sun*
This renowned Viennese snack bar offers a wide selection of small open-faced sandwiches with beer. Try the Swedish herring or the bacon with egg sandwich.

Beaulieu €€
Mediterranean **Map** 5 B2
Herrengasse 14, 1010
Tel *532 11 03* **Closed** *Sun*
The *coq au vin* and seafood risotto with saffron are a popular draw at this bistro. Look out too for the "dish of the day" or the plate of cheeses and breads, paired with local wines.

Café Central €€
Coffee House **Map** 5 B3
Herrengasse 14, 1010
Tel *533 37 63*
Once a gathering place for luminaries in art, literature, science and politics, this café has a long history and serves an excellent two-course lunch.

Café Demel €€
Coffee House **Map** 5 C3
Kohlmarkt 14, 1010
Tel *535 17 17 0*
Oozing with style and finesse, the grand Café Demmel has

Dining on the outdoor terrace at Café Mozart

been serving scrumptious cakes, scones, sweets and pastries since 1786.

Café Mozart €€
Coffee House **Map** 5 C4
Albertinaplatz 2, 1010
Tel *24 100 200*
This quaint spot is crowded at lunchtime, due to a very inviting and inexpensive set menu. Graham Greene worked on the screenplay of Orson Welles's Vienna-set movie *The Third Man* here.

DK Choice

Ilona Stüberl €€
Austro-Hungarian **Map** 5 C3
Bräunerstrasse 2
Tel *533 90 29*
Founded in 1957, this family-run restaurant is a highly regarded part of Vienna's culinary scene. A menu in eight languages covers veal, pork, fish, beef and vegetarian dishes, as well as salads, pastas, soups and hearty desserts. The waiters are amateur historians, well-versed in the 1867 unification of Austria and Hungary under Emperor Franz Josef.

Palmenhaus €€
Brasserie **Map** 5 B4
Burggarten 1, 1010
Tel *533 10 33*
In a Jugendstil greenhouse overlooking a pond, this is a charming location for brasserie-style light meals, as well as being a great lounging spot for just sampling wines.

Regina Margherita €€
Italian **Map** 5 B3
Wallnerstrasse 4, 1010
Tel *533 08 12*
The handmade pizzas at Regina Margherita are topped with the freshest produce and high-quality

olive oil. The menu also includes pastas, grilled meats and fish, and some Neapolitan dishes.

Restaurant im Ambassador €€
Modern Austrian **Map** 6 D4
Kärntner Strasse 22, 1010
Tel *961 61 0*
The Ambassador hotel's restaurant has established itself as a strong force in the city's culinary circles with its variety of flavourful dishes.

Restaurant Kanzleramt €€
Traditional Viennese **Map** 5 B3
Schauflergasse 6, 1010
Tel *533 13 09*
Here diners will find simple and price-conscious menus listing Viennese comfort food, such as calf's liver or dumplings. There is an outdoor terrace in summer.

Restaurant Lohmann €€
Traditional Viennese **Map** 5 C3
Bräunerstrasse 8, 1010
Tel *532 30 11*
Located on a quiet side street off the busy Graben in the old Palais Cavriani, Lohman is traditional in every way. Generous portions and good service.

Sky Restaurant €€
Modern Austrian **Map** 5C5
Kärntner Strasse 19, 1010
Tel *513 17 12*
The view of Vienna rooftops brings diners to this unusual contemporary bar and restaurant on the top floor of the Steffl department store. The menu is small but wide-ranging.

YOHM €€
Asian Fusion **Map** 5 C3
Petersplatz 3
Tel *533 29 00*
Sushi is the focus here, but there are other Asian dishes, including Thai, and everything is based on innovation and inspiration, making every visit exciting.

For more information on types of restaurants *see pages 200–203*

Sapori Restaurant €€€
Mediterranean **Map** 5 B2
Herrengasse 12, 1010
Tel 227 80 0 **Closed** *Sat & Sun*
Diners come here for a tasty modern take on flavourful Mediterranean fare. The braised lemon chicken with almond polenta, and beetroot and anchovy salad with Dijon mustard are truly delicious.

Schottering and Alsergrund

Café Stein €
Café **Map** 5 A1
Währinger Strasse 6–8, 1010
Tel 319 72 41
Popular with students, this coffee house serves hearty breakfasts and wholesome sandwiches all day, until 1am.

CaffèCouture €
Café **Map** 1 B4
Garnisongasse 18, 1090
Tel 0676 33 22 076 **Closed** *Sun*
This hip café uses a state-of-the-art coffee machine to make amazing coffees in a convivial atmosphere. Guests share a large communal table.

I Vecchi Amici €€
Italian **Map** 1 C3
Lichtensteinstrasse 24, 1090
Tel 319 12 86
Experience the warmth of the Mediterranean at I Vecchi Amici. The chalkboard menu, hanging on the tangerine-coloured walls, lists freshly cooked pizzas, pastas and seasonal specials.

Konzert-Café Weimar €
Coffee House **Map** 1 B3
Währinger Strasse 68, 1090
Tel 317 12 06
This is one of the last classic Viennese coffee houses run

Enjoy coffee and cakes at the trendy CaffèCouture

Bright interior of the charming Café Eiles, Josefstadt

in traditional style, serving coffee, pastries, cakes, snacks and *Schnitzel* dishes.

Rembetiko €€
Greek **Map** 1 C3
Porzellangasse 38, 1090
Tel 317 64 93
This blue-and-white-tiled taverna transports diners to the cobbled backstreets of Athens. Fresh pork kebabs, feta salads and lamb chops are all cooked to order in a rustic kitchen.

Restaurant Ragusa €€
Croatian **Map** 1 C4
Berggasse 15, 1090
Tel 317 15 77 **Closed** *Sun*
This eatery is highly praised for its fish menu and attention to presentation. One of the house specialities is the grilled branzino, served with seasonal garnish, accompanied by a rich Croatian wine.

Servitenwirt €€
Modern Austrian **Map** 2 D3
Servitengasse 7, 1090
Tel 315 23 87
Highly regarded for its quality of food-to-price ratio, and crowded with locals more than tourists, Servitenwirt has a large outdoor terrace under the trees.

Stomach €€
Modern Austrian **Map** 1 C3
Seegasse 26, 1090
Tel 310 20 99 **Closed** *Mon & Tue*
This intimate, hole-in-the-wall restaurant with gorgeous bloom-filled gardens is a well-hidden secret. Modern interpretations of traditional Austrian classics are served in fresh, light portions. Cash only.

Trattoria Martinelli €€
Italian **Map** 2 D5
Freyung 3, 1010
Tel 533 67 21
Open every night until midnight, this unassuming trattoria offers a true taste of Italy, focusing on Neapolitan cuisine. It is child-friendly, and there is a summer courtyard, too.

Livingstone €€€
Steakhouse **Map** 2 D4
Zelinkagasse 4, 1010
Tel 533 33 93 0
Slow-moving ceiling fans, giant potted palms and wooden floors create a distinctive plantation-style interior. Angus and Wagyu beef are aged and cooked on a stone grill. Huge choice of American wines.

Museum and Townhall Quarter

Café Eiles €
Coffee House **Map** 1 B5
Josefstädter Strasse 2, 1080
Tel 405 34 10
This unassuming café remains a favourite haunt of writers, actors, dancers and theatre critics. Go for breakfast, a light meal, or cake and a coffee. Faded black-and-white photographs adorning the walls chronicle a fascinating past.

Café Leopold €
Mediterranean **Map** 3 C1
Museumsplatz 1, 1070
Tel 523 67 32
This café in the Leopold Museum avoids traditional Austrian fare; the menu includes tandoori chicken wrap and falafel with hummus and olives. It has a club atmosphere on weekend nights, with live DJs and music.

Café Maria Haag €
Konditorei **Map** 5 B2
Helferstorferstrasse 2
Tel 676 941 81 80
Stop by at this café for coffees, teas and freshly baked cakes and pastries. The menu changes daily, depending on seasonal fruits. The apricot tarts and *Strudels* are particularly recommended.

Centimeter II am Spittelberg €
Traditional Austrian **Map** 3 B1
Stiftgasse 4
Tel 470 0606
This is one of several meat restaurants in Vienna that are famous for inexpensive burgers, ribs and sausages served in hearty portions.

For key to prices *see page 210*

Elegant dining room of Vestibül, inside the Burgtheater

Amerlingbeisl
Beisl €€
Map 3 B1
Stiftgasse 8, 1070
Tel *526 16 60*
This is basically a pub that offers good home-cooked traditional dishes on a limited menu at attractive prices. It is open daily until 2am.

Café Bellaria
Traditional Viennese €€
Map 3 C1
Bellariastrasse 6, 1010
Tel *523 53 20*
For superb coffee and live piano music, visit this café where the owner hosts operetta and Lieder evenings. Traditional dishes are served by charming waiters.

Halle Café
Modern Austrian €€
Map 3 C1
Museumsquartier 1, 1070
Tel *523 70 01*
A popular Museum Quarter restaurant, Halle Café in the Kunsthalle Wien serves food from morning until 2am. On the menu are good-value daily specials such as pork with red cabbage and *Rösti*, along with salads, snacks and desserts.

Kunsthistorisches Museum Café & Restaurant
Traditional Austrian €€
Map 3 C1
Burgring 5, 1010
Tel *649 66 45 46*   **Closed** *Mon*
The beautiful, opulent Cupola Hall of the Kunsthistoriches Museum provides an idyllic setting for the popular Sunday brunch or a romantic fine-dining supper.

Landtmann Café
Coffee House €€
Map 1 C5
Universitätsring 4
Tel *241 00 100*
Sigmund Freud, Hillary Clinton, Sir Paul McCartney and other famous figures have graced this elegant café, which dates back to 1873. Live piano music on Monday and Tuesday evenings.

Lebenbauer
Vegetarian €€
Map 1 C5
Teinfaltstrasse 3, 1010
Tel *533 55 56*   **Closed** *Sat & Sun*
One of Vienna's most upmarket vegetarian restaurants, Lebenbauer boasts an especially creative meat-free menu. Its recipes use mainly organic produce and are cooked without fat, eggs or flour. The pumpkin risotto is a menu highlight.

Pizzeria-Osteria Da Giovanni
Italian €€
Map 3 B1
Sigmundsgasse 14
Tel *523 77 78*   **Closed** *Sun*
At this simple and welcoming restaurant the menu comprises Italian favourites such as bruschetta, soups, salads, pastas and pizzas, all made from fresh ingredients. The home-made traditional desserts are delicious.

Prinz Ferdinand
Traditional Austrian €€
Map 1 A5
Bennoplatz 2, 1080
Tel *402 94 17*
This restaurant serves authentic Austrian cuisine. The *Wiener Schnitzel*, which comes with a delectable potato salad, and the wild garlic soup are highly recommended.

Witwe Bolte
Traditional Austrian €€
Map 3 B1
Gutenberggasse 3, 1070
Tel *523 14 50*
Tuck into mouthwatering *Tafelspitz*, the popular *Schnitzel* and heavenly plum pancakes. In summer, patrons can eat in a beautiful outdoor seating area.

Schnattl
Modern Austrian €€€
Map 1 B5
Lange Gasse 40, 1080
Tel *405 34 00*   **Closed** *Sat & Sun*
Discerning gourmets visit Schnattl for its extensive three- or nine-course tasting menus. Lovely courtyard terrace.

DK Choice

Vestibül
Modern Austrian €€€
Map 1 C5
Universitätsring 2, 1010
Tel *532 49 99*   **Closed** *Sun*
This accolade-winning restaurant in the Burgtheater specializes in wholesome dishes made with seasonal ingredients. Everything is home-made from scratch, from stock to elderberry juice. Buy a sauce from the kitchen to recreate favourite dishes at home.

Zu ebener Erde und erster Stock
Traditional Viennese €€€
Map 3 B1
Burggasse 13, 1070
Tel *523 62 54*   **Closed** *Sat & Sun*
This delightful café in Biedermeier style offers an authentic Viennese experience, from candlelit à la carte dinners to set-price meals of *Schnitzel* and potato dumplings.

Opera and Naschmarkt

Café Drechsler
Coffee House €
Map 3 C2
Link Wienzeile 22, 1060
Tel *581 20 44*
Despite a 21st-century style makeover, Drechsler retains its classic charm. It serves breakfasts, coffee and traditional Viennese cuisine every day until midnight.

Café Ritter
Coffee House €
Map 3 B2
Mariahilfer Strasse 73, 1060
Tel *587 82 38*   **Closed** *Sun*
Choose from a wide menu for breakfast, lunch, afternoon tea, dinner, or just a snack. Special dishes include grilled bream with spinach. Excellent wine list.

Café Sperl
Coffee House €
Map 3 C2
Gumpendorferstrasse 11, 1060
Tel *586 41 58*
Come to Café Sperl for a breakfast of ham, eggs and freshly baked breads. It also serves snacks, lunches and dinners, from dumpling soups to rabbit stews, and many cream-topped coffees.

For more information on types of restaurants *see pages 200–203*

Café Westend
Traditional Viennese €   Map 3 A3
Mariahilfer Strasse 128, 1070
Tel *523 31 83*
Close to the Westbahnhof, this quirky café serves good coffee, pastries and basic dishes. It often has art displays.

Neni
Mediterranean €   Map 3 C2
510 Naschmarkt, 1060
Tel *585 20 20*   **Closed** *Sun*
Open 24 hours a day, Neni is a lively, simple restaurant with a menu that favours Middle Eastern ingredients and dishes. Be sure to try the flatbreads with *hummus*, tahini and olives, lamb *shish kebab*, Israeli salad or lentil soup.

Tewa
Asian Fusion €   Map 3 C2
672 Naschmarkt, 1040
Tel *676 84 77 41 211*   **Closed** *Sun*
Fresh and exciting food is offered at this trendy restaurant. Regulars come here for the honey toast or croissants for breakfast, then wash them down with mango lassi. The lunchtime wraps and soups are great.

DK Choice

Café Sacher
Coffee House €€   Map 4 D1
Philharmonikerstrasse 4, 1010
Tel *514 56 0*
One of Vienna's most stylish venues, Café Sacher's speciality is the original *Sachertorte* (a rich chocolate cake). This is a popular meeting place for exquisite coffees, classic cakes (the *Apfelstrudel* is also highly recommended) and dishes such as *Wiener Schnitzel* in an elegant historic setting. There is a lovely open terrace in summer.

Kostas
Greek €€   Map 4 D2
Friedrichstrasse 6, 1010
Tel *5863729*   **Closed** *Sun*
This friendly restaurant offers diners a taste of authentic Greek cuisine including moussaka delicious *gyros* and crisp salads.

Mama Liu & Sons
Asian €€   Map 3 C2
Gumpendorfstrasse 29, 1060
Tel *586 36 73*   **Closed** *Mon*
While it is not to everyone's taste – because it is said to be authentic rather than adapted to Austrian palates – this Chinese

Chandelier-lit dining room of the traditional Café Sperl

eatery serves vegan meals, fondues and spicy dim sum that are so popular that reservations are essential.

Restaurant Hofbräu
Traditional Austrian €€   Map 3 B2
Mariahilfer Strasse 47
Tel *941 2332*   **Closed** *Sun*
Don't be fooled by the bright, fun decor of this diner – it is very serious about food. Try the breaded cheese with plum compôte or venison ragoût with potato dumplings.

DK Choice

Saint Charles Alimentary
Vegetarian €€   Map 3 C2
Gumpendorferstrasse 33, 1060
Tel *581 15 41*   **Closed** *Sat & Sun*
Laid out like a dispensary with medicine jars, pill bottles and apothecary trappings, this quirky restaurant focuses on organic and healthy cuisine. The selection of delicious and hearty dishes include such offerings as the wild root soup.

Aux Gazelles
French-Moroccan €€€   Map 3 C2
Rahlgasse 5, 1060
Tel *585 66 45*   **Closed** *Sun & Mon*
This is an unusual complex of bar, deli and upscale restaurant, including spa facilities, in an old brick factory. Smoking is permitted but only using a hookah. Couscous and other North African dishes are specialities.

Restaurant Anna Sacher
Modern Austrian €€€   Map 4 D1
Philharmonikerstrasse 4, 1010
Tel *514 56 0*   **Closed** *Mon*
One of the grandest dining experiences in Europe, from the massive chandelier and the green themes of carpet, wall and ceiling to the attentive service from waiters who seem right out of the Imperial age to the food itself, which covers both Austrian classics and fare from foreign seas and pastures. The dessert menu is in a class of its own.

Belvedere Quarter

Café Dialog
Café €   Map 5 E2
Rennweg 43, 1030
Tel *712 62 08*
Eat and drink while reading the newspapers at this authentic café, popular with locals. Endless coffee refills are offered in a cosy atmosphere. Alcohol is served 20 hours a day.

Café Museum
Coffee House €   Map 4 D2
Operngasse 7, 1010
Tel *241 00 62 0*
Since 1899 this lovely café has played host to numerous creative talents, including artists Gustav Klimt and Egon Schiele, composer Oscar Straus and architects Otto Wagner and Adolf Loos. Choose from a range of hearty dishes and enjoy the live evening piano music at weekends.

Heuer am Karlsplatz
Modern Austrian €   Map 4 D2
Treitlstrasse 2, 1040
Tel *890 05 90*
This eatery is very popular with a hip young crowd. The menu changes daily, and there are always vegan options. In summer, there is a DJ on the outdoor terrace.

Tempting desserts on display at the elegant Café Sacher

Café Schwarzenberg, a traditional Viennese coffee house

Bistro Menagerie €€
Bistro **Map** 4 F4
Prinz-Eugen-Strasse 27, 1030
Tel *320 11 11*
Indulge in creatively presented dishes here, including perfectly cooked pink seared tuna, juicy polenta-stuffed chicken and a mouthwatering array of exquisite Viennese desserts.

Café Schwarzenberg €€
Coffee House **Map** 4 E2
Kärntner Ring 17, 1010
Tel *512 89 98*
Choose from dozens of tea varieties as well as great coffees. The glass-fronted cabinet is full of tempting sugar-frosted buns, shiny tortes and yummy fruit pies. This is definite value for money.

Entler €€
Traditional Austrian **Map** 4 D3
Schlüsselgasse 2, 1040
Tel *504 35 85* **Closed** *Sun & Mon*
After an appetizer of nutty rye bread and carrot dipped into a herby oil, savour main course highlights such as venison and duck at this informal restaurant with cheerful, warm decor.

Salm Bräu €€
Tradtional Austrian **Map** 4 F3
Rennweg 8, 1030
Tel *799 59 92*
Try smoked venison and garlic bread or dumpling-topped brown beer soup at this popular beerhall with a convivial atmosphere. The daily specials are good value.

Shiki €€
Japanese **Map** 6 D5
Krugerstrasse 3, 1010
Tel *512 73 97* **Closed** *Sun & Mon*
Shiki is an upscale, fashionable brasserie-style establishment that serves mostly Japanese

dishes. However, it also has some Austrian standards on the menu.

Wiener Wirtschaft €€
Beisl **Map** 4 D3
Wiedner Hauptstrasse 27–29, 1040
Tel *221 11 36 4*
Popular with locals and visitors alike, this restaurant offers generous portions of well-prepared dishes, plus a variety of wines, draft beer and Austrian spirits including schnapps.

DK Choice

Bristol Lounge €€€
Modern Austrian **Map** 4 D2
Kärntner Ring 1, 1010
Tel *515 16 53 3*
Proximity to the State Opera House draws a somewhat formal crowd, not intimidated by the prices. There is live piano music, an open fireplace and a focus on seasonal organic produce. Try the venison *Gulasch* among the traditional dishes. It also has one of the best wine lists in Vienna.

Opus Restaurant im Imperial €€€
Modern Viennese **Map** 4 D2
Kärntner Ring 16, 1010
Tel *501 10 63 56* **Closed** *Mon*
Located in the grand Hotel Imperial, where Austrian monarchs gaze down from gilt frames, this restaurant has a plush yet understated dining room. Feast on exquisitely prepared meals.

Further Afield

Café Aida €
Café-Konditorei
Maxingstrasse 1, 1130
Tel *890 89 88 20 4*
Konditorei chain with over 20 branches in the city. The theme

is pink, from the cakes, cups, and sweets to the waitresses' outfits. Buy a box of chocolates to take home as a souvenir.

Café Cobenzl €
Traditional Austrian
Am Cobenzl 94, 1190
Tel *320 51 20*
A popular venue for cakes and excellent coffee, Café Cobenzl does daily specials and serves its *Strudel* with a large dollop of whipped cream.

Café Cuadro €
Modern Austrian **Map** 3 C4
Margaretenstrasse 77, 1050
Tel *544 75 50*
The chrome, beech and opaque glass decor lends this café a Scandinavian feel. It serves great-value breakfasts, burgers and cocktails, and is busy after dark.

Café Europa €
Traditional Austrian **Map** 3 B2
Zollergasse 8, 1070
Tel *526 33 83*
Excellent breakfasts are served all day here. The *Schnitzel* is delicious. DJs spin club classics in the back room at weekends.

Café Goldegg €
Traditional Austrian **Map** 4 E4
Argentinierstrasse 49, 1040
Tel *505 91 62*
This fine old café with leather chairs and a pool table serves full English breakfasts and club sandwiches, in addition to traditional local fare.

Café Schmid Hansl €
Traditional Viennese **Map** 1 A2
Schulgasse 31, 1180
Tel *406 36 58* **Closed** *Sun*
Open until 2am, with live piano music and frequent classical recitals, Café Schmid Hansl is a large and comfortable space that is perfect for lounging. Good local dishes are served.

Bristol Lounge, one of Vienna's most acclaimed restaurants

For more information on types of restaurants *see pages 200–203*

Opulent crystal chandeliers and red couches at Café Dommayer

Dellago €
Italian
Payergasse 10, 1160
Tel *957 47 95*
This bar and small eatery serves authentic Italian cuisine. Portions are big, and prices are low. Good coctail list.

Frisch WOK €
Asian
Schwaigergasse 10, 1210
Tel *966 88 88*
Come here for a quick fix of inexpensive soups and wraps, some very spicy. Limited seating but takeaway is available. Generous portions are served, and the place is lively late at night.

Gasthaus Reinthaler €
Beisl
Stuwerstrasse 5
Tel *726 82 82* **Closed** *Sat & Sun*
Locals flock to this friendly inn for tasty, home-cooked dishes such as juicy meat-filled cabbage rolls followed by apricot dumplings served with vanilla ice cream. The daily specials are great value.

Gmoa Keller €
Beisl **Map** 6 F5
Heumarkt 25, 1030
Tel *712 53 10* **Closed** *Sun*
The traditional Viennese ambience of this 19th-century inn is complemented by a menu of classic Austrian dishes and excellent selection of wine and beer.

The Golden Harp €
Irish Pub
Erdbergstrasse 27, 1030
Tel *715 13 93*
Locals outnumber tourists at this lively spot, where bands take to the stage on weekends. It offers

a "full Irish breakfast" and pub grub all day. Open until 2am.

DK Choice

Kunst-Café im Hundertwasserhaus €
Traditional Austrian
Lowengassestrasse 41, 1030
Tel *713 86 20*
This welcoming family-run place, although small, is highly praised for its *Apfelstrudel* (apple strudel) and chai latte. Art objects in the Hundertwasser style abound and are available to purchase. There is also an interesting video on Hundertwasserhaus *(see pp166–7)* that can be watched in multiple languages.

Liman €
Turkish
Payergasse 2, 1160
Tel *402 02 90*
Mostly Turkish cuisine is served here, like cabbage rolls filled with rice and meat, but there are also some Lebanese salads and grilled meats, all halal. This popular place is open daily until 4am.

Rasouli €
Modern Austrian
Payergasse 12, 1160
Tel *403 13 47*
This is a student and bohemian hangout with an appreciative audience for a limited but constantly changing menu with Turkish and Asian influences.

Rote Rübe €
Vegetarian **Map** 3 A1
Zieglergasse 37, 1070
Tel *065 07 91 38 60* **Closed** *Mon*
An arty café with a distinctive white-and-red decor, Rote Rübe

boasts a completely meat-free menu. Crêpes and frittatas are full of Greek flavours. Local produce is used to create good-value delicious meals.

Schweizerhaus €
Traditional Austrian
Prater 116
Tel *7280 1520*
Inside the Prater amusement park, you'll find this large beer garden with family tables and very good-value hearty meals of chicken, beef and sausages – in short, all kinds of Austrian comfort food.

Sri Thai Imbiss €
Thai
Baumgasse 18, 1030
Tel *707 92 96* **Closed** *Sat & Sun*
Diners can watch Mrs Sri herself cooking a range of authentic northern Thailand delicacies with fresh ingredients in the open kitchen. The menu features noodles, curries and rice dishes.

Strandcafé €
Traditional Austrian
Florian-Berndl Gasse 20, 1220
Tel *203 67 47*
Big portions of hearty dishes, usually using pork, steak, fish or pasta, are the trademark of this well-known waterfront restaurant. Make the most of the view and choose a table out on the deck.

Vegetasia €
Vegetarian
Ungargasse 57, 1030
Tel *713 83 32* **Closed** *Mon & Tue*
The theme here is "experimental soya", and the lunch buffet offers all you can eat. Other meal options include lentil soups, olive breads, tofu stir-fry, aubergine stew and pesto pasta.

Wetter €
Italian
Payergasse 13, 1160
Tel *406 07 75* **Closed** *Sun*
This former launderette has been transformed into a busy little eatery with distinctive industrial decor – including a rubber floor. Visit for wholesome north-western Italian dishes and Ligurian wines.

Café Dommayer €€
Coffee House
Dommayergasse 1, 1130
Tel *877 54 65 0*
Relax with a steaming cup of *melange* (similar to a cappuccino) in the shaded garden or on a comfortable red couch under crystal chandeliers at this classically stylish café.

Café-Restaurant Cobenzl €€
Traditional Viennese
Am Cobenzl 94, 1190
Tel *320 51 20*
A highlight at this historic, romantic restaurant, with views over Vienna, is a local delicacy – boiled beef fillet with mustard and herbs.

DK Choice

Das Loft €€
French-Austrian **Map** 6 F2
Praterstrasse 1, 1020
Tel *906 16 0*
At the top of the Sofitel Hotel, sparkling decor plus dazzling city views create a wonderful atmosphere to go with Das Loft's excellent menu. Try the scallop ceviche and the roasted suckling pig. A huge selection of wines complement the dishes.

Lusthaus €€
Traditional Austrian
Freudenau 254, 1020
Tel *728 95 65* **Closed** *Wed*
Once the meeting point for imperial hunting parties, Lusthaus serves classic Austrian cuisine in an elegant setting. Try the truffle gnocchi or the roasted pikeperch. There is an in-house patisserie too.

Motto €€
Asian fusion
Schönbrunnerstrasse 30, 1050
Tel *587 06 72*
Serious cuisine is served in a dining room protected from the DJ and dancing, which goes on until 4am on weekends. This hip place is very popular with

celebrities and for its unique cocktails. The menu includes Austrian and Asian fare.

Oktogon Am Himmel €€
Traditional Austrian
Himmelstrasse 125, 1190
Tel *328 89 36* **Closed** *Mon & Tue*
This space is an actual octagon of two-storey glass giving diners rural views. It is fashionable with an upmarket menu but has a casual clientele. Traditional dishes offered include the likes of *Schnitzel* and pork belly.

Ramasuri €€
Vegetarian
Praterstrasse 19, 1020
Tel *676 466 80 60*
This foodies' favourite offers mostly vegetarian and some vegan dishes, but beef and chicken dishes also feature. Outdoor seating is under a red-striped awning by the Johann Nepomuk Nestroy memorial.

Residenz €€
Traditional Austrian
Kavalierstrakt 52, 1130
Tel *241 00 30 0*
Come here for a hearty breakfast, a coffee and a pastry, or a hot meal – there is a fine range of game dishes on the menu. Grab a table on the terrace or sit in the relaxed dining area.

Santa Lucia €€
Italian/Indian
Salesianergasse 10, 1030
Tel *714 21 63*
This long-established Italian eatery serves deep-pan pizzas but also offers daily specials of Indian curries and other dishes

from the subcontinent. Free tiramisu with every dinner.

Tempel €€
Modern Viennese **Map** 6 F1
Praterstrasse 56, 1020
Tel *214 01 79* **Closed** *Sat lunch, Sun & Mon*
This charming restaurant, located close to the house where the "Blue Danube Waltz" was penned, pairs beautifully presented dishes with excellent Austrian wines. Staff are very attentive.

Xu's Cooking €€
Vegetarian/Vegan
Kaiserstrasse 45, 1070
Tel *523 10 91*
Nutrition is taken very seriously at Xu's, where the Chinese dishes are rich in proteins, vitamins and minerals and free from mono-sodium glutamate. The buffet is excellent value for money.

Flatschers €€€
Steakhouse
Kaiserstrasse 113–115, 1070
Tel *523 42 68*
Dishes such as beef tartare, smoked meats, chilli steak wrap and burgers with a huge choice of toppings satisfy a loyal clientele at this popular venue. Try the signature dish of Argentine fillet steak.

Mraz und Sohn €€€
Gourmet **Map** 2 E1
Wallensteinstrasse 59, 1200
Tel *330 45 94* **Closed** *Sat & Sun*
The creative cuisine here shows global influences and includes acclaimed saddle of lamb with barley, as well as a nine-course menu with wine pairings.

The bright, flashy decor of the fashionable Motto

For more information on types of restaurants *see pages 200–203*

SHOPS AND MARKETS

Since Vienna is a compact city, it is a pleasant place to shop. The main shopping area is pedestrianized and full of pretty cafés, and you can browse around at a leisurely pace. Austrian-made glassware, food and traditional crafts all make for good buys. Although the main shops tend to cater to comparatively conventional and mature tastes, the flea markets appeal to every whim and budget.

The pedestrian shopping areas of Kärntner Strasse, the Graben and Kohlmarkt are fun for window-shoppers. A surprising number of shops of all kinds, including coffee shops, now feature online shopping. But nobody goes home empty handed from the street markets selling antiques and outright junk. For more details of shops and markets see the Directory on page 225.

Best Buys

Many of the best buys in Vienna are small and readily transportable. Coffee addicts shouldn't forget to buy freshly ground coffee – the city imports some of the best.

If you have a sweet tooth, you couldn't be in a more appropriate city. Vienna is justly famous for its cakes, pastries and *Torten (see pp206–7)* and any good *Café-Konditorei* (cake shop and café) will ship cakes back home for you. In November and December, try the buttery Advent *Stollen* available from **Julius Meinl am Graben** *(see p223)* or any good baker. Stuffed with fruit and nuts and dusted with icing sugar, it is a tasty Christmas loaf.

Alternatively, buy some prettily packaged *Sachertorte (see p207)*, available year round. The specialist chocolate shops *(see p223)* are worth a visit, both for the unusual packaging and the chocolate itself.

Sweet *Eiswein* (so-called because the grapes are left on the vines until the first frosts) is

an unusual and delicious dessert wine. **Zum Schwarzen Kameel** *(see p223)* sells the rarer red version as well.

Other Austrian-made goods include clothes manufactured in the felt-like woollen fabric known as *Loden (see p223)*. If you feel like treating yourself and have space in your car or suitcase, buy custom-made sheets or high-quality down pillows or duvets made in Austria *(see p222)*. Petit point embroidery, which adorns anything from powder compacts to handbags, is a Viennese speciality *(see p222)*.

Glassware – including superb chandeliers – and **Augarten** porcelain *(see p222)* tend to be highly original, although expensive. Many people collect crystal ornaments made by Swarovski and should head to **Ostovics** *(see p222)*, a good crystal and glass shop.

Trachten (Austrian costume) shops *(see p223)* are fun; they have a wide selection of hats, children's dresses, jackets and blouses. **INLIBRIS Gilhofer**

Chest of drawers chocolate box from Altmann & Kühne *(see p223)*

(see p223) stocks old prints and maps. Early editions of works by writers such as Freud, Kraus or Rilke can be found in Vienna's antiquarian bookshops *(see p223)*.

Opening Hours

Shops usually open at 8:30 or 9 in the morning and close at 6 or 7 in the evening. Some of the smaller shops close for an hour at lunchtime. Traditionally stores were required to close at noon on Saturday, though all now stay open until 5pm. On Sundays, the food and clothing stores at shopping malls in the railway stations remain open, as do small supermarkets found at petrol stations. Many bakeries are also open on Sunday mornings.

How to Pay

As in most modern cities, Vienna's shops, on the whole, accept major credt and debit cards. Visitors should carry some

The famous Julius Meinl am Graben delicatessen in Vienna

cash, however, as the odd shop, café or restaurant may still be cash-only.

Where to Shop

The pedestrian shopping areas of Graben, Kohlmarkt and Kärntner Strasse have many of the best-known and most expensive shops in Vienna.

A less pricey area is along Mariahilfer Strasse, where there are department stores selling household goods, and well-known chain stores such as H & M.

Rights and Services

If a purchase is defective you are usually entitled to a refund, provided you have proof of purchase. This is not always the case with goods bought in the sales – inspect them carefully before you buy. Many shops in Vienna will pack goods for you – and often gift-wrap them at no extra charge – and send them anywhere in the world.

VAT Exemption

VAT (value added tax) or MWSt (Mehrwertsteuer) is normally charged at 20 per cent. If you reside outside the European Union (EU), you are entitled to claim back the VAT on goods purchased in Austria. This is only the case, however, if the total purchase price (this can include the total cost of several items from one shop) exceeds €73. Take along your passport when shopping and ask the shopkeeper to complete Form U34 at the time of sale. This should also bear the shop's stamp and have the receipt attached. You may choose to have the refund credited to your credit card account, have it posted home, or pick it up at the airport.

Purchased goods must not be used prior to exportation. If you leave Vienna by air, present the form at Customs before checking in, and have it stamped as proof of export. You may also have to show your purchases at Customs,

Kohlmarkt, one of Vienna's pedestrian shopping streets

so pack them somewhere accessible. Then post the stamped form to the Austrian shopkeeper or collect the refund at the airport (there is a handling fee). If leaving by car or train, present the form to Customs at the border, where you can also claim a refund. If you are not disembarking the train at the border, there is sometimes a customs official on the train to stamp your form.

When you have goods sent directly to your home outside the EU, VAT is deducted at the time of purchase. Since Austria is a member of the EU, EU citizens cannot claim back VAT.

The elegant Freyung Passage in Ferstel Palace, with beautiful vaulted ceilings

Sales

The bi-annual sales are held in January and July. The best bargains are usually in fashions. Electrical and household goods are also much reduced.

Shopping Centres

There are a handful of shopping centres dotted across Vienna, including **Ringstrassen-Galerien**, **Lugner City**, **Wien Mitte The Mall** and the **BahnhofCity Wien West** in the Westbahnhof station. Built in the same style as the Café Central *(see pp60–63)*, **Freyung Passage** is an arcade of elegant shops in the Palais Ferstel *(see pp110 and 112)*.

DIRECTORY

Shopping Centres

BahnhofCity Wien West
Westbahnhof, Europlatz 2.
Map 3 A2.

Freyung Passage
Palais Ferstel 1, Freyung 2.
Map 2 D5 & 5 B2.

Lugner City
Gablenzgasse 1–3.
Map 3 A2.

Ringstrassen-Galerien
Kärntner Ring 5–7.
Map 6 D5.

Wien Mitte The Mall
Landstrasser Hauptstrasse 1B.
Map 4 F1 & 6 F4.

Shops and Boutiques

Service in Vienna's shops is more courteous and informed than in some other countries, and English is invariably understood. Ease and efficiency of public transport and VAT-free prices attract astute shoppers looking for art, antiques and Austrian speciality products such as loden waterproof garments. Austrian glassware is justly famous, and cut-glass items are of a high quality. A few shops, such as **Knize** (in the Graben), designed by Adolf Loos, are in themselves worth a visit simply to admire the Jugendstil architecture.

Speciality Shops

Vienna still manufactures leather goods, although nowadays a lot is imported from Italy. **Robert Horn** designs and manufactures leather travel cases and accessories. He maintains that even he has been unable to improve on the design of a briefcase carried by Metternich at the Congress of Vienna, which he has only slightly modernized.

Petit point embroidery is another Viennese speciality. Some of the most attractive pieces can be found at **Petit Point** (where even the shop's door handle is embroidered) and at **Maria Stransky**.

Near Stephansplatz, **Steiff** is a den of teddy bears, cuddly toys and hand-carved wooden figures. The novelty and joke shop **Witte Zauberklingl** stocks masks, fancy dress outfits and, beautiful old-fashioned paper decorations that are designed for use at Viennese festivals. **Pirker**, a shop specializing in beeswax, sells its own candles and candlesticks. It also stocks other gift items such as honey cakes and boxes of chocolates.

Music

As you would expect in the "City of Music", the range of recordings available is rich and varied. The shops with the widest range of classical CDs are **EMI** and **Gramola**. However, don't expect to find many bargains: CDs are more expensive in Austria than in most other countries in Europe. **Arcadia** specializes in opera

and operetta. **Doblinger** focuses on contemporary Austrian music and is excellent for sheet music; it also has a second-hand CD department. The staff in all these shops are usually very knowledgeable.

Jewellery

Viennese jewellers have long been famous for their fine workmanship. Fruit and flower brooches carved in semi-precious stones and sometimes studded with diamonds are a recent Austrian innovation. **Juwelier Wagner** always has a good selection. Both **Köchert** and **Heldwein** were jewellers to the Imperial Court and their workshops still produce beautiful jewellery today. Köchert also sells antique pieces and Heldwein are known for their multi-coloured chains of semi- precious stones. In 2010, one of the pieces designed by **Schullin** won the prestigious Diamonds International award organized by De Beers for innovative design. Their small window usually attracts a crowd of admirers to view their latest creations. Don't let that put you off – prices start at a reasonable level.

Glassware

Chandeliers at Vienna's Opera House and the Metropolitan Opera in New York are by **J & L Lobmeyr**, as are chandeliers in numerous palaces throughout the world – including the Kremlin. This company – now run by

a fifth generation of the same family – has produced beautiful glassware and crystal chandeliers since the early 19th century, often commissioning famous artists. One range of glasses still in production today was designed by Josef Hoffmann (see pp56–9) in Jugendstil style. Its famous *Musselinglas*, a type of glass so fine that it almost bends to the touch, is exquisite. There is a small but superb glass museum on the first floor and, apart from its own glassware, Lobmeyr also sells select items of Hungarian Herend porcelain.

Interiors

Albin Denk, founded in 1702, is the oldest porcelain shop in Vienna and was the official purveyor to the court. It has a vast range of beautiful objects. **Augarten**, the second oldest porcelain maker, was founded in 1718 and taken over by the Habsburgs in 1744. Ever since, its products have been marked with their banded shield coat of arms. Each piece of porcelain at **Schloss Augarten** is still hand-finished and painted: patterns and shapes are based on original designs from the Baroque, Rococo, Biedermeier and Art Deco periods or are created by present-day artists. The Schloss Augarten factory is open to visitors. **Ostovics** stocks glass and porcelain as well as kitchen-ware, and is good for gifts.

Founded in 1849, **Backhausen** is known for its exclusive furnishing fabrics, woven in the original Jugendstil patterns, and for its silk scarves and matching velvet handbags. In addition it has a good selection of duvets and household linens. Quality bedding and linens are available at **Gans**, which conveniently has a shop at Vienna's Schwechat airport for last-minute purchases.

Gunkel stocks household linen and bath robes, and for generations the Viennese have patronized **Zur Schwäbischen**

Jungfrau, founded in 1720, where fine linens can be made to order as well as purchased ready-made.

Food and Wine

One of Vienna's most renowned and almost revered food and wine shops, **Zum Schwarzen Kameel** *(see p212)*, sells mouth-watering produce. **Julius Meinl am Graben** food hall, on the pedestrianized Graben, also offers a wide selection of delicacies. Enter via its Lukullus Bar in Naglergasse if you want to stop for a snack and a drink. There is a good chain of wine merchants called **Wein & Co**, one of whose branches is situated on the Jasomir-gottstrasse. **Altmann & Kühne** is famous for its tiny, handmade chocolates sold in beautiful boxes shaped like miniature chests of drawers, books, horses and angels.

Gifts

Successor of the famous Wiener Werkstätten, the outfit called **Österreichische Werkstätten** has a selection of almost exclusively Austrian goods. It stocks a range of enamelled jewellery designed by Michaela Frey, ceramics, mouth-blown glass, candles and, from late autumn onwards, Christmas tree decorations. The arts and crafts markets *(see p224)* are also good hunting-grounds for knick-knacks. The Tirol-based firm of **Swarovski** produces high-quality crystal. Their necklaces, pins and earrings are popular worldwide, as are their animal figurines and accessories.

Books

Located in the Jewish District is **Shakespeare & Co**, which stocks an extensive selection of books in English, as does **Frick International**. For music books in English, visit **Doblinger** *(see p222)*. Rare old books – as well as new ones, including novels and autobiographies – can be purchased at **Heck**. Old prints and maps are available at the specialist **INLIBRIS Gilhofer**.

Newspapers and Periodicals

Most newspaper kiosks located within the Ringstrasse stock foreign newspapers – and so do the best coffee houses, where they can be read free of charge. There is no English-language Viennese newspaper. **Morawa** sells a variety of newspapers and periodicals in practically any language.

Clothes and Accessories

Viennese clothes are well made and tend to be quite formal. **Loden-Plankl** is famous for jackets, coats and capes made from *Loden*. This is a warm, felt-like fabric traditionally in dark green or grey, but now produced in a range of colours.

Tostmann is best known for traditional Austrian costumes or *Trachten*: its *Dirndl* (dresses) are made from a variety of fabrics, including beautiful brocades. Its clothes for children are particularly delightful.

Hämmerle has fashion shops all across Austria, but the showcase for elegant eveningwear is the stylish shop on Mariahilferstrasse. The flagship store of **Peek & Cloppenburg** sells casual and sporty clothing as well as accessories. A trusted and old-established Viennese name is **Knize**. Designed by Adolf Loos, in imperial times this was a famous tailoring establishment, but the shop now stocks ready-to-wear clothes for men and women. It also sells its own scent. **Kettner** – almost hidden down a nearby side street – stocks outdoor *Trachten* for both men and women. **Steffl** department store has seven floors of fashion, toys and stationery.

All the shoes at **Bally** are imported from Italy; the quality, as you would expect, is excellent. **D'Ambrosio**, which has several branches, stocks trendy, up-market Italian-style shoes for both men and women at moderate prices. **Denkstein Comfort** is another shoe retailer with stock at reasonable prices.

Younger, trendier shoppers should head straight to Judengasse – this street has plenty of boutiques with styles to suit every taste. **Paul Vienna** is a menswear store that stocks some of the more popular designer labels as well as casual clothing. The branch of the trendy clothes chain **H & M**, on Graben, is worth a visit if only to view the gilded birdcage of a lift.

Back in 1980, an optician called **Erich Hartmann** bought a shop that had a large stock of horn and tortoiseshell. Today he sells a range of handmade spectacles, combs and chains, all made from horn.

Size Chart

Women's clothes

Austrian	36	38	40	42	44	46	48	50
British	10	12	14	16	18	20	22	24
American	6	8	10	12	14	16	18	20

Shoes

Austrian	36	37	38	39	40	41	42	43
British	3½	4	5	5½	6½	7	7½	8
American	6	6½	7½	8½	9	9.5	10	10½

Men's shirts

Austrian	44	46	48	50	52	54
British	34	36	38	40	42	44
American	S	M	M	L	XL	XL

Antiques, Auctions and Markets

Many districts in Vienna have their own markets – and a few have several – where you can buy arts and crafts, food, flowers and imported and second-hand goods. The city is also known for its Christmas markets, popular with locals in the evenings. If you are interested in antiques and bric-a-brac, it is worth looking in both the specialist antique shops and the main auction house. The Naschmarkt, Vienna's main food market, is packed with bustling ethnic stalls and a mix of cultures, making it the perfect place for browsing.

Antiques

Vienna is justly famous for its antique shops. Most are located in the Stephansdom Quarter and along Schön-brunner Strasse, where stock ranges from valuable antiques to second-hand goods. The **Dorotheum** *(see Auctions)*, the **Kunst und Antikmarkt** and the **Flohmarkt** *(see Artisan Markets)* should not be missed. Jewellery and antique paintings can be particularly good finds. The Vienna silver specialist is **Kulscar**, which is also a good place to go for bronze sculptures and porcelain.

If you are interested in old jewellery, gold and other antiques, **Edith Stöhr** is worth a visit. For larger pieces, try **Sonja Reisch** on Bräunerstrasse. **Kovacs** by the Palais Lobkowitz has perhaps Vienna's finest antique furniture, as well as decorative pieces focusing on the Art Nouveau period.

Auctions

Opened in 1707 as a pawn-broker for the "new poor", and appropriately called the *Armen Haus* (poor house), Vienna's **Dorotheum** is now the city's most important auction house. In 1788 it moved to the site of a former convent called the Dorotheerkirche, which contained an altarpiece dedicated to St Dorothea – hence the name. This is an interesting place to browse, and since buying is not restricted to auction times, you can often purchase items over the counter. It has other branches dotted around the city.

Food Markets

Between the Linke and Rechte Wienzeile, the **Naschmarkt** *(see p142)* is worth visiting even if you don't buy anything. Exotic fruit and vegetables, notably Greek, Turkish and Asian specialities, crowd the stalls and are piled high in the shops. It is a fascinating place to wander around and observe life. Open all year round, it acts as a meeting point for people of different nationalities who come to buy and sell fruit and vegetables, tea, herbs and spices. The section near the Karlsplatz contains the more expensive Viennese-run stalls. These gradually give way to colourful stands stocking a range of international treats.

In addition to the exotic food stalls, you will see Czechs selling hand puppets, Russians selling Babushka dolls and Turks with stalls piled high with clothes. The market is also a good spot for late-night revellers to feast on highly spiced fish snacks in the early hours of the morning.

Food lovers should not miss the farmers' market known as the **Bauernmarkt**. A whole range of organic country produce is on sale here on Friday and Saturday.

Artisan Markets

Antique markets and arts and crafts markets are fairly new to Vienna, but the **Flohmarkt** (flea market) at the end of the Naschmarkt *(see p142)* and the **Antiquitätenmarkt** are established hunting grounds for second-hand goods and antiques. The price quoted is probably not the price that you are expected to pay – it's usually assumed that you will bargain.

For better-quality hand-crafted goods, head to the **Spittelberg** market *(see p119)* near the Volkstheater. Here artists and craftspeople sell their own products rather than mass-produced factory goods. This is a fashionable and attractive part of Vienna and, although the market is small, you are likely to find gifts to take back home. There are also small galleries and cafés where artists exhibit their works.

The **Kunst und Antikmarkt Am Hof** is the place to buy exquisite antique paintings, books and coins. Intricately designed stone, clay and porcelain vessels, Asian artworks and wooden toys are also available here, while rustic stalls sell delicious sausages and beer.

Festive Markets

Christmas markets in Vienna are very special, the most famous of all being the **Christkindlmarkt** *(see p66)* held in front of the Rathaus. Attractions vary from year to year, but there are always sideshows, decorated trees, performances on a temporary stage and lots of stalls, as well as a workshop for making Christmas presents and baked goodies. Items for sale include honey cakes, beeswax candles, Christmas decorations and various crafts, although the main attraction is the joyous atmosphere. It is especially magical at night when everything is lit up.

The **Alt Wiener Christ-kindlmarkt** *(see p66)* at the Freyung is a smaller affair. Two weeks before Easter there is also an Easter market here with a large selection of blown and hand-painted eggs. Other Christmas markets take place in the Spittelberg area, Schloss Schönbrunn, Karlskirche, Heiligenkreuzerhof and on Maria-Theresien-Platz.

DIRECTORY

Speciality Shops

Maria Stransky
Hofburg Passage 2.
Map 5 C4.
Tel 5336098.

Petit Point
Kärntner Strasse 16. **Map**
4 D1 & 6 D4. **Tel** 5124886.

Pirker Lebkuchen
Stephansplatz 7. **Map** 2
E5 & 6 D3. **Tel** 5123433.

R Horn's Wien
Bräunerstrasse 7.
Map 5 C4. **Tel** 5122507.

Steiff
Bräunerstrasse 3.
Map 4 D1 & 5 C4.
Tel 5124896.

Witte Zauberklingl
Linke Wienzeile 16.
Map 3 A4. **Tel** 5864305.

Music

Arcadia
Kärntner Strasse 40. **Map**
4 D2 & 5 C5. **Tel** 5139568.

Doblinger
Dorotheergasse 10.
Map 5 C3. **Tel** 515030.

EMI
Kärntner Strasse 30.
Map 4 D1 & 6 D4.
Tel 5123675.

Gramola
Graben 16. **Map** 2 D5 & 5
C3. **Tel** 5335034.

Jewellery

Heldwein
Graben 13. **Map** 5 C3.
Tel 5125781.

Juwelier Wagner
Kärntner Strasse 32.
Map 4 D1. **Tel** 5120512.

Köchert
Neuer Markt 15.
Map 5 C4. **Tel** 5125828.

Schullin
Kohlmarkt 7.
Map 2 D5 & 5 C3.
Tel 5339007.

Glassware

J & L Lobmeyr
Kärntner Strasse 26.
Map 2 D5 & 6 D4.
Tel 512050888.

Interiors

Albin Denk
Graben 13. **Map** 2 D5 & 5
C3. **Tel** 5124439.

Augarten
Spiegelgasse 3.
Map 2 D5 & 5 C3.
Tel 5121494.

Backhausen
Kärntnerstrasse 6.
Map 4 D1 & 6 D4.
Tel 2852 5020.

Gans
Brandstätte 1–3.
Map 4 D1 & 6 D3.
Tel 5333560.

Gunkel
Tuchlauben 11. **Map** 2 D5
& 5 C3. **Tel** 5336301.

Ostovics
Stephansplatz 9. **Map** 6
D3. **Tel** 5331411.

Schloss Augarten
Obere Augartenstrasse 1.
Map 2 E2. **Tel** 21124200.

**Zur Schwäbischen
Jungfrau**
Graben 26. **Map** 2 D5 &
5 C3. **Tel** 5355356.

Food and Wine

Altmann & Kühne
Graben 30. **Map** 2 D5 &
5 C3. **Tel** 5330927.

**Julius Meinl am
Graben**
Graben 19. **Map** 2 D5 &
5 C3. **Tel** 5323334.

Wein & Co
Jasomirgottstrasse 3–5.
Map 6 D3. **Tel** 507063121.

**Zum Schwarzen
Kameel**
Bognergasse 5.
Map 5 C3. **Tel** 5338125.

Gifts

**Österreichische
Werkstätten**
Kärntner Strasse 6.
Map 4 D1 & 6 D4.
Tel 5122418.

Swarovski
Kärntner Strasse 24.
Map 6 D4. **Tel** 3240000.

Books

Frick International
Schulerstrasse 1–3.
Map 6 D3. **Tel** 5126905.

Heck
Kärntner Ring 14. **Map** 4
E2 & 6 D5. **Tel** 5055152.

INLIBRIS Gilhofer
Rathausstrasse 19.
Map 1 C5. **Tel** 40961900.

Shakespeare & Co
Sterngasse 2. **Map** 2 E5 &
6 D2. **Tel** 5355053.

Newspapers and
Periodicals

Morawa
Wollzeile 11. **Map** 2 E5 &
6 D3. **Tel** 5137513450.

Clothes and
Accessories

Bally
Graben 12. **Map** 5 C3.
Tel 5130550.

D'Ambrosio
Jasomirgottstrasse 6.
Map 6 D3. **Tel** 533041623.

Denkstein Comfort
Stephansplatz 4.
Map 6 D3. **Tel** 5127465.

Flamm
Neuer Markt 12.
Map 5 C4. **Tel** 5122889.

H&M
Graben 8. **Map** 2 D5 & 5
C3. **Tel** 0810909090.

Hämmerle
Mariahilferstrasse 105.
Map 3 A3 & 5 A5.
Tel 5336053.

Hartmann
Singerstrasse 8, Corner of
Lilieng. **Map** 6 D3.
Tel 5121489.

Kettner
Plankengasse 7.
Map 5 C4. **Tel** 5132239.

Knize
Graben 13. **Map** 2 D5 & 5
C3. **Tel** 5122119.

Loden-Plankl
Michaelerplatz 6.
Map 5 C3. **Tel** 5338032.

Paul Vienna
Kärntner Strasse 14.
Map 6 D4. **Tel** 5129523.

Steffl
Kärntner Strasse 19.
Map 6 D3. **Tel** 930560.

Tostmann
Schottengasse 3a.
Map 5 B2. **Tel** 5335331.

Antiques

Edith Stöhr
Stallburggasse 2.
Map 5 C3. **Tel** 5128973.

Kovacs
Lobkowitzplatz 1. **Map** 4
D1 & 5 C4. **Tel** 5879474.

Kulscar
Spiegelgasse 19. **Map** 4
D1 & 5 C4. **Tel** 5127267.

Sonja Reisch
Bräunerstrasse 10.
Map 5 C4. **Tel** 5355215.

Auctions

Dorotheum
Dorotheergasse 17. **Map**
4 D1 &5 C4. **Tel** 515600.

Markets

Antiquitätenmarkt
Donaukanal-Promenade.
Map 6 F2. **Open** May–
end Sep: 2–8pm Sat,
10am–8pm Sun.

**Alt Wiener
Christkindlmarkt**
Freyung. **Map** 2 D5 & 5
B2. **Open** 17 Nov–24 Dec:
9:30am–7:30pm daily.

Bauernmarkt
Freyung. **Map** 2 D5 & 5
B2. **Open** 9am–6pm Fri
& Sat.

Christkindlmarkt
At the Neues Rathaus.
Map 1 C5 & 5 A2.
Open Mid-Nov–24 Dec:
10am–7pm daily.

**Kunst und
Antikmarkt Am Hof**
Map 5 C2. **Open** Mar–
Nov: 10am–6pm Fri & Sat.

Naschmarkt
Map 3 C2. **Open** 6am–
6:30pm Mon–Fri,
6am–6pm Sat.

Many of the listings have
multiple branches. Shops
will be happy to provide
information of their
nearest branch.

ENTERTAINMENT IN VIENNA

Vienna offers a wide range of entertainment, particularly of the musical variety. Grand opera is performed at the Staatsoper, or State Opera House, (see pp140–41) and the Theater an der Wien (see p142). Dignified orchestral concerts and elegant Viennese waltzes take place at great balls during the Carnival season, and waltzes are played in the relaxed atmosphere of the Stadtpark. The famous white Lipizzaner stallions dance to Austrian classical music at the Spanish Riding School, and the Vienna Boys' Choir perform at various venues. Vienna has some of the best German-speaking theatre in Europe and even one entire theatre group devoted to English-language productions. There is an IMAX super-size cinema, and most films are shown in English or subtitled. Within the Ringstrasse, the city buzzes with late-night revellers enjoying music clubs, such as the Roter Engel, discos and bars with live music. At the end of the night, there is public transport to take you home, and always a sausage stand open on the way.

The stage of the Theater in der Josefstadt (see p118)

Practical Information

The best way to find out what's on is to check the Vienna tourist office website (www.wien.info), which lists over 10,000 events. Other handy internet guides are vienna.eventful.com and vienna.inyourpocket.com.

Many of the most high-profile events are fully sold out several months in advance, but concierges at the more upmarket hotels generally know where the best shows are and how to obtain tickets.

Posters around town advertise upcoming events, shows and concerts, and daily newspapers, although in German, are also informative.

Booking Tickets

You can buy tickets from online agencies such as culturall.com, viennaclassic.com, vienna concerts.com, viennaticket. com and wien-ticket.at, and also direct from the appropriate box office (check opening hours, since these vary), or reserve them by telephone. The phone numbers and addresses for the booking offices are listed in the Music, Theatre and Cinema directories (see pp229–30). The four state theatres – the Burgtheater (see pp134–5), the **Akademietheater** (see p230), the Opera House (see pp140–41) and the Wiener Volksoper (see p228) – all have one central booking office, the **Bundestheaterkassen** (see p229). However, tickets for performances at any of these four theatres can also be purchased at the box office of the Wiener Volksoper and the Burgtheater.

Tickets usually go on sale two months before the performance. However, bear in mind that tickets for September performances of the Vienna State Opera are sold during the month of June.

Written applications for tickets for the state theatre must reach the Vienna State Opera ticket office (address as Bundestheaterkassen) no later than three weeks before the date of the performance. Standing-room tickets are sold at the evening box office one hour before the start of the performance.

Tickets for the state theatres, the Theater an der Wien (see p142), the **Raimund Theater** (see p229) and **Konzerthaus** (see p228) are also valid for public transport for two hours before, and six hours after, all performances.

At the Theatre

If you visit the theatre in person, you will be able to see the seating plan and make your choice accordingly. The monthly programme for the state theatres also contains

Billboard column

Dancing at the grand Opera Ball *(see p141)*

individual seating plans and it is a good idea to have them in front of you when booking your tickets by telephone. Most hotel porters will also have copies of seating plans for the principal venues.

If you book by telephone remember that *Parkett* (stalls) are in front and are usually the most expensive. In some theatres the front rows of the stalls are known as *Orchestersitze*. The *Parterre* (back stalls) are cheaper and the dress circle (the grand or royal circle) is called *Erster Rang*, followed by the *Zweiter Rang* (balcony). At the Burgtheater and Opera House, there are two extra levels called the *Balkon* and *Galerie*. The higher you go, the cheaper the seats are. Boxes are known as *Logen* and the back seats are always cheaper than the front seats.

At the **Wiener Volksoper** *(see p229)* they still have *Säulensitze*, seats where the view is partly obscured by a column. These cheap tickets are bought by music lovers who come to listen rather than to view. There are four tiers of boxes at the Volksoper, known in ascending order as *Parterre, Balkon, Erster Rang* and *Zweiter Rang*.

Buffets at Vienna's principal theatres provide alcoholic and non-alcoholic drinks, and tasty snacks which range from open sandwiches at the **Akademietheater** *(see p230)* and Volksoper to the more elaborate concoctions at the Opera House and Burgtheater. Sandwiches, made from a Viennese bread roll, are often filled with caviar, egg, smoked salmon, cheese or salami. Glasses of *Sekt*, a sparkling wine, are always available.

Buffets are usually open for up to one hour before the start of a performance and are often fairly empty. They are an ideal place to have a small bite to eat and something to drink, and the coffee is extremely good.

It is not usual to tip ushers at theatres, unless you are being shown to a box, but you may round up the price of a theatre programme.

Coats and hats have to be left in the cloakroom before you go to your seat. There is usually no fixed charge, and tipping is at your discretion.

Late Night

Many of the better restaurants stop serving food as early as 10pm. But music clubs such as U4 *(see p229)* carry on into the early hours. Restaurants with late hours are noted in the *Where to Eat and Drink* section *(see pp210–19)*. In addition to these, there are cafés open until 1am and scores of very late-night takeaway shops. But you have not been to Vienna until you have joined the 4am sausage devotees at a *Würstelstand*. North American fans of the cheese dog will become instant converts to the *Käsekrainer*.

Alternative

Vienna is not just about history and tradition. Explore the emerging hipster culture and street life, for free, in a 3-hour tour that is unique and entertaining. Visits to squats, artists' workspaces and street art in areas like Kirchengasse and along the canal are designed to show the other side of this city of tradition. Evening pub crawls are also arranged.

Facilities for the Disabled

Legislation in recent years has made Vienna, with its sometimes inconvenient old buildings, far more accessible, or "barrier-free", to use the local term. A comprehensive booklet in English can be downloaded at www.wien.info/en/travel-info/accessible-vienna. Many venues will assist those in wheelchairs to special viewing areas.

Transport

Normal service on the buses, trams and underground (U-bahn) lines shuts down around midnight, depending on the route. For night owls, the subway lines stay open 24 hours on Friday and Saturday nights and every night before a public holiday. Lines run every 15 minutes. There are also 26 bus routes running from midnight to 5am, some going deep into the suburbs. These night buses are marked "N-", with the number of their route, and they run every 30 minutes. Taxis will not be found cruising looking for fares; instead, they wait at designated taxi stands or at hotels. They can also be requested by phone.

Music in Vienna

The Vienna Opera House (see pp140–41) is one of the greatest of its kind in the world and, as one of four state theatres, is heavily subsidized. The acoustics are excellent – the world-famous conductor Arturo Toscanini advised on the rebuilding of the theatre after it was destroyed in 1945. The city supports two principal orchestras: the Wiener Philharmoniker and the Wiener Symphoniker. Musicians invited to join the Philharmonic are all members of the State Opera House orchestra. Most operas are sung in the original language. There are also a number of chamber music ensembles and visiting artists. Church music is often of concert quality. You can hear more informal music in the Stadtpark, where a small orchestra regularly plays waltzes in summer. Live rock music is popular in clubs, and there is an annual jazz festival (see p65).

Opera and Operetta

The **Staatsoper** (State Opera House; see pp140–41), performs 300 times a year and with an astonishing diversity, featuring ballet and operas from every period and including five premieres a year. Tickets must be booked one month in advance and are expensive. But performances are streamed live on the website or via the mobile app for free, and some appear on a huge screen outside the Opera. The New Year's Eve performance is always *Die Fledermaus* by Johann Strauss, and famous guests sometimes make surprise appearances during the Second Act.

The **Wiener Volksoper** is renowned for its superb operetta productions of works by composers ranging from Strauss, Millöcker and Ziehrer to Lehár and Kálmán. There are also performances of musicals and light opera by Mozart, Puccini and Bizet, sung in German. Prices range from €3 to €86, and the season is exactly the same as the Opera House.

One of Vienna's most vibrant stages is the **Theater an der Wien** (see p142), near the Naschmarkt. Built in 1801 and once the temporary home of the State Opera, it is now rebranded as "the new opera house", with a range of dance, concerts and operas, often built around a theme. Productions at Theater an der Wien are planned in conjunction with those at the smaller **Wiener Kammeroper**, or Chamber Opera, in the Stephansdom quarter. A diverse programme, with younger performers appealing to a younger audience, sometimes tiptoes into rock music. Today, musical theatre productions, including world premieres, flourish under the direction of the VBW group at two venues. The **Raimund Theater**, in the Westbahnhof area, with an operetta pedigree, is Vienna's first exclusively musical theatre venue, with its own orchestra. The **Ronacher**, once a vaudeville hall, stages original works as well as popular musicals.

Tickets for all Vienna's most famous venues, including the State Opera and the Volksoper, can be purchased at the central ticket service of the **Bundestheaterkassen**. Tickets go on sale one month in advance. A limited number of standing tickets go on sale one hour before a performance.

Classical Concerts

The **Musikverein** is Vienna's single most famous concert venue. Built in Classical style with pillars and pedestals, the Musikverein's main auditorium is known as both the Grosser Musikvereinssaal (Great Hall), and the Goldener Saal (Golden Hall). It is world-famous for its impeccable acoustics, that are all the more remarkable because, at the time of construction in 1863, modern acoustic materials and theories were unknown. These concert areas are devoted to jazz and next-generation artists. But the Musikverein is most renowned as the home of what is considered one of the very finest orchestras in the world, the Vienna Philharmonic, or **Wiener Philharmoniker**. Each New Year's Day, the Musikverein's Great Hall echoes to the annual Philharmonic concert. The concert is so popular that tickets are sold by lottery, and the music is streamed live to 80 countries.

Complementing the Musikverein, and not far away, is the **Wiener Konzerthaus**. Built in 1913, the Konzerthaus retains its period opulence. But the showpiece Great Hall, which seats 1,840 and houses Austria's largest organ, is now equipped with the latest technology, and musicians can be projected onto huge screens. Music here is eclectic. The only thing that does not vary is the quality. Baroque music is as likely to be heard as Bob Dylan.

Church Music

Details of the many church concerts performed in Vienna are published in all the daily newspapers. Look out particularly for details of Sunday Mass at the following places: Augustinerkirche (see p104), Minoritenkirche (see p105), the Jesuitenkirche (see p79), Stephansdom (see p75) and Michaelerkirche (see p94). In July and August, many other churches hold organ recitals.

The Vienna Boys' Choir, or **Sängerknaben** (see p41), can be heard during Mass at the **Hofburgkapelle** (Imperial Chapel; see p105), on Sundays and religious holidays at 9:15am (except July–mid-September). The choir has its own performance hall near the school where it rehearses. This modernist structure is called **MuTh**, for music and theatre. Concerts are scheduled frequently.

Informal Music

The description just outside **Konzertcafé Schmid Hansl** reads, "the home of Viennese song". The original owner of this small café, which serves hot food until it closes, was Hansl Schmid, a very fine singer and musician. Guests would often visit the café just to hear him sing, and sometimes a famous artist might join him in a duet or give a solo performance. The present owner, Hansl Schmid's son, once a member of the Vienna Boys' Choir, has kept up this tradition, and you may well encounter opera stars coming in to perform unexpectedly.

Another Viennese favourite is the **Wiener Kursalon**. Dinner and waltz evenings with the Johann Strauss Salonorchester are held daily throughout the year along with classical ballet performances. Concerts take place in the Stadtpark during the summer months.

Rock, Pop and Jazz

What is popular one week in Vienna's lively music scene may very well be out of fashion the next. Many nightclubs have live music on certain nights or for a limited period.

U4 club has a different style every night (from industrial to flower power); Monday is Open Stage night for upcoming acts. **Volksgarten Clubdiskothek** is the oldest disco in town, with music ranging from house to hip-hop and salsa. **Roter Engel** in the Bermuda Triangle has live music every night.

The **Praterdome**, situated near the Ferris wheel in the Prater, has popular theme nights.

Live concerts are held at **Chaya Fuera**, **Jazzland**, and on Sundays at **Chelsea**. The **Sass Music Club** plays the best of electronic music.

A must for jazz fans is **Jazz & Music Club Porgy & Bess**, with live music and dancing, and the **Jazzfest** held in the first two weeks of July, with concerts at various venues, such as the Opera House (see pp140–41), the Volkstheater (see p230) and the Neues Rathaus (see p132), as well as many open-air events.

All styles, including electro, house and alternative music, can be found at **Schikaneder Bar** and **Flex**.

DIRECTORY

Opera and Operetta

Bundestheaterkassen
Central Ticket Office.
Operngasse 2. **Map** 5 C4.
Tel 514447810 (10am–9pm daily). **Open** 8am–6pm Mon–Fri, 9am–noon Sat. w **bundestheater.at**

Raimund Theater
Wallgasse 18. **Tel** 58885.
w **musicalvienna.at**

Ronacher
Seilerstatte 9.
Map 4 E1 & 6 D4.
Tel 58885.
w **musicalvienna.at**

Staatsoper
Openring 2. **Map** 4 D1 & 5 C5. **Tel** 514442250.
w **wiener-staatsoper.at**

Wiener Kammeroper
Fleischmarkt 24.
Map 2 E5 & 6 D2.
Tel 58885.
w **kammeroper.at**

Wiener Volksoper
Währinger Strasse 78.
Map 1 B2. **Tel** 514443670.
w **volksoper.at**

Classical Concerts

Musikverein
Bösendorferstrasse 12.
Map 6 D5. **Tel** 5058190.
w **musikverein.at**

Wiener Konzerthaus
Lothringerstrasse 20. **Map** 4 E2 & 6 E5. **Tel** 242002.
w **konzerthaus.at**

Wiener Philharmoniker
Bösendorferstrasse 12.
Map 4 E2 & 6 D5.
Tel 50565250.
w **wienerphilhar moniker.at**

Church Music

Hofburgkapelle
Hofburg, Schweizerhof.
Map 4 D1 & 5 B4.
Tel 5339927.
w **hofmusikkapelle. gv.at**

MuTh
Am Augartenspitz 1.
Map 2 E3. **Tel** 3478080.
w **muth.at**

Sängerknaben
Augartenpalais.
Map 2 E3. **Tel** 2163942.
w **wienersaenger knaben.at**

Informal Music

Konzertcafé Schmid Hansl
Schulgasse 31. **Map** 1 A2.
Tel 4063658. **Open** 5pm–4am Mon–Fri.
w **cafeschmidhansl.at**

Wiener Kursalon
Johannesgasse 33.
Map 6 E5. **Tel** 5125790.
w **soundofvienna.at**

Rock, Pop and Jazz

Chaya Fuera
Kandlgasse 19–21.
Map 3 A1.
Tel 5440036250.
w **chayafuera.com**

Chelsea
Lerchenfeldergüertel,
U-Bahnboegen 29–32.
Tel 4079309.
w **chelsea.co.at**

Flex
Donaukanal Augartenbrücke. **Map** 1 D3.
Tel 5337525.
w **flex.at**

Jazzfest
Tel 4086030
w **viennajazz.org**

Jazzland
Franz-Josefs-Kai 29.
Map 2 D5 & 6 D2.
Tel 5332575.
w **jazzland.at**

Porgy & Bess
Riemergasse 11.
Map 5 E4. **Tel** 5128811.
w **porgy.at**

Praterdome
Riesenradplatz 7.
Tel 9081 1920.
w **praterdome.at**

Roter Engel
Rabensteig 5.
Map 6 D2. **Tel** 5354105.
w **roterengel.at**

Sass Music Club
Karlsplatz 1.
Map 5 C5. **Tel** 4116116.
w **sassvienna.com**

Schikaneder Bar
Margaretenstrasse 22–24.
Map 3 C3. **Tel** 5852867.
w **schikaneder.at**

Volksgarten Clubdiskothek
Burgring/Heldenplatz.
Map 5 B4. **Tel** 5324241.
w **volksgarten.at**

U4
Schönbrunner Strasse 222. **Map** 3 A4. **Tel** 817 11920. w **u-4.at**

Theatre and Cinema

Vienna is far more famous for its music, but theatre and film also flourish, both with the old classics and with avant-garde new productions. Many theatre houses are architectural gems. Almost all cinemas show films in German, but the latest Hollywood films are always shown in English. The city itself has been the backdrop to famous films such as *The Third Man*, but it also features in other movies, including *The Night Porter* from 1974 and indie classic *Before Sunrise* (1995).

Theatres

Viennese theatre productions are some of the best in Europe and the **Burgtheater** (*see p134*), one of the city's four state theatres, is the most important venue. Classic and contemporary plays are performed here and even if your understanding of German is limited, you might still enjoy a new production (which can often be avant-garde) of a Shakespeare play. The **Akademietheater**, part of the Burgtheater, also stages a range of plays.

The **Theater in der Josefstadt** (*see p118*) is worth a visit for its interior alone. As the house lights slowly dim, the crystal chandeliers float gently to the ceiling. It puts on excellent productions of Austrian plays, as well as classics from other countries, and the occasional musical. **Kammerspiele** is the Josefstadt's "little house". The old and well-established **Volkstheater** hosts more modern plays as well as the occasional classic and even some operetta performances.

Vienna has a wide range of fringe theatre, from one-man shows to *Kabarett* – these are satirical shows, not cabarets – but fluent German is needed to appreciate them. German-speakers will also enjoy the highly recommended **Kabarett Simpl**, featuring top name acts. Theatres that host performances in English include **Vienna's English Theatre**, which is the oldest English-language theatre in Europe. Plays staged here are cast and rehearsed in London or New York before opening in Vienna. Although some run for only a short period, they often include famous international stars among the cast.

Cinemas

Most films are dubbed and shown in German; those that can be watched in their original language are always advertised as such in the programme. **Burg Kino**, **Haydn Kino** and the **Artis International** show new releases in English. **Österreichisches Filmmuseum**, **Filmhaus Stöbergasse**, **Filmcasino**, and **Votiv-Kino** show both classic and contemporary cult films. The Filmmuseum is only open to members. But visitors can get a guest membership for just €10.50, which includes a full day's admission. Both historical retrospectives and emerging world cinema are featured. **Apollo** is the ultimate in cinema in Vienna. It has 12 screens, one of which shows IMAX presentations, and it offers some English-language films.

DIRECTORY

Theatres

Akademietheater
Lisztstrasse 1, A-1030.
Map 4 E2.
Tel 514444740.
W burgtheater.at

Burgtheater
Dr Karl-Lueger-Ring,
A-1014. **Map** 1 C5 & 5 A2.
Tel 514444145.
W burgtheater.at

Theater in der Josefstadt
Josefstädter Strasse 26,
A-1080. **Map** 1 B5.
Tel 427000.
W josefstadt.org

Kabarett Simpl
Wollzeile 36, A-1010.
Map 2 E5 & 6 E3.
Tel 5124742.
W simpl.at

Kammerspiele
Rotenturmstrasse 20,
A-1010.
Map 2 E5 & 6 E2
Tel 42700300.
W josefstadt.org

Vienna's English Theatre
Josefsgasse 12, A-1080.
Map 1 B5. **Tel** 40212600.
W englishtheatre.at

Volkstheater
Neustiftgasse 1, A-1070.
Map 3 B1. **Tel** 52111400.
W volkstheater.at

Cinemas

Apollo
Gumpendorfer Strasse 63,
A-1060. **Map** 3 A4 & 5 B5.
Tel 5879651
W cineplexx.at

Artis International
Schultergasse 5, A-1010.
Map 1 A2.
Tel 5356570.

Burg Kino
Opernring 19, A-1010.
Map 4 D1 & 5 B5.
Tel 5878406.
W burgkino.at

Filmcasino
Margaretenstrasse 78,
A-1050.
Map 3 C3.
Tel 5879062.
W filmcasino.at

Filmhaus Stöbergasse
Stöbergasse 11–15,
A-1070.
Map 3 B5.
Tel 5466630.

Haydn Kino
Mariahilfer Strasse 57,
A-1060.
Map 3 B2.
Tel 5872262.
W haydnkino.at

Österreichisches Filmmuseum
Augustinerstrasse 1,
A-1010.
Map 4 D1 & 5 C4.
Tel 5337054.
W filmmuseum.at

Votiv-Kino
Währinger Strasse 12,
A-1090.
Map 1 C4.
Tel 3173571.
W votivkino.at

Sport and Dance

Famed for its waltz, it's no surprise that one of Vienna's favourite pastimes is dance and many of the city's dance schools hold special waltz classes during the Carnival season *(see p67)*. Ice-skating is hugely popular and open-air rinks are well-attended, as is the rink at the Stadthalle, which also boasts bowling alleys and a pool. Vienna is home to the nation's two most successful football (soccer) teams, the bitter rivals Austria Vienna and Rapid Wien. Their matches against each other are particularly lively. Horse racing in Vienna is perhaps less raucous than in some other countries.

Ice-Skating

Outdoor ice-skating is very popular in Vienna. Locals make good use of the open-air rinks at the **Wiener Eislaufverein** and Vienna Ice Dreams *(see p234)*.

Swimming

Vienna can be very warm in summer and has many outdoor pools, including the Schönbrunner Bad in the Schönbrunn Palace park *(see pp174–7)*. The **Krapfenwaldbad** has wonderful views over Vienna, and the **Schafbergbad** is pleasant for families. The **Therme Wien** is a privately owned thermal spa; it is sometimes known as Oberlaa. The Familienbad Augarten *(see p234)* is popular with children, and they can be left in the

shallow pool to be watched by the attendants. Beach huts on the Alte Donau coast can be hired daily from **Strandbad Gänsehäufel** or **Strandbad Alte Donau**, where you can also hire boats. Strandbad Gänsehäufel has a beach, a heated pool, table tennis and Punch and Judy shows. **Donauinsel** water park is run by the city and is open 24 hours, with free admission.

Football

The Viennese are enthusiastic football fans, and there are two covered football stadiums in the city. The **Ernst Happel Stadion**, the national stadium, is in the Prater and the **Hanappi Stadion**, home to Rapid Vienna, is at Hütteldorf.

Horse Racing

The Prater offers a wide range of activities *(see pp164–5)*, including trotting races at the **Krieau**.

Dancing and Dance Schools

During the Carnival season *(see p67)* many balls, and some fancy dress dances, are held in Vienna. Venues include the Hofburg, the Neues Rathaus *(see p132)* and the Musikverein *(see p150)*. The grandest event is the Vienna Opera Ball *(see p141)*, which takes place on the Thursday before Ash Wednesday. The opening ceremony includes performances by vocal soloists, the orchestra and the ballet company of the Vienna State Opera. An invitation is not needed, you just buy a ticket. The Kaiserball is held at the Neue Burg on New Year's Eve *(see pp67 and 97)*. A special ball calendar is issued by the Vienna Tourist Office *(see p238)*.

The Summer Dance Festival *(see p65)* runs from July to August. Dance classes for all ages and in all styles are popular among locals and tourists alike. There are a number of schools, such as the **Elmayer-Vestenbrugg** dance school, which also teaches etiquette.

CHILDREN'S VIENNA

Vienna is a child-friendly city with plenty of attractions to avoid any cries of boredom. There are white dancing stallions to see at the Spanish Riding School and huge fairy-tale palaces to explore. Many museums have hands-on interactive displays that are not only educational but also fun. Vienna also offers Amusement park rides, boat rides on the Danube, a zoo and theaters dedicated to the little ones. There are also a number of special activities organized for children throughout the year. Hotels that are family-friendly are reviewed on pages 197–9. At the majestic Hotel Sacher, for example, children have their own concierge and are given complimentary toys.

Families relaxing in Stadtpark in the sunshine

Practical Advice

When walking on pavements with children, it is important to be aware that cyclists riding on the same pavement – if lanes are so marked – have right of way at all times.

Children up to the age of 6 can travel for free on public transport. Those between the ages of 6 and 14 can buy a half-price ticket. During the summer holidays (the end of June to the end of August) children under 15 can travel free provided they can show some form of identification when buying a ticket.

It is a good idea to carry some small change, as there is often a charge to use public lavatories. These are usually clean.

The concierges at many hotels, particularly the larger establishments, can arrange for a baby-sitter for parents wanting an evening out. Hotel Sacher offers the most comprehensive children's service in Vienna (see p199). Kids have a concierge reserved for them, their own spa treatments and free toys and games to keep.

Children's Shops

Traditional Austrian clothing, which is still worn by some children in Vienna, can be purchased from **Lanz Trachtenmoden** on Kärntner Strasse. Traditional dress includes *Lederhosen*, leather shorts, for boys and the *Dirndl*, a traditional dress, for girls. The *Dirndl* is worn with a white lace blouse and an apron. A little bag is sometimes carried as well. Lanz Trachtenmoden also stocks a range of beautiful knitwear in myriad colours and designs, including fine embroidered woollen slippers made in the Tyrol.

Dohnal has half a dozen shops selling baby clothes and prams. International chains such as **H&M** carry standard children's ranges. But exclusive to Vienna are the four shops of **Herzilein**, selling Vienna-designed and hand-sewn traditional garments and accessories.

Herr und Frau Klein is Austria's first concept shop for mothers and babies, with clothing, furniture and toys all in one store. **Spielzeugschachtel-Spielwaren** has, since 1963, offered excellent children's toys and books. It has a policy not to carry any kind of "violent" toy.

Dressing up in traditional costume is popular during Fasching (see p67)

Eating Out

Almost all tourist restaurants have children's menus and chairs for toddlers. Dedicated play areas are harder to find. Some restaurants offer special Sunday brunch buffets for families. The best is probably the **Vienna Marriott** (see p197), where

Children on a day out visiting Josefsplatz in the Hofburg

Humboldt penguins at Schönbrunn Zoo in the palace gardens

children under 6 eat free and 6- to 11-year-olds are charged half price. The hotel also provides a playroom with a child minder. The **Hotel Daniel** (see p197) offers a brunch deal.

Heurigen, where you can sit outside in summer, are usually less formal and therefore a good option for families with small children. The best time to go is from 4pm, when most of them open, as they are likely to get busier as the evening goes on. Heuriger Zimmermann on Armbrustergasse in Grinzing (see pp188–9) has a small zoo where children may stroke the animals.

Fast food and takeaway food, from burgers to Asian cuisine, is available throughout the city, and ice creams are sold in most pastry shops. **Eis-Greissler** is one of the most popular and central of ice-cream shops. Just south of Belvedere is **Tichy**, which is a great place to take the kids for a treat, as huge ice-cream sundaes are on offer here. In the centre, **Haas & Haas** is a palace of exotic teas. **Wienerwald** is a city-wide chain of chicken restaurants, with fast and inexpensive food and a family-friendly ambience.

Sightseeing with Children

Vienna has an amazing variety of attractions that will appeal to children of all ages, including theme parks, funfairs, museums, sports and the zoo.

It usually costs around half the adult entrance fee for children to get into museums, though at several places children and young adults up to the age of 19 can enter for free. Most museums and attractions now have changing-room facilities. Breastfeeding in public is widely practised in Vienna and throughout Austria.

Vienna has plenty of parks, but some are designed more for admiring from the pathways than running around in. Watch out for signs warning *Bitte nicht betreten*, which means "Please don't walk on the grass". Details of some of the more child-friendly parks and nature reserves are given on page 234, and there are several playgrounds along the first stretch of the Prater Hauptallee. These parks are ideal for a picnic, and food and drink can easily be obtained from a supermarket.

Children's playgrounds in Vienna are generally safe and well equipped.

Zoo and Nature Reserve

The Schönbrunn Zoo (see p175), or Tiergarten, is the oldest in the world. In the palace gardens, the zoo houses giant pandas, a koala house, kangaroos and lions, in addition to orangutans and both ice and coral-reef environments. There is an adventure trail for kids with a climbing wall and the rope-bridge Treetop Trail. If that is not enough, there are guided night-time tours where children can watch nocturnal animals with infrared binoculars.

In the Vienna Woods, the Lainzer Tiergarten (see p173) is a nature reserve where children can see deer, wild boar and horses. There are also playgrounds and a pond. An easy walk takes you to Hermesvilla hunting lodge, with its café and nature-based exhibitions.

Funfair and Children's City

A great spot for a family outing is the atmospheric **Prater** (see pp164–5) with its wonderful Ferris wheel. The Prater park also has sandpits, playgrounds, ponds and streams. Located at the entrance of the park, **Madame Tussauds Wien** has waxworks of Austrian and international personalities including historical figures and sports and music stars.

Family out cycling, a familiar sight at the Prater

Ice skating on the seasonal rink that is set up in front of the city hall each winter

Children's Sports

Vienna has some excellent swimming baths that are free for children under six. The **Stadionbad**, one of the city's largest leisure pools, has three children's pools and a water slide. The **Familienbad Augarten** is a shallow pool and free for children between the ages of 6 and 15. Single adults without children are not allowed.

In summer, you can swim in the Donauinsel coves (see p231). Wintertime can be spent bathing in the hot geysers at Thermalbad Oberlaa (see p231) or ice-skating at **Wiener Eislaufverein** and at **Vienna Ice Dreams** in front of the Rathaus. Ice Dreams, or Eistraum, has free skating for children and beginners.

Entertainment

Although virtually all theatre is performed in German, the **Märchenbühne der Apfelbaum** marionette theatre sometimes puts on shows of favourite fairy tales in English. Fairy stories with music and song can also be seen at the **Lilarum** puppet theatre, which also has a cinema for children. The **Wiener Konzerthaus** and Musikverein hold regular concerts for children six times a year on Saturday or Sunday afternoons. In November and December the Opera House (see pp140–41) and the Wiener Volksoper (see p229) put on traditional children's programmes (Kinderzyklus). Productions include Mozart's The Magic Flute and the most popular opera at the Volksoper, Engelbert Humperdinck's Hansel and Gretel.

Several cinemas in Vienna show films in their original language – check in the Standard newspaper's foreign films section. See also Entertainment in Vienna on pp226–31.

Special Activities and Workshops

The Neues Rathaus (see p132) has children's activities once a month (details from the town hall), and from mid-November there is a Christmas market (see pp224–5) which includes a children's train, pony rides and stalls selling toys, chestnuts and winter woollens. A Christmas workshop is held at the Volkshalle in the Rathaus from 9am to 7pm daily (to 4pm on 24 December). The activities include baking, silk painting and making decorations.

Museums

Vienna has a range of museums that children will enjoy. The Naturhistorisches Museum (see pp130–31) boasts an impressive collection of towering reconstructions of dinosaurs. The **Haus des Meeres** (Vienna Aquarium) contains over 3,000 sea creatures, including crocodiles and sharks. Feeding time is 3pm.

Popular exhibits at the Weltmuseum Wien (see p97) include exotic musical instruments, African masks and figurines, and other treasures. Children aged 10 and under can visit the **Kunst Haus Wien** for free. Designed by Friedensreich Hundertwasser, this private gallery has undulating floors and colourful paintings. **Remise Transport Museum** in an old tram depot allows children to clamber over old trams and experience a 3D view of the route from a driver's perspective.

The big wheel is a familiar landmark in the Prater park (see pp164–5)

The Heeresgeschichtliches Museum *(see pp168–9)* chronicles the history of the Austrian military from primitive days through to aircraft and boats, and allows kids to experience the trenches and bunkers but with the slogan "Wars Belong in Museums". Vienna's best children's museum is ZOOM Kindermuseum *(see p122)*, with special hands-on learning programmes for kids as young as eight months. Older children can make their own movies and music videos. At the **Circus- und Clownmuseum**, more static displays show old costumes and photographs.

A Christmas market stall in front of the Rathaus *(see p132)*

DIRECTORY

Children's Shops

Dohnal
Kärntner Strasse 12.
Map 4 D1 & 6 D4.
Tel 5127311.

H&M
Kärntner Strasse 28.
Map 4 D1.
Tel 810909090.

Haas & Haas
Teehandlung,
Stephansplatz 4.
Map 2 E3 & 6 D3.
Tel 5129770.

Herzilein
Wollzeile 17.
Map 2 D5 & 5 C3.
Tel 676 6577106.

Lanz Trachtenmoden
Kärntner Strasse 10.
Map 4 D1 & 6 D4.
Tel 5122456.

Spielzeugschachtel-Spielwaren
Rauhensteingasse 5.
Map 2 E1 & 6 D4.
Tel 5124494.

Eating Out

Eis-Gressler
Rotenturmstrasse 14.
Map 2 E5 & 6 D3.
Tel 02647 4295055.

Tichy
Reumannplatz 13.
Tel 6044446.

Wienerwald
Annagasse 3.
Map 4 D1 & 6 D4.
Tel 5123766.
Goldschmiedgasse 6.
Map 6 D3.
Tel 5354012.

Funfair and Children's City

Madame Tussauds Wien
Riesenradplatz 5.
Tel 8903366.
Open 10am–6pm daily.

Children's Sports

Familienbad Augarten
Karl Meissl Strasse.
Map 2 E1. **Tel** 3324258.
Open May–Sep:
10am–8pm daily.

Stadionbad
Prater, Krieau.
Tel 7202102.
Open May–Sep: 9am–7pm Mon–Fri (to 8pm Jul & Aug), 8am–7pm Sat, Sun & hols (to 8pm Jul & Aug) .

Vienna Ice Dreams
Rathausplatz.
Map 5 A2.
Tel 4090040.
Open end of Jan–Mar:
9am–11pm daily.

Wiener Eislaufverein
Lothringerstrasse 28.
Map 4 E2.
Tel 7136353.
Open mid-Oct–early Mar:
9am–9pm Tue, Thu & Fri,
9am–8pm Sat–Mon,
9am–10pm Wed.

Entertainment

Lilarum
Göllnergasse 8.
Tel 7102666.

Märchenbühne der Apfelbaum
Kirchengasse 41.
Map 3 B1.
Tel 523172920.

Wiener Konzerthaus
Lothringerstrasse 20.
Map 4 E2 & 6 E5.
Tel 242002.

Museums

Circus- und Clownmuseum
Ilgplatz 7.
Tel 6764068868.
Open 10am–1pm Sun,
7–9pm every 1st or 3rd
Thu of month.

Haus des Meeres
Fritz Grünbaum Platz 1.
Map 3 B2.
Tel 5871417.
Open 9am–6pm daily.

Kunst Haus Wien
Untere Weissgerber-strasse 13.
Tel 7120491.
Open 10am–7pm daily.

Remise Transport Museum
Erdbergstrasse 109.
Tel 7909 46803.
Ⓦ remise.wien

SURVIVAL
GUIDE

PRACTICAL INFORMATION

Walking is the best way to experience Vienna, allowing you to see and smell the roasting chestnuts in winter and to stop and sample sidewalk cafés in summer. From Stephansdom (St Stephen's Cathedral) to Belvedere Palace and Gardens in the south, it is no more than a 30-minute stroll. A useful map with up-to-date information on Vienna's museums and *Wien Programm*, a monthly listings guide, can be obtained free of charge from tourist offices. Except for shopping malls in train stations, most retail businesses are closed on Sundays, and many shops also close early on Saturdays. Churches may restrict visitors, or not allow them at all, when services are under way.

Visas and Passports

Austria is part of the Schengen common European border treaty, which means those going from one Schengen country to another are not subject to border controls. Schengen residents need only show an identity card when entering Austria. Visitors from the UK, Ireland, USA, Canada, Australia or New Zealand will need to show a full passport. Travellers from these countries do not need visas for stays of up to three months. Non-EU citizens wishing to stay in the country longer than three months will need a visa, obtained in advance from their country's Austrian embassy or consulate. All visitors should check requirements before travelling.

Travel Safety Advice

Visitors can get up-to-date travel safety information from the Foreign and Commonwealth Office in the UK, the State Department in the US and the Department of Foreign Affairs and Trade in Australia.

Customs Information

Nationals of EU countries, including Britain and Ireland, may take home unlimited quantities of duty-paid alcoholic drinks and tobacco goods, as long as these are intended for their own consumption and it can be proven that the goods are not intended for resale. Citizens of the US and Canada are limited to a duty-free maximum of 200 cigarettes or 50 cigars. Americans may bring home 1 litre (33.8 fl oz) of wine or spirits, while Canadians are allowed 1.5 litres (50.7 fl oz) of wine, or a total of 1.14 litres (38.5 fl oz) of any alcoholic beverages, or 8.5 litres (287 fl oz) of beer or ale. Residents of other countries should ask their customs authority for more details. Information is included in the free *Zollinfo* brochure available at the Austrian border and allowances are listed on the Vienna Tourist Board website. The **Austrian Foreign Ministry** website also has information on tax-free goods.

Tourist Information

For help planning your visit you can contact the **Österreich Werbung** (Austrian National Tourist Office) and the **Wiener Tourismusverband** (Vienna Tourist Board). The main Tourist Board office is located on Albertinaplatz, just by the Hofburg palace complex. The information booth at Schwechat Airport *(see p246)* can provide maps, brochures, public transport schedules and assistance with hotel bookings. Tickets to musical and theatrical performances are sold at the Albertinaplatz office, including discounted tickets for same-day events. The Austrian National Tourist Office can also assist with planning day trips from Vienna *(see pp178–81)*.

Tourists walking near the Hofburg complex *(see pp98–9)*

Wien Xtra-Youth Info offers information for toddlers and youths up to 26, organizing workshops and excursions for the whole family.

Admission Prices and Opening Hours

All major attractions charge admission. A number of museums allow those under 19 to enter for free, and children under 12 generally enter for half-price. There are also reductions for senior citizens. Museums grouped together, such as at Neue Burg, have tickets offering admission to multiple museums. Some multi-day Wiener Linien transport tickets grant free or discounted admission to certain attractions. Popular attractions like the Art History Museum and Belvedere complex of palace and gardens charge €15 per adult. The Natural History Museum charges €10, and a guided tour of the State Opera House costs

Tourist Information office in central Vienna

€7.50. Prices may change with no notice. Many museums are closed on Mondays and on the public holidays of New Year, Easter, May Day (the workers' holiday) and Christmas.

Public Toilets

Viennese public toilets (signed as "WC") are clean, safe and well maintained. Most charge a nominal fee payable by machine or to an attendant in small change. Many are open until late, especially those in underground stations. Vienna's "toilet art" is renowned, and the beautiful Art Deco WC on the Graben, designed by Adolf Loos, is well worth a visit. Other lavatorial highlights include the Opera Toilet at the Karlsplatz underground station and the Toilet of Modern Art in the Hundertwasserhaus housing estate.

Travellers with Disabilities

Vienna is relatively easy to navigate as a disabled traveller. Most of the major museums have entrances and ramps designed for wheelchairs; detailed information is available from the Vienna Tourist Office. Trams and buses are equipped with seats for disabled travellers (see p254). Most major underground stations have lifts unless otherwise indicated. Travellers who need assistance from airline or train staff should contact the airline at least 48 hours in advance.

Senior Travellers

The Viennese are extremely respectful of older people. Senior travellers in Vienna are often given priority seating on public transport and many theatres, cinemas, attractions and museums offer generous discounts to travellers with senior ID. There is no free travel for seniors, though they can buy the Obb 50 per cent discount card for a full year for only €29, if 62 or older. Some ski resorts offer free skiing for those over-80.

Student Travellers

Vienna's main theatres sell cheap standing-room and unsold tickets at the box office before a performance. For popular shows, you may need to queue for several hours. A university ID card or international student card also entitles students to discounts on some museum admission fees and occasionally on rail tickets. Tourist offices provide a list of cheaper hotels as well as a list of Vienna's youth hostels (see p194).

Electricity

Austria's voltage is 220V AC/50Hz and electrical sockets take European round 2-pin plugs.

Responsible Tourism

Austria is one of the world's leading destinations for sustainable tourism. About 70 per cent of energy is generated from non-fossil-fuel sources and about 60 per cent of all waste is recycled. Guests will notice that many hotels ask that they reuse towels instead of exchanging them daily. Recycling is rigorously adhered to but not mandatory.

The *Österreichisches Umweltzeichen* (Austrian Eco Label) is a seal of approval awarded to hotels and restaurants that meet high environmental and waste-reduction standards. **Hotel Stadthalle**, near to Westbahnhof station, was the first hotel in Vienna to be awarded the *European Ecolabel* for its green credentials. This hotel uses solar panels to heat up water and collects rain water to flush its toilets.

The eco-friendly Hotel Stadthalle

Personal Security and Health

Vienna is one of Europe's safest capital cities and visitors are unlikely to encounter any violence. Crime rates are low (although there has been an increase in petty crimes such as pickpocketing in busy tourist areas). Most incidents involving tourists are crimes of opportunity, involving theft of personal belongings. Visitors should take the normal precautions, such as not leaving baggage unattended Austrian police are trusted and are easy to contact for both minor incidents and in the case of an emergency. Pharmcists are respected and their advice is often sought by locals. A visit to a pharmacy, unless the problem is serious, is probably the easiest choice if you are feeling unwell.

Police

Vienna police are part of the national force, called *Bundespolizei*, and are generally armed. Most speak English and are happy to assist tourists with directions and questions. They wear blue uniforms and often patrol on bicycles. It is not uncommon to see strong security forces, including officers armed with advanced weapons, at airports and train stations. Often trains will be patrolled by teams with dogs. In rare cases, police will ask for identification, which by Austrian law, should be carried at all times. A national identity card or photo identification like a driving licence will suffice.

Viennese police officers
in uniform

To report a crime, go in person to the nearest police station or call the emergency number: 133. You will need to give a detailed account of the incident and any items stolen. The police will prepare a statement, which you will need to sign. You can ask for an interpreter to translate any German-language documents or terms you don't understand. Should the police need to detain you for questioning, be sure to request the services of a solicitor. You are also entitled to contact the local branch of your country's embassy or consulate for assistance *(see p239)*. The police also run lost property departments *(Fundbüro)*, which can be found in any district police station.

What to be Aware of

Vienna is ranked as the safest capital city anywhere in Europe. Nonetheless, Vienna police report a rise in petty crime such as pickpocketing at city train stations and aboard trains themselves. The area around St Stephan's Cathedral has also had incidents. For the latest advice, consult a hotel concierge or speak to your host for local advice. Keep your cash in a discreet money belt and other valuables, such as cameras and mobile phones, well out of sight. Carry bags

on your front with the strap worn across your shoulder.

There are a few places to steer clear of in Vienna. Unlit parks should be avoided at night. Prostitution is legal in Austria, but Vienna has no designated "red light" district. Always avoid street gambling and illegal money changers, as they are likely to be using counterfeit notes. Street cons and late-night petty theft are common in the Bermuda Triangle area *(see p86)*. Walking in Vienna's cycle lanes is forbidden and dangerous at any time of day or night.

In an Emergency

Austrians are approachable, community-minded and often more than willing to help a person in need. Before you arrive in Austria, make a list of the emergency numbers you may require for events such as credit card theft, emergency repatriation or any specialized critical medical care you may need. Also take a photocopy of your passport, medical insurance and ID cards. Your country's consulate in Austria will be able to help in the first instance with most emergency situations. All under-ground stations have SOS points for emergencies from which you can call the station supervisor. There is also a special SMS emergency service for the deaf.

Red Cross sign

Lost and Stolen Property

Victims of theft should visit the police station in **Stephansplatz** as soon as possile to file a crime report. The report will take some time to complete, but you will need a copy to claim against an insurance policy for stolen property. For items misplaced on the rail-ways or the Schnellbahn, go in person to the lost-and-found office at the **Westbahnhof**. For lost or stolen credit cards,

Police car

Ambulance

Fire engine

called in all medical emergencies by dialling 144.

Minor Hazards

Most visitors to Vienna will only ever need medical advice for minor ailments, such as sunstroke during the city's hottest months. More common is altitude sickness among high mountain hikers and skiers venturing well above 3,000 m (9,850 ft). The symptoms are nausea and headache, and the only cure is a quick return to valley level. Hotels will be able to recommend a doctor.

contact the issuing company's office *(see p242)*. For items lost elsewhere, call the **Lost Property Bureau** *(Fündbüro)* and consult your embassy for help *(see p239)*.

Hospitals and Pharmacies

Vienna's many pharmacies are a good source of information on medicines and the treatment of minor ailments. To locate an *Apotheke* (pharmacy), look out for a bright red "A" sign; there is generally one on every major street. Pharmacies operate a night and Sunday rota system. Closed pharmacies will display the address of the nearest one open, and the number of the **Pharmacy Information Line**.

For more serious illnesses and injuries, call the **ViennaMed** doctors' hotline for visitors. Vienna has several private hospitals, clinics and medical centres, but the main facility is **Vienna General**, the largest hospital in Austria. Most doctors, paramedics and clinic staff in Vienna speak English. An ambulance *(Rettungsdienst)* should be

Travel and Health Insurance

Medical care is expensive in Vienna, so it pays to be fully insured for health purposes, however short your visit. Britain, like many other European countries, has a reciprocal arrangement with Austria whereby emergency hospital treatment is free upon presentation of a British passport. Keep all receipts for medical services, as you may need to claim costs back after you return home. EU citizens with a European Health Insurance Card (EHIC) are entitled to state-provided healthcare at a reduced fee or sometimes free. The card comes with a booklet of advice and information on the procedure for claiming free medical treatment.

A travel insurance policy will also provide cover for other expenses and losses. Health and travel policies vary dramatically, so be sure to shop around for a policy that suits your particular needs, especially if you are planning on participating in adventure sports, or if you have an existing medical condition.

Banking and Local Currency

Outside almost every bank, in every train station and on the streets of every district of Vienna you will find an ATM, known in Austria as a *bankomat*, that accepts international credit and debit cards. Cash is dispensed in euros. Debit and credit cards are accepted by almost all shops and restaurants, though sometimes not for very small purchases. Cards equipped with the contactless function can be used for amounts under €25. The use of traveller's cheques is steadily being phased out – so cash or card is recommended.

Banks and Currency Exchange

The best place to change money is at a bank. Although you can use travel agents, hotels and currency-exchange offices (*Wechselstuben*), banks give a better rate. Commission applies on all currency changed. The two banks that have the most branches – Bank Austria and Erste Bank – charge either 3% commission or a minimum handling fee of €5.50.

Exchanging a larger amount of money at one time can save on commission. You can also exchange foreign bank notes for euros at the automatic money-changing machines or even in large department stores.

Most banks are open from 8am to 3pm Monday to Friday (to 5:30pm on Thursdays). Some banks, generally those located at the main railway stations and at airports (*see Directory*), stay open for longer.

The façade of Bank Austria in central Vienna

ATMs

A convenient and easy way to change money is at an ATM (*bankomat*). Most ATMs accept foreign credit and debit cards with 4-digit PIN codes (check with your bank before travelling that you don't have the older 6-digit code). Normal precautions should be used to protect your PIN To find a cash point that accepts your card, check the logos on the machine. Visa and MasterCard are generally accepted but few machines take American Express. Instructions are generally given in English and some other languages. Be aware that money drawn out using a credit or debit card often incurs a considerable fee. The daily limit for withdrawals is usually £250 (about €350).

Bankomats can be found outside all banks or within the bank lobby; these are usually accessible 24 hours a day. ATMs are also easy to find in Vienna's central shopping and main tourist areas. Train and bus stations, as well as hotels, usually have an ATM in the vicinty. The website bankomat finder.at is a handy way of finding your nearest ATM.

Credit Cards and Currency Cards

Almost all shops, restaurants, hotels and petrol stations take major credit and debit cards. **Visa** and **MasterCard** are very common; **American Express** is less widely accepted. Shops often require a minimum spend, such as €20, for card use. Contactless technology is fast being adopted across the city enabling small payments (no more than €25) to be made quickly using a contactless-enabled card or mobile device. However, it is advisable to carry some cash, which is often preferred by smaller establishments such as side-street boutiques and cafés. Some banks offer credit cards for international travel that do not incur currency-conversion surcharges.

Another useful way to carry money is with a prepaid currency card. As with a debit card, you can use it in shops and restaurants, and withdraw money from cash machines. It is easy to top up the cards online or with an app. Currency cards can easily be obtained online.

DIRECTORY

Banks

Bank Austria Creditanstalt
Kärntner Ring 1. **Map** 4 D2 & 6 D5. **Tel** 05 050547150.
Stephansplatz 2. **Map** 2 E5 & 6 D3. **Tel** 05 050532120.
Stock-Im-Eisen-Platz 3–4. **Map** 5 C3. **Tel** 05 050532300.

Bank Austria Kunstforum
Freyung 8. **Map** 2 D5 & 5 B2. **Tel** 01 537330.

Erste Bank
Graben 21. **Map** 2 D5 & 5 C3. **Tel** 50 10010100.

Meinl Bank
Bauernmarkt 2. **Map** 2 E5 & 6 D3. **Tel** 01 531880.

National Bank of Austria
Otto-Wagner-Platz 3. **Map** 1 B4 **Tel** 01 404200.

Lost or Stolen Credit Cards

American Express
Tel 0800 900 940.

MasterCard
Tel 0800 218 235.

Visa
Tel 0800 200 288.

Currency

The euro (€) is the common currency of the European Union. It went into general circulation on 1 January 2002, initially for 12 participating countries. Austria was one of those 12 countries and the Austrian schilling was phased out in the same year.

EU members using the euro as sole official currency are known as the Eurozone. Several EU members have opted out of joining this common currency. Euro notes are identical throughout the Eurozone, each denomination portraying designs of fictional architectural structures. The coins, however, have one side identical (the value side), and one side with an image unique to each country.

Banknotes

Euro banknotes come in seven denominations. The €5 note (grey in colour) is the smallest, followed by the €10 note (pink), €20 note (blue), €50 note (orange), €100 note (green), €200 note (yellow) and €500 note (purple). All notes show the stars of the European Union.

€5

€10

€20

€50

€100

€200

€500

€2

€1

50 cents

20 cents

10 cents

Coins

The euro has eight coin denominations: €1 and €2; 50 cents, 20 cents, 10 cents, 5 cents, 2 cents and 1 cent. The €2 and €1 coins are both silver and gold in colour. The 50-, 20- and 10-cent coins are gold. The 5-, 2- and 1-cent coins are bronze.

5 cents

2 cents

1 cent

Communications and Media

Staying in touch in Vienna is easy. Making national and international telephone calls is uncomplicated, thanks to well-organized mobile and landline networks, and the city is saturated with high-speed internet and Wi-Fi networks. Post offices across the city offer a range of mailing options. It is well-served by TV (terrestrial and satellite) and radio channels and there is a range of domestic and foreign-run newspapers and magazines.

An Austrian public telephone box, an increasingly rare sight

International and Local Telephone Calls

Making calls within Austria and to overseas numbers is straight-forward but can be pricey. For international calls it is best to avoid phoning from hotels as they tend to add a hefty surcharge. Cheap-rate calling times for international calls from Austria is between 6pm and 8am and at week-ends; for domestic calls it is between 8pm and 6am, and weekends. A cheap way to make calls to international numbers from a regular phone is with a phonecard, which can be purchased from any post office or from newsagents. Travellers are also increasingly using VoIP (Voice over Internet protocol) services such as Skype. This system permits you to make phone calls anywhere in the world from a mobile, tablet or computer providing you have the right software installed.

Mobile Phones

Visitors with Android or Apple smartphones should download and install a free VOIP app like Skype in order to make free or low-cost phone calls inside Austria and internationally. The EU has massively reduced roaming charges for users from European Union member states. Others should make sure their data and phone plans are not prohibitively costly from Vienna. Use of mobile phones in museums and churches is generally forbidden.

Remember, also, that Austrian electrical sockets take a European round 2-pin plug, and you may need an adaptor in order to charge your phone.

If your handset is unlocked, you may be able to purchase a SIM card from one of the local mobile phone providers, such as **A1 Telekom, tele.ring** or **Yesss**. Pay-as-you-go handsets can be bought from super-markets such as Merkur or Hofer for around €15–20.

Public Telephones

As in other parts of the world, public payphones are now not easily found in Vienna, but transport hubs such as main railway stations still have them. They usually take debit or credit cards, as well as 10-, 20- and 50-cent, and €1- and €2- coins.

Most public phones have instructions in English and other languages. Directories are usually missing or too tatty to use. Post offices have directories in good condition; your hotel may help you find a number, or contact directory enquiries *(see Reaching the Right Number, below)*.

Internet

Vienna was one of the first cities to install fibre-optic internet connections. Free Wi-Fi is everywhere, even in the most traditional coffee houses. Many establishments demand a password, given freely to clients. But visitors will find most parts of the city offering open access, from

Tourists using an internet café in central Vienna

Reaching the Right Number

- For directory enquiries (including EU numbers), dial 118877.
- For international directory enquiries (excluding EU numbers), dial 0900 118877.
- All directory enquiries cost €2.17 per minute.
- For wake-up service, dial 0900 979720.
- To phone the **USA**, dial 001 followed by the number.

- To ring the **UK**, dial 0044 followed by the number (omit the 0 from the area code).
- To ring **Australia**, dial 0061 followed by the number.
- To ring **New Zealand**, dial 0064 followed by the number.
- To ring the **Irish Republic**, dial 00353 followed by the number.
- The front pages of the A–Z telephone directory list codes for each country.

libraries and museums and businesses streaming signals into public squares. The average speed in Vienna is 30 mbps, from many different providers. A number of phone apps, such as Freewave (freewave.at), serve as location finders for free Wi-Fi signals (hot spots). Most hotels and public libraries have free computer terminals for visitors. Some hotels still charge a fee per day, which can be expensive.

As a consequence of ubiquitous free Wi-Fi, Vienna's internet cafés have largely disappeared. Vienna has embraced the internet culture, and booking restaurants is more often done online than by phone. Almost all speciality shops, including antiquarian shops and artisanal bakeries, offer online shopping, frequently with same-day delivery. The Viennese have also taken to internet-based taxi services like Uber. And both train and tram tickets can be bought online and either printed out or used as barcode-type symbols on screen.

The Austrian government blocks a number of filesharing websites, and visitors will not be able to access their subscription streaming services like Netflix or Amazon Prime. Access to BBC iPlayer is also blocked from Austria.

Postal Services

Austrian post offices are clearly identifiable by their bold yellow signs. They provide postage stamps (Briefmarken), can send registered letters, and arrange the delivery of packages. Phonecards and collectors' stamps are also sold. Other services include Post Restante or Postlagernd (to be called for) and some financial services.

The Austrian postal system is reliable and efficient. Postage is charged by weight. Customers can choose between two postal tariffs: priority and economy. For quick delivery of a package, international couriers such as **DHL** and **FedEx** offer a reliable service.

Newspapers and Magazines

As befits coffee-house culture, Austria is still a land of newsprint, though tablets, smartphones and laptops outnumber newspapers in many traditional coffee houses. For German speakers, the tabloid Kronen Zeitung is Austria's most widely read newspaper by far. The second-largest, Der Kurier, is less sensationalist and focuses on national and international news, politics and current affairs. Die Presse is the oldest of Austria's dailies, as well as the best-selling quality paper, while independent broadsheet Der Standard is popular with students. Falter is Vienna's main listings magazine. English-language newspapers and magazines are widely available, some appearing the same day they are published in New York or London. Larger newsagents have a wide range of English-language magazines, including sports and political periodicals. It is also possible to find a good selection of English-language paperbacks at most train stations and even at street kiosks and hotel shops.

TV and Radio

The main television broadcaster is state-owned ORF, with a wealth of channels. Private broadcasters include ATV, Pulse 4 and Servus. All these broadcast in German. Many hotels, however, will have the full range of BBC channels, as well as international channels like CNN and MSNBC.

Distinctive yellow sign outside one of Vienna's post offices

Austrian and international newspapers on sale at a street kiosk

Austria has two main radio stations. Ö1 specializes in classical music and Ö3 plays popular tunes. Radio FM4 broadcasts in English from 1am to 2pm daily on 103.8 MHz. Vienna Cable Radio transmits on FM100.8. Although terrestrial broadcast TV is German-language, many international films are shown with subtitles. Almost every hotel and sports bar has satellite television, on which large numbers of international programmes and English-language channels are broadcast.

GETTING TO VIENNA

Getting to Vienna is easier and quicker now than it's ever been in the past. Most visitors to the city arrive by air. There are direct flights to Schwechat airport from main European cities as well as from the USA, Canada, Japan and Australia. Shuttles from the airport into the centre of Vienna take as little as 15 minutes. There are good rail and coach links, too, but from Britain this involves a long journey, often overnight, and is not significantly cheaper than air travel. One of the most comfortable journeys is by train. Vienna is now served by one of the highest-speed trains in Europe, travelling significantly faster than the motorway speed limit for cars. The motorway network throughout Austria and motorway links between Austria and the rest of Europe are extensive; the roads are clearly signposted and well maintained.

The modern exterior of Schwechat International Airport

Arriving by Air

Vienna International Airport, known locally as Schwechat Airport, is well served by most international airlines. Several flights per day link London and regional UK airports with Vienna. The main airlines with regular direct flights between the UK and Vienna are **British Airways** and **Lufthansa**, along with several low-cost carriers such as **easyJet** and **Flybe**. The main Austrian carrier is **Austrian Airlines**.

Austrian Airlines is the only carrier offering direct non-stop flights from North America, with a choice of departure cities including Miami, New York and Toronto.

Schwechat Airport

Schwechat International, one of Europe's most modern airport facilities, is located 19 km (12 miles) southeast of the city centre. With two terminals, the airport is used by over 100 airlines. It is served by the super-efficient CAT (City Airport Train), which runs to and from Wien Mitte station in 16 minutes.

Schwechat has all the facilities of a major international airport, including business lounges, restaurants and over 50 shops. These shops range from supermarket chains to luxury clothing. It is even possible to buy a pay-as-you-go Austrian mobile phone, to save on roaming charges.

All the major car-rental agencies are in the arrival hall, and there are always taxis waiting outside. Direct access to bus and train transport is right at the airport. All areas of the airport are wheelchair-accessible, and electric carts to deliver passengers to boarding gates can be requested in advance.

Schwechat now offers the Vienna Airport app for Apple or Android tablets and smartphones. With this app, information about changing departure or arrival times can be viewed on your device. An airport map and information about parking availability as it changes, as well as schedules of buses and trains, are all provided.

Passengers travelling to Schwechat from Wien Mitte station on CAT can get their boarding passes and seat reservations right in the centre of Vienna at the CAT counter. This check-in can be done the night before flying. Passengers have the luxury of depositing their bags at the CAT counter instead of carrying them to the airport. This service is entirely free.

Tickets and Fares

To get the best deal on air fares, shop around and book well in advance. Cheaper tickets on scheduled flights can often be booked up to six months before the date of travel. Discount agencies also sell cut-price APEX tickets at less than the normal full fare. Charter flights are often available at very competitive prices. No-frills budget airlines represent excellent value for money, although many charge extra for checked luggage, stowed sporting equipment, priority boarding and other services. There's also an additional charge for meals. Being flexible with the date and time of travel allows passengers to get the best from low-cost airlines. Another option from Europe is a weekend package, which may include a two-night stay at a good Viennese hotel for less than the price of an economy-class airline ticket.

Travellers checking in at Schwechat International Airport

Transfers from the Airport

The most utilized route from the airport into the centre of Vienna is with the sleek and modern **CAT (City Airport Train)**. CAT's 16-minute ride beats the half-hour taxi drive and the Schnellbahn train, which takes about 35 minutes. The CAT trains, with free Wi-Fi and laptop charging points, run every 30 minutes from the basement terminal inside the airport. They arrive at Vienna's Wien Mitte station, which has the biggest shopping mall in the city and is also a terminal for the U3 and U4 underground U-bahn lines. Mitte is a 10-minute walk from Stephansplatz and is also on several bus and tram lines.

Tickets can be bought online in advance, and be printed out or saved as digital files on smartphones. If tickets are bought on the train there is a €2 surcharge. If At airport counters or platform machines, single fares to the city cost €12 (€11 online), with round trips at €20

(€19 online). Children under 15 always travel free on CAT.

Another efficient option is the non-stop high speed **ÖBB** Railjet (Austrian National Railways), which runs from the airport to Vienna's main railway station, the Hauptbahnhof, in just 15 minutes. ÖBB Railjet trains depart Vienna International Airport every 30 minutes. These are the most modern and luxurious carriages in Austria. A one-way ticket costs only €3.90. Note, though, that the Railjet's terminus is at the main Hauptbahnhof station, much less convenient for central hotels than the Wien Mitte station, where both the CAT and the urban transport train the Schnellbahn deposit passengers.

Taxis can be delayed by congestion, but they have the advantage of taking you exactly where you want to go. Fares from the airport to a central location are always a fixed €36, plus a customary 10 percent gratuity. Limousines are also available at the airport.

DIRECTORY

Airports

Schwechat Airport
Tel 7007 32300.
W viennaairport.com

Airlines

Austrian Airlines
Tel 517661000.
Airport: Tel 700762520.
W austrian.com

British Airways
Tel 79567567.
W ba.com

easyJet
W easyjet.com

Flybe
Tel 020 7308 0812 (UK).
W flybe.com

Lufthansa
Tel 0810 10258080.
W lufthansa.com

Transfers from the Airport

CAT (City Airport Train)
Tel 25250.
W cityairporttrain.com

ÖBB
Tel 51717.
W oebb.at

Vienna Airport Lines
W viennaairportlines.at

Wiener Linien
W wienerlinien.at

Aside from taxis, the most flexible way to get from the airport into Vienna is by bus. **Vienna Airport Lines** departs every half-hour from Schwechat. There are three routes, with terminuses at Westbahnhof, Schwedenplatz and Donaustadt, with 14 local stops along the way. The buses have free Wi-Fi and cost €8 one way or €13 return. Tickets can be bought on the bus or online with the airport app. Under-6s travel free, and those under 14 pay half price.

Part of Vienna's tram and bus network run by **Wiener Linien**, the urban rapid-transit Schnellbahn, or S-bahn, No. 7 runs every half-hour and takes about 35 minutes. Tickets can be bought onboard for €2.30.

CAT (City Airport Train) linking Schwechat to the centre of Vienna

Arriving by Rail

Rail travel from all of Europe to Vienna has become faster and more comfortable. The Austrian Federal Railways (ÖBB Railjet) has sophisticated trains. Since opening in 2014, Vienna Central Station, the Hauptbahnhof, has seen a rerouting of train lines for greater efficiency.

It is now possible to travel from London to Vienna in 14 hours, changing in Brussels and again in Frankfurt. The 230 km/h (143 mph) Railjet trains run across Austria and into neighbouring countries. Cityjet sleeper trains offer the highest level of luxury in an overnight train. They are the only trains that require advance reservations.

Railjet offers business-, first- and second-class seating. All classes have free movies, free Wi-Fi and electrical charging-stations for laptops. Business-class travellers have leather reclining chairs. and get meals served at their seat.

All international trains go to the Hauptbanhof, sometimes signposted simply as Wien HBF. It is the nation's hub but is not the most central station, being off to the southeast, within walking distance of the Belvedere Palace and Gardens. The Hauptbahnhof has its own BahnhofCity shopping mall and is served by the main U-bahn line number 1, as well as by tram lines O and 18, bus lines 13A and 69A, and the rapid transit Schnellbahn lines S-1, S-2, S-3, S-7, S-60 and S-80.

Visitors to Vienna's centre are more likely to travel through the

A Railjet train standing at the station awaiting passengers

Wien Mitte station, within easy walking distance of Stephansdom, the cathedral. Mitte also has a huge shopping mall. Mitte handles 650 trains a day and is the home of the airport shuttle CAT. It is a busy hub itself, at the junction of the U3 and U4 underground U-bahn lines and Schnellbahn routes S-1, S-2, S-3 and S-7. Mitte is further served by the O-tram and the 74A bus.

With the opening of the Hauptbahnhof, Vienna's formerly busy Westbahnhof has seen a decline in traffic, though trains from the west of Austria do stop here. Trains coming from the northeast of the country use the Franz-Josefs-Bahnhof, in the north of the city.

It is not necessary to reserve a seat on Austrian trains, except for overnight sleepers. However, it is highly advisable to make an advance booking if special facilities, such as space for wheelchairs, are required. The

State Federal Railways can handle such requests in as little as 3 hours. But it is advisable to alert the ÖBB Mobility Centre at 05-1717-5 or by using the online form as early as possible.

Seats on any train can be reserved three months in advance, at a minimum price of €3, with no extra charge for business- or first-class travellers.

Arriving by Coach

International coach travel is a cheap way to travel. A coach ticket on Eurolines from London can cost between €100 and €200. Vienna's main coach station, the Vienna International Bus Terminal (VIB), is located close to Erdberg U3 underground station. Run by **Eurolines**, coaches still arrive here from major European cities. Operated by the natiomal train company ÖBB, Austria's **Postbus** runs everywhere in Austria and also into Bratislava, using its own bus terminal at the Hauptbahnhof, right on the U1 underground line.

Arriving by Car

Austrian roadways are well maintained, and fewer accidents occur than the EU average. All cars must be equipped with a first-aid kit, warning triangle and high-visibility vest. In winter, on mountain roads, chains must be used when conditions warrant, even on cars with snow tyres.

All non-EU drivers must have an international driving licence. Drivers must be at least 18 years of age and carry car registration,

Vienna's Hauptbahnhof, or Central Station

insurance documents and driving licence at all times. The maximum speed limit is 130 km/h (81 mph). Children under 12 cannot ride in front seats.

Tolls are compulsory on all motorways in Austria and a *vignette* sticker should be purchased and attached to the inside of the windscreen before travel on motorways. *Vignettes* are available for 10 days (€8.70), two months (€25.30) or one year (€84.40) and can be purchased at fuel stations and newsagents. All hire cars should have a *vignette* provided. Drivers without a valid *vignette* can be fined up to €3,000.

There are four main routes into Vienna by road. The Südautobahn, comprising the A2 and A23 motorways, provides access to the city from the south. The Donau-uferautobahn (A22) is the main northen motorway. The A1 (Westautobahn) and the A4 (Ostautobahn) enter Vienna from the west and east respectively. Motorways converge on the outer ring road (Gürtel). The city centre is marked *Zentrum*. The **Austrian Automobile Club (ÖAMTC)** provides daily reports on road conditions.

Arriving by Boat

From April to October you can arrive in Vienna by boat along the Danube from Bratislava, the Wachau and Budapest. Companies such as **Viking River Cruises** also run cruises into Vienna from Budapest. Boats dock at the **DDSG–Blue Danube** landing station at the Reichsbrücke bridge, close to the Vorgartenstrasse U-Bahn station on the U1 line. An information counter at the dock sells tickets and provides city maps and schedule information. A seasonal hydrofoil links Vienna, Budapest and Bratislava. Discounts apply for children (aged 2–14) and students (ID required).

DIRECTORY

Arriving by Rail

Austrian Federal Railways
W oebb.at

Öbb Call Centre
Tel 051717 (rail information).

Arriving by Coach

Eurolines
W eurolines.com

Postbus
W postbus.at

Arriving by Car

Austrian Automobile Club
W oeamtc.at

Arriving by Boat

DDSG–Blue Danube
W ddsg-blue-danube.at

Viking River Cruises
W vikingrivercruises.co.uk

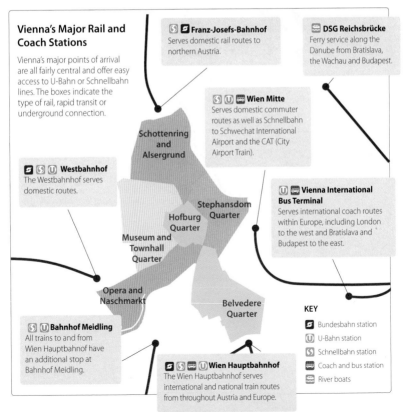

Vienna's Major Rail and Coach Stations

Vienna's major points of arrival are all fairly central and offer easy access to U-Bahn or Schnellbahn lines. The boxes indicate the type of rail, rapid transit or underground connection.

Franz-Josefs-Bahnhof
Serves domestic rail routes to northern Austria.

DSG Reichsbrücke
Ferry service along the Danube from Bratislava, the Wachau and Budapest.

Wien Mitte
Serves domestic commuter routes as well as Schnellbahn to Schwechat International Airport and the CAT (City Airport Train).

Westbahnhof
The Westbahnhof serves domestic routes.

Vienna International Bus Terminal
Serves international coach routes within Europe, including London to the west and Bratislava and Budapest to the east.

Schottenring and Alsergrund

Stephansdom Quarter

Hofburg Quarter

Museum and Townhall Quarter

Opera and Naschmarkt

Belvedere Quarter

Bahnhof Meidling
All trains to and from Wien Hauptbahnhof have an additional stop at Bahnhof Meidling.

Wien Hauptbahnhof
The Wien Hauptbahnhof serves international and national train routes from throughout Austria and Europe.

KEY

- Bundesbahn station
- U-Bahn station
- Schnellbahn station
- Coach and bus station
- River boats

GETTING AROUND VIENNA

With so much to see, central Vienna is best explored on foot. Footpaths are well maintained, with signposts marking major sights and attractions. Traffic-free areas offer pedestrians the opportunity to shop and sightsee away from tooting horns and congestion. Numerous cobblestone plazas, gardens, parks and cafés offer plenty of places to stop, draw breath, check the map and enjoy a cup of coffee. Viennese drivers are dissuaded from driving in the city centre by a complicated and frustrating one-way system and fairly expensive parking tariffs. However, if the legwork gets too much, the public transport system is cheap and efficient to use. One ticket buys access to five underground U-bahn lines, 29 trolley car tram routes and 127 bus routes. Fridays and Saturdays subways run 24 hours, and there are always night buses.

Tourists walking in the gardens at Schönbrunn Palace

Green Travel

As one of the greenest cities in Europe, Vienna has invested heavily in an impressive array of environmentally-friendly transport initiatives. A highly efficient public transport system and 1,300 km (800 miles) of bicycle paths offer viable eco-friendly alternatives to driving through the city. Over 1,000 rechargeable electrically powered ebikes are available for hire at very affordable rates from nearly 100 strategically positioned stations throughout the city (see Cycling). Almost every part of the metropolis is accessible by public transport and timetables for trams, buses, underground and trains neatly dovetail each other. Inexpensive tickets and discounted fares for combined use of all modes of transport ensure the network is very popular with locals and tourists alike.

The ultimate green transport-ation in Vienna are the pedicab taxis known as **Faxi Taxi** (see p252). These have fixed, inexpensive rates for runs to public transport hubs but can carry only two passengers with minimal bags.

Cycling is important to Vienna's environmental concerns, and an entire vehicle-free housing development has been built in the capital. "Bike City" focuses on the needs of cyclists with the whole complex benefitting from easy access bicycle paths and excellent direct links to public transportation.

Walking

There is no better way to see the city than to walk around Vienna at your own pace. Major sights and attractions are conveniently clustered together in close proximity and attractive streets are peppered with inviting cafés and cake shops. The area around Kärntner Strasse, Stock-im-Eisen-Platz and Graben is entirely traffic free. Numerous tour companies offer multilingual guided walks with a wide variety of cultural themes and historical topics. Contact the *Wiener Tourismusverband (see p238)* for more information.

Exploring Vienna on foot is not without its hazards. Traffic rarely stops at pedestrian crossings, so it is wise to be cautious when crossing the road. British and Australian visitors should remember that motorists drive on the right. In addition, keep an eye out for cyclists; some official cycle lanes are actually on the pedestrian pavement, and bikers have legal right of way. At all times, pedestrians should take care not to walk along bike paths and tramlines, as this is prohibited. On the Ringstrasse, trams run against the traffic, so looking both ways is essential. Jaywalking is illegal in Vienna, and this law is enforced by police – even if the roads are quiet. To avoid a hefty fine, it is important to abide by the signals at the pedestrian crossings; do not cross a road when a red figure is showing.

Fiaker

Traditional horse-drawn open carriages or Fiakers, many driven by a bowler-hatted and whiskered coachman, are a novel and relaxing way to get around. Remember that part of the route is on the busy Ringstrasse. You can hire a Fiaker at Stephansplatz, Heldenplatz or Albertinaplatz. A 20-minute ride from Stephansplatz to Michalerplatz with **Carriage**

Tourists in a horse-drawn cab outside the Michaelertrakt at the Hofburg Complex

Company Wulf costs around €55 for four persons, rising to €105 for an hour.

Cycling

With 1,300 km (800 miles) of dedicated bike paths, Vienna is a great city for cyclists. A 7-km (4-mile) cycle path round the Ringstrasse takes you past many historic sights, and there are also bike paths to the Prater *(see pp164–5)* and to the Hundertwasserhaus *(see p166)*. If you are a keen cyclist, look out for *Radkarte*, a booklet illustrating all of Vienna's cycle routes, which is available from bookshops. Bicycles can be rented at some train stations (discounts are given with a train ticket), or from any of the 100 or so **Citybike** stations. To use a Citybike, you need to register first with a debit or credit card, either online or at the station's terminal, for a one-off fee of €1; when the bike is returned, the charge (maximum €4 per hour) is calculated automatically and debited from your account.

Some cycle lanes are on pavements, and cyclists have right of way. It is permitted to ignore one-way rules in residential districts.

Guided Tours

Vienna Sightseeing is the largest operator of group tours by bus. But there are also hundreds of individual guides with expertise in specific

buildings and periods, as well as themes like cuisine.

Trams are a good way of seeing the 19th-century buildings in the Ringstrasse because you can choose where to get on and off. Organized tours are run by the **Tram Museum** in a 1920s tram from a meeting point at Otto Wagner's Karlsplatz Pavilions *(see pp150–51)*. Private groups may also hire a vintage tram to go to the Prater or a *Heuriger*, or simply to tour the city.

DDSG–Blue Danube organizes tours on the Danube River and the Danube Canal to sights such as Otto Wagner's Nussdorf locks. From April to October the **Twin City Liner**, a high-speed catamaran, makes a round trip to Bratislava three times a day.

From May to September, cycling enthusiasts can book tours through Pedal Power (pedalpower.at) or **Vienna Explorer**, which offers ebikes for older folks and seats for children. **Segway public tours** run from April to October, and the 3-hour excursion includes a brief lesson on how to ride the Segway personal transport.

Driving

Priority is always given to the right unless a yellow diamond indicates otherwise. Unlike in other EU countries, Austrian stoplights blink rapidly in green before switching to amber. Trams, buses, police cars, fire engines and ambulances all have right of way. Vienna's speed limit is 50 km (30 miles) per hour. Police carry out checks with infrared guns and can issue fines on the spot. The limit for alcohol is 0.5 mg per ml of blood (about 1/3 litre [11 fl oz] of beer or 1–2 glasses of wine). Spot checks are common and anyone exceeding the limit is likely to face a hefty fine and loss of licence.

EU drivers need no extra documentation. But North American and other non-EU drivers are required by law to have an international driving licence to complement their own country's documents.

Parking

Parking regulations can be confusing. The standard red circle with red X inside, denoting a forbidden zone, in Vienna also has *Anfang* (beginning) and *Ende* (end) signs to mark the zone. The City of Vienna operates a park and pay scheme in districts 1–9, 12, 14–17 and 20 from 9am to 10pm Mondays to Fridays *(see p252)*. Parking disks are sold at newsagents *(Tabak Trafiken)*, some banks and petrol stations. Usually, a maximum stay of 2 hours is allowed in any space. In other districts, a blue line by the kerb indicates a pay and display scheme. Underground parking in the city centre can cost €8 for one hour or €40 per day.

Cycling by the Danube Canal

Faxi Taxis lined up on a Vienna street

Taxis

Taxis are not flagged down, like they are in New York or London. They wait at official taxi stands outside stations, hotels and elsewhere. There are taxi apps for Android or Apple devices, and taxis can be summoned by phone on 60160, 40100 and 31300. A short ride can cost €10, with surcharges outside normal hours or for baggage. The fare to the airport is fixed at €36. A 10 per cent tip is expected. **Uber**, **Blacklane** and **MyDriver** are smartphone-based taxi services. Limousine services, both to the airport and for city destinations, are also bookable.

Vienna's Faxi Taxi pedicab is a quick way to get around the centre of the city (*see p250*). Find them at taxi stands or flag one down in the street. Journeys up to 2 km (1 mile) cost €5. One-way journeys more than 2 km cost €10.

Public Transport

Vienna's transport network is made up of trams (*Strassen-bahn*), buses (*Autobus*), underground (U-Bahn) and commuter trains to outlying districts (S-Bahn). The city's transport system, **Wiener Linien**, works on an honour system. The absence of ticket barriers at stations speeds transit, but tourists must never travel without a ticket, as there are spot checks on-board, with fines of over €100 demanded on the spot. Tickets cannot be purchased on the tram or bus. Smoking is banned in stations and on public transport. Children under 6 travel for free year-round while those aged between 6 and 14 qualify for half-price single tickets. The latter can also travel free during holidays providing they can show proof of age. Rush hour runs weekdays from about 7am to 9:30am, then again from about 4:30pm to 6:30pm.

Tickets and Travel Cards

Vienna's public transport ticketing system is less confusing than it appears at first glance. Buying a ticket in advance is the easiest option. Tickets are sold at newsagents (*Tabak Trafiken*), from ticket machines at stations or over the counter at U-Bahn and S-Bahn offices. Vienna city is zone 100 of the regional fare system; a standard ticket covers all areas of the city and allows passengers to change trains and lines and switch from the underground to a tram or a bus, as long as they take the most direct route and don't break their journey. A single ticket costs €2.20 bought in advance or €2.30 on board.

Weekly season tickets (€16.20) are valid from Monday to Monday at 9am. These are good value for anyone using public transport for more than four days. The *8-Tage-Karte* (€38.40) is best for groups of travellers and consists of eight strips which, when stamped, are valid for a day. Up to eight people may stamp the same ticket; start with strip one or you will invalidate the other seven. Also available are 24-, 48- and 72-hour tickets costing €7.60, €13.30 and €16.50 respectively. The Vienna Card is a 24-, 48- or 72-hour ticket (€13.90/18.90/21.90) valid on all transport. It comes with additional discounts and benefits and only needs punching once.

DIRECTORY

Green Travel

Faxi Taxi
Tel 0699 12005624.
W faxi.at

Fiaker

Carriage Company Wulf
Tel 0699 18154022.

Cycling

Citybike
Tel 0810 500 500.
W citybikewien.at

Pedal Power
Tel 7297234.
W pedalpower.at

Guided Tours

DDSG–Blue Danube
Handelskai 265. Tel 58880.
W ddsg-blue-danube.at

Segway tours
Elisabethstrasse 13.
Tel 7297234.
W segway-vienna.at

Tram Museum
Ludwig-Kössler-Platz.
Tel 790946803.

Twin City Liner
Schiffsstation Wien City, Schwedenplatz, between Marienbrücke and Schwedenbrücke bridges.
Map 6 E2. Tel 72710137.

Vienna Explorer
Tel 8909682.

Vienna Sightseeing Tours
Operngasse Top 3.
Map 5 C5.
Tel 7124683.

Parking

Parkgarage Am Hof
Map 2 D5 & 5 C2.

Parkhaus City
Stephansplatz 6/ Schulerstrasse.
Map 2 E5 & 6 D3.

Taxis

Tel 60160. W 60160.at
Tel 40100. W 40100.at
Tel 31300. W 31300.at

Blacklane
W blacklane.com

MyDriver
W mydriver.com

Uber
W uber.com

Public Transport

Wiener Linien
Tel 7909100.
W wienerlinien.at

Travelling by Underground

Vienna's underground system (U-Bahn) is one of Europe's most modern networks and is a clean, fast and reliable way of crossing the city. Construction commenced in the late 1960s, with the inaugural journey taking place in the mid-1970s. It has since undergone phases of refurbishment and expansion to a total length of 80 km (50 miles). A new U5 line is under construction, and five stations opened in 2017.

The Underground System

The U-Bahn is safe (see p240), but in case of emergencies there are help points on most platforms. Smoking is prohibited on U-Bahn platforms and on the trains themselves. Displays above the train doors show stations and connections, and a recorded voice announces stops and also connections to trams and buses. Signs indicate where prams can be stored by the doors. Bicycles are allowed on a few carriages, although not before 9am or between 3 and 6:30pm Mon–Fri. Be aware that doors are opened manually and can be stiff and heavy. The U-Bahn operates seven days a week. From Sunday to Thursday, it runs from about 5am to after midnight, with trains departing every 5–15 minutes. A 24-hour service runs Fridays, Saturdays and public holidays. Outside these hours, the U-Bahn service is complemented by Vienna NightLine buses (see pp254–5).

The U-Bahn's five colour-coded lines are U1, U2, U3, U4 & U6. There is no U5 line yet, but it is being built. The Vienna U-Bahn continues to expand as part of an ongoing city transport project that is expected to run until 2030. This will involve extending the U2 line and completing the U5 line.

Making a Journey by Underground

1 Look for your destination on a U-Bahn map. The five lines are distinguished by colour and number. Make a note of whether and where you need to change lines. Connections to other forms of transport are also shown.

2 Insert your ticket into the ticket-stamping machine in the direction of the arrow. Wait for the ping indicating that it is validated, and pass through the barrier. Follow the signs (with the number and colour of the line) to your platform.

3 On the platform, check the indicator boards for the direction and destination of the trains.

4 Stops along the line are shown on a plan in the train.

5 At your destination, follow *Ausgang* signs to reach street level.

6 At stations with more than one exit, use the map of the city to check which street or square you will come out at.

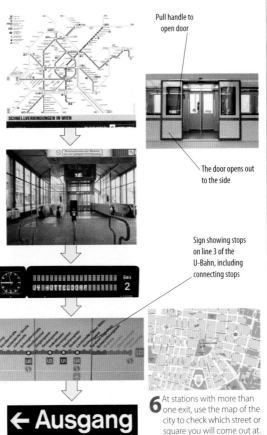

Pull handle to open door

The door opens out to the side

Sign showing stops on line 3 of the U-Bahn, including connecting stops

← Ausgang

Travelling by Tram, Bus and Train

Tram, bus and train travel in Vienna is safe, inexpensive and efficient. There are 29 red-and-white trams (or trolley cars) and 127 bus routes. Little hopper buses serve the city centre, while larger buses run from the inner suburbs, Ringstrasse and Prater to the outer suburbs. Excursions to the most remote valleys are offered by the national postal bus service (ÖBB Postbus). Used mainly by commuters, the Schnellbahn (S-Bahn) runs beyond the city limits to the outer suburbs and further afield.

On New Year's Eve, buses and other forms of public transport run all night. All buses in Vienna are wheelchair-accessible.

Trams

Vienna's tram network is one of the largest in the world. Known locally as "Bim" for its distinctive bell sound, the tram is a delightful way to get around the city. For the ultimate experience, seek out one of the old, traditional models with their wooden seats and vintage interiors.

The yellow Vienna Ring Tram is the only tram that makes an unbroken circuit of the Ring. The €9 ticket includes an audio and video commentary. Trams depart from Schwedenplatz every 30 minutes all year round, from 10am to 5:30pm.

Vienna trams are equipped with seats for disabled travellers. However, the modern low-riding trams are a more wheelchair-friendly option. Look for vehicles with the ULF (Ultra Low Floor) sign.

Buses

Buses are comfortable, air-conditioned and equipped with CCTV. Bus stops are marked by a green "H" for *haltestelle* or stop. All stops display bus numbers, destinations, timetables and route maps. Buses should stop automatically at all bus stops but if you are in any doubt, flag it down. Tickets purchased from the driver will be valid for one bus journey only. If you have already purchased a ticket from a newsagent or ticket machine, you will need to validate it in the blue ticket-stamping machine on the bus. If you have already made part of your journey by tram or U-Bahn, there is no need to stamp your ticket again. Limited services run on holidays and Christmas Day.

Night Buses

Vienna's night bus service operates every night of the week starting at 12:30am and then at 30-minute intervals until 5am in the morning. There is some variation between the services operating on weekday nights (Sunday to Thursday) and those at weekends and on public holidays. Night buses are marked by the letter "N". All night buses in Vienna start from Schwedenplatz, the Opera and Schottentor, and together serve most suburbs. Tickets can be purchased from the driver and all other pre-bought tickets and passes are valid. Passengers can pre-arrange a taxi to wait at the destination stop if they are staying some distance from a night bus route. A number for a local taxi firm can be obtained from the Transport Office in Schwedenplatz or from the Wiener Linien hotline (7909100).

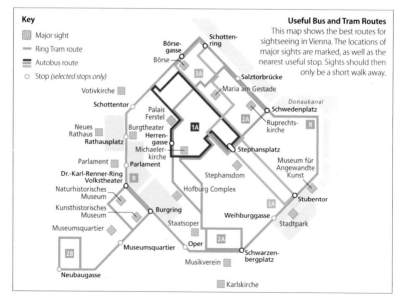

Key
- Major sight
- Ring Tram route
- Autobus route
- ○ Stop (selected stops only)

Useful Bus and Tram Routes
This map shows the best routes for sightseeing in Vienna. The locations of major sights are marked, as well as the nearest useful stop. Sights should then only be a short walk away.

An S-Bahn train at Wien Mitte Station

Trains

Known colloquially as the S-Bahn, the Schnellbahn (Fast Train) is recognizable by its blue and white logo and is primarily a commuter service. A metropolitan route has stops in the centre of Vienna interconnecting with mainline stations *(see p249)* but is generally used as a means of getting farther afield. The local Bundesbahn is also a commuter service and is sometimes called the Regionalbahn on maps and timetables to distinguish it from national routes. Timetables are available from station information offices and is displayed on departure boards. When travelling within the city, all public transport tickets and passes are valid on the Schnellbahn. For Schnellbahn journeys outside of Vienna a ticket must be purchased in advance. See the **Austrian Federal Railways** website for more information and a useful journey planner.

DIRECTORY

Austrian Federal Railways
Tel 51717.
W oebb.at

Wiener Linien
Tel 7909100.
W wienerlinien.at

Travelling Beyond Vienna

Vienna is a great base from which to discover other parts of Austria, as well as neighbouring European destinations. The historic cities of Salzburg, Innsbruck, Graz and Linz are well served by public transport from the city, and car hire is a viable option to reach more rural areas.

Wien Hauptbahnhof station

Domestic Flights

Frequent domestic flights with **Austrian Airlines** link Vienna with Graz, Klagenfurt, Salzburg, Innsbruck and Linz. In terms of cost, flying is always more expensive. A round-trip flight to Innsbruck, for example, is about €200, compared to €120 for the train. The train takes 4 hours; the plane, 1 hour.

Trains

Trains to destinations throughout Austria depart from Wien Hauptbahnhof, and there are hourly services to Salzburg. Routes from Franz-Josefs-Bahnhof station connect Vienna with Tulln, Krems an der Donau and the Wachau region.

Car Hire and Road Travel

Some car-hire firms require drivers to be at least 25. Non-EU drivers must have an international driving licence. If driving your own car, a motorway toll sticker for the windscreen is mandatory. It costs under €9 for ten days.

Boats and Hydrofoil

Boat trips regularly set off from Vienna along the Wachau Valley. Alternative trips in the other direction head to Bratislava (1.5 hours) and Budapest (4 hours). All vessels have restaurants and sundecks.

A hydrofoil service runs from the landing station at the Reichsbrücke, connecting Vienna with Budapest and Bratislava. Return fares cost €38 to Bratislava and €125 to Budapest.

DIRECTORY

Domestic Flights

Austrian Airlines
W austrian.com

Car Hire

Avis City
Airport **Tel** 7007 32700.
W avis.at

Europcar
Tel 7146717.
Airport **Tel** 7007 32812.
W europcar.at

Boats and Hydrofoil

LOD
Praterstrasse 40 **Tel** 958 0808.
W lod.sk

Budapest-Vienna Hydrofoil Lines
Tel +36 70 604 8050.
W vienna-hydrofoil.hotels-in-budapest-hungary.com

STREET FINDER

The map references for all the sights, hotels, restaurants, bars, shops and entertainment venues described in this book refer to the maps in this section. A complete index of street names and all the places of interest marked on the maps can be found on the following pages. The key map *(right)* shows the area of Vienna covered by the *Street Finder*. This map includes sightseeing areas as well as districts for hotels, restaurants and entertainment venues.

All the street names in the index and on the *Street Finder* are in German – *Strasse* translating as street and *Gasse* meaning lane. *Platz* or *Hof* indicate squares or courtyards. Throughout this guide, the numbers of the houses follow the street names, in the same way that you will see them written in Vienna.

Vienna's rooftops as seen from Am Hof *(see p89)*

Key to Street Finder

- ▦ Major sight
- ▦ Places of interest
- ▢ Other building
- Ⓤ U-Bahn station
- 🚆 Bundesbahn station
- 🚋 Badner Bahn stop
- Ⓢ Schnellbahn station
- 🛈 Tourist information office
- ✚ Hospital with casualty unit
- 🚓 Police station
- ✝ Church
- ✡ Synagogue
- — Railway line
- Pedestrian street

Scale of Maps 1–4 & 5–6 respectively

0 metres	250	
0 yards	250	1:14,000

0 metres	125	
0 yards	125	1:9,000

Section of the Austria fountain (1846) by Schwanthaler *(left)* and side view of the Schottenkirche *(see p112)*

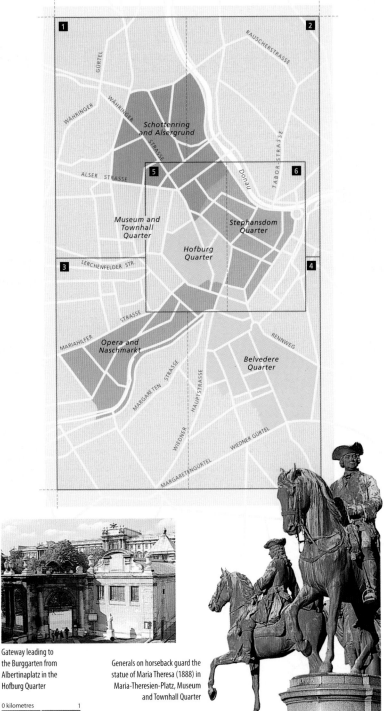

Gateway leading to
the Burggarten from
Albertinaplatz in the
Hofburg Quarter

Generals on horseback guard the
statue of Maria Theresa (1888) in
Maria-Theresien-Platz, Museum
and Townhall Quarter

0 kilometres   1

0 miles   0.5

Street Finder Index

Vienna's street and place names are generally spelled as one word; -platz, -strasse or -kirche are put at the end of the name, as in Essiggasse for example. Occasionally they are treated as separate words, for instance Alser Strasse. Abbreviations used in this index are Dr as in Doctor-Ignaz-Seipel-Platz, and St as in Sankt Josef Kirche. Some entries have two map references. The first refers to the smaller-scale map that covers the whole of central Vienna, the second refers to the large-scale inset map that covers the Stephansdom and Hofburg Quarters.

Useful Words

Gasse	lane, alley
Strasse	road, street
Platz	square
Hof	courtyard
Kirche	church
Kapelle	chapel
Dom	cathedral
Denkmal	monument
Markt	market
	(often the site of a former market)
Brücke	bridge

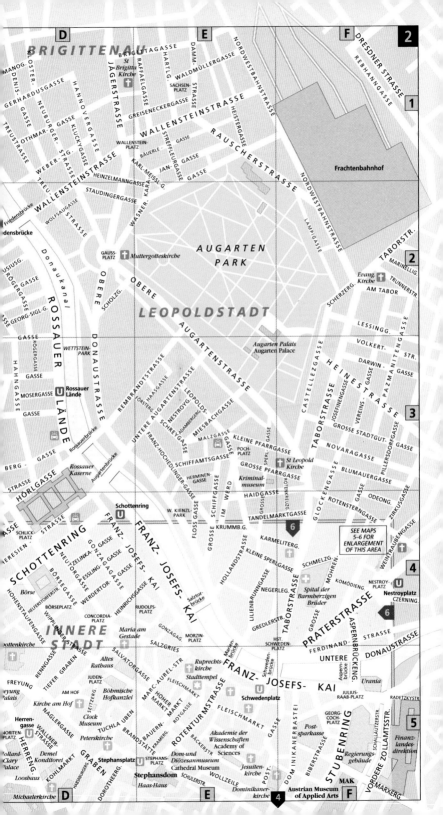

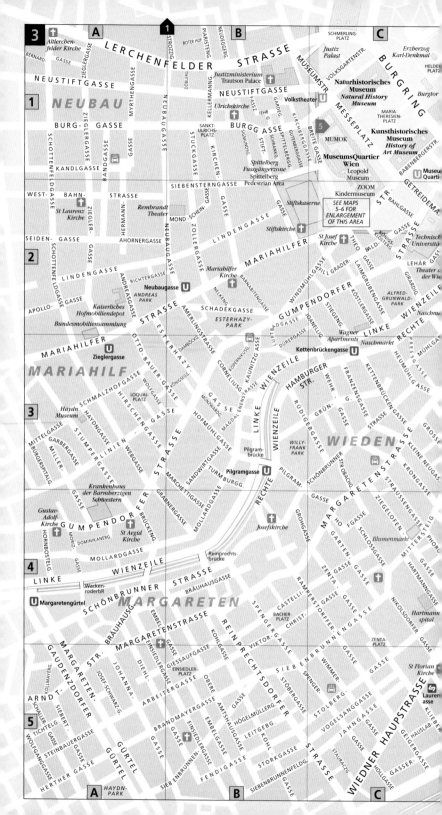

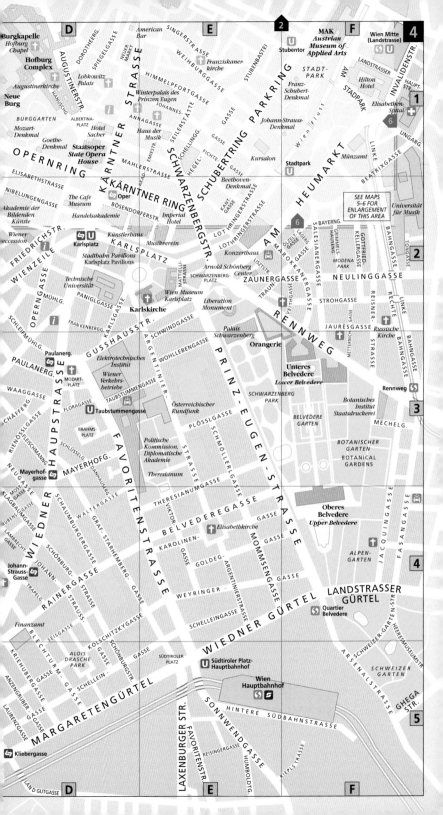

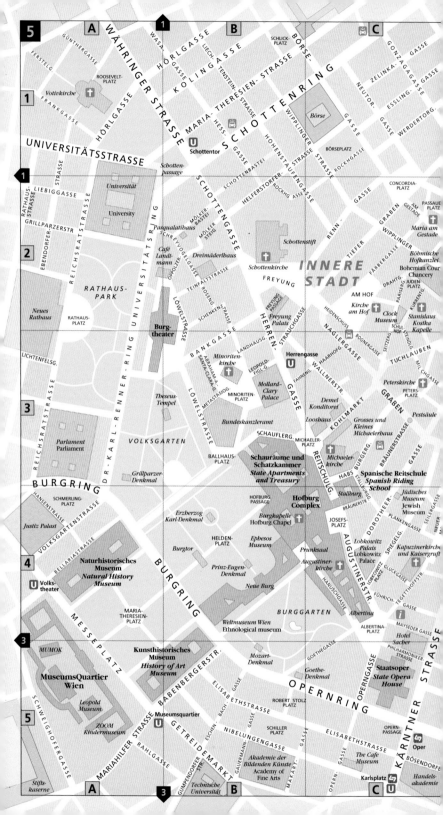

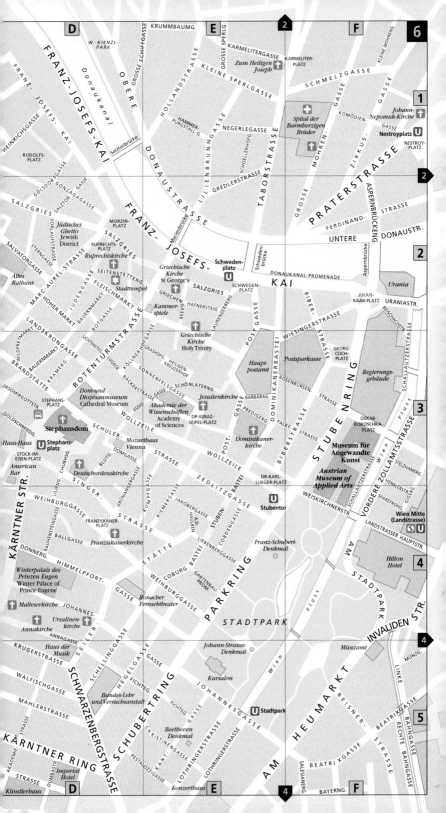

General Index

Acknowledgments

Dorling Kindersley wishes to thank the following people who contributed to the preparation of this book.

Main Contributor

Stephen Brook was born in London and educated at Cambridge. After working as an editor in Boston and London, he became a full-time writer in 1982. Among his books are *New York Days, New York Nights; The Double Eagle; Prague, L.A. Lore* and books on wine. He also writes articles on wine and travel for many newspapers and periodicals.

Additional Contributors

Gretel Beer, Rosemary Bircz, Caroline Bugler, Dierdre Coffey, Fred Mawer, Nicholas Parsons, Christian Williams, Sarah Woods.

Proofreader

Kate Berens, Diana Vowles.

Design and Editorial

Managing Editor Carolyn Ryden
Managing Art Editor Steve Knowlden
Senior Editor Georgina Matthews
Senior Art Editor Vanessa Courtier
Editorial Director David Lamb
Art Director Anne-Marie Bulat
Consultant Robert Avery
Language Consultant Barbara Eichberger

DTP

Vinod Harish, Vincent Kurian, Azeem Siddiqui.

Revisions Team

Louise Abbott, Ashwin Adimari, Emma Anacootee, Ros Angus, Parnika Bagla, Claire Baranowski, Marta Bescos, Tessa Bindloss, Jane Edmonds, Gadi Farfour, Emer FitzGerald, Fay Franklin, Rhiannon Furbear, Camilla Gersh, Sally Gordon, Emily Green, Alistair Gunn, Swati Gupta, Elaine Harries, Mohammed Hassan, Paul Hines, Laura Jones, Bharti Karakoti, Sumita Khatwani, Priya Kukadia, Joanne Lenney, Alison McGill, Carly Madden, Hayley Maher, Ella Milroy, Deepak Mittal, Sonal Modha, Kate Molan, Catherine Palmi, Garima Pandey, Helen Partington, Sangita Patel, Susie Peachey, Alice Peebles, Helen Peters, Marianne Petrou, Robert Purnell, Rada Radojicic, Nicki Rawson, Rituraj Singh, Sadie Smith, Sands Publishing Solutions, Simon Ryder, Andrew Szudek, Samia Tadros, Hollie Teague, Ajay Verma, Lynda Warrington, Susannah Wolley Dod, Johanna Wurm.

Additional Illustrations

Kevin Jones, Gilly Newman, John Woodcock, Martin Woodward.

Cartography

Uma Bhattacharya, Mohammad Hassan, Jasneet Kaur, Peter Winfield, James Mills-Hicks (Dorling Kindersley Cartography), Colourmap Scanning Limited, Contour Publishing, Cosmographics, European Map Graphics, Street Finder maps: ERA Maptec Ltd (Dublin).
Map Co-ordinators Simon Farbrother, David Pugh
Cartographic Research Jan Clark, Caroline Bowie, Claudine Zante.

Additional Photography

DK Studio/Steve Gorton, Ian O'Leary, Poppy, Rough Guides/ Natascha Sturny, Steve Shott, Clive Streeter, Peter Wilson, Daniel Wurm.

Factcheckers

Dieter Löffler, Melanie Nicholson-Hartzell, Doug Sager.

Special Assistance

Marion Telsnig and Ingrid Pollheimer-Stadtlober at the Austrian Tourist Board, London; Frau Preller at the Heeresgeschichtliches Museum; Frau Wegscheider at the Kunsthistorisches Museum; Frau Stillfried and Mag Czap at the Hofburg; Herr Fehlinger at the Museen der Stadt Wien; Mag Schmid at the Naturhistorisches Museum; Mag Dvorak at the Österreichischer Bundes-theaterverband; Dr Michael Krapf and Mag Grabner at the Österreichische Galerie; Robert Tidmarsh and Mag Weber-Kainz at Schloss Schönbrunn; Frau Zonschits at the Tourismusverband.

Photography Permissions

Dorling Kindersley would like to thank the following for their kind permission to photograph at their establishments:

Alte Backstube, Bestattungsmuseum, Schloss Belvedere, Bundesbaudirektion, Deutschordenskirche and Treasury, Dom und Diözesanmuseum, Sigmund Freud Gesellschaft, Josephinum Institut für Geschichte der Medzin der Universität Wien, Kapuzinerkirche, Pfarramt St. Karl, Stift Klosterneuburg, Wiener Kriminalmuseum, Niederösterreichisches Landesmuseum, Österreichischer Bundestheaterverband, Österreichische Postsparkasse (P. S. K.), Dombausekretariat Sankt Stephan, Spanische Reitschule and Volkskunde Museum. Dorling Kindersley would also like to thank all the shops, restaurants, cafés, hotels, churches and public services who aided us with photography. These are too numerous to thank individually.

Picture Credits

a = above; b = below/bottom; c = centre; f = far; l = left; r = right; t = top.

Works of art have been reproduced with the permission of the following copyright holders: *Brunnenhaus* Ernst Fuchs © DACS, London 2011; *The Tiger Lion* 1926 Oskar Kokoschka © DACS, London 2011 157t; © **The Henry Moore Foundation:** 146bl.

The Publishers are grateful to the following individuals, companies and picture libraries for permission to reproduce their photographs:

4corners Images: Damm Stefan 11br.
Alamy Images: Luise Berg-Ehlers 60tr; David Coleman 238cra; Bernhard Ernst 39bl; Christopher Gannon 250cla; imagebroker/ Christian Handl 205tl; CTK 248tr, 248bl; ImageBROKER 61cr, 64bl, 214tc; INSADCO: Photography/ Martin Bobrovsky 205c; Hackenberg-Photo-Cologne 50tr; Art Kowalsky 10cla; John Lens 178cr; Yadid Levy 100–101tc; LOOK Die Bildagentur der Fotografen GmbH 12tr; Stefano Politi Markovina 61tl; Barry Mason 207c; Willy Matheisl 194br; mediacolor's 178 cla, 206cla; David Noble 207tl; B. O'Kane 111br; Robert Harding Picture Library Ltd/ Richard Nebesky 204cla; Jack Sullivan 241cla; vario images/ Stefan Kiefer 245tr, 251crb; vario images/ Thomas Jantzen 245bc; Viennaslide 60br; volkerpreusser 220bl; Ken Welsh 10bc; **Graphic Sammlung Albertina,** Wien: 28–9; **Ancient Art and Architecture Collection:** 26b(d), 27tc, 31cra; **AKG-Images:** 18(d), 11tc(d), 21br(d), 23bc, 24–5, 26cla, 26–7, 27cb, 27bl, 28cla, 28br(d), 29tc, 30cl, 30br(d), 31tc, 30–31, 30cl, 31bl, 32cl, 34cl, 34br, 35bc, 36br, 38tl, 40bl, 89b(d), 100cl, 112br(d), 149cra, 154clb, 174bl, 237 inset; Erich Lessing 11tl, 40clb, 41crb; **Austrian Archives:** 37tl
Bank Austria. UniCredit Bank Austria AG: 242bl; **Hotel Beethoven GmbH & Co KG:** 198bc; **Belvedere, Vienna:** 158br; Thomas Preiss 159cra; Margherita Spiluttini 159br; **Bildarchiv Preussischer Kulturbesitz,** Berlin: 25bl, 37cb, 94tr; **Bildarchiv Österreichische Nationalbibliothek,** Wien: 92cl, Johannes Hloch 4tc; **Casa Editrice Bonechi,** Firenze: 169cra; **Boutique**

Hotel Stadthalle: 196bc; Christian Brandstätter Verlag, Wien: 22ca, 33crb(d), 35tl, 36bl, 85tc, 101c; Bridgeman Art Library, London: 135bl(d); Albertina, Wien 48br; Bonhams, London 26cl; 21bl(d); Kunsthistorisches Museum, Wien 21tr(d), 48cl; Museum der Stadt Wien 35tr, 40cr(d), 40clb, 41cl; Österreichische Galerie 37tc; Hotel Bristol: 192cra, 193br, 217br; ©1999 Bundesgärten, Wien: 174cl; Bundesministerium Für Finanzen: 29cb(d); Burghauptmannschaft In Wien: 103ca, 103cra, 103br. CaffèCouture: 214bl; Archäologischer Park Carnuntum: 23tc; Casinos Austria: 227cra; Cephas Picture Library: Mick Rock 163br, 208tr; Wine Magazine 240br; Citybike Wien: 251tl; Contrast Photo: Milenko Badzic 67ca; Franz Hausner 170crb; Michael Himml/ Transglobe 154tr; Hinterleitner 227br; Peter Kurz 65b, 141tll, 233br; Boris Mizaikoffl/Transglobe 65cra; Tappeiner/Transglobe 234c; H Valencak 180b.
Dellago: 203br; Do & Co Hotel: 197tl; Café Dommayer: 218tl; Dreamstime.com: Amoklv 144; Andreykr 13br, 90, 147crb; David Bailey 12bc; Baloncici 212tl; Belish 164tr; Maciej Bledowski 121bl; Boggy 70; Boris Breytman 31cr, 106bl; Chaoss 2-3; Marco Clarizia 60cla; Mike Clegg 160; Dafrei 108; Digitalpress 147tc, 236-7; Freesurf69 180cl; Eugeniu Frimu 255cl; Ginasanders 114; Denitsa Glavinova 5cr; Gunold 138bl; Jorg Hackemann 247tl; Fritz Hiersche 96tl; Andrei Kaplun 43bl; Anna Lurye 43cl; Meinzahn 42; Roman Milert 244cl; Monysasi 96bl; Miruna Niculescu 182; Irina Papoyan 17tc; Ariadna De Raadt 43c; Radub85 190-91, 255tl; Arseniy Rogov 241cl; Romasph 4cr; Rosshelen 2-3; Sborisov 16cl; Jozef Sedmak 55clb, 179cr; Toxawww 251tl; Tupungato 68-9; Robert Zehetmayer 142tr, 181tr; Café-Restaurant Dunkelbunt: 200cr. Et Archive, London: 40br; Museum für Gestaltung, Zurich 36cl; Museum der Stadt Wien 28bc, 33tl, 40ca; European Commission: 243; Mary Evans Picture Library, London: 20cla, 20bl, 20crb, 21tl, 24c, 27br, 29br, 32ca, 32bl, 32br, 37br, 41t, 74tr, 177b.
F. A. Herbig Verlagsbuchhandlung GmbH, München: 100bl, 100br, 101bl, 101br. FAXI Das Fahrradtaxi: 252tl.
Getty Images: Ralph Crane 38tr, Neil Farrin 136; Imagno 170cla; De Agostini / A. Dagli Orti 8-9; Wolfgang Kaehler 234tl; Samuel Kubani 239bc; Stringer / Erich Auerbach 39tc.
Robert Harding Picture Library: Larsen Collinge International 44clb; Adam Woolfitt 64cra, 139cra, 152tl; Heeresgeschichtliches Museum, Wien: 49br, 168cla, 168bl, 169tc, 169br; Hertz: 255cb; Historisches Museum Der Stadt Wien: 19b, 23ca, 23crb, 30crb, 34cb, 34bl, 35cla, 35crb, 45tr, 49tl, 51cl, 141cra, 141tr, 147ca, 171tl; Hollmann Beletage, Vienna: 193t; Hulton-Deutsch Collection: 40br(d); The Hutchison Library: 202tl.
Hotel Imperial: 192br; iStockphoto.com: benedek 221bc.
Josefstadt Theatre: 226cl.
Wilhelm Klein: 25tl, 28clb; Kunsthistorisches Museum, Wien: 26cb, 43crb, 48tr, 50bl, 58cl, 97tc, 97bc, 101t, 102 all, 124-5 all, 126-7 all, 128-9 all, 177tc.
J & L Lobmeyr, Wien: 51tr; Leopold Museum-Privatstiftung: Selbstbildnis, 1910, by Egon Schiele 48bla, Hockender Weiblicher Akt, 1910, by Egon Schiele 122tr, Self Portrait with Chinese Lantern, 1912, by Egon Schiele 120tr, Die Schnitter, 1922 by Egger-Lienz 122t; Lonely Planet Images: Richard Nebesky 233tl.
Magnum Photos: Erich Lessing 20tr, 22cl, 22bl, 22br, 23tl, 23clb, 24clb, 25ca, 28c, 31br, 32-3, 33b; MAK: Lois Lammerhuber 85cb;

Katrin Wißkirchen 84tr, 84bc; MAK-Osterreichisches Museum fur ange wandte Kunst: 84cl Restaurant Motto: 219b; Cafe Restaurant Mozart bei der Opera GsmbH: 201t, 213br; Museum Judenplatz: Votava/PID 88tl; Museumsquartier, Errichtungs-und Betriebsgesmbh: Lisi Gradnitzer 120br; Rupert Steiner MQ E+B GesmbH 43br, 121tl; MUMOK, Museum of Modern Art Ludwig Foundation Vienna: Homme accroupi, 1907, by André Derain, © ADAGP, Paris & DACS, London 2011, 121br; The Red Horseman, 1974 by Roy Lichtenstein, © Estate of Roy Lichtenstein/DACS, London 2011, 122bl.
Narodni Museum, Praha: 20br; Naturhistorisches Museum, Wien: 48cla, 130-31 except 131bl, 235c.
Österreichische Galerie, Wien: 49crb, 156clb, 157 all, 158bl, 159br; Österreichisches Museum Für Angewandte Kunst, Wien: 30cla, 49cra, 58tr, 59clb, 84-5 all except 85t; Österreichische Nationalbibliothek, Wien: 22crb, 25crb, 38cb; Österreich Werbung: 29cra, 33tc, 33cra, 36ca, 46bl, 100cbl, 103tc, 140br, 165cr, 165bl, 174t, 181cl, 232cra.
Photolibrary: Merten Merten 159tl.
Raiffeisenbank Wien: Gerald Zugman 36ca; Manya Rathmore 153br; Restaurant at Eight: 202b, 212br; Retrograph Archive, London: Martin Ranicar-Breese 193clb; Rex Features, London: Action Press 38bc, Adolfo Franzo 39tl, Sokol/Sipa Press 123crb; GEORG RIHA: 75t; Ronacher Variety Theatre/CMM: Velo Weger 226t.
Café Sacher: 201br, 216br; Hotel Sacher: 195tr, 199br; Hotel Sans Souci: 194tl, 198tl; Schloss Schönbrunn Kultur-und Betriebsges Mbh, Wien: Alexander E. Koller 30bl; Professor Gerhard Trumler 174cl, 175 all except 175b, 176 all, 177tr; Schloss Schönbrunn Kultur- und Betriebsges MBH 1999: Wolfgang Voglhuber 143br; Cafe Sperl: 216tc; SYGMA: Habans/ Orban 39tr, Viennareport 39ca; Surfland Internetcafe: 244crb. Travel Library: Philip Entiknapp 221tr.
Restaurant Vestibül: 203tr, 215tl; Vienna Airport: 246cla, 247bl; Vienna Police: 240bl, 241tl; Vienna Secession: Jorit Aust 57br; Vienna Tourist Board: 238bl; Viennaslide: Harald A Jahn 232bc; Karl Luymair 232cla; Museum Für Völkerkunde, Wien: 51br, 235bc; Votava, Wien: 165tc.
Werner Forman Archive: Museum der Stadt Wien 62c; St Stephens Cathedral Museum 25cr; Wiener Linien GmbH & Co KG: 25cr, 253c, 253cb, 253br; Wien Museum: 88br, Longcase Clock c.1762-69 David A.S. Cajetano 88cb; Wiener Sängerknaben: 41br, 66bl; Wiener Stadt- Und Landesbibliothek, Wien: 38ca, 38bl.
Zoom Kindermuseum: Alexandra Eizinger 120cla.

Front Endpaper: Dreamstime.com: Amoklv Rbr; Andreykr Rcr; Dafrei Rtc; Goran Bogicevic Rtr; Ginasanders Lcl; Getty Images: Neil Farrin Lbl.

Map Cover: 4Corners: Olimpio Fantuz / SIME.

Cover: Front and spine – 4Corners: Olimpio Fantuz / SIME; back – 123rf.com: Matthew Dixon.

All other images © Dorling Kindersley. For further information see: www.dkimages.com

Special Editions of DK Travel Guides

DK Travel Guides can be purchased in bulk quantities at discounted prices for use in promotions or as premiums. We are also able to offer special editions and personalized jackets, corporate imprints, and excerpts from all of our books, tailored specifically to meet your own needs.

To find out more, please contact:

in the US specialsales@dk.com

in the UK travelguides@uk.dk.com

in Canada specialmarkets@dk.com

in Australia penguincorporatesales@
penguinrandomhouse.com.au